Psychology
and
Personal
Growth

SEVENTH EDITION

PSYCHOLOGY AND PERSONAL GROWTH

Nelson Goud
*Indiana University–
Purdue University Indianapolis*

Abe Arkoff
University of Hawaii at Manoa

PEARSON

Boston   New York   San Francisco
Mexico City   Montreal   Toronto   London   Madrid   Munich   Paris
Hong Kong   Singapore   Tokyo   Cape Town   Sydney

Editor-in-Chief: Susan Hartman
Editorial Assistant: Deborah Hanlon
Senior Production Administrator: Donna Simons
Cover Administrator: Kristina Mose-Libon
Composition Buyer: Linda Cox
Manufacturing Buyer: JoAnne Sweeney
Editorial-Production Service: Omegatype Typography, Inc.
Electronic Composition: Omegatype Typography, Inc.

For related titles and support material, visit our online catalog at www.ablongman.com.

Between the time website information is gathered and then published, it is not unusual for some sites to have closed. Also, the transcription of URLs can result in typographical errors. The publisher would appreciate notification where these errors occur so that they may be corrected in subsequent editions. Thank you.

Library of Congress Cataloging-in-Publication Data

Psychology and personal growth / [edited by] Nelson Goud, Abe Arkoff.—7th ed.
    p.   cm.
  Includes bibliographical references.
  ISBN 0-205-46883-7 (paperbound)
  1. Psychology—Textbooks. 2. Maturation (Psychology)—Textbooks. 3. Self-actualization (Psychology)—Textbooks. I. Goud, Nelson. II. Arkoff, Abe.

BF149.P835 2006
158—dc22

                                                        2005053480

Printed in the United States of America

10 9 8 7 6 5 4 3 2   09 08 07 06

For my children David and Debbie.
To Bonnie.
For former and current students in
my Developing Human Potential course.
—*Nelson Goud*

For my fellow growers,
Susan, Amy, and Ty.
—*Abe Arkoff*

CONTENTS

SECTION SIX   A QUALITY LIFE   **299**

PREFACE

In 1845, when he was 28 years old, Henry Thoreau began his experiment in living at Walden Pond. He wrote that he went to the woods because "I wished to live deliberately, to front only the essential facts of life, and see if I could not learn what it had to teach, and not, when I came to die, discover that I had not lived" (Thoreau, 1854/1962, p. 172).*

One essential fact of life is how to choose and create an authentic life, a life that is truly lived. Knowing who you are and who you want to be—your being and becoming—does not require a two-year visit to Walden Pond. You can explore your essence right where you are, right now. This book offers one way to begin this quest of knowing yourself and the life paths you are pursuing. Over eighty readings and forty applied activities are offered that apply psychology to personal growth. These selections focus on six themes: identity, human communication, growth dynamics, human relationships, emotions and feelings, and a quality life.

Some of the selections will have immediate relevance and application. Others may take some thought, discussion, or writing to fully comprehend their message. Each article has a Follow-Up section that provides guidance in interpreting the ideas. You are strongly encouraged to answer at least one of these questions for each assigned article.

Applied Activities are offered at the end of each of the six sections. These exercises apply and extend the main ideas of the section. Completing these activities will aid in integrating what you've learned into your life.

To Instructors

This book is designed so that most of the articles can be read within a semester. Depending on your teaching style, the articles can be used for small and large group discussion, student journal assignments, or as launching pads for related topics. Some articles are supplemented by short features entitled "Along These Lines," which amplify and expand the points made in the articles and give the reader more to think about. Some students need little or no guidance and others need a great deal of structure in interpreting a reading.

*Thoreau, H. (1854/1962). *Thoreau: Walden and and other writings*, J. W. Krutch, Ed. New York: Bantam Books, Inc.

I have found it helpful to have students complete at least one of the Follow-Up items for every assigned article. I would also recommend that at least one Applied Activity be assigned per section. If you use small groups as part of your instruction, it is suggested that students read Section Two (Human Communication) prior to any group interaction. Additional teaching suggestions are offered in the supplemental Instructor's Manual and Test Bank, which are available to qualified instructors. Please contact your local Allyn and Bacon representative for details concerning policies, prices, and availability of these supplements, as some restrictions do apply.

An Invitation

Students and instructors are invited to share their comments, reading suggestions, or other ideas with me at the address below:

Nelson Goud, Ph.D.
School of Education
Indiana University–Purdue University at Indianapolis
902 W. New York Street
Indianapolis, IN 46202
e-mail: ngoud@iupui.edu

THANKS

A note of thanks to those who made it possible to complete this book.

Section One   Identity

Carl Rogers. "The Search for Identity." From *Freedom to Learn*, Third edition, by Carl Rogers & H. Jerome Freiberg. Copyright © 1994. Reprinted by permission of Prentice-Hall, Inc., Upper Saddle River, NJ.

Jon Kabat-Zinn. "Mindfulness." From *Wherever You Go, There You Are*. Copyright © 1994. Hyperion.

Richard Cohen. "Suddenly I'm the Adult?" Reprinted by permission of the author.

Goud, N. "The Emerging Adult: Challenges." Excerpts from *Quarterlife Crisis* by Alexandra Robbins and Abby Wilner. Copyright 2001. Reprinted by permission of Jeremy P. Tarcher/Putnam, New York, NY.

Silbert, Sarah. (2001). "The Rivers We Call Ourselves." From *The Sun*, October 2001. Reprinted by permission of the author.

Goud, N. "The Emerging Adult: The Work World." Excerpts from *Conquering Your Quarterlife Crisis* by Alexandra Robbins. Copyright 2004. Reprinted by permission of Perigree, New York, NY.

Christopher A. Schaefer. "Occupational Exploration." Reprinted by permission of the author.

Craig Mosher. "Woodworker." From *The Humanist*, January/February 1975. Reprinted by permission of the author.

Aaron R. Kipnis and Elizabeth Herron. "Ending the Battle between the Sexes." Reprinted by permission of the authors.

Sam Keen. "On Being a Man." From *Fire in the Belly: On Being a Man*. Copyright © 1991. New York: Bantam Books.

Denise Karuth. "If I Were a Car, I'd Be a Lemon." From *Ordinary Moments: The Disabled Experience*, 1984, Ed. Alan J. Brightman, by University Park Press. Reprinted by permission of Alan J. Brightman.

"Think 'People First'" was developed by Ohio Public Images/Public Images Network.

Section Two   Human Communication

Warner Burke. "Interpersonal Communication." Reprinted with permission from NTL Institute. From the Selected Series Reading Nine, *Behavioral Science and the Manager's Role*, pp. 78–84, edited by Warner Burke. Copyright © 1969.

Carl Rogers. "To Hear and to Be Heard." From *Freedom to Learn* by Carl Rogers. Copyright © 1969. Reprinted by permission of Prentice-Hall, Inc., Upper Saddle River, NJ.

"John Steinbeck on Listening." From *Log from the Sea of Cortez*. Copyright © 1976. New York: Penguin Books.

Deborah Tannen. "You Just Don't Understand." From *You Just Don't Understand* by Deborah Tannen. Copyright © 1990. Reprinted by permission of HarperCollins Publishers.

Arthur J. Lange and Patricia Jakubowski. "Assertive, Nonassertive, and Aggressive Behavior." Adapted from *Responsible Assertive Behavior*. Copyright © 1976 by Research Press. Used by permission of Research Press, Champaign, IL.

Lou Beeker Schultz. "Personal Journaling as a Life Companion." Reprinted by permission of the dedicated journaler and "comma writer," Lou Beeker Schultz.

Frances Vaughan. "Awakening Intuition." From *Awakening Intuition* by Frances E. Vaughan, Copyright © 1979 by Frances E. Vaughan. Used by permission of Doubleday, a division of Random House, Inc.

Ernest Hartmann, M.D. "Nature and Uses of Dreaming." From *USA Today Magazine*, March 1999.

"Intuitive Problem-Solving through Guided Imagery" activity. Adapted from *Awakening Intuition* by Frances E. Vaughan. Used by permission.

Section Three   Growth Dynamics

Abraham Maslow. "Self-Actualizing and Beyond." From *Challenges of Humanistic Psychology*, 1967, James Bugental, McGraw-Hill. Used by kind permission of James Bugental.

Harold Bloomfield and Robert B. Kory. "Getting Unstuck: Joyfully Recreating Your Life." From *Inner Joy*. Used by permission of Harold H. Bloomfield. Copyright © 1980 by Harold H. Bloomfield, M.D., and Robert B. Kory.

Morton Hunt. "The Lesson of the Cliff." From *Parade*, July 14, 1985. Copyright © 1985 by Morton Hunt. Reprinted by permission of Georges Borchardt, Inc., for the author.

Tom Keating. "Herbie." From *Indiana Faces and Other Places* by Tom Keating. Published by Indiana Only Press in arrangement with Central Newspapers, Inc. and *The Indianapolis Star*. Copyright © 1982. Reprinted by permission of Frank Caperton, Indianapolis Newspapers, Inc.

Allan Mallinger, M.D., & Jeanette DeWyze. "Too Perfect." From *Too Perfect: When Being in Control Gets out of Control* by Allan Mallinger, M.D. & Jeanette DeWyze. Copyright 1992. Reprinted by permission of Fawcett Columbine, New York, NY.

Poe Ballantine. "Advice to William Somebody." From *The Sun*, June 2000. Used by permission of Poe Ballantine.

Jenny Montgomery. "Left Behind." Originally titled "Suicide Leaves Friends Bewildered." From *The IUPUI Sagamore*, Sept. 19, 2000. Used by permission of Jennifer Montgomery.

"Courage." Adapted from Rollo May's *The Courage to Create,* 1976, Bantam Books.

"The Pace of Growth." Quotations taken from John Knowles (1966), *Indian Summer,* New York: Random House; and Nikos Kazantzakis (1952), *Zorba the Greek,* New York: Simon & Schuster.

Daphne Haygood-Benyard. "No One's Perfect." From *The Doors Are Always Open.* Copyright © 1994 by Daphne's Creations. Reprinted by kind permission of the author.

Section Four   Human Relationships

Abe Arkoff. "Intimate Relationship Choices." From *Exploration in Personal Growth.* Copyright © 1988. Boston: Allyn and Bacon.

John Gottman and Nan Silver. "Making Marriage Work." From *The Seven Principles for Making Marriage Work* by John M. Gottman and Nan Silver. Copyright © 1999 by John Mordechai Gottman and Nan Silver. Reprinted by permission of Crown Publishers, a division of Random House, Inc.

Tom Keating. "Sometimes It Rains." From *Indiana Faces and Other Places* by Tom Keating. Published by Indiana Only Press in arrangement with Central Newspapers, Inc. and *The Indianapolis Star.* Copyright © 1982. Reprinted by permission of Frank Caperton, Indianapolis News papers, Inc.

Dianne Hales. "Are Money Fights Ruining Your Marriage?" From *Women's Day,* April 1, 1992. Used by permission of Dianne Hales.

Meghan Daum. "Internet Romance." From *The New Yorker.* Reprinted by permission of International Creative Management, Inc., Copyright © 1998, and Meghan Daum.

"Kinds of Friends." Adapted from *Necessary Losses* by Judith Viorst (1986), Simon & Schuster.

Mark Murrmann. "Lamenting the Fading of Friendships." From *The Indianapolis Star,* August 19, 1995. Reprinted by kind permission of the author.

Martin Shepard. "Parents." From *The Do-It-Yourself Psychotherapy Book.* Copyright © 1976 by Martin Shepard. Reprinted by permission of the author.

David W. Johnson. "Resolving Interpersonal Conflicts." From *Reaching Out: Interpersonal Effectiveness and Self-Actualization.* Copyright 2000. Reprinted by permission of Allyn & Bacon, Boston, MA.

"Love Maps" activity. Adapted from *The Seven Principles for Making Marriage Work,* by John Gottman and Nan Silver. Copyright © 1999. Three Rivers Press. Used by permission.

Section Five   Emotions and Feelings

Daniel Goleman. "What's Your Emotional I.Q.?" From *Emotional Intelligence* by Daniel Goleman, Copyright © 1995 by Daniel Goleman. Used by permission of Bantam Books, a division of Random House, Inc.

Wayne Dyer. "Worry." From *Your Erroneous Zones.* © 1976 by Wayne W. Dyer. Reprinted by permission of HarperCollins Publisher, Inc.

Section Six   A Quality Life

vention Services, Inc. email: ncis@uslink.net. Reprinted by permission of the author.

Michael Jones. "Who Will Play Your Music?" From *Creating an Imaginative Life*, Conari Press, 1995. Copyright © 1995 by Michael Jones. Reprinted by the kind permission of the author who is equally adept on the keyboard as he is with words (his book includes a free CD of his professional solo piano recordings).

AND MORE THANKS

There are several pieces in this book that have unnamed authors. These contributions are from students in the senior author's Developing Human Potential course. They wish to remain anonymous but are willing to share their thoughts. I applaud their articulate and caring excerpts, all of which provide a personalized perspective of the book's themes.

All of the illustrations were drawn by tom mcCain, a professional cartoonist, illustrator, and an old friend. Copyright © 1996 by tom mcCain and reprinted with permission. Thanks "½" for the usual outstanding work.

All photos and captions are by Nelson Goud, copyright © 2001.

Great appreciation is extended to those who assisted in the many tasks needed to complete a finished manuscript: Bonnie Beaumont, Rae Kornbroke, and Dr. Khaula Murtadha, who performed excellent "bounder" leadership. Executive editor Karon Bowers gave just the right amount of encouragement and her editorial assistant, Deb Hanlon, provided timely assistance. Thanks to Diana Neatrour and the team at Omegatype Typography, Inc. for their customary high-quality work.

I would also like to extend my appreciation to the reviewers for this edition: Robert Bridges, Pennsylvania State University; Tom Caldwell, Middle Georgia College; Juan Kenigstein, Breyer State University; Susann S. Shepard, Middle Georgia College; Jeanne M. Slattery, Clarion University; and Lois Willoughby, Miami-Dade Community College.

Psychology
and
Personal
Growth

IDENTITY

What am I? Where am I? Who am I?
No one can answer these questions—
Why have I been so afraid to try?
I know if I look it's all there to see;
So I opened one small door to look inside,
And from out of that door a small voice cried,
"Have you come to set me free?"
It scared me a bit—Should I close the door?
No, I had to find out whose voice had cried,
Should I step inside and ask the voice to say more?
Perhaps if I took just one small glance inside—
So I peered through the door, but all was dim;
Could I summon the courage to step within—
And find the voice before its echo died?

—Anonymous

Who am I? This is the essential question of identity. It is rarely asked in public, thankfully, but is almost always raised during times of personal change. Throughout our lifetime we will be redefining who we think we are. Our identity, or self-concept, is crucial for positioning ourselves in life. It is the center of how we view others and the world. For a brief check of the current status of your identity, provide ten answers to the question "Who are you?" Just list your answers as quickly as you can.

_____   _____

_____   _____

_____   _____

_____   _____

Your answers may offer some helpful clues about your identity. You may define yourself primarily by *roles* such as age, gender, race, major or occupation, marital status, organizational membership, and so on. You may define yourself by *individual qualities* such as how you think, believe, or feel. Imagine yourself ten years ago looking at the list you just wrote. You probably would have wondered "Who is this person?" Our identity both initiates and reflects our development as a person.

The confidence you have in your identity will vary. Sometimes you will have a strong sense of who you are and where you are going in life. Then there are times of questioning and doubt about who this person is inside your skin. Identity changes can occur rapidly or gradually. Some identity changes are forced on a person, whereas others are natural developmental shifts, and even others are the products of deliberate effort. Most identity change does not occur in the manner hoped for by this undergraduate student:

I am very confused. I am glad I decided to go to a therapist so I can know who I am and where I should be going career-wise. I am glad there is a break before next semester so I can spend time with God and discover who I am and where I am going. I hope I will know before next semester starts.

Maybe this student found her identity during the holiday break—it *could* happen, but it's unlikely. This student, however, stated what most of us want when confronted with an identity crisis—a quick solution because it is so unsettling.

This section focuses on major issues in identity formation. The articles selected examine identity from several perspectives.

- In "The Search for Identity," Carl Rogers, a major theorist and therapist, discusses how the struggle to discover an identity is a modern problem. He explains how finding and creating an identity is a lifetime journey. His account of how artist Georgia O'Keeffe discovered her artistic identity has relevance for us all.

- In "The Basic Relationship," Abe Arkoff suggests that the way we come to see and regard ourselves is our most fundamental relationship.
- Nelson Goud elaborates on a little-known concept of the pioneering psychologist Abraham Maslow, called "Rubricizing." He discusses how we place people, including ourselves, into identity categories, and how rubricizing helps or hinders.
- Being aware of what we are experiencing now is the focus of "Mindfulness" by Jon Kabat-Zinn.
- In "Suddenly I'm the Adult?" Richard Cohen provides a personalized history of his identity milestones. Of particular emphasis is how he became an adult. Most of us will quickly spot parallels in our own lives.
- Themes of the quarterlife crisis are highlighted in "Challenges of the Emerging Adult" by Nelson Goud.
- When her basic priorities changed, so did her identities. Sarah Silbert explores how one's life shifts when fundamental values are altered in "The Rivers We Call Ourselves."
- Seeking careers that fit and adjusting to the working world are central issues in "The Emerging Adult: The Work World" by Nelson Goud.
- In "Occupational Exploration," Christopher A. Schaefer describes how his careers evolved in a natural process.
- Craig Mosher explains how a self-employed option fits him the best in "Woodworker."
- The differing and sometimes baffling interactions between men and women are discussed in "Ending the Battle between the Sexes."
- The male role is the theme of a brief piece, "On Being a Man" by Sam Keen.
- Sometimes part of what you are is forced on you. Such is the case for Denise Karuth, who describes her world living with a physical disability in "If I Were a Car, I'd Be a Lemon." You may be surprised at Karuth's point of view in this piece.
- Language and disability are highlighted in "Think 'People First.'"

You are encouraged to attempt one or more of the Follow-Up questions at the end of each article. At the end of this section are Applied Activities that extend and apply the ideas presented in the articles.

The Search for Identity: A Modern Problem

Carl Rogers

We are, perhaps all of us, engaged in a struggle to discover our identity, the person we are and choose to be. This is a very pervasive search; it involves our clothes, our hair, our appearance. At a more significant level, it involves our choice of values, our stance in relation to parents and others, the relationship we choose to have to society, our whole philosophy of life. It is, in these days, a most perplexing search. As one college woman says:

I'm confused. Just when I think I'm getting my head together, I talk with some fellow who's sure he knows what life is all about. And because I'm uncertain, I'm really impressed. And then when I get away I realize that's his answer. It can't be the answer for me. I've got to find my own. But it's hard when everything is so loose and unsure.

I see this search for one's real self, for identity, as much more of a problem today than it was in the historical past. During most of history, it made little difference whether the individual discovered himself. Perhaps he lived a more comfortable life if he did not because the identity he lived was defined for him. It is interesting to imagine ourselves back in feudal times. The serf was expected to be a serf throughout his life, as were his children after him. In return he was permitted to eke out a meager living, most of his work going to support the lord of the manor, who in turn protected him. The nobleman was, in a more luxurious way, also constricted. He was the lord, responsible for his followers, and his children would continue the role of the nobleman. In our own country, during one dark period of our history, the slave was always the slave and the master always the master. The difficulties of abandoning these role identities are still painfully with us. While the rigidity of the defined role seems incredibly restrictive to us now, it should not blind us to the fact that such rigidity made life simpler in many ways. The cobbler knew that he and his sons would always be cobblers; his wife knew that she and her daughters would always be primarily servants of their husbands. There were almost no options, and peculiarly enough this gave people a type of security that we have left behind. Perhaps one of the few analogies that are comprehensible to us is the peacetime army. Many men and women have come to accept army life with more satisfaction than they had supposed possible. There are almost no decisions: they are told what to wear, how to behave, where to live, and what to do. They can gripe as freely as they wish, without any responsibility for their lives. They are given an identity, told who they are; and the agonizing personal search that most of us must go through is at least temporarily abrogated.

It is for reasons of this sort that I say the search for one's real self is a peculiarly modern problem. The individual's life is no longer defined (though it may be influenced) by one's family, social class, color, church, or nation. We carry the burden ourselves of discovering our identity. I believe the only person today who does not suffer this painful search for self is the person who voluntarily surrenders his or her individual identity to some organization or institution that defines the purposes, the values, the philosophy to be followed. Examples include people who completely commit themselves to some strict religious sect that is sure of all the answers; those who commit themselves to a rigorous ideology (whether revolutionary or reactionary) that defines their philosophy, their life-style, and their actions; those who give themselves completely to science or industry or traditional education (though there are large cracks in the certainties of all these institutions); or, as I mentioned, those who give their lives to the military. I can thoroughly understand the satisfactions and securities that cause individuals to make such commitments, one of which is to gain a certain comfort.

The transition from conformity to freedom creates a strong sense of disequilibrium and discomfort. Yet I suspect that the majority of young people prefer the more painful burden of choosing the uniqueness that is involved in discovering the real self. I know that is my choice. Still, one of the most common fears of people trying to discover who they really are inside is that this undiscovered "me" will turn out to be a worthless, bizarre, evil, or horrible creature. Something of this fear is expressed by a searching student:

I feel my mind is open, kind of like a funnel, and on top there are sparks and exciting things, but down deeper in the funnel it's dark, and I'm afraid to go down in there because I'm scared of what I might find. I'm not going to do it just now.

This attitude is a very common one indeed. There are a number of ways in which individuals pursue this goal of becoming themselves. Some lives have been badly distorted or warped by early childhood. For them, the search for solidity in themselves, for their own real self, may be a long or painful one. Others more fortunate are already in the process of discovery and have an easier time. Some are sufficiently frightened by the risks involved in the search that they endeavor to freeze themselves as they are, fearful of any road that would lead into unknown territory. I

will briefly describe several of the ways in which people venture, as they search for the real self.

THE LIFETIME JOURNEY OF SELF-DISCOVERY

This process of self-discovery, self-acceptance, and self-expression is not something that goes on only in therapy or in groups. Many people have neither of these experiences. For those who do, the therapy or the group exists for only a limited time. But for all of us, the search to become the person we most uniquely are is a lifetime process. I believe this is one reason why biography holds a fascination for so many readers. We like to follow the struggle of individuals to become what they are capable of becoming. For me, this is illustrated by the book I have just finished reading: the life story of artist Georgia O'Keeffe [*Portrait of An Artist: A Biography of Georgia O'Keeffe*, by L. Lisle (1980)]. There are many steps in her development. At fourteen, the inwardly independent but outwardly conforming girl won a gold medal for her ladylike deportment at a strict Catholic school. But by the age of sixteen, she was beginning to dress in a "tailored, midwestern corsetless style" (in 1903!), which was to be a characteristic throughout her many years. And at age twenty-nine she locked herself into her studio and analyzed all her work up to that point with "ruthless detachment." She could tell which paintings had been done to please one professor and which to please another. She could tell which had been influenced by well-known artists of the day.

> Then an idea dawned on her. There were abstract shapes in her mind integral to her imagination, unlike anything she had been taught. 'This thing that is your own is so close to you, often you never realize it's there,' she later explained.... 'I could think of a whole string of things I'd like to put down but I'd never thought of doing it because I'd never seen anything like it.' ... She had made up her mind. This was what she would paint. (p. 81)

As you can imagine, this decision was the initial step toward becoming the great artist of her mature years. Even in her nineties, she relentlessly pursued that goal of painting her own unique perceptions of the desert, of bleached bones, of huge and gorgeous flowers—to the point that one has only to look at one of her paintings to realize "That's an O'Keeffe."

Like Georgia O'Keeffe, each of us is the artist or the architect of his or her own life. We can copy others, we can live to please others, or we can discover what is unique and precious to us and paint that, become that. It is a task that takes a lifetime.

YOU CAN *BE YOURSELF*

Let me try to summarize what it means to me to find one's real self. In the first place it is a process, a direction, not some static achievement. In my estimation no one is ever completely successful in finding all her real (and ever-changing) self. But there are certain characteristics of this process. Persons move away from hiding behind facades and pretenses, whether these have been held consciously or unconsciously. They move toward a greater closeness to and awareness of their inward experiences. They find this development exceedingly complex and varied, ranging from wild and crazy feelings to solid, socially approved ones. They move toward accepting all of these experiences as their own; they discover that they are people with an enormous variety of reactions. The more they own and accept their inner reactions—and are unafraid of them—the more they can sense the meanings those reactions have. The more all this inner richness belongs to them, the more they can appropriately *be* their own experiences. An individual may become aware of a childish need to depend on someone, to be cared for and protected. In appropriate situations she can let herself be that childish, dependent self. She may discover that certain situations anger her. She can more easily express that anger as it

When you are very young, life, like these railroad tracks, appears to go on forever. We wonder and dream about what awaits us down the way. If there is an end, it is too distant to even think about. Sometimes our lifetrack feels just right. Other times we may have doubts about our lifetrack. Something isn't right, something is missing in our travels. Bernard Malamud's words begin to make sense—"If your train's on the wrong track, every station you come to is the wrong station." If this happens, it is often wise to choose another lifetrack. But just switching tracks is not sufficient because, as Will Rogers warned, "Even if you're on the right track, you'll get run over if you just sit there."

"The Right Track" by Nelson Goud. Copyright © 1996.

arises in the situation that arouses it, rather than suppress it until it pours out explosively onto some innocent victim. A man can discover soft, tender, loving feelings (which are especially difficult for men to own) and can express them with satisfaction, not shame. These people are becoming involved in the wider range of their feelings, attitudes, and potential. They are building a good relationship with what is going on within themselves. They are beginning to appreciate and like, rather than hate and mistrust, all their experiences. Thus, they are coming closer to finding and being all of themselves in the moment. To me this is the way that the person moves toward answering the question, "Who am I?"

Follow-Up

1. *Rogers quotes a college woman who is impressed with someone who knows for sure about life and his identity. She realizes that this is his answer, not hers, but she is confused on how to find her answers. When you are not sure of who you are, are you also easily influenced by confident and seemingly authoritative persons? Provide an example, if possible. Have you, like the above student, chosen to find your way and answers, even though this approach is loaded with doubts and uncertainties? If yes, try to give a real-life example.*

2. *Rogers discusses how even some modern day groups offer ready-made identities in which few decisions have to be made. He mentions the military, as well as political and religious sects. Do these kinds of identity solutions appeal to you? Why or why not? For further reading on this topic try the classic small book* True Believers, *by the longshoreman philosopher Eric Hoffer.*

3. *Rogers explains how the artist Georgia O'Keeffe found her artistic voice. She said that she locked herself in her studio and looked at her work with "ruthless detachment." She then realized that she had not been painting the images that seemed to exist only in her mind. These images became her artistic identity. She concluded that "this thing that is your own is so close to you, often you never realize it's there." Try looking at your own life with "ruthless detachment" to discover which parts are direct results of others' influence and which parts are uniquely yours. How can you blend the most significant of each into your own voice?*

4. *Rogers mentions that biography appeals to many because it provides some hints on how others struggle with identity issues. Have you experienced this effect? Consider reading a biography of someone you admire.*

5. *In the last paragraph of his article, Rogers talks about several characteristics of the process of becoming one's real self. One characteristic is moving away from facades and pretenses. Have you found that you become truer to your identity when you drop false fronts? Consider trying out some of the ideas in that paragraph. If you're interested in a fuller discussion of these characteristics, you will find them in* On Becoming a Person *by Carl Rogers.*

The Basic Relationship

Abe Arkoff

John Vasconcellos is a highly esteemed member of the California legislature, but he speaks candidly about his own early failure to value himself and of many later years of therapy to develop his self-esteem and personhood. Recently, recalling his own long trek to a better sense of self, he wrote:

> In school, I was a high-achiever, receiving awards and excellent grades. In adulthood, I became a prominent lawyer in a prestigious firm. My first campaign for a seat in the state legislature in 1966 was successful, and I have now been reelected eleven times.
>
> Yet, through it all, I had almost no sense of my self, no self-esteem. I worked for my successes only in a constant attempt to please others. My intellect functioned superbly, but the rest of my self barely functioned at all. I had been conditioned to know myself basically as a sinner, guilt-ridden and ashamed, constantly beating my breast and professing my unworthiness. I had so little self-esteem that I lost my first election (running for eighth-grade president) by one vote—my own (Vasconcellos, 1989, pp. xiv–xv).

Vasconcellos notes that personal experience has taught him the importance of valuing oneself. He has increasingly focused on the issue of self-esteem both to help himself and others develop "a strong sense of self." He is the author of legislation creating the California Task Force to Promote Self-Esteem and Personal and Social Responsibility, whose aim is to promote the well-being of the individual and society as a way of preventing, rather than just reacting to, serious social ills.

As a clinical psychologist, I have worked with many people who have come to me for help. Some were deeply troubled. Of these, I cannot recall a single one who had a good relationship with herself or himself. Not one was her or his own best friend. When they began to like themselves and trust themselves, I knew they were getting better. When they began to take some pride in themselves, I knew they were getting well.

Not long ago I heard a comedienne ask a group this question: "How many of you know how it feels to be the only person in a relationship?" This got a laugh, but thinking back on my clinical experience with human beings, it seems clear to me that the most important relationship we each have is the one with ourself. How strange that most of us do not think of this as a relationship at all. How strange that this is the relationship in which we sometimes appear least humane, treating ourselves in a way we would never treat somebody else.

Think about this with reference to your own self. You are always in your own presence, and just as you are aware of the world around you, you are aware of yourself. You think, you feel, you act. You also observe yourself thinking and feeling and acting. You reflect on yourself and come to know yourself. You have *reflective awareness*—the ability to consider your behavior as you observe it.

Because you have the power of reflective awareness, you are both actor and audience in your life. You perform and at the same time watch yourself perform. But you are not a passive audience. You, the audience, attend and consider. You weigh and evaluate. Sometimes you applaud, sometimes you hiss or jeer, sometimes rise and command. You (the actor) are influenced by you (the audience) just as you (the audience) are influenced by you (the actor).

Of course, there are other people in the audience too. In their responses to you, they tell you who they think you are and what you can and can't do and should and shouldn't do. You observe these others, observe them observing you, and you observe yourself. Out of all these observations you shape and reshape the idea of who you are, and you shape and reshape your relationship to yourself. Your relationship to yourself could be called "the basic relationship," because how you come to see and regard yourself becomes such a fundamental force in your life.

THE DYNAMIC SELF-IMAGE

The Self-Image and Behavior

Because of its influence on our perceptions, our self-image influences our behavior in many ways. Some psychologists believe that the basic human force is the striving to maintain and enhance our conception of ourselves (Combs, Richards, & Richards, 1976). We present ourselves to others in ways calculated to enhance our image in their eyes and in our own. We defend our image from attack, whether this be assault from without or doubts arising from within.

Our self-image serves us as a basic frame of reference—as a foundation or guide for our actions. We would be lost without it, and therefore we defend it against change. Some of us seem to be resistant to growth or positive movement in our lives, but this may be our way of being true to our picture of ourselves (Rosenberg, 1979).

Psychologists have suggested that when a person believes something to be so, he or she tends to behave in a way that makes it so; this is called a "self-fulfilling prophecy." If we see ourselves in a positive light, we are apt to try harder because we think our efforts will pay off, and we are more likely to succeed or define the outcome as successful. If we have a low opinion of ourselves, we may avoid a sit-uation or approach it halfheartedly, and we are more likely to fail or to interpret the results as failure (Langer & Dweck, 1973).

The Self-Image and Relationships with Others

Our self-image influences our perceptions of others and our relationships with them. There is considerable evidence that we tend to see others as we see ourselves. Emerson wrote, "What we are, that only can we see." Hamachek (1978) adds, "When we think we are looking out a window, it could be that we are merely gazing into a looking-glass" (p. 47). He suggested that a good way to find out what a person is really like is to find out what this person thinks others are like. He writes, "The man who tells us that people are basically trustworthy and kind—ignoring the plain fact that they can also be devious and cruel—may be saying more about himself than about the world" (p. 47).

People who like and accept themselves tend to accept others (Berger, 1952; Pirot, 1986). Research shows that individuals who hold themselves in high esteem tend to take a favorable view of others and also expect more acceptance and less rejection (Baron, 1974; Walster, 1965). And, of course, when others are approached in this light, they are more likely to respond favorably.

If we dislike or reject ourselves, we are more likely to view and treat others in the same way, and consequently our relations with others will suffer. Oscar Wilde observed that "all criticism is a form of autobiography." Hamachek (1978) suggests some personal research that one can do on this point. He writes, "Pay particular attention to your feelings about yourself for the next three or four days and note how they influence your behavior toward others. It may be that it is not our friend or our loved one or our children we are mad at; it is ourselves. What we feel toward ourselves gets aimed at others, and we sometimes treat others not as persons, but as targets" (p. 46).

We tend to form relationships with persons who are similar to us, who see us as we see ourselves and who confirm our own positive self-impressions (Swan, 1984; Taylor & Brown, 1988). It's hard for us to rest easy in the company of those who don't see us as we wish to be seen (Lang, Phillipson, & Lee, 1966). Joseph Joubert understood this prime requisite of friendship when he wrote, "When my friends are one-eyed, I look at their profile."

THE MULTIPLE SELF

Subpersonalities

Psychologist John Vargiu (1977) believes that we may not be a single self. He attributes our variability to a number of *subpersonalities*— semi-autonomous personages within us that are all striving for expression. He holds that we need to understand these subpersonalities better and bring them into harmony with each other; doing so, we become a single harmonized self.

You may recall seeing an acquaintance behave in a quite uncharacteristic way. You wonder, "What's gotten into him?" Or you think, "She's not herself today." Of course, she *is* herself—but a different one of her selves or subselves or subpersonalities.

Consider the inconsistencies or subpersonalities that may exist within yourself. Have you noted that you sometimes seem to get caught up in a particular way of being and behaving? You recognize it and could even give it a label because it is so salient and you have been caught up in it before. When you are under its spell, you see yourself and your world differently and you behave differently, perhaps in a way you like or don't like. You may be able to identify a number of these subpersonalities in yourself, some in harmony and some in conflict with each other.

It may be useful to identify and study the subpersonalities in yourself. When I did so, these subselves were most salient: The Creative but Tiring Soul (a subself that enjoyed creating something new or different and watching it develop—for a while), Dad (a caring, helpful subself), The Relentless Searcher (a subself that was always looking for something better but never quite finding it), and The Wise Old Man (an emerging subself, one with the ability to understand, accept, and enjoy things as they are). I was pleased to note that The Examiner (a subself that was constantly scrutinizing things to see if they measured up) had been largely decommissioned.

It is important not to confuse the concept of *subpersonalities*, which applies to normal behavior, with that of *multiple personality*, which is a serious and disabling disorder (Rowan, 1990). This latter condition is quite rare and better known to Hollywood and television script writers than to psychiatrists or psychologists. The added personalities in multiple personality disorder are quite autonomous, even with differences in handedness (left or right dominance) and in patterns of handwriting and brain waves (Putnam, 1984), and usually operate without the awareness of the original personality.

Accepting Ourselves

Some of the dictionary's definitions of the word *accept* are "to be favorably disposed toward," "to believe in," and "to receive as adequate or satisfactory." If we accept ourselves or show *self-acceptance*, we are favorably disposed toward ourselves and believe we are okay. That doesn't mean we don't want to be better, but it does mean whatever we are right now, it's all right to be. If we reject ourselves or show *self-rejection*, we don't like or believe in ourselves, and we feel inadequate.

Before considering self-acceptance more fully, it may be helpful to look at self-rejection— all the things self-acceptance is not. Following is a checklist of behaviors seen in those who find themselves personally unacceptable, which is adapted from larger listings by Wayne Dyer (1976) and by Bloomfield and Kory (1980). The list is presented here just to get you thinking about yourself—it's not a deep and definitive device. As you think, answer each item "yes" or "no."

_____ 1. Do you feel embarrassed by your abilities or accomplishments?

_____ 2. Do you give credit to others when you really deserve it yourself?

_____ 3. Do you put others above you when you are really their equal or superior?

_____ 4. Do you fail to stand up for the things you really believe in?

_____ 5. Do you put yourself down when you have made a mistake?

_____ 6. Do you let others put you down?

_____ 7. Do you have a cute name for yourself that reduces you in some way?

_____ 8. Do you depend on others to bolster your opinions?

_____ 9. Do you believe that others cannot possibly find you attractive?

_____ 10. Do you believe that others are being kind out of charity or some ulterior motive?

_____ 11. Do you find it hard to say no to a request because of what the person might think of you?

_____ 12. Do you find it hard to complain about poor treatment because you are afraid of making a fuss?

Because the items in the preceding list reflect self-rejection, each item to which you answered "yes" suggests an area for you to work on to change the "yes" to "no." But don't put yourself down for your "yeses"—that would be another bit of self-rejecting behavior.

Showing one's true face—even to oneself—can be a difficult task when it is a face one has somehow come to think is wrong or even evil.

Some lesbians and gays have written of their confusion or consternation at discovering their sexual orientation and of their struggle to come out of the closet and be who they truly are. In one study (Jay & Young, 1979), a woman reported that she didn't realize she was a lesbian until she was 20, and her coming out was traumatic. "I used to look at myself in the mirror and cry. I couldn't believe what I was. How could a good girl like me be something as wicked as a lesbian? Once I found the gay bars and gay community I found that there were many 'good girl' lesbians" (pp. 55–56). She noted that since then, her self-image had improved each year, and now she wouldn't want to be anyone other than who she is.

We must constantly seek to understand ourselves if we are to become ourselves; but the understanding does not come once and for all. It comes little by little as we observe ourselves in every new situation. In every situation, we can learn to tell whether we are being genuine and true to ourselves, or phony and unauthentic (Friedman, 1958).

For ten years, I was a volunteer working with hospice patients and those with life-threatening illnesses. Being with a number of persons as they faced death, I've come to believe that dying has been hardest for those who never really lived their lives—those who were losing both life and their last chance to become themselves. I am reminded of the story told about Rabbi Zusya as he approached death. Rabbi Zusya said that when he met the Holy One, he would not be asked, "Why were you not like Moses?" No, he would be asked, "Why were you not like Zusya?" Zusya added, "It is for this reason that I tremble."

References

Baron, P. (1974). Self-esteem, ingratiation, and evaluation of unknown others. *Journal of Personality and Social Psychology, 30,* 104–109.

Berger, E. (1952). The relation between expressed acceptance of self and expressed acceptance of others. *Journal of Abnormal and Social Psychology, 47,* 778–782.

Bloomfield, H. H., & Kory, R. B. (1980). *Inner joy: New strategies to put more pleasure and satisfaction in your life*. New York: Wyden.

Combs, A. W., Richards, A. C., & Richards, F. (1976). *Perceptual psychology: A humanistic approach to the study of persons*. New York: Harper & Row.

Dyer, W. W. (1976). *Your erroneous zones*. New York: Funk & Wagnalls.

Friedman, M. (1958). *To deny our nothingness: Contemporary images of man*. London: Macmillan.

Hamachek, D. E. (1978). *Encounters with the self* (2nd ed.). New York: Holt, Rinehart and Winston.

Jay, K., & Young, A. (1979). *The gay report*. New York: Summit Books.

Lang, R. D., Phillipson, H., & Lee, A. R. (1966). *Interpersonal perception: A theory and method of research*. New York: Springer.

Langer, E. J., & Dweck, C. S. (1973). *Personal politics: The psychology of making it*. Englewood Cliffs, NJ: Prentice-Hall.

Pirot, M. (1986). The pathological thought and dynamics of the perfectionist. *Journal of Individual Psychology, 42*(1), 51–58.

Putnam, F. W. (1984). The psychophysiologic investigation of multiple personality disorder: A review. *Psychiatric Clinics of North America, 7*(1), 31–39.

Rosenberg, M. (1979). *Conceiving the self*. New York: Basic Books.

Rowan, J. (1990). *Subpersonalities: The people inside us*. New York: Routledge.

Swan, W. B., Jr. (1984). Quest for accuracy in person perception: A matter of pragmatics. *Psychological Review, 91*, 457–477.

Taylor, S. E., & Brown, J. D. (1988). Illusion and well-being: A social psychological perspective on mental health. *Psychological Bulletin, 103*(2), 193–210.

Vargiu, J. G. (1977). Subpersonalities. In A. Arkoff (Ed.), *Psychology and personal growth* (3rd ed., pp. 22–27). Boston: Allyn & Bacon.

Vasconcellos, J. (1989). Preface. In A. M. Mecca, N. J. Smelser, & J. Vasconcellos (Eds.), *The social importance of self-esteem* (pp. xi–xxi). Berkeley: University of California Press.

Walster, E. (1965). The effect of self-esteem on romantic liking. *Journal of Experimental Social Psychology, 1*, 184–197.

Follow-Up

1. *Do you have a good relationship with yourself? Describe this relationship as it seems to you.*
2. *What subpersonalities can you detect in yourself? Name and describe each one and its influence on you.*
3. *How much insight into yourself do you have? How much of a puzzle are you? Discuss an important aspect of yourself that remains a mystery to you.*
4. *Is your life right for you? Are you on the way to becoming yourself? Give your evidence.*

Rubricizing

Nelson Goud

She was standing in line waiting to board the Denver to Seattle flight. In her 70s, she had gray-blue hair, a red dress, and a satchel clutched under her right arm. What she did not have was a left arm. I became immediately sympathetic as the old lady negotiated the movements necessary to board the plane. On the plane she was two seats away in the same row. About thirty minutes into the flight she pulled out a paperback novel, opened to a marked page, and held the book in her only hand. I snuck a look—readers cannot seem to help but check out what other readers read—and saw *Lake Wobegon Days* on the cover. I had read it a couple of months ago and could not resist the urge to ask how she liked it. Besides, this one-armed old lady just had to be lonely and probably experienced life on the fringe, a human satellite. "How's it going in Lake Wobegon lately?" I asked while eating lunch. She talked about the book a bit and seemed quite friendly. We kept chatting and somewhere in there music was mentioned. We discovered we were both big band fans. I droned on about my favorites and how I played the trumpet. She was politely attentive and when I finally took a breath she said, "I played in a big band once." This surprised me. "What did you play?" I asked. "Sax," she said. I asked if this was in high school. "Oh, no. I was 17 though. I played in an all-female professional big band which toured all the USO places in the U.S. and Europe in WWII." Not only did she know of my favorite big band leaders, but she saw and talked with them in their prime. After many minutes of answering my eager questions, I noticed that the one-armed old lady had "disappeared." She had become a different person.

I even forgot about her loss of an arm and asked if she still played the sax. She just smiled and said she hadn't picked it up in a while. We deplaned and she met her daughter and two friends and I knew then I was a better reader of books than people.

At a meeting during a national convention, I found myself seated next to a counselor dressed in the garb of a 1960s throwback—Army fatigues, long hair, beard, and a detached, peaceful gaze.

"I'm having a most fascinating time at this convention," he said during a break.

"Why is that?" I asked.

"Take a look at my nametag," he motioned.

It read "Rev. Bill Smith." He then explained that prior to reading his nametag, conventioneers react to him like they would to a hippie—that is, either ignoring him, staring, or engaging in the hippie lingo.

"The thing is," he continued, "I am not a man of the cloth. When they finally see the nametag they stop talking for a few seconds. You can sense the confusion going on as they try to figure out how to act with a 'hippie preacher.' Most people do not have that category and do not know what to say or do. I need the nametag to get into the workshops so I keep it on. So far I have learned more about people with my nametag than from the workshops."

Peace, brother, love, and that's a far out story, Reverend.

These are examples of *rubricizing* (pronounced roo-bri-sigh-zing), a term coined by Abraham Maslow. He believed that there are two major ways to perceive any experience. One is to observe its unique essence, how the experience is truly different and individualistic. The second, rubricizing, is to respond to an experience as a representative of a category (rubric). Rubricizing perception is similar to the actions of a file clerk who recognizes only what is minimally necessary to place a paper under A, B, Y, and so on. When we rubricize people, we quickly scan them for certain characteristics (often subconsciously) and place them into one of our mental file folders. A rubricized person becomes a member of a grouping: waiter, teenager, a Johnson kid, math major, jock, married, female, southerner, sorority type, and so on. Rubrics are categories of the mind.

RUBRICIZING CONTINUUM

Rubrics range from the stereotypic to the highly individualistic. A stereotype is a rubric with a prepackaged set of meanings. Common stereotype subjects are race, religion, occupation, gender, age, marital status, residence, and geographical locale. At the other end of the rubricizing continuum is the individualistic rubric that has meaning only for the perceiver (or possibly just a few others). For instance, I know a person who can glance at the shoes of a person and then tell you his or her food and clothing tastes, social status, and several personality characteristics. To her, people have an astrology chart on their feet. There are also rubrics that fall between these extremes.

NEGATIVE AND POSITIVE ASPECTS

Rubrics can have negative or positive meanings. It is easy to understand why one dislikes being placed in a negative rubric (e.g., "She comes from _____ and you know they never amount to much."). It is also a burden to be rubricized into a positive rubric. This is common for those who stand out in some valued quality like "outstanding student," "talented musician/dancer/artist," "really good looking." Many of the latter also resist being rubricized. Some find the pressure to uphold this image too daunting over the long haul. But the major cause of resistance is that every person has multiple dimensions to his or her identity that also call for expression and recognition. To always be seen characterized in reference to the outstanding quality becomes a constraining and limiting existence.

Rubricizing can be either an enhancing or hindering form of perception. It enhances one's life whenever one is required only to respond to familiar, repetitive tasks or to quickly recognize a single feature. By having only to exert partial attention to a situation, one is then freed to devote more energy to a more difficult activity (or several low-challenge activities at one time). One can, for example, plan other activities during a boring committee meeting without missing a key point, or one can watch TV and talk to another on surface topics simultaneously.

Rubricizing is a hindrance whenever a situation calls for attention to uniqueness, complexity, wholeness, and change. Trying to understand another person's life, solving a difficult problem, creating something, self-examination—these are kinds of actions that demand more than a quick, cursory scan. One must be open to the shifting multiple dimensions of what is being presented. Carl Rogers explains that this kind of perception requires an "openness to experience" and provides an example:

One of the most satisfying experiences I know—is just fully to appreciate an individual in the same way that I appreciate a sunset. When I look at a sunset . . . I don't find myself saying, "Soften the orange a little on the right hand corner, and put a bit more purple along the base, and use a little more pink in the cloud color" . . . I don't try to control a sunset. I watch it with awe as it unfolds. It is this receptive, open attitude which is necessary to truly perceive something as it is.

It is important to know that rubricizing is usually our *first* perceptual response. One must therefore be especially vigilant in the situations described previously in which rubricizing is a hindrance. In addition, once something is rubricized it tends to keep this meaning unless a stronger, countering experience changes this perception.

Rubricizing can freeze how a person is perceived, so that if major changes occur, they go unnoticed. You may be a significantly different person compared to earlier years, but on a visit back home or reuniting with friends, find that they treat you as you were back then. Those very close to us are not immune to rubricizing. We have very strong rubrics about our parents (and they of us). I realized I had rubricized my grandmother. Although we had an affectionate relationship, I noticed at the age of 30 that I was acting toward her the same way I did at 13. It was ritualistic—she was Grandma and I was Grandson. I happened to ask her about her decision to come to America (she was a Dutch immigrant). Telling her life story as a young girl and woman revealed whole new dimensions of her as a person besides being a grandmother. A rubric has been broken whenever you hear or say, "You surprised me by your interest (or background) in . . ." or "I didn't know you had that in you." Take another look at those close to you to see if some rubricizing is going on.

Rubricizing diminishes the people or things that you value. Rubricizing can be accurate or inaccurate, but it is always an *incomplete* form of perception. Everything has multiple facets of which we only perceive a portion. Sometimes we unintentionally slip into a rubricizing mode. I know a physical therapist who was talking to a friend who had to have some surgery to heal a fracture. The physical therapist said to her friend, "I have been learning about patients just like you." Her friend replied, "You have not been learning about patients just like me because there is no one like me. You probably mean that you have been learning about injuries similar to mine." The friend naturally resisted being totally classified by a type of injury.

APPLICATIONS

Here are some guidelines for lessening negative rubricizing:

- Be alert to the *language* signals of rubricizing—"She is the *type* who. . . ," "He's that *kind*," "I can *peg* a person by how. . . ."
- The most frequent rubricizing questions are, "What do you do?" or "What is your major?" If answered, it is very likely that this will be the only dimension of your life that is discussed. It becomes the central identity rubric. Some prefer to be perceived primarily in this rubric. However, there are other choices if you desire to place your occupational identity in a larger context. You can refrain from initially asking a new person, "What do you do?" When introducing or meeting someone for the first time, guide the conversation first to other life activities. You can do the same if asked by someone else. I find it helpful to reply "I do quite a few things. I know you're asking about what I do for a living, but I'd like to talk first about . . . (a new book, jazz, a recent trip, a new idea)." Some of my best conversations started this way; sometimes, though, others persist on finding out my occupational identity (or even shift to another rubric ritual—"What is your sign?").

  During the first weeks of a graduate course I request that students refrain from revealing their occupation or major, age, marital status, religion, and residence. Their ideas and feeling on course topics become the central focus rather than their rubrics. Only later, in the larger context of telling life stories, do the above identity markers emerge.
- Start to observe your system of "rubric triggers"—for example, appearance, occupational/major categories, residence,

mannerisms, clothing, names, family background, social interaction style, language usage, and so on. Stereotypic rubrics are relatively easy to spot. Try also to uncover the individual system of rubrics that exist primarily for you.

- Check the accuracy of initial rubricizing. Through observation and interaction one can find out if the first impressions are erroneous or too restrictive. Rubricizing is counteracted by discovering new facets of a person. Even if it is not realistic to look for new facets (e.g., being served by a waiter), your basic human respect is enhanced in just knowing that this person, like you, has many dimensions that are not seen.
- Try to thaw out a frozen rubric you have of someone close to you. This usually means talking about new topics or doing different activities than what you customarily do.
- Develop further skills in non-rubricizing, receptive perception. Kazantzakis' Zorba seemed to have the secret—"Like the child, he sees everything for the first time. He is forever astonished and wonders why and wherefore . . . each morning when he opens his eyes he sees trees, sea, stones and birds, and is amazed. 'What is this miracle?' he cries" (1952, p. 151). Unless we are alert, rubricizing can gradually erode experiences that were previously delightful. A pretty flower loses its appeal because we see it several times or find out its name. A favorite song, painting, book, or poem are now given a glance instead of the full absorption that made them delightful in the first place.

One simple idea to try is to focus on a commonly rubricized object you see each day. Maybe it's a tree on the way to work. Try to discover how it is different from other trees, whether it has lost or grown leaves, how the bark looks different after a rain, and whether it is a home to birds.

- Have you considered that you can rubricize yourself? It is possible to freeze your own identity so that all that is left are repeating familiar patterns. Here are some typical self-rubricizing statements: "I am a methodical and prudent type so it is almost impossible to be spontaneous," "As a teacher I am really not qualified to do anything else but teach children," "People from my (family, school, town, etc.) don't try to do . . . , they'll fail."

All the concepts of rubricizing others also apply to ourselves. Self-rubricizing blunts the adventuring edge so necessary for realizing one's potentialities. Ask yourself, what do *you* do?

References

Kazantzakis, N. (1952). *Zorba the Greek.* New York: Simon and Schuster.

Follow-Up

1. *Describe an instance where you:*
   - *Have been rubricized*
   - *Rubricized another*
   - *Rubricized yourself*
2. *Choose two statements from the article that have meaning for you and tell why.*
3. *Attempt one or more of the applications explained in the final section of the article.*

Mindfulness

Jon Kabat-Zinn

Mindfulness means paying attention in a particular way: on purpose, in the present moment, and nonjudgmentally. This kind of attention nurtures greater awareness, clarity, and acceptance of present-moment reality. It wakes up to the fact that our lives unfold only in moments. . . . The key . . . is an appreciation for the present moment and the cultivation of an intimate relationship with it through a continual attending to it with care and discernment. It is the direct opposite of taking life for granted. . . .

The best way to capture moments is to pay attention. . . .

You can easily observe the mind's habit of escaping from the present moment for yourself. Just try to keep your attention focused on any object for even a short period of time . . . you may have to remember over and over again to be awake and aware . . . to look, to feel, to be. . . .

The impulse frequently arises in me to squeeze another this or another that into this moment. Just this phone call, just stopping off here on my way there. . . . I've learned to identify this impulse and mistrust it. I work hard at saying no to it. It would have me eat breakfast with my eyes riveted to the cereal box, reading for the hundredth time the dietary contents. . . . This impulse doesn't care what it feeds on, as long as it's feeding. . . . I like to practice voluntary simplicity to counter such impulses and make sure nourishment comes at a deep level. It involves intentionally doing only one thing at a time and making sure I am here for it. . . . Voluntary simplicity means going fewer places in one day rather than more, seeing less so I can see more, doing less so I can do more, acquiring less so I can have more. . . .

A commitment to simplicity in the midst of the world is a delicate balancing act. It is always in need of retuning, further inquiry, attention. . . . You don't get to control it all. But choosing simplicity whenever possible adds to life an element of deepest freedom which so easily eludes us, and many opportunities to discover that less may actually be more. . . .

Try: Asking yourself in this moment, "Am I awake?," "Where is my mind right now?"

Suddenly I'm the Adult?

Richard Cohen

Several years ago, my family gathered on Cape Cod for a weekend. My parents were there, my sister and her daughter, too, two cousins and, of course, my wife, my son and me. We ate at one of those restaurants where the menu is scrawled on a blackboard held by a chummy waiter and had a wonderful time. With dinner concluded, the waiter set the check down in the middle of the table. That's when it happened. My father did not reach for the check.

In fact, my father did nothing. Conversation continued. Finally, it dawned on me. Me! I was supposed to pick up the check. After all these years, after hundreds of restaurant meals with my parents, after a lifetime of thinking of my father as the one with the bucks, it had all changed. I reached for the check and whipped out my American Express card. My view of myself was suddenly altered. With a stroke of the pen, I was suddenly an adult.

Some people mark off their life in years, others in events. I am one of the latter, and I think of some events as rites of passage. I did not become a young man at a particular year, like 13, but when a kid strolled into the store where I worked and called me "mister." I turned around to see whom he was calling. He repeated it several times—"Mister, mister"—looking straight at me. The realization hit like a punch: Me! He was talking to me. I was suddenly a mister.

There have been other milestones. The cops of my youth always seemed to be big, even huge, and of course they were older than I was. Then one day they were neither. In fact, some of them were kids—short kids at that. Another milestone.

The day comes when you suddenly realize that all the football players in the game you're watching are younger than you. Instead of being big men, they are merely big kids. With that milestone goes the fantasy that someday, maybe, you too could be a player—maybe not a football player but certainly a baseball player. I had a good eye as a kid—not much power, but a keen eye—and I always thought I could play the game. One day I realized that I couldn't. Without having ever reached the hill, I was over it.

For some people, the most momentous milestone is the death of a parent. This happened recently to a friend of mine. With the burial of his father came the realization that he had moved up a notch. Of course, he had known all along that this would happen, but until the funeral, the knowledge seemed theoretical at best. As long as one of your parents is alive, you stay in some way a kid. At the very least, there remains at least one person whose love is unconditional.

For women, a milestone is reached when they can no longer have children. The loss of a life, the inability to create one—they are variations on the same theme. For a childless woman who could control everything in life but the clock, this milestone is cruel one indeed.

I count other, less serious milestones—like being audited by the Internal Revenue Service. As the auditor caught mistake after mistake, I sat there pretending that really knowing about taxes was for adults. I, of course, was still a kid. The auditor was buying none of it. I was a taxpayer, an adult. She all but said, Go to jail.

There have been others. I remember the day when I had a ferocious argument with my son and realized that I could no longer bully him. He was too big and the days when I could just pick him up and take him to his room/isolation cell were over. I needed to persuade, reason. He was suddenly, rapidly, older. The conclusion was inescapable. So was I.

One day you go to your friends' weddings. One day you celebrate the birth of their kids. One day you see one of their kids driving, and one day those kids have kids of their own. One day you meet at parties and then at weddings and then at funerals. It all happens in one day. Take my word for it.

I never thought I would fall asleep in front of the television set as my father did, and as my friends' fathers did, too. I remember my parents and their friends talking about insomnia and they sounded like members of a different species. Not able to sleep? How ridiculous. Once it was all I did. Once it was what I did best.

I never thought that I would eat a food that did not agree with me. Now I meet them all the time. I thought I would never go to the beach and not swim. I spent all of August at the beach and never once went into the ocean. I never thought I would appreciate opera, but now the pathos, the schmaltz and, especially, the combination of voice and music appeal to me. The deaths of Mimi and Tosca move me, and they die in my home as often as I can manage it.

I never thought I would prefer to stay home instead of going to a party, but now I find myself passing parties up. I used to think that people who watched birds were weird, but this summer I found myself watching them, and maybe I'll get a book on the subject. I yearn for a religious conviction I never thought I'd want, exult in my heritage anyway, feel close to ancestors long gone and echo my father in arguments with my son. I still lose.

One day I made a good toast. One day I handled a headwaiter. One day I bought a house. One day—what a day!—I became a father, and not too long after that I picked up the check for my own. I thought then and there it was a rite of passage for me. Not until I got older did I realize that it was one for him, too. Another milestone.

Follow-Up

1. *See the Applied Activity titled "Are You An Adult?" at the end of this readings section.*
2. *In this article, Richard Cohen describes several life events that he calls milestones. These milestones caused shifts in how he viewed himself and added dimensions to his identity. We all have these identity milestones, little or great, that tell us that we have changed, that we have entered another phase of life, or that we have shifted some basic way of seeing and being in the world. What have been some of your identity milestones?*
3. *Complete the statement "I know I'm getting older when . . ."?*

   Samples
   * *I cannot name or tolerate the top three rock groups.*
   * *I am referred to as* sir *or* ma'am.
   * *I read or watch the news.*
   * *Cops are my age or younger.*
   * *I hear my parent's voice coming out of my mouth.*
   * *I really need consistent sleeping hours.*
   * *I have a high school reunion.*

   What are some other indicators that you're getting older?

The Emerging Adult: Challenges

Nelson Goud

The twentysomething age group is often referred to as the period of
emerging adulthood. Some say that being 30 is now equivalent to being
age 21 a generation ago. The term *quarterlife crisis* was coined to describe
the problems and issues facing twentysomethings (see Robbins & Wilner,
2001). According to recent college graduates, the quarterlife crisis is a
"response to overwhelming instability, constant change, too many
choices, and a panicked sense of helplessness" (Robbins & Wilner, 2001,
p. 3). Indecision and apprehension are common companions during this
period. On leaving the protective spheres of family and college, twentysomethings encounter disorientation and confusion regarding identity,
career choices, living arrangements, establishing independence, discovering and harnessing a life passion, and creating new social networks. One
twentysomething encapsulates the doubts of many in this age range:

> It was this whirling downward spiral, a rapidly increasing cycle, like a con-
> centric circle that kept expanding and suffocating all of my other thoughts.
> There was just no room for anything else to think about. I kept asking myself
> things like, "What will I do with my life?" "Can I ever be happy at a job or
> will it always be just work?" "Is all of adulthood this stifling and monoto-
> nous?" "Will I ever be sure enough about somebody to marry him if I can't
> even be sure about myself?" "Am I going to feel this hopeless for the rest of
> my life?" "Why is everyone else handling this more easily than I am?" and
> there were more and more of these questions that I just couldn't get around.
> I gave myself headaches because I was worrying about this relentlessly. I
> withdrew from my friends and incessantly snapped at my boyfriend, who
> tried to understand what I was going through. (p. 88)

Having little experience at making major life decisions and accepting
responsibility for them places twentysomethings in a transition zone of
trying to find guideposts on what to do, where to go, and who to be. It is
a time of trial and error, making premature resolutions, and sometimes
paralysis due to indecision. Following are interview excerpts that characterize the dilemmas of the quarterlife crisis.

DASHED EXPECTATIONS

For all their lives, twentysomethings have been told that they can be whatever they want to be, do whatever they want to do—which was great to hear
when they were formulating childhood dreams and aspirations. But once
they get to the point where it is time to make those goals happen, twentysomethings often realize that not everything is attainable. "I always envisioned postcollege life as a time of uninhibited freedom. I would travel the

country and the world; I would hold a variety of interesting and challenging jobs; I would meet new people and make new friends," she says. "But travel requires money, and I won't have any money until I secure a job. So here I am at home, living with my parents, working at my old summer job where I do nothing more interesting than stacking CDs on shelves. I feel like instead of progressing forward into more freedom, more opportunity, and a more interesting life, I slid backward. It's like I'm still in college, except without the college part to look forward to. It's almost like being in high school again. I know I can move out as soon as I am offered and accept a job, but despite the assurances of well-meaning adults that this is the best job market in years, no job seems forthcoming. I grow increasingly despairing and hopeless as I languish in a sea of boredom. Who wouldn't be easily frustrated in this position?"(pp. 111–112)

LIFESTYLE CHANGES

A frustrating adjustment in lifestyle for many twentysomethings is the change in structure after college or graduate school. While there may have been a set agenda in place in school that directed students toward the end goal of graduating with a degree, daily schedules were never so rigid that they were set in stone. . . . "Transitioning from college to the real world has been tremendously difficult because basically you have to leave an environment where you're free to do what you want all day long," says Kevin, the 1999 Colgate University graduate. "You have classes and responsibilities, but they're flexible. If you're feeling tired, you can skip a class and catch up. You can grab food when you want it, you can go to sleep at whatever time you want to, depending on what you want to do that day. Then you transition from that to a world where you have to wake up and be at work at a certain time." (pp. 187–188)

THE UNKNOWN NEXT

Some twentysomethings follow a well-defined plan upon graduation and accomplish their goals only to wonder "What do I do next?" As one states:

For the first time in my life, I felt like there was no new topic in my outline. . . . I got what I had zeroed in on. And now I was wondering, what do I do next? There has to be a "next." There has always been a "next" in my life. After high school there was "go to college," after college there was "get a job," and then in your job it was "work hard and get promoted." So there I was, a twentysomething single, successful marketing manager, wondering what in the world the next step should be for me. I still haven't figured it out. But what I did learn is that all that time I spent wondering why I didn't have a plan and trying to figure out how to get one, my real life was passing me by. (p. 21)

THE BURDEN OF MANY CHOICES

I tend to just let my life unfold and stay open-minded about what opportunities come before me. I don't think there'll ever be a time when my whole life is settled, and I'm kind of glad. To be honest, that's what's best about the twenties—we're so free. No mortgages, no kids, no job that we've been at for fourteen years. The problem, though, as I've tried to explain a million times to my mom, is that freedom is really a big burden. When all options are available, it's really easy to sit on your bun and choose nothing. . . . It's great to actually have something in my life that I'm certain of. The uncertainty can kill you. (p. 35)

I think I struggle with wanting everything. I want to pursue my personal fantasies, desires, interests. At the same time I want the guarantee of financial stability. (p. 91)

At times, the freedom to change is an escape.

We believe change will resolve some of the fears we have because it wipes the slate clean—a change of scenery, a new set of coworkers to substitute for ones you hated. Come on. The majority of the time, it's an excuse to avoid reality. (p. 92)

Then there is the fear of making wrong choices.

[We] are intimidated by making changes, taking risks. I mean, how can we throw away financial security and career opportunities to do something creative, interesting, inspiring—to throw caution to the wind and join the Peace Corps? What would our friends, families, colleagues say? What if I make the wrong choice and have lost out on success, respect, and money by leaving it all behind? How will I get back into step with the level of success and financial viability of my friends who stuck with it? (pp. 92–93)

Extended discussion of these and other issues for the emerging adult are covered in the following references:

The Quarterlife Crisis: The Unique Challenges in Your Twenties by Alexandra Robbins and Abby Wilner, Penguin Putnam, 2001.
Conquering Your Quarterlife Crisis by Alexandra Robbins, Perigee, 2004.
Quarterlife Crisis: www.quarterlifecrisis.com. This website includes a network of support groups.
Alexandra Robbins: www.alexandrarobbins.com. This website includes additional twentysomething stories.

Some guidelines from these books are mentioned in other Emerging Adult sections throughout this book. Many of the points discussed in these pieces will also apply to other age groups.

Reference
Robbins, A., & Wilner, A. (2001). *The quarterlife crisis: The unique challenges in your twenties.* New York: Penguin Putnam.

Follow-Up

1. *Discuss whether you think being 30 now is equivalent to being 21 a generation ago.*
2. *Are the problems of being a twentysomething today more difficult or just different from being a twentysomething in earlier generations? Why?*
3. *Select two statements from this article and explain how they apply (or don't apply) to your experience being a twentysomething.*

The Rivers We Call Ourselves

Sarah Silbert

Until the age of twelve, I yearned to be a rock star. Janis Joplin, Jimi Hendrix, Jim Morrison—I idolized those who raged and loved in gargantuan volumes. Every day, I mimicked them, stomping and screaming and wiggling my hips on the rim of the bathtub and on my bed. Like them, I sought to be loud and impossible to ignore. I wanted to be a magnet for light and attention—spotlights and strobes, camera lenses and multitudes of young faces. Sometimes at night, in the woods behind my parents' house, I sang about purple planes and bombs and chains (I routinely misheard the words of my favorite songs) and tossed my fuchsia-and-gold-dyed hair while trying to grab handfuls of the summer-warm air above my head. I felt all the light of the galaxy focus upon me, and I reflected that light back, glowing like a jewel, a treasure, a human-shaped star.

I yearned for the splash and glamour of the rock star's life because I was convinced that intense attention made a thing real, while lack of attention robbed it of existence. If a tree fell in the forest and no one heard, I thought, then its death was insignificant. For the fall to be meaningful, a crowd of media and fans needed to encircle the tree as it swayed and groaned and finally came crashing down. I applied the same ruthless judgment to myself: if I fell and no one saw—and so gave me no pity, praise, or attention—then the fall did not count.

After my first year of high school, I began to listen less to the loud, raging words of rock stars (who were getting old and dying, one after the other) and instead listened to stars of a different sort—the kind who gave off an eternal, divine light.

Part of me had long been aware of the values of wisdom and compassion. When I was seven, one of my mom's friends had told me the story of Buddha, who'd sat beneath the Bodhi tree, waiting for enlightenment. I'd envisioned him as a clear-skinned, faithful youth gradually growing old beneath the tree until, when he was a man of my father's age, a small pulse of light began to beat over his left breast. A saint, I'd realized, was one who generated his or her own light from some source of energy within. Saints didn't need electricity or camera lenses or even other people—just a strong heart.

Now I thought more of Buddha: how had he known that he did not have to hurry, strain, and scream to win eternal fame? For answers, I studied the words of Rabindranath Tagore, Mahatma Gandhi, Martin Luther King Jr., and Henry David Thoreau. They all wrote enchantingly about the golden light of truth—which, for them, was synonymous with freedom. They spoke out against greed, war, slavery, and submission to arbitrary authority, and advocated, instead, time to appreciate earthly beauty and the opportunity to live out one's destiny unrestrained.

To be unrestrained, I saw, one needed more than simply a fair government: one needed to pray, to purify, to quiet the "monkey mind" and open oneself to inner peace. I began fervently to study the poetic and religious texts that promised to help me do this. I let my dyed hair grow out to a natural dirty blond. I wore fewer sequins and more cotton. I wrote in a journal daily. At the age of fifteen, I lay on my bed and copied out the poems, letters, and essays of my favorite authors with the same intensity with which I had once screamed out the lyrics of Janis and Jimi. I learned stanzas, paragraphs, even whole pages by heart, and eventually absorbed so many words that the authors seemed to reside within me. Rather than ponder the world from my own confused perspective, I listened to their voices for advice. Tagore, Gandhi, King, and Thoreau sat at a round table in my head, their hands folded and resting on its shiny surface, and whenever I had a decision to make—should I break up with my current boyfriend? what should my college major be?—these wise men would confer amiably across the table and come up with a course of action for me to follow.

More than anything else, my inner advisors urged me to put down their books and work actively on behalf of the causes they espoused. Thanks to them, much of my late-adolescent life was dedicated to serving others' needs rather than my own. I volunteered at a homeless shelter and a food-salvage organization, and I devoted a year to working for Mother Teresa's Sisters of Charity in Calcutta. I had gone from seeking glamour to fulfilling moral obligations, but what hadn't changed was my belief about existence: If I felt sympathy for a woman sleeping on a sidewalk in twenty-degree weather, but didn't approach her and ask her to come home with me for a meal—and perhaps create with her a campaign to open another women's homeless shelter in our neighborhood—then my feelings weren't real. Nothing was real, for me, if it was not affecting other people. Can you be a rock star without an audience? Can you claim to feel compassion if you are sitting still in solitude, touching no one? If a tree falls, if a dream falls, if a faith fails, and there is no one to witness it, who will know, who will care, what will happen?

As a result of my philosophy, I was always exhausted and usually guilty. I could never do enough: suffering, sickness, and deprivation remained despite my frenzied activities. I often woke before 5 A.M. and did not stop working till nine at night. I didn't go to parties or movies; I didn't drink alcohol; I ate mainly bread and rice; I gave up reading and writing

in order to be an ever available worker. Still, the men at the round table suggested that I could do more. What mattered was using my energy to benefit others in a material way. All else was insubstantial, and therefore nonessential.

Looking back on that time, I see some accomplishments I am proud of and some activists with whom I feel fortunate to have worked. And yet, I also see a very lost and tired girl who, despite her large black boots and determined stance, had weary eyes and a spirit bent double under the weight of questions about her worth and about the value of human life in general.

On the day of my twenty-sixth birthday, a Monday, I woke up sick with a fever and a deep cough. I remember thinking, *I am ill,* and yet, at the same time, sensing that the flu was my birthday gift. I felt that I needed to use it. As if under orders, I called in sick to work and, ignoring the aches in my joints and the pain in my chest, dressed for a hike up Mount Monadnock, an hour and a half away in New Hampshire. The philosophers I'd read had each made a pilgrimage, an ascension, a half-random journey in search of a sign, and now I needed to make one, too.

The day was cold—zero degrees, at best. The wind was fierce, and my boots were old and not well-made. Climbing the mountain, I had to stop every ten minutes to catch my breath and wipe the fever-induced sweat from my neck and face. Still, I was enchanted by the beauty that surrounded me. The beech, birch, and poplar trees were white-and-silver skeletons rattling winter's hollow bones all around. The few fir trees I saw made me think of Christmas, with their dark green branches bowed with crisp white drifts of snow. The sky was white, too, pressing low upon the ground, softening the rocky rises and dips into one smooth, opaque pathway.

About five hundred feet from the summit, I had to stop. The wind was rising, and snow had begun to fall in a thick, silent curtain across the mountain. Resting for one last moment before heading back, I leaned against a hunk of granite the size of three men. Along its side, I noticed a waterfall frozen in midstream. I brushed the snow from it: miniature rose-gold stars bloomed within its shiny, translucent surface. Running my hand along its curves, I felt as if I were touching a living being—a dolphin, an orca, an undiscovered creature soon to be released down the mountain by the oncoming spring.

As my imagination played with the thick slab of ice, my chest began to feel squeezed until I could hardly breathe. The cause was not my cold, nor the exertion of the hike: it was sadness. I realized, at that moment, that I had spent so many years denying the beautiful, the inexplicable. I had become a severe and limited person leading a severe and limited life. And, for once, the wise men in my head had nothing to say. For the first time in a long while, I knew quiet.

I didn't want to let that sensation of quiet end. I returned from the mountain and took the next three days off from work—something I had never done before. I requested the time off partly because the flu had sunk deep into my lungs and made me dizzy, but also because I genuinely did not want to return to work. Instead, lying on my side and blowing my nose, simultaneously sweating and feeling chilled, I wrote a short story about a hip-high, fat gray monster trudging through a make-believe world in search of "my twenty-one lost years." I sent the story, along with an application, to an artists' colony, and was accepted. Within a few months, I was back in New Hampshire, at the base of Mount Monadnock, this time living alone in a one-room cabin. I wrote every day for a month, beginning by recording my own immediate feelings in a journal, then slipping into the voices of several teenage girls. Some were in jail, others in math class, still others trapped behind shop windows: all wanted out of whatever confines surrounded them.

None of the stories sold. Strangely, I didn't mind. I had lived in them anyway. No one needed to read the stories or witness my hard work in order for that activity to be real.

After that, I chose to be my own teacher for a while. I didn't want a crowd of advisors around me (or inside my head). To experience the meaningfulness of solitude, I found, is to feel whole, self-contained, to be both the seer and the seen. And to miss out on such an experience would be to doom my creative being to too narrow a life. Before my pilgrimage up Mount Monadnock, I had calculated the worth of my spirit by counting my actions, and I had judged the worth of those actions by the number of people they affected positively. But beyond such number games lay a vast terrain—limitless and immeasurable—that I now wanted to explore on my own.

Oddly, once I'd committed myself to looking inward, I began to see the outside world more clearly. I was no longer distracted by other voices and perspectives: my own heart—and mine alone—beat within me, and I could see and hear without confusion. In my mind, I returned often to my brief moment atop Mount Monadnock: First, there was the quiet. Then the wind pushing at my front and back, filling me, it seemed, with snow, until all I could see and feel was dense and white. My body was like a hollow vessel full of the chilled stillness of winter, and yet deep inside me was a frightened young girl. She was not me, exactly, but rather a figure of humanity's common suffering—a small voice within the larger chorus.

Suffering, I could see then, was natural, a part of being human, impossible to wipe away. Social work and shelters and free blankets would not chase it out of our cities, nor our souls. Yearning and loss were inevitable parts of our lives because all of us were less the result of will or desire or morality, and more a fallout of weather, timing, luck, and what so many of us resignedly call fate.

Acknowledging the power of fate does not, of course, release any of us from our political and personal responsibilities. It merely puts politics and personhood in perspective.

And I needed that perspective. I needed to feel the vast openness of the world, as opposed to the narrowness of my own mind.

I did not know then that fate was about to knock me down and hold me there, for years.

I first saw Jeff when I was twenty-four, two years before my climb up Mount Monadnock. He was behind the counter in a coffee shop, and I stared at him through the large window as if he were waving bright white wings and calling out to me—which he was not. He was serving drinks to a line of customers, and I was standing outside amid a crowd of other pedestrians who, as soon as the crossing light flashed WALK, nudged me along toward the entrance to the subway.

Over the next two years, I thought often of that man in the coffee shop. I did not know his name, and I did not enter his cafe—I was too busy, I told myself. But whenever my roommates asked me why I didn't date or why I wouldn't let them set me up with so-and-so, I always answered, "Because I'm saving myself for the man at the Someday Cafe."

Not long after my pilgrimage, I returned to the coffee shop, and, this time, I went inside.

It was a rainy Monday. Jeff looked glum. Cautiously, I made small talk with him. He told me about the cafe and about his growing wish to leave it; I confessed my slow shift from committed activist to less-active thinker and writer. After an hour of conversation, I no longer felt shy. After seven hours, I was in love. And after a month of daily long conversations, I was committed to this man for life.

Jeff and I shared our first kiss on Plum Island, Massachusetts, where the wind whipped the Atlantic's waves into a frenzy and blew snow and sand against our backs. When Jeff turned my face to meet his, I felt a frozen sting against my cheek, then the soft touch of his lips on mine. Later, clutching each other's blue fingers, we ran back to the nearby tourist town, where we drank wine in a booth, glowing like rock stars on a stage.

Within a year, we were engaged and building a small post-and-beam cabin in Vermont—our first home. We were as full of life as milkweed seedpods about to burst and bloom. Then, on September 13, 1998, Jeff was diagnosed with cancer.

How strange life is! What a story! No matter how many times I write about it or ponder it, it still stuns me and makes my stomach hurt, forcing me to lie down, sometimes for hours.

What makes life strange, I believe, is its single defining characteristic: movement. A brook runs by our Vermont cabin—which is now built, plumbed, and wired—and I often walk for miles along its banks, in winter and in summer. At every step, the brook changes; it becomes deep or shallow, wide or narrow, silent and frozen or splashing over logs and stones. I see now that we are like that water, carving our experience into life's terrain. At certain places along the brook's length, I recall the past. I see myself fighting with a nurse, screaming, "No more chemo!" I also see—at the miniature waterfall that borders the neighbor's property—Jeff, ruddy and muscled, approaching me on skis, hugging me, and pushing me down in the snow.

The disease came upon Jeff without warning. The day we arrived at the hospital, doctors told us he could die before dawn. They said his cancer was terminal, but mentioned an experimental cure that would entail a year or two of debilitating, excruciating chemotherapy treatments.

Within two years, Jeff diminished from a man of Paul Bunyan's fortitude to an invalid who hadn't the strength to hold my hand. Between Jeff's month-long stays in the ward, we slept in other people's living rooms and dens or rented subsidized housing units at the hospital. Everything we owned fit into the trunk of my car. I worked only sporadically, usually at night, so I could be around to monitor Jeff's IVs, help him eat, massage him, and try vainly to complete the endless list of errands that illness creates. The day I turned thirty, Jeff was infused with so many steroids and immunosuppressants that his muscles shook like flags battered by the wind. He could not even turn the pages of a book.

That was March 2000. I began this essay on Christmas morning of the same year, and our rivers have traveled another hundred miles since then. Jeff has been cancer-free for eleven months. His hair has grown to a length of three inches, and his arms are developing a curve of muscle (though his legs are still pencil thin). He looks like no one I have ever seen, and he moves slowly, gracefully, like an animal walking through trees at night. Occasionally, he brings home a bottle of wine for dinner and presses me against the sink with kisses before I can even open it. We have walked the brook together on many occasions, and on New Year's Day, Jeff is planning to ski for the first time in three years. Every day feels like an anniversary: we celebrate each one for how different it is from the same date in recent years.

But here's the trick: this, too, shall change. Jeff's cancer could return, or a new one could bloom inside of him as a result of those toxic treatments. A house fire, a flood, a baby, a new idea—every human event, doctrine, and song acknowledges the movement and continual transformation of the rivers we call ourselves. Sometimes we rail against this truth; other times we may try to hurry it along. But movement is the inevitable reality.

A few days ago, a friend of Jeff's dropped by unannounced with his wife. Jeff and I had just returned from hiking three miles through snow up to our hips, climbing up ice-slick rocks and then slipping down them, marveling at the dream blue sky, a set of fox tracks, a distant coyote, the way the beech trees still held on to their tattered golden leaves. When the visitors arrived, Jeff and I were piled upon each other like kindling by the fire—winded, wet, and a little giddy. Kissing Jeff's face, neck, and chest, I tasted salt and what I liked to believe was new life.

"Knock, knock!" the friend called to us from behind the glass door.

I looked over my shoulder: a beard, a woman's smile over a purple-and-red scarf, hands waving.

Jeff and I pulled apart and sat up, and the couple came in to chat. They had been driving around Vermont all weekend, looking at properties. (Ever since Jeff and I had found our land, they'd wanted some, too.) They'd seen three properties so far, none of them any good. They sighed as they sat down, snow melting off their boots and jackets and pooling on the floor around them.

"We did find two places to rent for the summer, though," Jeff's friend said happily. "Our boy Carl loves farm animals: big toys!" He laughed. They had two kids, a boy and a girl, and wanted very much to raise them in greener, gentler territory.

The conversation tripped on, but Jeff and I didn't stand up, didn't offer food or drink. Without knowing why, I felt defeated.

After maybe an hour, clouds moved in, and a fine snow began to fall. To avoid a messy drive, our visitors decided to leave. I watched through the window with relief as they shook the snow from their boots before getting into their Jeep. I still didn't understand my cold reaction to them, but the magic of the morning seemed to have departed with their arrival, and the cabin now felt empty and eerie, like a museum after hours.

Jeff was rubbing the back of his neck, which was often tight and sore—a side effect of a medication he still took twice a day. I noticed the folds of skin around his eyes; there were so many of them. I placed a hand on his forehead, still damp from our earlier romp, and ran my palm over his head. Though getting longer, his hair was still very thin.

"They're ten years older than us," I said of our guests, "and they seem ten years younger."

I knew then what it was that bothered me: I envied our visitors' smooth, round faces, the way they flung their hands in the air when announcing plans. I thought of their two children, whose faces looked so similar to theirs. I felt like a Third World refugee looking at advertisements in an out-of-date U.S. newspaper—grapes, sofas, lingerie, the models' straight white teeth and long bare arms. I started to cry.

"Hey," Jeff said, putting his arms around me. "Hey."

Usually, I tried not to express sadness, especially around Jeff: what was the point of giving voice to the obvious? I let Jeff hold me and waited for the sadness to go, but I couldn't help thinking that he and I might as well be twenty years older than our visitors—or thirty, or forty: old people whose children have left them in a home for good, never to return. We had only each other now—fragile, mutable beings no more substantial than open windows, through which anything at all might fly: an owl, a bluebird, the final specter.

I turned my head so that we could kiss and pushed my hands up under Jeff's damp T-shirt, along his bare skin. Although I continued to cry, the tears did not all come from sadness, but also from some more raw, unnamable emotion. For why lament that our skin was loosening more quickly than others'; that it was scarred; that one day—perhaps sooner rather than later—we would pour right out of these sacks called bodies and onto the floor of a very different world? Life, for the moment, was inside us both, and no one else needed to know how it thrummed with such energy between us. We would flow on regardless, rivers that we are. What was distant would become near; what was invisible would become material. And still, in that inevitable movement, we would always be more mystery than flesh—to each other, and to ourselves.

Follow-Up

1. *The author fully committed to her ideals. She also changed her ideals, which resulted in significant life identity shifts. Discuss this style of living. How is it similar to or different from the way you shape your identity?*
2. *Silbert says that life is defined by movement. She makes an analogy to a brook by her cabin. Explain why you do or do not agree with this comparison.*
3. *Choose one statement from this article and discuss its meaning for your life.*

The Emerging Adult: The Work World

Nelson Goud

Two developmental tasks dominate the twentysomething age group: establishing intimacy and having a satisfactory vocation. Regarding the latter, Robbins and Wilner (2001) found that "while many twentysomethings claim they don't want to define themselves by their careers, nearly all of the ones we spoke to still responded to questions about their identities by talking about their jobs" (p. 30). Exploring career options is especially prevalent during this age period. Job-hopping is not as stigmatizing as it was a generation ago. A trial-and-error process in changing jobs is common among emerging adults. Some are still hoping for the ideal career.

> I think that I do not want to be mediocre. I want to be special. I know that I have talents. It is just a matter of finding that right blend of activities that challenges me on all planes—physical, spiritual, and mental. I want a job that is challenging and uses my skills. (Robbins & Wilner, 2001, p. 31)

Others resist being classified and defined by their jobs.

> I couldn't really say that the job I have right now—jewelry design and sales— really describes me as a person, even though I like it a lot. It's not my life's work. (Robbins & Wilner, 2001, p. 17)

Some emerging adults look elsewhere to engage in life-fulfilling endeavors (e.g., extracurricular activities, outside-of-work interests).

WHAT TO DO IF YOU HATE GOING TO WORK

In *Conquering Your Quarterlife Crisis,* Robbins (2004) offers these guidelines for those who dislike their jobs. She recommends to first isolate those factors that cause the dissatisfaction and not let one factor taint the entire field. Robbins asks

> What specifically, do you hate about work? Is it the particular company you don't like, the kind of work you're doing, the people you're working with, the city you're working in, the lifestyle of your position, or the entirety of your field?
>
> (For the lawyers, this translated to, Is it the particular firm you don't like, the type of law you're practicing, the people you're with, the city in which you work, the hours you're working, or the act of lawyering?)
>
> Once the lawyers thought, really thought, about separating these aspects of their work, I heard a variety of answers that illustrated the importance of separating the job from the field. One, for example, wasn't happy with his firm and the way it treated associates, but he found the other aspects of

his job tolerable. Once he found a similar position at another firm, he was much happier going to work. Another didn't like the kind of law he was practicing. When he was able to convince the partners to switch him to a different practice within the firm, his job satisfaction skyrocketed. Another couldn't stand the cold days in Boston, so he transferred to an office in another city. Again, a sudden change of attitude.

CAN YOU MAKE WORK BETTER?

Another common reason twentysomethings initially balk about going to work is the culture shock of the monotonous desk-job routine: wake up early, commute (bus, subway, car), sit behind desk, sit behind desk, sit behind desk, meeting, sit behind desk, commute (bus, subway, car), sleep, repeat. Many of us merely need to get used to the routine . . . and will find that eventually the process will fade to the background of our working lives as we get more involved in and enthused about the work itself. If after years of this, the routine still sends you into the "this can't be the rest of my life" panic, you *do* have other options.

CHANGE YOUR ROUTINE

First, if you like the work itself, or at least the path that the work will eventually lead to, it's definitely worth asking your employer if you can work out a different arrangement. Companies today understand much more than they did ten years ago that our generation doesn't put a whole lot of stock in "face time." Rather than prove we're doing our job by sitting at the office for a prescribed number of hours during a required time frame (9 a.m. to 6 p.m., 8 a.m. to 8 p.m., etc.), many of us would rather have a project-based scenario: as long as we do the work by the time it's due, it doesn't matter where we do it. Ask your supervisor if you might be able to telecommute a certain number of days per week. Or suggest a comp-time or flex-time arrangement in which you can bank extra hours you work on one day and take them off on another day. If your boss is open to it, you can even come up with your own creative ideas: work late on Wednesdays in order to take Friday afternoons off, for instance. It's worth asking your employer or potential new employers about the possibility of these arrangements. One twentysomething I know disliked his job until he requested to telecommute three days a week, and his boss agreed. He still gets the work done, but three days a week he does it from home, which makes a huge difference in his lifestyle and his attitude. (pp. 100–102)

Another option that is increasingly being chosen is self-employment. A 2004 survey by the National Association for the Self-Employed found that 15 percent of its members were in their 20s or early 30s. Experts suggest enrolling in courses on self-employment or thoroughly researching an area prior to starting a business. Self-employment can be a long-term investment or as short-term as freelancing while searching for a more traditional career.

References

Robbins, A., & Wilner, A. (2001). *Quarterlife crisis*. New York: Penguin Putnam.

Robbins, A. (2004). *Conquering your quarterlife crisis*. New York: Perigee.

Follow-Up

1. *Select one statement from this section and discuss your reaction.*
2. *Apply one or more of the ideas suggested if you dislike your job.*
3. *See also "Occupational Exploration" by Christopher Schaefer in this section.*

Occupational Exploration

Christopher A. Schaefer

When I first entered college as an undergrad, I was a product of my parents' wishes—they wanted me to become a physician, so that's what I worked toward. But the courses were mind numbingly boring, and I realized that the course they had set for me was not what I wanted. The problem was, I didn't know what I wanted either.

After dropping out of school, finding a job and supporting myself for several years, I decided that being a blue collar worker (a shipping dock worker at a meat packing plant in Chicago) wasn't really me either. I enjoyed the money and the independence, but felt I was not fulfilling my potential, that I could do better and find a fulfilling career. So I decided to go back to school and get a very practical business degree (this after several other part-time "false starts"). While pursuing my business degree, I took a required computer course and decided—Ah, this is something I enjoy, that I want to do. This was a key turning point in my life—it was the first time I discovered something I really wanted to do and pursued it.

After graduation, I got a position in the computer field and enjoyed the challenge of my new responsibilities and the prestige of my own office. I now felt much closer to "Me," but there was still something missing, something within me still unfulfilled. I had always enjoyed helping others, and found the most enjoyable aspect of my new job was the time I spent training and teaching them. This was a life thread that felt like "Me." So in need of some extra money anyway, I decided to look for a part-time teaching job. To do this, I had to cope with a lifelong fear of public speaking. It wasn't easy, but the reward was worth the risk. I feel I have finally found a direction for myself that's "with the grain."

Follow-Up

1. *Sometimes it takes some actual experience to find out what you like and dislike in a job. Schaefer kept trying different jobs and taking courses until he found a position that matched his strengths and identity. What has been your job history and level of satisfaction? Do you think you will be in a continual search to find or create a job that matches your identity?*

Woodworker

Craig Mosher

As my hands press the plane forward, a smooth shaving curls up from the keen edge, filling the air with the tangy scent of freshcut pine. There is a soothing rhythm to the strokes of the plane and a delightful uniqueness in each spiraled shaving.

My chisel and mallet seek some more-organic form hidden within a block of Hawaiian koa wood. The power saw that cuts the block is no respecter of the flowing lines of light and dark that mark the pattern of growth. Sometimes, when my efforts at seeking the life-lines in the wood succeed, the form seems to take on a liveliness reminiscent of the forces that shaped the once tall and supple tree.

Now, as I seek to shape my life in more flexible, natural ways, the schools and offices that claimed so many of my years seem like a buzz saw that cut me into blocks irrespective of the life forms hidden within.

There are so many joys in my new vocation I wonder that I did not find it sooner. Perhaps, my life had to be cut into blocks in order for me to know that was not the form I sought. Yet, there are connections, too. The enjoyment I once got from organizing ideas and programs and peace marches I now find in planning the sequence of tasks and gathering materials to build a table. It is satisfying to see my hands transforming boards and glue into functional and even beautiful objects.

Working for myself I have a flexibility and a discipline that is rarely found in offices that structure work into eight-hour days and fifty-week years. I find freedom within my work, not just during my "time off." Even when I choose to discipline myself to eight-hour days, I feel more free knowing that I am choosing that schedule, either as self-discipline or so I can conveniently work with others. I struggle, when working for myself, to find a balance between demanding regular eight-hour days of myself in order to earn money, learn new skills, and do quality work, on the one hand, and taking time to play with my family, on the other.

I have time between jobs for other activities. I can take a day off each week to build projects for my own pleasure. In fact, the line between work and play blurs because I have such fun at my work. Tools become toys when I go to play in the shop.

As a free-lance woodworker I work for myself or for a client with whom I have some personal contact. The client knows that it is I and not some impersonal factory or machine creating the product. Both praise and criticism come directly to me. Expectations for the form and quality of the job are set by me, alone or in dialogue with the client. In either case I participate directly in setting expectations for my work, and thereby find myself committed to them. This brings pleasure when the product meets the standard and anguish when I sometimes fall short. As in any demanding personal endeavor, part of myself becomes invested in my work, so that I am happy when it is going well and sometimes depressed when I do poorly.

I am also learning more about my relationship to authority. I find it easier to use external authority—like a foreman's or client's expecting me on the job at 8 a.m. each morning—to motivate myself to work. Yet, I find greater satisfaction when I can internalize the authority and muster the self-discipline to go to work regularly in my own shop when only I know how many hours I work. I learned such self-discipline as a student, but then it was under the external threat of grades and disapproving teachers, which I came to internalize as guilt. The wide range of available jobs, from wood carving in my own shop to framing houses on a crew or even working in a factory, provides many levels of internal and external authority, so I have some flexibility to choose the level at which I feel comfortable at any given time.

There is clarity and concreteness in the woodworking craft. I work with materials rather than ideas or personalities. Most of my work is sequential, orderly, and structured. Work proceeds step by step. Foundations must be built before walls, wood cut before being finished. Progress is easily seen as walls are raised and rafters set. Sometimes work goes fast and sometimes slow, but at the end of every day I can see what I have done. I find this continually rewarding.

These rewards are immediate and "self-bestowed." I need not wait for a teacher or boss to tell me whether a cabinet is square or a floor level. Once I have learned the standards of high quality for a particular type of work, I decide for myself whether the job is properly done. I enjoy the freedom to judge my own work and also the challenge to my integrity that is implicit in every decision I make about quality.

I find satisfaction in discovering the direct link between the form and the function of the things I build. There is pleasure in erecting a house that will warmly shelter a family and provide spaces that facilitate their particular living patterns. The same is true of a child's pull toy, which both evokes laughter and withstands considerable knocking about. When I understand and observe the direct relation between the form and the function of a project, I get a sense of clarity that makes the work flow more smoothly.

Every job seems to pose new challenges to my growing skills. There is such variety in the types of work available that when I get bored I simply choose a different area of my work.

When I tire of framing houses, I build furniture. When I get lonely in the shop, I seek bigger jobs with other workers. The range of skills that can be developed is so broad that I know I will spend many years as an active learner, enduring the frustrations and cherishing the joys of that process.

The many different woodworking skills can be generalized and transferred, so I rarely feel completely at a loss about how to solve a new problem. Relevant past experience is usually available to guide new learning. This range of transferable skills also gives me the secure feeling that I will likely be able to find work in almost any place at almost any time. The work is not always steady. There are seasonal fluctuations and changes dependent upon the state of the economy, but there are so many kinds of work that something is almost always available.

The key to finding plenty of work seems to be developing a reputation for quality and efficiency (that is, reasonable cost). I am encouraged by an increasing demand in the nation for quality hand craftsmanship. Perhaps it is a passing fashion, or perhaps it is a real trend away from the dreary uniformity of mass-produced goods, large factories, anonymous, alienated employees, and concentrations of power and wealth in the hands of a few capitalists.

A client once told me that he felt guilty asking me to remodel his garage for him while he sat in his office, since he was capable of doing the job himself. I realized that I was very happy it was he and not I going to his office every day in a suit and tie and that I was glad he had the money to pay me to do work I enjoy.

Most of the skills I have were learned on the job—what John Dewey and his followers called "learning by doing." Sometimes I learn slowly by my own trials and errors. I learn more quickly when I work with someone more skilled than I who can offer advice and answer questions. Apprenticeship is one of the oldest and most effective teaching-learning strategies. This teacher-apprentice relationship has, in my experience, also been an opportunity for forming friendships that make the work flow more smoothly. My woodworking teachers shared their skills and knowledge so that together we could do the work more quickly and accurately—quite unlike some authoritarian teaching styles I experienced in classrooms.

I am intrigued by the possibilities for cooperation inherent in the crafts and trades. Their variety, flexibility, and lack of officially determined credentials make for fewer barriers caused by specialization and less emphasis on hierarchical measures of status, all of which should make it easier for people to form cooperative work groups in which they can share their tools and skills, as well as themselves. The friendships and group cohesion that can develop in such a cooperative endeavor make the work all that much more enjoyable.

I now find myself with a set of useful skills that contribute to a sense of identity based on concrete work and achievements. These skills and the work I can produce give meaning to my life, meaning that is tangible, self-renewing, and growing—and very personal. To the extent that my craft becomes art my individuality is expressed through work that others can use and enjoy.

It is, after all, more healthy, both personally and socially, for me to gain pleasure and self-esteem through the quality of my craftsmanship and the beauty and functionality of my work than through struggling for a position of wealth, authority, and power over other people. And it is certainly more fun.

Follow-Up

1. *Mosher feels that being self-employed provides him with several intrinsic satisfactions: flexible scheduling, using his skills, designing products, creating quality work, discipline, and pride in his work. What aspects of Mosher's career appeal to you and why? Which do not?*
2. *Bureaucratic organizations, according to Mosher, "cut me into blocks irrespective of the life forms hidden within." Explain how this statement does or does not apply to your life.*
3. *Select two statements from this article and offer your commentary.*

Ending the Battle between the Sexes

*Aaron R. Kipnis
and Elizabeth Herron*

Relations between women and men are rapidly changing. Often, however, these changes are seen to benefit one sex at the expense of the other, and the mistrust that results creates resentment. Most men and women seem unable to entertain the idea that the two sexes' differing perspectives on many issues can be equally valid. So polarization grows instead of reconciliation, as many women and men fire ever bigger and better-aimed missiles across the gender gap. On both sides there's a dearth of compassion about the predicaments of the other sex.

For example:

- Women feel sexually harassed; men feel their courting behavior is often misunderstood.
- Women fear men's power to wound them physically; men fear women's power to wound them emotionally.
- Women say men aren't sensitive enough; men say women are too emotional.
- Women feel men don't do their fair share of housework and child care; men feel that women don't feel as much pressure to provide the family's income and do home maintenance.
- Many women feel morally superior to men; many men feel that they are more logical and just than women.
- Women say men have destroyed the environment; men say the women's movement has destroyed the traditional family.

- Men are often afraid to speak about the times that they feel victimized and powerless; women frequently deny their real power.
- Women feel that men don't listen; men feel that women talk too much.
- Women resent being paid less than men; men are concerned about the occupational hazards and stress that lead to their significantly shorter life spans.
- Men are concerned about unfairness in custody and visitation rights; women are concerned about fathers who shirk their child support payments.

It is very difficult to accept the idea that so many conflicting perspectives could all have intrinsic value. Many of us fear that listening to the story of another will somehow weaken our own voice, our own initiative, even our own identity. The fear keeps us locked in adversarial thinking and patterns of blame and alienation. In this frightened absence of empathy, devaluation of the other sex grows.

In an attempt to address some of the discord between the sexes, we have been conducting gender workshops around the country. We invite men and women to spend some time in all-male and all-female groups, talking about the opposite sex. Then we bring the two groups into an encounter with one another. . . .

We've heard many permutations of this same conversation:

Gina, a 32-year-old school teacher in Washington, D.C., asks, "Why don't men ever take no for an answer?"

Arthur, a 40-year-old construction foreman, replies that in his experience, "some women *do* in fact say no when they mean yes. Women seem to believe that men should do all the pursuing in the mating dance. But then if we don't read her silent signals right, we're the bad guys. If we get it right, though, then we're heroes."

Many men agree that they are in a double bind. They are labeled aggressive jerks if they come on strong, but are rejected as wimps if they don't. Women feel a similar double bind. They are accused of being teases if they make themselves attractive but reject the advances of men. Paradoxically, however, as Donna, a fortyish divorcée, reports, "When I am up front about my desires, men often head for the hills." . . .

Some of our gender conflict is an inevitable by-product of the positive growth that has occurred in our society over the last generation. The traditional gender roles of previous generations imprisoned many women and men in soul-killing routines. Women felt dependent and disenfranchised; men felt distanced from feelings, family, and their capacity for self-care.

With almost 70 percent of women now in the work force, calls for women to return to the home full time seem ludicrous, not to mention financially impossible. In addition, these calls for the traditional nuclear family ignore the fact that increasing numbers of men now want to downshift from full-time work in order to spend more time at home. So if we can't go back to the old heroic model of masculinity and the old domestic ideal of femininity, how then do we weave a new social fabric out of the broken strands of worn-out sexual stereotypes?

Numerous participants in the well-established women's movement, as well as numbers of men in the smaller but growing men's movement, have been discovering the strength, healing, power, and sense of security that come from being involved with a same-sex group. Women and men have different social, psychological, and biological realities and receive different behavioral training from infancy through adulthood.

In most pre-technological societies, women and men both participate in same-sex social and ceremonial groups. The process of becoming a woman or a man usually begins with some form of ritual initiation. At the onset of puberty, young men and women are brought into the men's and women's lodges, where they gain a deep sense of gender identity.

Even in our own culture, women and men have traditionally had places to meet apart from members of the other sex. For generations, women have gathered over coffee or quilts; men have bonded at work and in taverns. But in our modern society, most heterosexuals believe that a member of the opposite sex is supposed to fulfill all their emotional and social needs. Most young people today are not taught to respect and honor the differences of the other gender, and they arrive at adulthood both mystified and distrustful, worried about the other sex's power to affect them. In fact, most cross-gender conflict is essentially *conflict between different cultures.* Looking at the gender war from this perspective may help us develop solutions to our dilemmas.

In recent decades, cultural anthropologists have come to believe that people are more productive members of society when they can retain their own cultural identity within the framework of the larger culture. As a consequence, the old American "melting pot" theory of cultural assimilation has evolved into a new theory of diversity, whose model might be the "tossed salad." In this ideal, each subculture retains its essential identity, while coexisting within the same social container.

Applying this idea to men and women, we can see the problems with the trend of the past several decades toward a sex-role melting pot. In our quest for gender equality through sameness, we are losing both the beauty of our diversity and our tolerance for differences. Just as a monoculture is not as environmentally stable or rich as a diverse natural ecosystem, androgyny denies the fact that sexual differences are healthy.

In the past, perceived differences between men and women have been used to promote discrimination, devaluation, and subjugation. As a result, many "we're all the same" proponents—New Agers and humanistic social theorists, for example—are justifiably suspicious of discussions that seek to restore awareness of our differences. But pretending that differences do not exist is not the way to end discrimination toward either sex.

Our present challenge is to acknowledge the value of our differing experiences as men and women, and to find ways to reap this harvest in the spirit of true equality. Carol Tavris, in her book *The Mismeasure of Women*, suggests that instead of "regarding cultural and reproductive differences as problems to be eliminated, we should aim to eliminate *the unequal consequences that follow from them.*"

Some habits are hard to change, even with an egalitarian awareness. Who can draw the line between what is socially conditioned and what is natural? It may not be possible, or even desirable, to do so. What seems more important is that women and men start understanding each other's different cultures and granting one another greater freedom to experiment with whatever roles or lifestyles attract them.

Lisa, a 29-year-old social worker from New York participating in one of our gender workshops, told us, "Both Joel [her husband] and I work full time. But it always seems to be me who ends up having to change my schedule when Gabe, our son, has a doctor's appointment or a teacher conference, is sick at home or has to be picked up after school. It's simply taken for granted that in most cases my time is less important than his. I know Joel tries really hard to be an engaged father. But

the truth is that I feel I'm always on the front line when it comes to the responsibilities of parenting and keeping the home together. It's just not fair."

Joel responds by acknowledging that Lisa's complaint is justified; but he says, "I handle all the home maintenance, fix the cars, do all the banking and bookkeeping and all the yard work as well. These things aren't hobbies. I also work more overtime than Lisa. Where am I supposed to find the time to equally co-parent too? Is Lisa going to start mowing the lawn or help me build the new bathroom? Not likely."

In many cases of male-female conflict, as with Lisa and Joel, there are two differing but *equally valid* points of view. Yet in books, the media, and in women's and men's groups, we only hear about most issues from a woman's point of view or from a man's. This is at the root of the escalating war between the sexes.

For us, the starting point in the quest for gender peace is for men and women to spend more time with members of the same sex. We have found that many men form intimate friendships in same-sex groups. In addition to supporting their well-being, these connections can take some of the pressure off their relationships with women. Men in close friendships no longer expect women to satisfy *all* their emotional needs. And when women meet in groups they support one another's need for connection and also for empowerment in the world. Women then no longer expect men to provide their sense of self-worth. So these same-sex groups can enhance not only the participants' individual lives, but their relationships with members of the other sex as well.

If men and women *remain* separated, however, we risk losing perspective and continuing the domination or scapegoating of the other sex. In women's groups, male-bashing has been running rampant for years. At a recent lecture we gave at a major university, a young male psychology student said, "This is the first time in three years on campus that I have heard anyone say a single positive thing about men or masculinity."

Many women voice the same complaint about their experiences in male-dominated workplaces. Gail, a middle management executive, says, "When I make proposals to the all-male board of directors, I catch the little condescending smirks and glances the men give one another. They don't pull that shit when my male colleagues speak. If they're that rude in front of me, I can only imagine how degrading their comments are when they meet in private."

There are few arenas today in which women and men can safely come together on common ground to frankly discuss our rapidly changing ideas about gender justice. Instead of more sniping from the sidelines, what is needed is for groups of women and men to communicate directly with one another. When we take this *next step* and make a commitment to spend time apart and then meet with each other, then we can begin to build a true social, political, and spiritual equality. This process also instills a greater appreciation for the unique gifts each sex has to contribute.

Husband-and-wife team James Sniechowski and Judith Sherven conduct gender reconciliation meetings—similar to the meetings we've been holding around the country—each month in Southern California. In a recent group of 25 people (11 women, 14 men), participants were invited to explore questions like: What did you learn about being a man/woman from your mother? From your father? Sniechowski reports that "even though, for the most part, the men and women revealed their confusions, mistrust, heartbreaks, and bewilderments, the room quickly filled with a poignant beauty." As one woman said of the meeting, "When I listen to the burdens we suffer, it helps me soften my heart toward them." On another occasion a man said, "My image of women shifts as I realize they've been through some of the same stuff I have."

Discussions such as these give us an opportunity to really hear one another and, perhaps, discover that many of our disagreements come from equally valid, if different, points of view. What many women regard as intimacy feels suffocating and invasive to men. What many men regard as masculine strength feels isolating and distant to women. Through blame and condemnation, women and men shame one another. Through compassionate communication, however, we can help one another. This mutual empowerment is in the best interests of both sexes, because when one sex suffers, the other does too.

Toward the end of our meetings, men and women inevitably become more accountable for the ways in which they contribute to the problem. Gina said, "I've never really heard the men's point of view on all this before. I must admit that I rarely give men clear signals when they say or do something that offends me."

Arthur then said, "All my life I've been trained that my job as a man is to keep pursuing until 'no' is changed to 'yes, yes, yes.' But I hear it that when a woman says no, they want me to respect it. I get it now that what I thought was just a normal part of the dance is experienced as harassment by some women. But you know, it seems that if we're ever going to get together now, more women are going to have to start making the first moves."

After getting support from their same-sex groups and then listening to feedback from the whole group, Joel and Lisa realize that if they are both going to work full time they need to get outside help with family tasks, rather than continuing to blame and shame one another for not doing more.

Gender partnership based on strong, interactive, separate but equal gender identities can support the needs of both sexes. Becoming more affirming or supportive of our same sex doesn't have to lead to hostility toward the other sex. In fact, the acknowledgment that gender diversity is healthy may help all of us to become more tolerant toward other kinds of differences in our society.

Through gender reconciliation—both formal workshops and informal discussions—the sexes can support each other, instead of blaming one sex for not meeting the other's expectations. Men and women clearly have the capacity to move away from the sex-war rhetoric that is dividing us as well as the courage necessary to create forums for communication that can unite and heal us.

Boys and girls need regular opportunities in school to openly discuss their differing views on dating, sex, and gender roles. In universities, established women's studies courses could be complemented with men's studies, and classes in the two fields could be brought together from time to time to deepen students' understanding of both sexes. The informal discussion group is another useful format in which men and women everywhere can directly communicate with each other (see *Utne Reader* issue no. 44 [March/April 1991]). In the workplace the struggle for gender understanding needs to go beyond the simple setting up of guidelines about harassment; it is essential that women and men regularly discuss their differing views on gender issues. Outside help is often needed in structuring such discussions and getting them under way. Our organization, the Gender Re-

lations Institute, trains and provides "reconciliation facilitators" for that purpose.

These forums must be fair. Discussions of women's wage equity must also include men's job safety. Discussions about reproductive rights, custody rights, or parental leave must consider the rights of both mothers and fathers—and the needs of the children. Affirmative action to balance the male-dominated political and economic leadership must also bring balance to the female-dominated primary-education and social-welfare systems.

We call for both sexes to come to the negotiating table from a new position of increased strength and self-esteem. Men and women do not need to become more like one another, merely more deeply themselves. But gender understanding is only a step on the long road that must ultimately lead to fundamental institutional change. We would hope, for example, that in the near future men and women will stop arguing about whether women should go into combat and concentrate instead on how to end war. The skills and basic attitudes that will lead to gender peace are the very ones we need in order to meet the other needs of our time—social, political, and environmental—with committed action.

Follow-Up

1. *Explain why you agree or disagree with the authors' contention that in cases of male–female conflict there are two differing but equally valid points of view.*
2. *Discuss or write about your views on any two statements in this article.*
3. *What is one major issue or question you would like answered by the opposite gender? Consider asking a few members of the opposite gender and report the responses and your analysis.*
4. *Complete the Applied Activity "Gender Roles: Positive and Negative" at the end of this section.*

On Being a Man

Sam Keen

The year I was seventeen I received many messages from my class-mates, my family, and my culture about what was required to be a *real man:*

> *Join the fraternity.*
> *Get a letter in football, baseball, or basketball.*
> *Screw a lot of girls.*
> *Be tough; fight if anybody insults you or your girl.*
> *Don't show your feelings.*
> *Drink lots of beer (predrug era).*
> *Be nice—don't fight or drink.*
> *Dress right—like everybody else: penny loafers, etc.*
> *Get a good job, work hard and make a lot of money.*
> *Get your own car.*
> *Be well liked, popular.*

* * *

Today I look at an old picture of that seventeen-year-old boy…. His clandestine life included many activities not on any list of re-quirements for being a *real man:* keeping a diary; exploring nearby woods and longing for the wilderness;…wondering about the limits of his mind; exploring his dark moods; writing poetry;…loving his par-ents;…wanting to do something to make the world better….

The popular cliché says that men think and do, women feel and emote. It's a half-truth worth playing with. Most of us learned that real men were supposed to control their feelings…. Little did we understand that by doing the manly thing, girding up our loins, pulling in our guts, pushing out our chests, tightening our jaws, and constricting our breath-ing, we forced most feelings into exile in our unconscious….

Perhaps the greatest price men have paid for their obsession with fearlessness is to have become tough on the outside but empty within. We are hollow men. The connection between fearlessness and feeling-lessness should be obvious…. Men and women seem to have different styles of fearing. Men's fears focus around loss of what we experience as our independence, and women's around the loss of significant relationships….

…Men are more fearful of death than women…. Men make lousy patients. Ask any doctor. Disease and disability frighten us more than they do women…. Sickness raises the specter of all that men have been taught to fear: weakness, dependency, passivity….

Men usually do not talk much about their sexual fears and disappointments. Sex is a big thing for us. And we judge it in more absolute terms than women do. It is either/or. Up or down.

Follow-Up

1. *Either as a man, or in your experiences with men, how accurate are Keen's views about manhood today?*
2. *Select one of Keen's statements and discuss your reaction.*

If I Were a Car, I'd Be a Lemon

Denise Karuth

This morning the plumber for my building stopped by. I assured him that my barking Labrador retriever wouldn't bite by explaining that she was a seeing eye dog.

"You aren't blind are you?"

"Yes, but I used to be able to see better."

"But you're . . . you're in a wheelchair . . . You're not," he hesitated, "a cripple, too, are you?"

"I have multiple sclerosis," I answered. "Some of us just have all the luck."

"Holy Jesus! God bless you, ma'am. I'm really sorry. God bless you. If you ever have any trouble with your sink or electricity you just call this number." He placed his card on the arm of the couch. "Call any time, even at night. Just tell them you're a handicapped apartment and they'll come right out. God bless you. Jesus God!"

Sometimes the reactions are even stronger.

I would never willingly cause pain to anyone, so it makes me sad when perfect strangers walk up to me and burst into tears. My first reaction is to think that their tears are somehow my fault. As it happens, some of the people who cry have lost family members or friends to disabling illness, and in two instances, deaf senior citizens cried from a sense of empathy and community with me. In most cases, though, the tears are shed because of peoples' bleak notions of what life must be like for me, the "helpless blind cripple."

I'm not talking only about "the man in the street." The same misconceptions are held as well by students and professionals. Back when I was "just" blind, a middle-aged man passed me on campus and remarked to his companion, "Oh my God, Martha. Look at that. She's blind!"

"Yes," I replied, "but she isn't deaf!"

Then, of course, there are the rehabilitation counselors and the doctors, professionals who deal with disabled people *on a regular basis.* How much they, too, have yet to learn. For example, during my last eye exam at a leading teaching hospital in Boston, one of the top ophthalmologists said (in my presence) to three of his students: "When the retinal damage is not too severe, many of these patients can lead a normal life. But in a case like this, a normal life is impossible."

This pro may have known about my eyes. He knew very little about me.

Another doctor once told me, "You can't possibly have MS. Lightning just doesn't strike twice in the same place." Would that he had been right.

I would like to be able to sit people down and say, "Look, I appreciate your concern, but my life isn't that bad. Sure, it's not quite uninterrupted bliss, but whose life is? It's a good life. I work and play and have friends and make love and mistakes and get bored now and again just like you. So put your handkerchiefs away. First impressions aside, I'm a lot more like you than you probably imagine."

MORNING THOUGHTS

It's 6:30 a.m., and the solar alarm clock beckons through the patio doors; it refuses to be ignored. I savor a few last moments of rest and begin to plan the day ahead. It's Saturday. My weekend shower and hairwash are behind me, as are bladder irrigation and bowel care; with regard to personal care, this should be an easy day. I read over a long list of ongoing projects and responsibilities compiled over the last 2 days and select several items to work on. (With MS, memory can be affected, and mine needs all the help it can get; hence, the list.)

What's this? A Stravinsky attack! I am back at Symphony Hall where last night I heard the Dumbarton Oaks Concerto, a piece long familiar to me from my years as a music major and an orchestral musician. I must hear it again—now—and am compelled to roll over in bed to search for it in a small box of cassettes. I find it and slip it in the deck.

Having been an orchestral musician was one of the high points of my life. Orchestral playing has to be one of the most complex and beautiful group endeavors (a team sport, if you will) yet devised by humanity. Football pales to insignificance in comparison.

As a 17-year-old who had been ardently playing double bass for only 2 years, Chamber Orchestra helped me discover the exhilaration of overcoming overwhelming inexperience, the joy of sharing in the creation of something unsurpassingly wonderful, and of intimate involvement with a plane of music that I would have thought far beyond my understanding.

My intense involvement with music was like an express train to enlightenment: Regardless of what happens at the end of the line, one is always grateful for the ticket. People often wonder that I am not bitter about having to give up my orchestral playing. Sometimes I miss it so much that I cry. Mostly, though, I am grateful for having had the opportunity and for having learned, importantly, from it. So I cannot complain. My life now presents me with many of the same challenges and opportunities as did Stravinsky's music. The stakes, of course, are higher, but the price of defeat is more than I am willing to pay.

The joy of living with meaning and with purpose is worth considerable effort. In the long run, I do not have a great deal of control over what is happening to me physically. But if I let my physical disability paralyze my spirit, my life would become a well of self-pity, anger, and despair. I cannot allow that to happen.

THE NORMAL ASPECTS

What's my life been like? I was born 2 months prematurely in November 1954, the middle child of three. My family lived in the Adirondack Mountains and in Buffalo, New York. I attended public schools in Cheektowaga and Amherst, both neighbors to Buffalo. In 1972 I won a New York State Regents' Scholarship that paid my tuition to the State University of New York at Buffalo. In 1976 I graduated magna cum laude with a degree in music. That September, my brother Ed, our closest friend Fred, and I moved to Boston where I attended graduate school and received a master's degree in rehabilitation counseling.

My faith education stressed the importance of serving others and working for justice and peace. I am a member of the local chapters of the American Friends' Service Committee, Mobilization for Survival, Amnesty International, and IMPACT, a national ecumenical political action network. I have also lobbied at both state and national levels concerning U.S. involvement in Latin America, U.S. food policy, nuclear disarmament, civil rights for the disabled, and human services legislation and cutbacks. I have supported the Infant Formula Action Coalition, INFACT, which fights the unethical promotion of infant formula in Third World countries and helped organize a Legal Defense Fund for a friend who was unjustly arrested at the Seabrook nuclear power plant site in New Hampshire (all charges against him were later dropped). I have written a review of an accessible art exhibit for the Cambridge women's magazine *Sojourner*, and have had requests to do further writing. I also have been involved with two area food co-ops.

For fun, I run Irene, my black Labrador retriever, around Jamaica Pond every week in good weather. I entertain and visit friends, play some piano and recorder, and take walks in my motorized wheelchair either with friends or on my own.

So much for the many "normal" aspects of my life. As I focus on my experience as a disabled individual, I hope that you, the reader, will not lose sight of the similarity of the life we share.

COUSIN CAROL'S PREGNANT?

Being legally blind, with a small amount of residual vision, is like living in a bizarre fun house where what you see is not necessarily what you get. First off, I can see things up close far better than things any distance away. I can see my fingers, for example, if I hold them 2 inches from my face, but I cannot see my toes (although, when the lighting is right, I can see a blur where my foot is). If the contrast is right, I can make out Irene's dark shape; but, then, I have also mistaken a low stool or my black skirt or my black coat lying on the bed for Irene, even in the best light.

As my sight deteriorated, I found myself asking questions of store mannequins, I mistook full-length mirrors for doorways, and I tried to find the "Push for Walk" button on trees.

Many people think that either you can see or you can't. How difficult it is to write about vision, since no common vocabulary exists that adequately explains the variability of sight.

Being blind with residual vision means that you "see" your relatives and friends on the Boston trolleys and buses . . . even though those relatives never left Buffalo. It means looking both ways before crossing the street and then walking out into the side of a school-bus. It means entering an unfamiliar room and being visually bombarded by confusing patterns of light and dark. It means getting so accustomed to familiar places that your friends accuse you of being able to see, or worse, they forget to warn you about newly placed obstacles.

Being blind means getting so thoroughly lost that sometimes you have no idea where you are, much less how to get where you're going. It means having people come up to you in the street, say "Hi!" and disappear, before you can figure out who they were. (*Always* identify yourself to your blind friends, especially if your meeting occurs in a place where they're not used to seeing you.)

Being blind means not knowing that Aunt Trudy has lost weight, or that cousin Carol is 8 months pregnant (until you embrace them). It means brushing up against wet paint, waltzing down the street with silver-streaked coat and hair, and wondering why people are taking notice of you. It means being the only person in the theater who does not dive under a chair when Audrey Hepburn's ankle is grabbed by her assailant in "Wait Until Dark." It means being utterly confused by cars making right and left turns on red. It means spending too much time looking for house-keys, dark glasses, the checkbook, or the vegetable steamer. And it means knowing how to take notes into exams by a method so wonderfully clever that I will not reveal it here.

In my case being blind is compounded by poor memory, difficulty with sense of touch, and the fact that I rely on others to do so much for me that things are often put away without my knowing where to find them again.

In short, being blind means having to become adept at assembling an image of reality from a jumble of jigsaw puzzle pieces—and doing so in the shortest possible time.

MS. It stands for multiple sclerosis, a chronic, disabling, neurologic disease. In my book it also stands for the Marquis de Sade, who, if given the chance to invent a disease, would have been hard pressed to come up with anything more diabolical.

No one knows what causes MS or how to cure it. There isn't even a fool-proof diagnostic test to see if you've got it. Many MS'ers are told that their symptoms are caused by depression, anxiety, hysteria, and even conversion reaction. It's not uncommon for as many as 8 years to elapse before the diagnosis is confirmed.

MS presents with dozens of different symptoms and affects each individual who has it quite differently. Textbook cases of MS are found only in textbooks.

One of the most disabling aspects of the disease is fatigue. There are 168 hours in a week. In a good week I can spend about 15 hours away from home in a wheelchair doing things like working, socializing, attending meetings and church, and the like. About 85% of my time is spent in bed in a mixture of work, resting up, and planning ahead. Being able to condense much of life into 15 hours a week and developing strategies for a constructive invalidism should earn me an honorary degree as a management consultant.

When I finally moved into an accessible apartment and acquired my two electric wheelchairs (the second because my first was unsuitable for outdoor use), the sense of freedom came rushing in like a wave. The second day I had my outdoor chair, I took it and Irene on an 8 mile walk, four times longer than any walk I'd been able to take in 5 years! The wheelchair had liberated me from the limits of my walking, and from a fair amount of the pain that walking and standing had intensified.

There are times now when I almost take for granted my ability to glide down streets for distances that were formerly unthinkable. I pass places where I spent hours waiting for buses to go distances I can now wheelchair in minutes. I remember how much it hurt to stand and wait for trains and buses, how I sat down on curbs and on floors of trolleys, banks, and supermarkets in an attempt to lessen the overwhelming pain and fatigue. I remember the times I cried walking down the street, doing dishes, or waiting for transit.

Whose turn is it to ask for a ride to church? (My dislike of asking people for rides to church is outmatched only by my love of choir, which rehearses earlier than the local wheelchair transit service can get me there.) Some would think that dependency and illness simplify life in that one is no longer faced with the burdens of work and self-reliance. On the contrary, a severely disabled person generally has more details to keep track of and a harder time doing it.

An able-bodied person does not have to:

- Know exactly where everything is in the house (from Elmer's Glue and electrical tape to hair barrettes and catheter clamps) because the able-bodied person can easily get up and search for things. A disabled person who spends a great deal of time in bed has to be able to tell others where things can be found.
- Set aside substantial amounts of time or plan in advance for things like bowel movements and catheter irrigation.
- Plan activities 5 business days in advance to meet the requirements of the wheelchair transit system.
- Make sure that a list of approximately 20 medical and surgical supplies are in stock and close at hand, along with whatever prescription drugs are required.
- Keep a particularly close watch on the budget so he or she can afford to pay attendants even when the reimbursement checks from Medicaid are 3 to 4 months behind.
- Budget time so that not more than 5 hours a day are spent out of bed.
- Hassle with things like wheelchair acquisition, maintenance, and repair or bills that providers did not submit to Medicaid.

In general, the less you are able to do for yourself, the more health problems you have that require specialized care. Also, as it gets harder to remember things, the more things there are to be remembered, planned, and kept track of.

The more disabled you are, the more of a magician you have to be simply to lead a normal life.

My best friend is most remarkable. She has congenital deformities of both hands, no intelligible speech, and she functions at a 3- to 4-year level. She is nearsighted, color blind, short statured, and dependent on others for assistance with personal care. She is also black, which many would agree is an additional handicap in today's society.

Yet, after a 3-month vocational training program, and with only a minimum of adaptive equipment, my best friend is now successfully employed in a skilled job that many able-bodied individuals would find daunting.

My best friend's name is Irene. Irene is my guide dog.

She has a black silky coat that looks like it's been polished, and a wonderfully expressive face with big brown eyes that could melt glaciers. Her favorite pastimes are eating, sleeping, playing, and being lovable. Her favorite food is virtually anything organic.

Irene, I am told, is a Greek word meaning peace. My best friend couldn't have a better name.

Irene is loyalty incarnate. She even goes with me into the too-little stalls in public bathrooms. As I write this, she is sleeping in a chair at the foot of my bed. The space is much too cramped for her, but she prefers to stay there, close to me, rather than stretching out comfortably on the double bed or the couch in the other room.

Irene and I have been together for the past 5½ years. Twenty-four hours a day. Seven days a week. We've enjoyed a truly symbiotic relationship.

How does Irene guide me? In the wheelchair I am so close to the ground that I can hold the leather leash very near to her collar. In this way, I'm able to follow her moves without having to hold the metal harness. She, of course, stops for curbs and steps, just as she did when I could walk. But now, in addition, she aims for curb-cuts and driveways.

Oh love of my life, dog of my dreams, hound of my heart. How can I possibly describe this relationship of ours? Should I write of our first week in training school when we were waiting to cross Massachusetts Avenue? You were eager and pulling my arm, but I told you that the light was against us. "Relax," I said. You looked up at me as if to say, "You mean that?" and promptly lay down (in complete disregard of standard guide dog behavior). Or should I tell about the time we went to see the Boston Ballet and you reacted to a bizarre, musically dissonant piece by climbing in terror upon my lap? Or should I write about the 160 or more days we've spent together in various hospitals? How you always knew when to put on the "Lassie act" to impress administrators and Nursing Supervisors.

Remember the time we walked on the subway platform and a disturbed lady greeted us with a cry of "Lord, strike down this demon dog led by a demon!"? Or when you had a gland infection and couldn't wag your tail? Or when you held your ground, even after I'd given the "Forward" command, and saved me from being hit by a car on Newbury Street?

Maybe I should write about how you joyously proceed with choir on Sunday mornings, snore during the sermon, and always know when the worship is over. Or about all the great romps we've had together. (How you love to play and make friends.) Or about how I'm convinced I can tell what you're thinking at any point in time.

I should write about your talent for being able to remember routes we've taken or people we've met only once before. Or about your adaptability in learning to locate curb-cuts, driveways, and elevators. Or your eagerness to shepherd others who travel with me. Maybe I should even mention that I've only run over your paws once in the 2 years I've been in a wheelchair.

I'm so proud of you that I don't care if people stare as we glide together down the street with your leash in my left hand and the wheelchair control in my right.

All in all, you are my pride, my love, and my joy. I can't conceive of life without you. If someone gave me a choice between losing my right arm or losing you permanently, I would part, reluctantly, with my right arm.

But then, what are best friends for?

MY BODY, MY WIMP

Right now it is 8:45 on a Sunday night, and I've been in bed for 5 hours. I want to continue to write, but my body wants to sleep. Can you remember being a little kid and wanting to stay up late, but your mother wouldn't let you? It's frustrating and aggravating to have a mother who never gives in, not even once. Sometimes I want to shout: "I'm 27 years old! Can't I even stay up until 10:00?" But I know from long experience that my protests are of no avail, that my only option is to give in. But not before I negotiate.

"Give me just 20 minutes," I say. "Maybe even 15." I find that I negotiate with my body a lot. "If we go to Jamaica Pond this afternoon and to choir this evening, I promise to stay in all day tomorrow." Or, "I know you're tired, but it's an important meeting, and I really should be there." I even apologize to it: "Chastity (one of my nicknames for my genital area), I'm sorry. Being catheterized is a bitch. What can I say? Let's hope we don't have to do it again for awhile."

For years before it became irrefutably clear that my increasing weakness, fatigue, and pain were the result of illness, I was at war with my body, always pushing it beyond its limits. Now I realize that I treated it like a traitor instead of a besieged ally. I gave it years of grief that it did nothing to deserve,

Time's up. It's 9:00. I got my 15 minutes in. Now I'm negotiating with a body that is busy spacing out. "Let's put the writing board away, take our evening medications, pull up the covers, and go to sleep."

I'll have to leave the lights on since Fred is out. I used to feel badly that I had to trouble someone else to close doors and turn out lights that I couldn't get to. The paradox of their physical closeness and inaccessible distance hit home. Now I rarely think about it. I guess that's adjustment.

It's 9:05, and I'm reluctantly going to sleep. That's adjustment, too. "You know, body," I tease affectionately, "you're really a wimp."

Follow-Up

1. *If you do not have a physical disability: Think of instances in your life when you have seen or interacted with people who have physical disabilities. Describe your thoughts and feelings about these encounters. Are you confused about how to talk to a person who has a disability or to know what is "proper"?*

   If you do have a physical disability: What have been your experiences with people without disabilities? Were they similar to those described by Denise Karuth?

2. *Select one or more of these statements and offer your reactions:*
   - *"I do not have a great deal of control over what is happening to me physically. But if I let my physical disability paralyze my spirit, my life would become a well of self-pity, anger, and despair."*
   - *"As I focus on my experience as a disabled individual, I hope that you, the reader, will not lose sight of the similarity of the life we share."*
   - *To her best friend Irene, Denise says "'If someone gave me a choice between losing my right arm or losing you permanently, I would part, reluctantly, with my right arm.'"*

- *"I was at war with my body, always pushing it beyond its limits. Now I realize that I treated it like a traitor instead of a besieged ally."*

3. *In another section of the article, Denise Karuth says that the biggest environmental barriers faced by individuals who use wheelchairs are, of course, architectural. She estimates that 60% of "accessible" architecture is flawed, with about 20% posing insurmountable difficulties. If you do not use a wheelchair, as you go through your day imagine doing your activities in a wheelchair. If you know someone who uses a wheelchair, ask about the challenges of getting around. If you do use a wheelchair, would you agree or disagree with Karuth?*

4. *Karuth could spend a maximum of 15 hours per week away from home in a wheelchair. Faced with similar constraints, what would your life be like?*

5. *Try one or more of the suggestions in the accompanying piece titled "Think 'People First'."*

6. *See the Applied Activity at the end of this section titled "A New Identity." Choose a disability for your identity transformation.*

Think "People First"

Language is a reflection of how people see each other. That's why the words we use can hurt. It's also why responsible communicators are now choosing language which reflects the dignity of people with disabilities—words that put the person first, rather than the disability. Read on for a short course on using language that empowers.

1. Think "people first." Say "a woman who has mental retardation," rather than "a mentally retarded woman."
2. Avoid words like "unfortunate," "afflicted," and "victim." Also, try to avoid casting a person with a disability as a superhuman model of courage. People with disabilities are just people, not tragic figures or demigods.
3. A developmental disability is not a disease. Do not mention "symptoms," "patients" or "treatment," unless the person you're writing about has an illness as well as a disability.
4. Use common sense. Avoid terms with obvious negative or judgmental connotations, such as "crippled," "deaf and dumb," "lame," and "defective." If you aren't sure how to refer to a person's condition, ask. And, if the disability is not relevant to your story or conversation, why mention it at all?
5. Never refer to a person as "confined to a wheelchair." Wheelchairs enable people to escape confinement. A person with a mobility impairment "uses" a wheelchair.
6. Try to describe people without disabilities as "typical" rather than "normal."

Applied Activities for Section One

CHILDHOOD SURVEY

The purpose of this activity is to try to see and feel like a child (birth to age 12). Attempt to recall your memories and impressions in the areas listed below. You are not expected to disclose any information that is uncomfortable to you. If you cannot think of a response to an item, let it sit for awhile (also consider talking to someone who knew you at this age). Looking at photos of yourself at this age may help also. Try to complete at least ten of the items.

1. My earliest memory is _____

   _____

2. My favorite toys as a preschooler were _____

   _____

3. My favorite non-school activities as an elementary student were_____

   _____

4. Describe the interior of your home(s) and which rooms were your favorite

   _____

   _____

5. What was a favorite place outside of your home and why? _____

   _____

6. How would you describe your typical peer relationship as an elementary child (e.g., loner, leader, many but few close friends, etc.)? _____

   _____

7. What were some special interests, fascinations, etc. for you?_____

   _____

8. What current skills and aptitudes started to show at this age? _____

   _____

9. What were some aptitudes and interests that you have *not* retained or developed further as you aged beyond childhood? _____

_____

10. Who were your heroes/heroines during childhood?_____

_____

11. Who were your "villains" (who you were told not to be like)?_____

_____

12. What were your summers like? _____

_____

13. Describe a special time or event with a parent/guardian _____

_____

14. What are some beliefs or ideas you had as a child that you now perceive to be untrue, unusual, etc.? _____

_____

15. What, if anything, was an imagined future or special destiny?_____

_____

16. What are two or three major events that stand out from this age? _____

_____

17. Who were major influential persons outside of your family? _____

_____

18. What caused you to be fearful or anxious at this age?_____

_____

19. What were the appropriate and inappropriate ways to be a boy or girl? ___

_____

20. Name one thing for which you are glad you are not a child now _____

_____

21. Name one quality you had as a child but do not have now (and wish you did) _____

_____

22. When and how did your childhood *end?* _____

_____

Follow-Up

1. Share your childhood memories with three or four others and look for differences and similarities.
2. How are you similar to your childhood years now? Different?
3. What are some learnings from completing this survey that have relevance for you today?

ARE YOU AN ADULT?

Most people offer psychological rather than legal reasons when describing how they knew they were adults. Richard Cohen, for example, discovered he was an adult when he paid a restaurant tab. Here are some other events that trigger adulthood realization (as obtained from interviews): the first day on a full-time job; buying a house; filling out income tax returns; attending the funeral of a friend or a parent; being referred to as *lady* by a patient; being asked to leave home by parents; and pursuing a dream (such as playing rock music for a living) that others consider impractical. One 23-year-old, a married college grad and a health professional, still does not feel like an adult "because my husband now does everything for me that my father used to do." Try to complete one of the following items:

1. I became an adult when

_____

_____

_____

_____

_____

2. I do *not* believe I am an adult yet because

_____

_____

_____

1. Ask others outside of class if they think they are adults.
2. Ask older family members when they considered themselves adults. Are you considered an adult by the people in your family?
3. Analyze the responses to the adulthood question for underlying themes (responsibility, independence, etc.).
4. Discuss (or write about) your findings.

ROLES AND AUTHENTICITY

Culturally defined roles constitute a major portion of one's identity. Some major roles include: male/female, acting your age, spouse/significant other, father/mother, son/daughter, employee/employer, student, member of a social/professional group, ethnic/racial identity, spiritual/religious orientation, volunteer. A role may use and draw out one's authentic needs, values, and aptitudes. Or, a role may demand behaviors that contradict one's authentic needs, values, and aptitudes. The degree of fit between roles and authenticity is a primary determinant of well-being.

In this activity, examine how roles match your authentic needs, values, and aptitudes.

Directions:
1. Select a major role in your life and write it in the space provided (some examples of roles were listed previously or you can list another of your choosing).
2. Analyze your self-role behavior according to the four categories described below. Try to list actual examples for each of the four categories if possible.

ROLE _____

Self-role behavior categories	Examples from your life
A. True to self and true to role: When the role expectations fit your needs, values, aptitudes.	
B. True to self but may not be true to role: Individualistic and authentic behavior that falls outside the "regular way of doing things." Sometimes results in signs of disapproval or actual sanctions.	

Self-role behavior categories	Examples from your life
C. Not true to self but true to role: When you act because "you have to" but it runs counter to your authentic needs, values, and aptitudes.	
D. Not true to self and not true to role: When you act in ways contrary to both role expectations and your authentic self (e.g., self-destructive/illegal behaviors).	

Follow-Up

1. Which of your role categories ranks *first* in reference to the time and energy invested in it? Discuss or write what this means to you.
2. There are strategies for enhancing one's self-role functioning. Here are a few to consider:
   (a) Attempt to increase the A category behaviors, and/or decrease behaviors in the B, C, and D categories.
   (b) In extreme situations you might consider *eliminating* a role when this is a possible choice.
   (c) Sometimes *adding a new role* can draw out more of your authentic needs, values, and aptitudes.
   Attempt and experiment with one of these options to see if it enhances your well-being.
3. Repeat this activity with different roles.

A NEW IDENTITY

You had a good night's sleep, but as you start to wake up you sense something is different, even strange. Crawling out of bed you pass a mirror and stop and stare. Somehow overnight you've changed into a person of the opposite gender. Take a few moments to ponder this change and try to address the following items:

1. Describe some major ways in which your life would be different.
2. Name one positive aspect of this new identity. Name one negative aspect of this new identity.

3. If given the choice to stay with this new identity or to revert back to your former one, which one would you choose? Why?

Describe your learnings and interpret them.

Variations: Instead of gender change, consider changes of race, age, nationality, or historical period. Answer the above questions for any of these other identity changes.

SYMBOLIC IDENTITY

Emerson said that objects in nature have corresponding mental likenesses. Carl Jung believed that one's inner life can be represented by outward objects. This activity is a strategy for discovering facets of one's identity through seeking parallels in one's environment. It is crucial to conduct this activity in a relaxed, receptive manner. Let the symbolic discoveries come to you rather than striving for them.

Instructions:
Go for a solitary stroll for at least 30 minutes. On this stroll you are to be receptive to something that reflects you as a person. You may see something, feel it, hear it, smell it, taste it, or even sense it intuitively. It is important to *not* force this parallel. Do not make it an intellectual task. Allow the surroundings to present you with the discovery. Just watch and observe with a free-floating attention. If this symbolic reflection appears, pause and enter it without analysis. Let it express itself to you. Once you feel that you have learned all you can, try to write it down. If nothing appears, then try again another time.

Here is one example of this technique: "On campus there is this pedestrian walkway over a busy street. It is tunnel shaped with a clear plastic enclosure. I was walking through this tunnel and gazing at the traffic passing below, couples walking hand-in-hand, and people hurrying to classes. It was then that I realized I was living my whole life in a tunnel. A big project had consumed so much of my life for over a year that I could only observe, but not participate in, a full life. To paraphrase a line in a Hemingway short story, I was there in real life but did not go to it anymore."

GENDER ROLES: POSITIVE AND NEGATIVE

Directions: Complete steps 1 and 2 individually. Form groups (2–6 members of the *same* gender) and discuss your results. Attempt one or more of the Follow-Up activities.

1. List two advantages and two disadvantages of being a *male* today.

Advantages _____

_____

Disadvantages   _____

_____

2. List two advantages and two disadvantages of being a *female* today.

Advantages   _____

_____

Disadvantages   _____

_____

Follow-Up

Compare and discuss* your results in one or more of the following ways:

1. In *mixed* gender groups (2–6 members).

2. Post all the lists on the wall. Have all participants read them. Conduct a whole class discussion on the perceptions and questions from these lists.

3. Discuss the following question in either mixed gender groups and/or with the whole class: What can be done to maximize the advantages and minimize the disadvantages for each gender?

4. Write about what you've learned after completing one or more of the above activities.

Note: Listening skills are essential with any of the above activities.

HUMAN COMMUNICATION

O ne of the things you can do that a squirrel cannot is talk. Another is to wonder why you are being compared to a squirrel. You can talk and wonder because of a part of the human brain called the cerebral cortex. Talking does not necessarily make us any wiser than the squirrels or other animals that do not have cerebral cortexes. We just do it a lot. We spend a good amount of our time hearing and watching others in person, in print, on TV, on the radio, and on all kinds of electronic technology. We tell about our experiences and listen to others' stories. We even talk to ourselves.

Humans seemingly have a need to put into words almost anything they experience. Communication research has shown that humans spend approximately 70 percent of their waking time in verbal communication. We communicate for instrumental reasons—our messages are means of obtaining information, objects, attention, affection, or influence, or explanation. We also communicate for expressive reasons. Our messages are valued for their own sake—we just enjoy the process of communicating. Being human means communicating.

Underlying all the reasons for communication is the need to make a connection with another person (or even with yourself). We all have a basic need to express what is going on in our life and have someone hear it in the way we intend. If this connection is appropriately made, we have genuine communication. If this connection is not achieved, humans often become angry, lonely, alienated, or even sick. The articles in this section feature some of the more significant concepts and techniques for making communication connections.

- In "Interpersonal Communication" Warner Burke provides a basic model of communication. He explains effective and ineffective approaches for sending and receiving messages.
- Psychologist Carl Rogers offers a personalized account of his experiences as a listener in "To Hear and to Be Heard." Rogers says that true listening is a source of deep joy and satisfaction.
- Is empathy automatically a good quality? This issue is addressed in "Johnny Bear and the Empath" by Nelson Goud.
- Additional views on possible kinds of listening are offered in "John Steinbeck On Listening" and "A Teacher Hears."
- Nelson Goud describes the dynamics of "Self-Disclosure" and offers guidelines for appropriate disclosure. Fusion communication is introduced in this piece.
- The different frameworks used by men and women in communication are the theme of Deborah Tannen's "You Just Don't Understand." Six patterns are discussed.
- Arthur J. Lange and Patricia Jakubowski distinguish three forms of expressing needs and rights in "Assertive, Nonassertive, and Aggressive Behavior." Guidelines are offered.
- A comprehensive treatment of personal journaling is offered by Lou Beeker Schultz in "Personal Journaling as a Life Companion."
- Intuition, the mode of knowing without thinking, is explained by Frances Vaughan in "Awakening Intuition."
- Developing your sensory intelligence is the focus of Nelson Goud's "Sensational Living."
- Making sense of those strange dreams is the topic of Ernest Hartmann's "The Nature and Uses of Dreaming."

Interpersonal Communication

Warner Burke

Communication, by definition, involves at least two individuals, the sender and the receiver. Consider yourself, first of all, as the sender of some message. There are certain filters or barriers (internal) which determine whether or not the message is actually transmitted. These barriers may be categorized as follows: (1) Assumptions about yourself—Do I really have something to offer? Am I safe to offer suggestions? Do I really want to share the information? Will others really understand? How will the communication affect my self-esteem? (2) Attitudes about the message itself—Is the information valuable? Do I see the information correctly, or understand it well enough to describe it to others? (3) Sensing the receiver's reaction—Do I become aware of whether or not the receiver is actually understanding? Or in other words, can I "sense" from certain cues or reactions by the receiver whether or not we are communicating?

Now consider yourself as the receiver. As a receiver you may filter or not hear certain aspects (or any aspect for that matter) of a message. Why? Because the message may seem unimportant or too difficult. Moreover, you may be selective in your attention. For example, you may feel that the sender is being redundant, so you quit listening after the first few words. You may be preoccupied with something else. Or your filtering or lack of attention may be due to your past experience with the sender. You may feel that "this guy has never made a point in his life and never will!"

Many times the receiver never makes use of his "third ear." That is, trying to be sensitive to nonverbal communication. The sender's eyes, gestures, and sometimes his overall posture communicate messages that the insensitive listener never receives.

There may be barriers that exist between the sender and the receiver, e.g., cultural differences. Environmental conditions may also cause barriers, e.g., poor acoustics. More common, however, are the differences in frames of reference. For example, there may not be a common understanding of purpose in a certain communication. You may ask me how I'm feeling today. To you the phrase, "How ya doing?" is nothing more than a greeting. However, I may think that you really want to know and I may tell you—possibly at length.

Now that some of the problems in interpersonal communication have been mentioned, let us delve somewhat deeper into this process of transferring a message from the brain and emotion of one person to the brain and emotion of another human being.

SENDING THE MESSAGE

In communicating a message effectively to another person, there are several obvious factors which are beneficial. Such things as correct pronunciation, lack of distracting brogue, dialect, or accent, or a pleasant resonance in one's voice usually facilitate the sending of a message.

Assuming the sender of a message really has a desire to be heard and understood and not just speak for the sake of speaking, he wants some assurance that he has communicated. The key to effective communication on the part of the speaker, then, is to obtain some feedback, of one form or another, from his listener(s). Some bright persons who really have something to say are ineffective speakers, be it lecturing or speaking to someone at a cocktail party, because they are unable to tell or care whether their listener(s) is understanding, or they do not make any effort to check on their effectiveness as a communicator. For example, many lecturers in a classroom situation are often unaware of when a listener is sound asleep. Unless there is interaction of some type between the speaker and his listener, the speaker is susceptible to "losing" his listener. Often the speaker must take the initiative in order to receive any feedback regarding the effectiveness of his communication. When speaking before a large group, I often resort to the simple act of requesting my audience to shake their head "yes" if they understand what I have just said, or "no" if they did not understand. Even though this technique is simple, I usually get considerable feedback quickly and I know immediately what I must do at that point to make my speech more effective or whether to continue on with my next point.

Even when talking to just one other person the speaker must often take the initiative, in an interactive sense, to determine whether his message is being understood. Even though I sometimes take the risk of "bugging" my listener, I often stop and ask him if he understands what I mean, or I occasionally ask him to tell me what he thinks I meant in my message.

There is a fairly small percentage of people who speak articulately and clearly enough to be understood most of the time. Most of us have to work at it, especially when we are attempting to communicate a message which is fairly abstract or when we want to tell something which is quite personal or highly emotional. In sending the message effectively, we must do two things simultaneously: (1) work at finding the appropriate words and emotion to express what we want to say, and (2) continually look for cues from the listener to get

some feedback even if we must ask our listener for some.

RECEIVING THE MESSAGE

In considering interpersonal communication, we might, at first thought, think that listening is the easier of the two functions in the process. If we assume, however, that the listener really wants to understand what the speaker is saying, then the process is not all that easy. The basic problem that the listener faces is that he is capable of thinking faster than the speaker can talk. In their *Harvard Business Review* article, Nichols and Stevens state that the average rate of speech for most Americans is about 125 words per minute. Most of our thinking processes involve words, and our brains can handle many more words per minute than 125. As Nichols and Stevens point out, what this means is that, when we listen, our brains receive words at a very slow rate compared with the brain's capabilities.

As you have experienced many times, you know that you can listen to what someone is saying and think about something else at the same time. As the "cocktail party" phenomenon illustrates, the human brain is truly remarkable in its ability to process a considerable amount of input simultaneously. Sometimes, at a cocktail party, I want to hear not only what the person in my small gathering is saying, but also what that lovely creature is talking about in the group about six feet away. If the overall noise level is not too loud, I can hear and understand both conversations.

The problem with listening, then, is that we have "spare" time in our thinking processes. How we use that spare time determines the extent of our listening effectiveness. It is easy for us to be distracted in listening, especially if the speaker talks slowly or haltingly or if he says something that stimulates another thought. For example, suppose you are listening to a friend who is telling you about a problem he is having in his department. In the process of describing the problem, he mentions a person whom you know, whereupon you start thinking about the person at length. Later, when your friend asks you what you would do about his problem, you're apt to respond, "what problem?"

Thus, a fundamental problem the listener must consider in the communicative process is the fact that his brain is capable of responding to a speaker at several different levels simultaneously. Naturally, this can be an asset to the listener rather than a problem. For example the listener can attend to nonverbal cues the speaker gives, e.g., facial expression, gesture, or tone of voice, as well as listen to the words themselves.

Besides a highly active brain, an effective listener has another factor to consider in the communicative process. This factor involves the process of trying to perceive what the speaker is saying from his point of view.

A BARRIER AND A GATEWAY

According to Carl Rogers, a leading psychotherapist and psychotherapy researcher, the major barrier to effective communication is the tendency to evaluate. That is, the barrier to mutual interpersonal communication is our very natural tendency to judge, to evaluate, to approve or disapprove the statement or opinion of the other person or group. Suppose someone says to you, "I didn't like what the lecturer had to say." Your typical response will be either agreement or disagreement. In other words, your primary reaction is to evaluate the statement from your point of view, from your own frame of reference.

Although the inclination to make evaluations is common, it is usually heightened in those situations where feelings and emotions are deeply involved. Thus, the stronger our feelings, the more likely it is that there will be no mutual element in the communication.

There will be only two ideas, two feelings, two judgments, missing each other in the heat of the psychological battle.

If having a tendency to evaluate is the major barrier to communication, then the logical gateway to communication is to become an active listener, to listen with understanding. Don't let this simple statement fool you. Listening with understanding means to see the expressed idea and attitude from the other person's point of view, to see how it feels to him, to achieve his frame of reference concerning his subject. One word that summarizes this process of listening with understanding is "empathy."

In psychotherapy, for example, Carl Rogers and his associates have found from research that empathetic understanding—understanding with a person not about him—is such an effective approach that it can bring about major changes in personality.

Suppose that in your next committee meeting you were to conduct an experiment which would test the quality of each committee member's understanding. Institute this rule: "Each person can speak up for himself only after he has first related the ideas and feelings of the previous speaker accurately and to that speaker's satisfaction." This would mean that before presenting your own point of view, it would be necessary for you to achieve the other speaker's frame of reference—to understand his thoughts and feelings so well that you could summarize them for him.

Can you imagine what this kind of approach might mean if it were projected into larger areas, such as congressional debates or labor-management disputes? What would happen if labor, without necessarily agreeing, could accurately state management's point of view in a way that management could accept; and management, without necessarily approving labor's stand, could state labor's case in a way that labor agreed was accurate? It would mean that real communication was established, and conditions would be more conducive for reaching a workable solution.

TOWARD MORE EFFECTIVE LISTENING

Some steps the listener can take to improve interpersonal communication have been stated. To summarize and be more explicit, let us consider these steps.

1. Effective listening must be an active process. To make certain that you are understanding what the speaker is saying, you, as the listener must interact with him. One way to do this is to paraphrase or summarize for the speaker what you think he has said.

2. Attending to nonverbal behavior that the speaker is communicating along with his verbal expression usually helps to understand the oral message more clearly. Often a facial expression or gesture will "tell" you that the speaker feels more strongly about his subject than his words would communicate.

3. The effective listener does not try to memorize every word or fact the speaker communicates, but, rather, he listens for the main thought or idea. Since your brain is such a highly effective processor of information, spending your listening time in more than just hearing the words of the speaker can lead to more effective listening. That is, while listening to the words, you can also be searching for the main idea of the message. Furthermore, you can attempt to find the frame of reference for the speaker's message as well as look at what he is saying from his perspective. This empathetic process also includes your attempting to experience the same feeling about the subject as the speaker.

These three steps toward more effective listening seem fairly simple and obvious. But the fact remains that we don't practice these steps very often. Why don't we?

According to Carl Rogers, it takes courage. If you really understand another person in this way, if you are willing to enter his private world and see the way life appears to him without any attempt to make evaluative judgments, you run the risk of being changed yourself. This risk of being changed is one of the most frightening prospects many of us face.

Moreover, when we need to utilize these steps the most, we are likely to use them the least, that is, when the situation involves a considerable amount of emotion. For example, when we listen to a message that contradicts our most deeply held prejudices, opinions, or convictions, our brain becomes stimulated by many factors other than what the speaker is telling us. When we are arguing with someone, especially about something that is "near and dear" to us, what are we typically doing when the other person is making his point? It's certainly not listening empathetically! We're probably planning a rebuttal to what he is saying, or we're formulating a question which will embarrass the speaker. We may, of course, simply be "tuning him out." How often have you been arguing with someone for 30 minutes or so, and you make what you consider to be a major point for your point of view, and your "opponent" responds by saying, "But that's what I said 30 minutes ago!"

When emotions are strongest, then, it is most difficult to achieve the frame of reference of the other person or group. Yet it is then that empathy is most needed if communication is to be established. A third party, for example, who is able to lay aside his own feelings and evaluation, can assist greatly by listening with understanding to each person or group and clarifying the views and attitudes each holds.

When the parties to a dispute realize that they are being understood, that someone sees how the situation seems to them, the statements grow less exaggerated and less defensive, and it is no longer necessary to maintain the attitude, "I am 100% right and you are 100% wrong."

SUMMARY

Effective communication, at least among human beings, is not a one-way street. It involves an interaction between the speaker and the listener. The responsibility for this interaction is assumed by both parties. You as the speaker can solicit feedback and adjust your message accordingly. As a listener, you can summarize for the speaker what you think he has said and continually practice the empathetic process.

One of the joys of life, at least for me, is to know that I have been heard and understood correctly and to know that someone cares enough to try to understand what I have said. I also get a great deal of satisfaction from seeing this same enjoyment on the face of a speaker when he knows I have understood him.

Follow-Up

1. *Choose one statement from this reading that describes one of your strengths as a communicator. Choose one statement that describes an area where you need improvement as a communicator.*
2. *Burke says that he sometimes initiates getting feedback from a listener to be sure he was understood. Consider trying this idea at times when you are not sure your message is understood.*
3. *Burke states that human thought is much faster than human speech. This fact often results in distracted thoughts and ineffective listening. Does this often happen to you? Try to focus on your listener more if it does.*
4. *Empathy is the ability to perceive another person's world as they do. Another option is to perceive a statement only from your own point of view. Try to understand what other people say from their point of view before you offer your viewpoint. What differences do you notice in the way you relate to one another? See the Applied Activity "Point of View" at the end of this section for a way to develop this skill.*
5. *Burke mentions that it takes courage to be an empathic listener because you run the risk of being changed yourself. You may hear something contrary to your existing beliefs that makes sense, then you have to reexamine your beliefs and possibly make major changes. This is threatening. Has this ever happened to you? Can you recognize when this is happening?*
6. *Burke states that when emotions are intense, true listening is especially important. But, of course, this is the time when listening is the most difficult. Experiment a few times with being a good listener during times when you can sense "hot" emotions. If this is done correctly, the defensiveness should decrease.*
7. *The Applied Activities at the end of this section allow you to apply most of the ideas mentioned in this article.*

To Hear and to Be Heard

Carl Rogers

The first simple feeling I want to share with you is my enjoyment when I can really *hear* someone. I think perhaps this has been a long standing characteristic of mine. I can remember this in my early grammar school days. A child would ask the teacher a question and the teacher would give a perfectly good answer to a completely different question. A feeling of pain and distress would always strike me. My reaction was, "But you didn't *hear* him!" I felt a sort of childish despair at the lack of communication which was (and is) so common.

I believe I know why it is satisfying to me to hear someone. When I can really hear someone it puts me in touch with him. It enriches my life. It is through hearing people that I have learned all that I know about individuals, about personality, about psychotherapy, and about interpersonal relationships. There is another peculiar satisfaction in it. When I really hear someone it is like listening to the music of the spheres, because beyond the immediate message of the person, no matter what that might be, there is the universal, the general. Hidden in all of the personal communications which I really hear there seem to be orderly psychological laws, aspects of the awesome order which we find in the universe as a whole. So there is both the satisfaction of hearing this particular person and also the satisfaction of feeling oneself in some sort of touch with what is universally true.

When I say that I enjoy hearing someone I mean, of course, hearing deeply. I mean that I hear the words, the thoughts, the feeling tones, the personal meaning, even the meaning that is below the conscious intent of the speaker. Sometimes, too, in a message which superficially is not very important, I hear a deep human cry, a "silent scream," that lies buried and unknown far below the surface of the person.

So I have learned to ask myself, can I hear the sounds and sense the shape of this other person's inner world? Can I resonate to what he is saying, can I let it echo back and forth in me, so deeply that I sense the meanings he is afraid of yet would like to communicate, as well as those meanings he knows?

I think, for example, of an interview I had with an adolescent boy, the recording of which I listened to only a short time ago. Like many an adolescent today he was saying at the outset of the interview that he had no goals. When I questioned him on this he made it even stronger that he had no goals whatsoever, not even one. I said, "There isn't anything you want to do?" "*Nothing* . . . Well, yeah, I want to keep on living." I remember very distinctly my feeling at that moment. I resonated very deeply to this phrase. He might simply be telling me that, like everyone else, he wanted to live. On the other hand he might be telling me, and this seemed to be a distinct possibility, that at some point the question of whether or not to live had been a real issue with him. So I tried to resonate to him at all levels. I didn't know for certain what the message was. I simply wanted to be open to any of the meanings that this statement might have, including the possible meaning that he might have at one time considered suicide. I didn't respond verbally at this level.

That would have frightened him. But I think that my being willing and able to listen to him at all levels is perhaps one of the things that made it possible for him to tell me, before the end of the interview, that not long before he had been on the point of blowing his brains out. This little episode constitutes an example of what I mean by wanting to really hear someone at all the levels at which he is endeavoring to communicate.

I find, in therapeutic interviews, and in the intensive group experiences which have come to mean a great deal to me in recent years, that hearing has consequences. When I do truly hear a person and the meanings that are important to him at that moment, hearing not simply his words, but *him*, and when I let him know that I have heard his own private personal meanings, many things happen. There is first of all a grateful look. He feels released. He wants to tell me more about his world. He surges forth in a new sense of freedom. I think he becomes more open to the process of change.

I have often noticed, both in therapy and in groups, that the more deeply I can hear the meanings of this person the more there is that happens. One thing I have come to look upon as almost universal is that when a person realizes he has been deeply heard, there is a moistness in his eyes. I think in some real sense he is weeping for joy. It is as though he were saying, "Thank God, *somebody* heard me. Someone knows what it's like to be me." In such moments I have had the fantasy of a prisoner in a dungeon, tapping out day after day a Morse code message, "Does anybody hear me? Is there anybody there? Can anyone hear me?" And finally one day he hears some faint tappings which spell out "Yes." By that one simple response he is released from his loneliness, he has become a human being again. There are many, many people living in private dungeons today, people who give no evidence of it whatever on the outside, where you have

to listen very sharply to hear the faint messages from the dungeon.

I LIKE TO BE HEARD

Let me move on to a second learning, which I would like to share with you. I like to *be heard*. A number of times in my life I have felt myself bursting with insoluble problems, or going round and round in tormented circles or, during one period, overcome by feelings of worthlessness and despair, sure I was sinking into psychosis. I think I have been more lucky than most in finding at these times individuals who have been able to hear me and thus to rescue me from the chaos of my feelings. I have been fortunate in finding individuals who have been able to hear my meanings a little more deeply than I have known them. These individuals have heard me without judging me, diagnosing me, appraising me, evaluating me. They have just listened and clarified and responded to me at all the levels at which I was communicating. I can testify that when you are in psychological distress and someone really hears you without passing judgment on you, without trying to take responsibility for you, without trying to mold you, it feels *damn good*. At these times, it has relaxed the tension in me. It has permitted me to bring out the frightening feelings, the guilts, the despair, the confusions that have been a part of my experience. When I have been listened to and when I have been heard, I am able to reperceive my world in a new way and to go on. It is amazing that feelings which were completely awful, become bearable when someone listens. It is astonishing, how elements which seem insoluble become soluble when someone hears; how confusions which seem irremediable turn into relatively clear flowing streams when one is understood. I have deeply appreciated the times that I have experienced this sensitive, empathic, concentrated listening.

I have been very grateful that by the time I quite desperately needed this kind of help, I had trained and developed therapists, persons in their own right, independent and unafraid of me, who were able to go with me through a dark and troubled period in which I underwent a great deal of inner growth. It has also made me sharply aware that in developing my style of therapy for others, I was without doubt, at some unconscious level, developing the kind of help I wanted and could use myself.

WHEN I CANNOT HEAR

Let me turn to some of my dissatisfactions in this realm. I dislike it in myself when I can't hear another, when I do not understand him. If it is only a simple failure of comprehension or a failure to focus my attention on what he is saying, or a difficulty in understanding his words, then I feel only a very mild dissatisfaction with myself.

But what I really dislike in myself is when I cannot hear the other person because I am so sure in advance of what he is about to say that I don't listen. It is only afterward that I realize that I have only heard what I have already decided he is saying. I have failed really to listen. Or even worse are those times when I can't hear because what he is saying is too threatening, might even make me change my views or my behavior. Still worse are those times when I catch myself trying to twist his message to make it say what I want him to say, and then only hearing that. This can be a very subtle thing and it is surprising how skillful I can be in doing it. Just by twisting his words a small amount, by distorting his meaning just a little, I can make it appear that he is not only saying the thing I want to hear, but that he is the person I want him to be. It is only when I realize through his protest or through my own gradual recognition that I am subtly manipulating him that I become disgusted with myself. I

know too from being on the receiving end of this how frustrating it is to be received for what you are not, to be heard as saying something which you have not said and do not mean. This creates anger and bafflement and disillusion.

WHEN OTHERS DO NOT UNDERSTAND

The next learning I want to share with you is that I am terribly frustrated and shut into myself when I try to express something which is deeply me, which is a part of my own private, inner world, and the other person does not understand. When I take the gamble, the risk, of trying to share something that is very personal with another individual and it is not received and not understood, this is a very deflating and a very lonely experience. I have come to believe that it is that experience which makes some individuals psychotic. They have given up hoping that anyone can understand them and once they have lost that hope then their own inner world, which becomes more and more bizarre, is the only place where they can live. They can no longer live in any shared human experience. I can sympathize with them because I know that when I try to share some feeling aspect of myself which is private, precious, and tentative, and when this communication is met by evaluation, by reassurance, by denial, by distortion of my meaning I have very strongly the reaction, "Oh, what's the use!" At such a time one knows what it is to be *alone*.

So, as you can see, a creative, active, sensitive, accurate, empathic, non-judgmental listening, is for me terribly important in a relationship. It is important for me to provide it. It has been extremely important especially at certain times in my life to receive it. I feel that I have grown within myself when I have provided it. I am very sure that I have grown and been released and enhanced when I have received this kind of listening.

1. *Try to think of a time when you, like Carl Rogers, felt a sense of enjoyment and satisfaction from really hearing someone.*
2. *Rogers claims that when you are really heard there is an inner release, a feeling of freedom, and a desire to share more of yourself. Has this been true for you? Has there been a listener in your life who hears you deeply?*
3. *Rogers is a highly influential therapist and theorist. However, even he dislikes himself "when I cannot hear the other person because I am so sure in advance of what he is about to say that I don't listen. . . . Still worse are those times when I catch myself trying to twist his message to make it say what I want him to say, and then only hearing that." Most of us engage in one or both of these non-listening behaviors. Monitor your listening behavior and attempt to catch yourself listening poorly. See if you can change your approach and just listen without imposing your thoughts.*
4. *Select any other point that Rogers makes in this article and offer your view on its validity.*
5. *Develop your listening skills by attempting one or more of the Applied Activities at the end of this section.*

Johnny Bear and the Empath

Nelson Goud

Could a greater miracle take place than for us to look through each other's eyes for an instant?"

—Henry Thoreau

Thoreau is asking us to experience empathy. Empathy, that quality of understanding how another feels and thinks. It is empathy that makes us wince when we see someone hitting a finger with a hammer or show joy or cry at a sentimental scene in a movie. Without empathy there would be no compassion, altruism or significant communication.

Not just any kind of empathy will suffice. Quasi-empathy guises would not qualify. One of these guises is described by John Steinbeck in *The Long Valley*. A village simpleton named Johnny Bear had the unusual ability to remember and exactly duplicate conversations he overheard—both in the content and tone of voice of the participants. Johnny Bear would overhear a conversation (often while hiding) and then go to the town tavern and repeat the exchange. If the bar patrons liked what they heard, they gave Johnny Bear a shot of whiskey. While he did not understand the words he repeated, Johnny Bear liked whiskey. He had some of the outer appearance of empathy, but was little more than a human sound recorder (with the thirst). Johnny Bear would now be said to have a medical condition known as "echolalia"—the repetition of words just spoken by others.

In a conversation between Don Quixote and his servant Sancho, another common quasi-empathy form appears:

> It is in the nature of good servants to share the grief of their masters and to feel what they are feeling, if only for appearances's sake.
>
> —Cervantes in *Don Quixote*

Quixote was doing all right until the last phrase. Pretending to show empathy falls several notches below the real thing.

True empathy goes beyond mere repetition and involves a *felt* experiencing of another's world. It is communicated through a caring attitude. An attitude much like this:

> He smiled understandingly—much more than understandingly.... It concentrated on *you* with an irresistible prejudice in your favor. It understood you just as far as you wanted to be understood, believed in you as you would like to believe in yourself.
>
> —F. Scott Fitzgerald, *The Great Gatsby*

Perhaps you have been understood like this in the past week. Most of us, though, find such understanding to be a rare event. We exert great energy to be understood in the world, and if we happen to come upon it, there is a release, a knowing that you are not alone. There never seems to be a surplus of empathy. Or is there?

In the original Star Trek television series, there was an alien who had empathic capacities so highly tuned that when another person received a cut, the alien would bleed in the corresponding body part. A full-time empath. Most of us have experienced a milder form of this ability having "sympathy pain" with another. Excessive empathy results in temporary merger identities where the boundaries vanish between one person and another. Such a state is rarely helpful (e.g., you cannot assist a person with a severe headache if you have one yourself). True empathy means to be able to perceive *as if* one were the other person without losing "as if" dimension.

One can also develop an exaggerated empathic mode of communicating with others. Here one habitually responds in an understanding manner but does not use any other mode. I knew a receptionist who would attentively listen to any staff member who approached her with a problem, explained a project or wanted to vent a minor concern. Her attitude was one of concern, and everyone who left her desk went away feeling understood and supported. She was the recipient of many visits. After a few months, however, I noted that she was never asked about herself nor did she share anything of her life. She was the office empath, the designated listener.

The empath garners several advantages: the constant reminders that you are useful and needed; knowing that others trust you with their disclosures; and possessing knowledge of what is going on with other persons. There are also possible adverse consequences of being an empath:

- becoming overwhelmed by both the number and nature of disclosures,
- some empaths cannot distinguish between their own selves and those of others,
- spending their time as full-time listeners, empaths often have great difficulty in self-disclosure. It takes a concerted effort for anyone to know the world of the empath (even if the latter desires to do so). Disclosure, like any communication mode, requires consistent practice to be maintained and developed. A deficiency in disclosure skills tends to lessen the chances of developing mutual, intimate relationships.

It is possible for most empaths to learn other communication modes. Usually it takes another person to encourage the empath to take gradual risks in assertiveness and disclosure (keeping in mind that the empath quite naturally will tend to turn any conversation back to another's needs).

In balanced empathy, according to Carl Rogers, one must temporarily enter another's world without prejudice and "you lay aside your self; this can only be done by persons who are secure enough in themselves . . . and they can comfortably return to their own world when they wish" (from *A Way of Being*). Johnny Bear and the empath are not capable of this empathy. How about you?

Follow-Up

1. *Provide examples from your life of quasi-empathy and excessive empathy. Discuss their effects.*
2. *Choose two statements from this article and explain how they relate to your experiences.*

John Steinbeck on Listening

We had had many discussions at the galley table and there had been many honest attempts to understand each other's thinking. There are several kinds of reception possible. There is the mind which lies in wait with traps for flaws, so set that it may miss, through not grasping it, a soundness. There is a second which is not reception at all, but blind flight because of laziness, or because some pattern is disturbed by the processes of the discussion. The best reception of all is that, which is easy and relaxed, which says in effect, "Let me absorb this thing. Let me try to understand it without private barriers. When I have understood what you are saying, only then will I subject it to my own scrutiny and my own criticism." This is the finest of all critical approaches and the rarest.

The smallest and meanest of all is that which, being frightened or outraged by thinking outside or beyond its pattern, revenges itself senselessly; leaps on a misspelled word or a mispronunciation, drags tricky definition in by the scruff of the neck, and, raging like a small unpleasant dog, rags and tears the structure to shreds. We have known a critic to base a vicious criticism on a misplaced letter in a word, when actually he was venting rage on an idea he hated. These are the suspicious ones, the self-protective ones, living lives of difficult defense, insuring themselves against folly with folly—stubbornly self-protective at too high a cost.

Follow-Up

1. *Describe examples and the effects of two kinds of reception mentioned above.*
2. *Describe the outcomes of applying Steinbeck's "best reception."*

A Teacher Hears

Listening, and hearing deeply, I feel, are the most important skills I must constantly strive to improve. Listening to my students tells me what they understand as opposed to what they can regurgitate. It tells me how they feel about the subject, about me, and about themselves.

Sometimes what I hear is silence. My classes are very active. No one goes quietly through the period. In the beginning of the year this surprises some students and even makes some uncomfortable. But soon they become accustomed to it. William was one of my new seventh-grade students this year. Early in the year I called on him. "So what law allows us to say that $3 + 7$ is the same as $7 + 3$? William? William? . . ." Nothing. No sound. No eye contact. Nothing. I approached him. My normal reaction was to tease. "Is there anybody in there?" Something in me said "not this time." I had never seen a reaction like this. I was to find out later that William was a victim of abuse. He was terrified of being hurt—of being wrong. Gradually as the year has progressed, William has learned to trust me. Although it has not been easy for either of us, I now can call on him, and he will look at me and softly, very softly, tell me what he knows.

Sometimes what I hear is non-verbal. Meghan is a bubbly, bright, tiny little girl in the same class as William. Meghan works very hard on a consistent basis to keep herself at the top of this class. In early June she took her final and completely fell apart. I recognized a full-blown case of test anxiety. The following day, the last day the class would meet, there was time left at the end of the period and the class visited among themselves. I approached Meghan's desk. As I began to ask her about how she felt taking the final, I saw eyes filling with tears, and a strong little girl trying very hard not to cry. We talked about what had happened, about her competitive drive, about how important her math *grade* had become in her mind, and about how we could attempt to conquer the problem next year. The entire time she sank lower in her chair, trying to answer my questions, but without much success. What a painful chord we had struck. As I left school later that day, I noticed a note attached to my windshield wipers. "Mrs. R., This year has been really great. I can't wait till next year. Meghan." It seems both of us had listened.

Sometimes I hear boredom. One day last year I looked up at my seventh-grade class and not one single student was "in attendance." Furthermore they weren't even being disruptive. It was like they had run into a really bad TV program! They were slouching and looking down or out the window. Total boredom had invaded that room. I was still in shock as I headed home that day. What I had heard in that room that period could not have been more clear if they, as a class, had gotten up and left!

Sometimes I hear confusion, frustration. Dara is an outstanding math student. She learns easily and well. Very often, however, when I am teaching a new concept, I often hear Dara say that "This is stupid" or "I don't like this." It was after a number of times of hearing this from her that I realized what I was really hearing was "I don't quite understand" or "I haven't completely processed what you are saying." In fact, she doesn't think it is stupid at all but rather is openly expressing a moment of confusion that she is experiencing.

And sometimes I fail to hear at all. Josh had done a beautiful job in math for three quarters. I'd had his older brother in past years, so he came to me already motivated. Suddenly in the fourth quarter he quit—missing or lost or half-done assignments, inattention in class. My response was annoyance, almost anger. After about three weeks of this, his mother called. Josh, it seemed, had had some bouts with depression and self-doubt in the past. Again it had flared up. He felt he had disappointed me and that I didn't "like" him. How could I have interpreted his behavior so wrongly? How could I have failed to hear what he was saying to me?

There are all kinds of hearing skills to be cultivated in teaching. It is the main link to the student–teacher chain, and perhaps is the most underrated of all the communication skills.

—A middle school teacher

Self-Disclosure

Nelson Goud

No man can come to know himself except as an outcome of disclosing himself to another person. . . . if we want to be loved, we must disclose ourselves.

—Sidney Jourard

I am afraid to tell you who I am, because, if I tell you who I am, you may not like who I am, and it's all that I have.

—John Powell

Self-disclosure is what we reveal about ourselves to others. As the above quotes illustrate, self-disclosure has the potential for great gains but also contains significant risks. We are continually faced with the choice of revealing or concealing ourselves from others.

Growth psychologists contend that the quality of authenticity is one of the marks of a mature, healthy person. In contrast is the person who primarily acts in the form of false fronts or facades. With an authentic person we do not have to always wonder "What is she or he *really* like?" Authenticity contains a good dose of naturalness and reality. The ability to self-disclose is one component of authenticity. Rogers (1961; Rogers & Freiberg, 1994) believes that a movement away from facades toward genuineness is a key sign of personal growth. Pearson (1985) summarized several studies that demonstrated a close relationship between self-disclosure and a person's level of self-esteem and self-actualization.

Learning to appropriately self-disclose is essential for establishing intimate relationships, avoiding social alienation, and knowing oneself. Some of the major dimensions of effective self-disclosure will be examined in the following discussion.

DISCLOSURE BREADTH AND DEPTH

Self-disclosure can be classified according to both breadth and depth. *Breadth* refers to the range of topics disclosed. *Depth* refers to the degree of intimacy and completeness (feelings and ideas) of a disclosure. In general, the more depth, the more risk and vulnerability. For example, casual relationships usually have breadth but little depth. Or, it is possible to have a relationship characterized by intense depth in one domain but little depth or breadth in other domains (a brief love affair would be an example).

What is considered low, moderate, and high disclosure varies greatly among individuals. You may feel very comfortable discussing your feelings about your age, but another may find this deeply personal and of a high disclosure nature. A person must be aware of these individual disclosure preferences if effective communication is to occur. Additionally, there are wide cultural differences in the appropriateness of disclosure levels (this article will emphasize general American norms). You may even experience variations in your willingness to disclose on the same topic to different people, or under different circumstances. Even with these individual variations, there are some common findings that relate to most people.

Several studies of self-disclosure have found that positive mental health is characterized by high disclosure to a few significant others; poorly adjusted persons tend to over-disclose or under-disclose to almost everyone (Cozby, 1973; Derlega & Chaikin, 1975; Johnson, 1993). Optimum disclosure depends on many factors: the purpose of disclosing, the nature of the relationship, the context of the disclosure, and the possible consequences. Most negative consequences result from either under- or over-disclosing.

UNDER-DISCLOSURE

There are many reasons why people may not reveal themselves. Derlega and Chaikin (1975) state that low revealers may not trust in the good will of others and may be "afraid of ridicule, rejection, or the possibility that the listener will reveal the information to others" (p. 14). Sometimes the low revealer is perceived to be a person of little emotion and as having few major problems. That person's uniqueness also is masked. If concealment becomes the predominant way of relating to others, there may be a number of detrimental consequences: loneliness, mistrust from others because they do not know how this person thinks or feels, little shared intimacy, loss of a major source of self-knowledge, and a higher-than-normal amount of psychological energy expended to maintain a persona.

Sidney Jourard (1971) contends that how people choose to fulfill their life roles can influence disclosure levels. Life roles refer to the expected behaviors based on gender, occupation, and age. A healthy person can perform these roles and also express other dimensions of personhood. However, some people define themselves entirely by the roles they perform and are unaware of their interior life. Self-disclosure depends on an awareness of this interior life. Role conformity can lead to a "normal existence" but, as Jourard says, "it is possible to be a normal personality and be absolutely miserable" (p. 28).

Low self-revelation may be purposeful for some but not for others. Verbal self-disclosure depends on the ability to first recognize what you are feeling and thinking, and second, to place these interior states into words. Some people have deficiencies in one or both of these capabilities. In many ways, self-disclosure is a learned skill. Without experience in recognizing emotions and how to verbalize them, it is not possible to disclose them. Ask a young child to express emotions and the majority fall into the "sad, bad, glad" categories. Many persons do not develop beyond this level because they are not taught or encouraged to do so. Even today, conventional socialization still tends to favor females over males in these abilities. Pearson (1985) cites many studies that demonstrate the greater facility of females in verbal and non-verbal emotional expression (and recognizing the same).

OVER-DISCLOSURE

> There's this girl on my floor in the dormitory who's really weird. She tells people she's just met about really personal things, like all these guys she's sleeping with. Everyone tries to avoid her. I think she really needs help (A college coed, as quoted in Derlega & Chaikin, 1975, p. 10).

In one of my first graduate counseling courses we formed a group and the instructor told us to share how we felt about ourselves. A man on my right was the first to volunteer. He said, "My name is John and for the past year I have been in a psychiatric hospital. For quite awhile I had been hallucinating about cadavers and talking with them. I decided to get help. It worked. I do not have my hallucinations very much anymore." No one knew how to react to John's revelation. His openness was respected, but we felt uneasy. His disclosure was introduced before most of us were really capable of hearing him. We did not know enough about each other to place his deeply revealing comment in context. Instead of creating a closeness, I felt more distanced from John—Was he really okay now? If he reveals at this level so readily, will he be able to keep our in-class disclosures confidential?

These instances are examples of what most would consider over-disclosing. Over-disclosing is characterized by immediate revelations of high intimacy without considering the context or others' readiness to hear. Instead of encouraging closeness, over-disclosing tends to produce avoidance behaviors. Many over-disclosers are perceived as strange or deviant. Being so open about their own private lives, over-disclosers may not be trusted with reciprocal disclosures from others. Over-disclosers may initially solicit some sympathy, but if they continue, others will begin to ignore them or become annoyed.

To engage in effective disclosure, a person must observe many cues. A good deal of sensitivity is required to accurately judge the changing conditions of trust, vulnerability, and context. Some guidelines to consider on the topic of self-disclosure are offered next.

GUIDELINES FOR EFFECTIVE SELF-DISCLOSURE

Interpersonal Relationships

The degree of intimacy in a relationship closely parallels the level of mutual self-disclosure. The more that you know of another, the deeper the foundation for trust (or in some cases, mistrust, as with some over-disclosers). Self-disclosure is a primary path to discovering shared interests, values, and life perceptions—all major components of intimacy (both romantic and non-romantic). Some basic findings are listed below.

1. For early stages of a relationship, the preferred pattern is to initially share a lot of information at low disclosure levels. Higher degrees of disclosure follow at a gradual rate. Each disclosure level change is generally reciprocated by each partner if the relationship is to deepen. Changing levels of disclosure requires one of the parties to take a risk. If the other party is willing to strengthen the relationship at that moment, a reciprocating disclosure will usually occur. The reciprocity of disclosure may not be as significant in advanced, established stages of intimacy. Here trust has already been developed and attention can be focused on the topic being divulged by one of the parties (Jourard, 1971; Pearson, 1985; Johnson, 1993).

2. Should I conceal or reveal? Some disclosures are so powerful that they can cause major shifts, positive or negative, in a relationship. You love her but you do not know if she "likes or loves" you. One night she says "I love you." This propels the relationship to a new dimension. A few months later you want to share your whole life because of this deep intimacy, but it includes (choose at least one): sexual fantasies with others, shameful past experiences, a disliked aspect of your partner. Will it be dishonest if you do not share yourself completely, or are some things best left unsaid?

Even the experts vary in their guidance on these issues. Harry Browne in Arkoff (1993) says that if you strive to be an honest person then "the only way to demonstrate your honesty is by simply responding honestly to everything (and to everyone)" (p. 322). Morton Hunt in Arkoff (1993) believes that people should be selective in what they reveal to intimates because often they release their own pain only to transfer it unnecessarily to the partner. "There are limits to intimacy," says Hunt, "not only for our own good, but for the good of those we love."

Carl Rogers, one of the most influential psychologists of this century, offers this example and guideline. He described a wife who was becoming increasingly sullen, angry, and guilty, and was expressing these feelings in ways that were damaging her marriage. She realized that some unresolved issues from affairs with married men prior to her marriage were part of the problem, but felt that she could not express these to her husband—he might change his mind about what kind of person she was to him (a loving "nice girl"). Deciding that concealing was doing as much or more harm, she revealed her feelings. She did not go into details, but focused on the effects of those affairs. In her case it was heard and understood, and cleared the way for a deeper relationship with her husband. She believed that her desire for a good marriage was worth the risk of disclosure.

Rogers offers a helpful guideline on whether to disclose in an intimate relationship: ". . . in any continuing relationship any persistent feeling had better be expressed. Suppressing it can only damage the relationship. The first sentence is not stated casually. Only if it is a significant continuing relationship, and only if it is a recurring or persistent feeling, is it necessary to bring the feeling into the open in the relationship. If this is not done, what is unexpressed gradually poisons the relationship" (Rogers, 1972, pp. 20–21).

Jennifer and Scott have gradually developed a close, intimate relationship. They find it exhilarating to be able to trust each other with deep disclosures. They both believe that they want a relationship based on total honesty. However, Jennifer still finds herself attracted to other men, though she does not act on these feelings. She wonders if she should share this with Scott (in order to be totally honest). She also knows that Scott is somewhat insecure about losing her. In this instance it would probably be premature for Jennifer to disclose her feelings of attraction to other men. The relationship would be unnecessarily threatened by feelings that are quite common and not strong enough to warrant a major negative shift in their developing relationship. If these feelings persist and influence her relationship with Scott, then disclosure should be considered.

There are many other instances in which non-disclosure is the appropriate choice given the multiple circumstances surrounding a relationship. What good does it do to mention a flaw of a friend, lover, or parent when it is not significant to a continuing relationship? There are many times when a leader, parent, or others in an authority position must *not* disclose their fears in order to keep a problem situation manageable for others. I remember how my own parents were somehow strong and lively during the whole period that I had a mild case of polio. If they had shared their fears with me as a ten year old, I would have been frightened for the duration of the illness. Through their actions I remained relatively confident and positive during my hospitalization and recovery.

Purposes of Self-Disclosure

As a sender and receiver it is important to realize the intent of a self-revelation. Knowing another's motive helps determine the kind of response to offer. Here are selected motives of self-disclosure, both negative and positive:

1. A genuine desire to establish more closeness or intimacy.
2. A catharsis or release of burdensome emotions. It is crucial here to consider the effects of this release on the receiver. Imagine that Carol has been suffering intense shame and hurt from abusive childhood experiences. She needs to express this to someone. Carol should consider talking to someone who can offer sound guidance, such as a counselor, spiritual advisor, or family doctor. In general, for disclosures that are primarily cathartic and confessional in nature, it is usually wise to initially share them with non-involved third parties.
3. Sometimes a person self-discloses to avoid responsibility. Instead of taking responsibility to right a wrong or to solve a

problem, a person may intentionally tell someone, hoping that person will shoulder the load.

4. Knowing that self-disclosure often creates affection and closeness, some persons take advantage of this knowledge in a self-serving manner, in what might be called manipulative intimacy. People may reveal just the right amount of information to be trusted, but the trust is used for their gain only (sexual, financial, or status). They have no intent of establishing a genuine relationship through this kind of self-disclosure.

Multiple Receivers

It is helpful to have several persons to whom you can disclose on different topics and intimacy levels. It is almost impossible for one person, even a spouse or close friend, to be an appropriate receiver for all your feelings and experiences. For example, you may need to talk *about* your spouse/friend, and this requires someone else you can trust. Most often a single receiver does not have all the needed background to understand everything you want to share. Think of a time when you tried to share an intense experience from your job, hobby, or school major but your receiver had no relevant experience. You undoubtedly found yourself explaining background information rather than the experience you wanted to share. I find there are some aspects of university life that are inaccessible to those outside of the university. Here I seek a university friend if I have a need to communicate. The same holds true for my trumpet-playing.

Context

For effective self-disclosure to occur, the circumstances must be considered. Some of the major circumstances include the following.

Emotional and Physical Readiness. It is difficult to send or receive high levels of disclosure when you are tired, rushed, anxious, in the midst of problem solving, and so on. While a person does not always have to be in a perfect mental or physical condition, make sure that at least minimal readiness levels are met.

Time Framework. Is there sufficient time to comprehend and discuss the disclosure (especially high level ones)? Try to avoid the last minute disclosure. In this approach a person delays a disclosure until the last possible moment to avoid possible further discussion or consequences. For example, counselors often hear the most important revelations in the last five minutes of a counseling session. Or imagine an ongoing couple at the end of a regular date. While about to leave, Rodolfo turns and says, "Oh, by the way, I think it might be good if we spent a little time apart—G'night."

Physical Setting. Attempt to be aware of the effects of the physical environment, such as temperature, noise level, and the presence of other people. Susie may be very comfortable disclosing in a crowded restaurant but Jake is not. Sometimes movement is a factor. I know of many people, including myself, who prefer to self-disclose while going on a walk, during breaks on a long bike ride, or driving in a car. My son and I have our best disclosure times during these kinds of activities. My daughter and I have our mutual disclosures while sitting out on the patio.

Dyad Effect. A two-person group (dyad) has been found to be the preferred number for self-disclosure (Pearson, 1985). Trust and confidentiality seem to occur more readily in dyads. Effective disclosure is possible in larger groups but there is more initial resistance.

Some Exceptions. There are two contextual circumstances in which high disclosure occurs faster than normal. One is during crisis situations such as disasters, accidents, serious illness or the death of a loved one, or being trapped in an enclosed space. In these situations, participants share a common and intense bond of danger or loss. The normal rules of disclosure are often shelved in order to restore a sense of safety and support.

The second instance is the stranger phenomenon first mentioned by the German sociologist Georg Simmel in the late 1800s. Here a person discusses intimate topics to a complete stranger at a bar, on a plane, in a hotel restaurant, on a park bench, and so on. Another and more recent version is to reveal oneself to strangers on the Internet. There are several reasons why a stranger may be the recipient of high self-disclosures. A stranger has little likelihood of using the information against the sender—in short, there is little threat. An Internet user does not have to worry about following up a disclosure or getting further involved. Sometimes a stranger may offer an outsider's point of view of your situation. Disclosures to strangers may be helpful, but only if not used as regular substitutes for genuine and consistent intimate relationships.

Fusion Communication

Usually the sender and receiver of a message are different people. It is possible for a person to be both the sender and receiver. I call this fusion communication. There are times when there are no appropriate receivers available to hear your disclosure. Or you cannot adequately verbalize certain feelings or experiences to others in a way they could understand, but you must express yourself. In this instance you may appoint yourself as the receiver. Some forms of fusion communication are discussed below.

Internal Dialogues. Internal dialogues include talking to yourself (silently or out loud); writing interpretive diaries or journals; or expressing your inner world through art forms—poetry, song, or dance. Anne Frank used fusion communication during her con-

finement by keeping a diary that functioned as a substitute friend.

Boomerang Dialogues. In boomerang dialogues, individuals seem to be disclosing to something else, but they are really communicating to themselves. You may, for example, speak to a pet about a current life dilemma or problem. Your message is bounced off the pet to you. Almost any external object can be a target of boomerang dialogue—plants, trees, a car, walls, the sky, or the ocean. Young children often disclose to real or stuffed animals or to invisible friends. Some forms of prayer function as fusion communication.

Deceased loved ones can also be recipients of self-disclosures. In *The Winter of Our Discontent,* John Steinbeck explains the essence of this form of fusion communication: "Much of my talk is addressed to people who are dead. . . . Nothing mysterious or mystic about that. It's asking for advice or an excuse from the inner part of you that is formed and certain" (p. 57).

Kempler (1987) discusses how some inner experiences have stages of maturity. To disclose them prematurely may damage their full expression. This is particularly true for new inspirations, emotional self-insights, and intuitive illuminations. Forms of fusion communication should be considered in these instances.

Fusion communication is one valuable self-disclosure strategy under the conditions described above. If it is the only form of self-disclosure, that indicates something is amiss. Interpersonal and fusion communication are both essential for a balanced life.

Self-Disclosure and Self-Knowledge

We gain knowledge of ourselves through several means. Two major sources are feedback from others and knowledge gained from our experiences. Talking about our inner reactions to experiences is also a primary path to self-awareness. Johnson (1993) says, "When you explain your feelings, perceptions, reactions, and experiences in words, they become clearer, better organized, and take on new meanings" (p. 35).

While disclosing some confused feelings or intuitions with someone you trust, you may suddenly stumble over an insight, or discover "I didn't know I felt this way." Jourard (1971) contends that without sufficient self-disclosure individuals may learn to conceal their own identities from themselves. One path to deep inner knowledge, he continues, is this: "When a person has been able to disclose himself utterly to another person, he learns how to increase his contact with his real self, and he may then be better able to direct his destiny on the basis of this knowledge" (p. 6).

Gender and Self-Disclosure

There are some gender differences in self-disclosure behavior. Below are selected findings as reported by Pearson (1985). These are group tendencies and do not automatically apply for every male or female:

- Women self-disclose more easily and more often than men.
- Women self-disclose more negative information.
- Women self-disclose more on intimate topics; both men and women self-disclose at similar levels on non-intimate topics.
- Increased eye contact and a closer personal space encourage self-disclosure for women, but decrease it for men.
- Positively interpreted touch increases self-disclosure for both men and women.
- Both men and women tend to disclose more as they get older; females disclose at higher levels at all age stages.

CONCLUSION

One requirement of an individual identity is boundaries. Without boundaries it is difficult to perceive where one person begins and an-

A sign points to the spot where campers can cast their rubbish. Campers leave the dumping station with lighter backs and more room in their tents.

Our minds could use a dumping station. A mind, too, functions better if it is lighter and has more room. It means that one must try to jettison unnecessary guilt, prolonged worry, immobilizing fear, or chronic mourning. It may mean talking it out with someone, doing more or doing less, or getting help. But cleaning out emotional debris is essential if life is to be lived as intended. Cleaning the mind starts with first knowing what to throw away. What would make your mind lighter?

"Dumping Station" by Nelson Goud. Copyright © 1996.

other ends. Sometime it feels nice to merge identities for awhile (such as the infant–mother bond or the initial stages of intense intimacy). Continuing these merged identities for too long, however, will eventually stunt full development. Our growth depends on realizing unique and individual potentialities.

Self-disclosure is closely tied to identity boundaries. Becoming close to another can be described as allowing another to enter—to pass through a boundary gate and see what is there. The further along another is allowed to pass boundary gates, the deeper the intimacy. In the most intimate of relationships there still may be some boundary gates that remain closed. We may have parts of ourselves that we wish not to reveal, or it may be that we just cannot explain some knowings of our interior life. Some of our unconscious stirrings are unknown to anyone, including us. Finally, we may purposely choose to have a hideaway that gives privacy in order to produce a sense of uniqueness, mystery, and constructive surprise.

The choice is ours. We can let everyone pass through our boundary gates at the costs of indistinct identities and interpersonal sameness. We can let no one in at the expense of loneliness, mistrust, and the loss of a major source of understanding oneself. Keeping our gates locked also means we cannot venture out; we, too, are locked out of others' lives. Or we can learn selectivity. We experiment and observe and even "goof." Eventually we will create and discover the art of knowing when to open and when to close our boundary gates, when to embrace the world and when to seek some privacy.

References

Arkoff, A. (1993). *Psychology and personal growth* (4th ed.). Boston: Allyn & Bacon.

Cozby, P. C. (1973). Self-disclosure: A literature review. *Psychological Bulletin, 79*, 73–91.

Derlega, V., & Chaikin, A. (1975). *Sharing intimacy.* Englewood Cliffs, NJ: Prentice-Hall.

Johnson, D. (1993). *Reaching out.* Boston: Allyn & Bacon.

Jourard, S. (1971). *The transparent self.* New York: Van Nostrand Reinhold.

Kempler, B. (1987). The shadow side of self-disclosure. *Journal of Humanistic Psychology, 27*, 109–117.

Pearson, J. (1985). *Gender and communication.* Dubuque, IA: Wm. C. Brown.

Rogers, C. (1961). *On becoming a person.* Boston: Houghton Mifflin.

Rogers, C. (1972). *Becoming partners: Marriage and its alternatives.* New York: Delacorte Press.

Rogers, C., & Freiberg, H. (1994). *Freedom to learn* (3rd ed.). New York: Merrill/Macmillan.

Steinbeck, J. (1962). *The winter of our discontent.* New York: Bantam Books.

Follow-Up

1. *Select two statements from the article that have relevance for your life.*
2. *Describe a time when you self-disclosed but wish you had not. What happened to make you feel this way? What did you learn about disclosure from this experience? (You do not have to reveal private details here, just general situations.)*
3. *Try to remember a time when you took a risk and self-disclosed and it turned out well. What did you learn about disclosure from this experience?*
4. *Overall, are you an under-discloser, an over-discloser, or an appropriate discloser? Explain why you see yourself this way.*
5. *Try to describe any experience or preference in fusion communication strategies. Under what conditions, if any, do you find them helpful?*
6. *Select one or more guidelines for effective self-disclosure and apply them in your current situation.*

You Just Don't Understand

Deborah Tannen

A married couple was in a car when the wife turned to her husband and asked, "Would you like to stop for a drink?"

"No, thanks," he answered truthfully. So they didn't stop.

The result? The wife—who had indeed wanted to stop—became annoyed because she felt her preference had not been considered. The husband, seeing his wife was angry, became frustrated. *Why didn't she just say what she wanted?*

Unfortunately, he failed to see that his wife was asking the question not to get an instant decision, but to begin a negotiation. And the woman didn't realize that when her husband said no, he was just expressing his preference, not making a ruling. When a man and woman interpret the same interchange in such conflicting ways, it's no wonder they can find themselves leveling angry charges of selfishness and obstinacy at each other.

As a specialist in linguistics, I have studied how the conversational styles of men and women differ. We cannot, of course, lump "all men" or "all women" into fixed categories— individuals vary greatly. But research shows that the seemingly senseless misunderstandings that haunt our relationships can at least in part be explained by the different conversational rules by which men and women often play.

Whenever I write or speak about this subject, people tell me how relieved they are to learn that what they had previously ascribed to personal failings is, in fact, very common. Learning about the different (though equally valid) conversational frequencies men and women are tuned to can help banish blame and help us truly talk to one another.

Here are some of the most common areas of conflict.

STATUS VS. SUPPORT

Men grow up in a world in which a conversation is often a contest—either to achieve the upper hand or to prevent other people from pushing them around. For many women, however, talking is typically a way to exchange confirmation and support. I saw this firsthand when my husband and I had jobs in different cities. When people made comments like "That must be rough" and "How do you stand it?" I accepted their sympathy.

But my husband would react with irritation. Our situation had advantages, he would explain. As academics, we had long weekends and vacations together.

Everything he said was true, but I didn't understand why he chose to say it. He told me that he felt some of the comments implied: "Yours is not a real marriage. I am superior to you because my wife and I have avoided your misfortune." It had not occurred to me there might be an element of one-upmanship, though I recognized it when it was pointed out.

I now see that my husband was simply approaching the world as many men do: as a place where people try to achieve and maintain status. I, on the other hand, was approaching the world as many women do: as a network of connections, in which people seek consensus.

INDEPENDENCE VS. INTIMACY

Since women often think in terms of closeness and support, they struggle to preserve intimacy.

Men, concerned with status, tend to focus on establishing independence. These traits can lead women and men to starkly different views of the same situation.

When Josh's old high-school friend called him at work to say he'd be in town, Josh invited him to stay for the weekend. That evening he told Linda.

Linda was upset. How could Josh make these plans without discussing them with her beforehand? She would never do that to him. "Why don't you tell your friend you have to check with your wife?" she asked.

Josh replied, "I can't say I have to ask my wife for permission!"

To Josh, checking with his wife would mean he was not free to act on his own. It would make him feel like a child or an underling. But Linda actually enjoys telling people, "I have to check with Josh." It makes her feel good to show her life is entwined with her husband's.

ADVICE VS. UNDERSTANDING

Eve had a benign lump removed from her breast. When she confided to her husband, Mark, that she was distressed because the stitches changed the contour of her breast, he answered, "You can always have plastic surgery."

This comment bothered her. "I'm sorry you don't like the way it looks," she protested, "but I am not having any more surgery!"

Mark was hurt and puzzled. "I don't care about a scar," he replied. "It doesn't bother me at all."

"Then why are you telling me to have plastic surgery?" she asked.

"Because *you* were upset about the way it looks."

Eve felt like a heel. Mark had been wonderfully supportive throughout her surgery. How could she snap at him now?

The problem stemmed from a difference in approach. To many men, a complaint is a challenge to come up with a solution. Mark thought he was reassuring Eve by telling her there was something she could *do* about her scar. But often women are looking for emotional support, not solutions.

INFORMATION VS. FEELINGS

A cartoon I once saw shows a husband opening a newspaper and asking his wife, "Is there anything you'd like to say before I start reading?" We know there isn't—but that as soon as the man begins reading, his wife will think of something.

The cartoon is funny because people recognize their own experience in it. What's not funny is that many women are hurt when men don't talk to them at home, and many men are frustrated when they disappoint their partners without knowing why.

Rebecca, who is happily married, told me this is a source of dissatisfaction with her husband, Stuart. When she tells him what she is thinking, he listens silently. When she asks him what is on his mind, he says, "Nothing."

All Rebecca's life she has had practice verbalizing her feelings with friends and relatives. To her, this shows involvement and caring. But to Stuart, like most men, talk is for information. All his life he has had practice in keeping his innermost thoughts to himself.

Yet many such men hold center stage in a social setting, telling jokes and stories. They use conversation to claim attention and to entertain. Women can wind up hurt that their husbands tell relative strangers things they have not told them.

To avoid this kind of misunderstanding, both men and women can make adjustments. A woman may observe a man's desire to read the paper, for example, without seeing it as rejection. And a man can understand a woman's desire to talk without feeling it an intrusion.

ORDERS VS. PROPOSALS

Diana often begins statements with "Let's." She might say, "Let's park over there" or "Let's clean up before lunch." This makes Nathan angry. He has deciphered Diana's "Let's" as a command. Like most men, he resists being told what to do. But to Diana, she is making suggestions, not demands. Like most women, she wants to avoid confrontation and formulates requests as proposals rather than orders. Her style of talking *is* a way of getting others to do what she wants—but by winning agreement first.

With certain men, like Nathan, this tactic backfires. If they perceive someone is trying to get them to do something indirectly, they feel manipulated and respond more resentfully than they would to a straightforward request.

CONFLICT VS. COMPROMISE

In trying to prevent fights, some women refuse to openly oppose the will of others. But at times it's far more effective for a woman to assert herself, even at the risk of conflict.

Dora was frustrated by a series of used automobiles she drove. It was she who commuted to work, but her husband, Hank, who chose the cars. Hank always went for automobiles that were "interesting," but in continual need of repair. After Dora was nearly killed when her brakes failed, they were in the market for yet another car.

Dora wanted to buy a late-model sedan from a friend. Hank fixed his sights on a 15-year-old sports car. Previously, she would have acceded to his wishes. But this time Dora bought the boring but dependable car and steeled herself for Hank's anger. To her amazement, he spoke not a word of remonstrance. When she later told him what she had expected, he scoffed at her fears and said she should have done what she wanted from the start if she felt that strongly about it.

As Dora discovered, a little conflict won't kill you. At the same time, men who habitually oppose others can adjust their style to opt for less confrontation.

When we don't see style differences for what they are, we sometimes draw unfair conclusions ("You're illogical," "You're self-centered," "You don't care about me"). But once we grasp the two characteristic approaches, we stand a better chance of preventing disagreements from spiraling out of control. Learning the other's ways of talking is a leap across the communication gap between men and women, and a giant step toward genuine understanding.

Follow-Up

1. *Describe an instance when you and someone of the opposite gender seemed to communicate on different wavelengths (or from distinctly separate frames of reference). Can you understand the other's framework?*
2. *Tannen shows how different gender mindsets result in different interpretations of the same situation. She gives examples from six conflicting patterns. Do you act in accordance with your gender in each of these six patterns? Explain why or why not.*
3. *Which of the six gender communication patterns were practiced by your parents or guardians in the way Tannen describes? How has this influenced your communication preferences?*
4. *Observe men–women conversations to see if Tannen's ideas hold true.*
5. *Attempt the "He Said, She Said" Applied Activity at the end of this section.*

Assertive, Nonassertive, and Aggressive Behavior

Arthur J. Lange and
Patricia Jakubowski

Assertion involves standing up for personal rights and expressing thoughts, feelings, and beliefs in *direct, honest,* and *appropriate* ways which do not violate another person's rights.[1] The basic message in assertion is: This is what I think. This is what I feel. This is how I see the situation. This message expresses "who the person is" and is said without dominating, humiliating, or degrading the other person.

Assertion involves respect—not deference. Deference is acting in a subservient manner as though the other person is right, or better, simply because the other person is older, more powerful, experienced, or knowledgeable, or is of a different sex or race. Deference is present when people express themselves in ways that are self-effacing, appeasing, or overly apologetic.

Two types of respect are involved in assertion: respect for oneself, that is, expressing one's needs and defending one's rights, as well as respect for the other person's needs and rights. An example will help clarify the kind of respect involved in assertive behavior.

A woman was desperately trying to get a flight to Kansas City to see her mother who was sick in the hospital. Weather conditions were bad and the lines were long. Having been rejected from three standby flights, she again found herself in the middle of a long line for the fourth and last flight to Kansas City. This time she approached a man who was standing near the beginning of the line and said, pointing to her place, "Would you mind exchanging places with me? I ordinarily wouldn't ask, but it's extremely important that I get to Kansas City tonight." The man nodded yes, and as it turned out, both of them were able to get on the flight.

When asked what her reaction would have been if the man had refused, she replied, "It would have been OK. I hoped he would say yes, but after all he was there first."[1]

In this example the woman showed self-respect for her own needs by asking whether the man would be willing to help her. Also, she respected the man's right to refuse her request and not fulfill her need.

How is respect shown when refusing another's request? It depends on how that request is refused. A request may be refused aggressively: "What do you mean you want to borrow my car! I don't know where you get your nerve!" Such aggressive refusals involve only one-way respect; that is, respect for one's right to refuse but not for the other person's right to ask. A request may also be refused nonassertively: "What can I say . . . I feel just awful saying this, really bad . . . I can't loan you my car. Oh gee, what a terrible thing to say!" Here the person refused the request, but did it in a way that showed lack of self-respect: It suggested that the refuser was a bad person who should not have denied the request. In addition, the nonassertive refusal did not respect the other person's right to be treated as a capable person who can handle a disappointment. In contrast, an assertive refusal would be: "I'd like to help you out, but I feel uncomfortable loaning my car." The assertive refusal shows the two-fold respect: self-respect in the self-confident way the request is refused and respect for the other person's right to ask.

In our view, the goal of assertion is communication and "mutuality"; that is, to get and give respect, to ask for fair play, and to leave room for compromise when the needs and rights of two people conflict. In such compromises neither person sacrifices basic integrity and both get some of their needs satisfied. The compromise may be one in which one person gets her needs taken care of immediately while the other party gets taken care of a little later. For example, one weekend the friends see a movie and the next weekend they bowl. Or the compromise may involve both parties giving up a little. They attend *part* of an outdoor concert and then take a short walk and talk. When personal integrity is at stake, a compromise is inappropriate and nonassertive.

We are opposed to viewing assertion as simply a way "to get what one wants" for three reasons. First, this view emphasizes success in attaining goals. Thus it can cause people to become passive when they believe that acting assertively will not get them what they want. Second, this view concentrates only on the asserter's right and not on the personal rights of both parties. Such an attitude increases the chances of people using aggressive or manipulative methods to get what they want. Third, it may lead to irresponsible behavior in which assertion is used to take advantage of other people. We have frequently heard people say that they can assertively ask for favors and it's just too bad that the other person is not strong enough to refuse their requests. In contrast, we advocate *responsible* asserting which involves mutuality, asking for fair play, and using one's greater assertive power to help others become more able to stand up for themselves. Interestingly, a by-product of responsible assertion is that people often do get what they want. Why? Because most people become cooperative when they are approached in a way which is both respectful of self and respectful of others.

Nonassertion involves violating one's own rights by failing to express honest feelings, thoughts, and beliefs and consequently permitting others to violate oneself, or expressing one's thoughts and feelings in such an apologetic, diffident, self-effacing manner that others can easily disregard them.[1] In the latter type of nonassertion, the total message which is communicated is: I don't count—you can take advantage of me. My feelings don't matter—only yours do. My thoughts aren't important—yours are the only ones worth listening to. I'm nothing—you are superior.

Nonassertion shows a lack of respect for one's own needs. It also sometimes shows a subtle lack of respect for the other person's ability to take disappointments, to shoulder some responsibility, to handle his own problems, etc. The goal of nonassertion is to appease others and to avoid conflict at any cost.

Aggression involves directly standing up for personal rights and expressing thoughts, feelings, and beliefs in a way which is often dishonest, usually inappropriate, and always violates the rights of the other person. An example of "emotionally dishonest" aggression is a situation where individuals who feel saddened by another person's mourning for the death of a loved one sarcastically degrade the mourner ("That's just what I like to see—a grown person sniveling like a two-year-old brat"), instead of revealing their own sad and helpless feelings.

The usual goal of aggression is domination and winning, forcing the other person to lose. Winning is insured by humiliating, degrading, belittling, or overpowering other people so that they become weaker and less able to express and defend their needs and rights. The basic message is: That is what I think—you're stupid for believing differently. This is what I want—what you want isn't important. This is what I feel—your feelings don't count.

NONVERBAL COMPONENTS OF ASSERTIVE, NONASSERTIVE, AND AGGRESSIVE BEHAVIOR

So far we've discussed the verbal components of assertive, nonassertive, and aggressive behavior. The nonverbal components of these behaviors are equally important, if not more so. Research has shown that the vast majority of our communication is carried out nonverbally.[2] Take a moment to consider how the statement "I like you" can be said as a sincere statement, a question, or a sarcastic remark, by simply changing voice inflection, facial expression, and hand gestures. Likewise, an otherwise verbal assertive statement can become nonassertive or aggressive depending on the nonverbal behaviors which accompany the verbal statement.

Eisler, Miller, and Hersen[3] have pinpointed some of the nonverbal behaviors which may be important in assertion: duration of looking at the other person, duration of speech, loudness of speech, and affect in speech. Research has generally supported the importance of these nonverbal behaviors[3] with the exception of the length of time it takes the person to respond to the other individual.[4] Other nonverbal behaviors which may be important in assertion, nonassertion, and aggression are described below.

In assertive behavior, the nonverbals are congruent with the verbal messages and add support, strength, and emphasis to what is being said verbally. The voice is appropriately loud to the situation; eye contact is firm but not a staredown; body gestures which denote strength are used; and the speech pattern is fluent—without awkward hesitancies—expressive, clear, and emphasizes key words.

In nonassertive behavior, the nonverbal behaviors include evasive eye contact, body gestures such as hand wringing, clutching the other person, stepping back from the other person as the assertive remark is made, hunching the shoulders, covering the mouth with the hand, nervous gestures which distract the listener from what the speaker is saying, and wooden body posture. The voice tone may be singsong or overly soft. The speech pattern is hesitant and filled with pauses and the throat may be cleared frequently. Facial gestures may include raising the eyebrows, laughs, and winks when expressing anger.

In general, the nonassertive gestures are ones which convey weakness, anxiety, pleading, or self-effacement. They reduce the impact of what is being said verbally, which is precisely why people who are scared of acting assertively use them. Their goal is to "soften" what they're saying so that the other person will not be offended.

In aggressive behavior, the nonverbal behaviors are ones which dominate or demean the other person. These include eye contact that tries to stare down and dominate the other person, a strident voice that does not fit the situation, sarcastic or condescending tone of voice, and parental body gestures such as excessive finger pointing.

EXAMPLES OF ASSERTIVE, NONASSERTIVE, AND AGGRESSIVE BEHAVIOR

In each example, the first response is aggressive, the second, nonassertive, and the third is assertive.

Confronting a Professor Who Gives Inappropriate and Excessive Amounts of Work—

1. Dr. Jones, you have some nerve giving me this kind of work. I know you have control over me, but I don't have to take this stuff. You professors think you can use grad students for anything you please—Well not this time!

2. OK, Dr. Jones, I'll do it. I guess you must have a reason for asking me to do this stuff . . . even if it isn't related to my assistantship. I don't suppose you'd consider letting me off the hook this time? Huh?

3. Dr. Jones, when you give me work that's not related to your class, I'd have to put in extra hours beyond what's appropriate for my assistantship. For those reasons I need to say no on this extra work.

Talking with Someone Who Has Just Made a Sexist Remark—

1. Who the hell do you think you are? God's gift to women?
2. Oh come on (ha ha). You know how much that irritates me when you say things like that (ha ha).
3. Frankly, I think that remark demeans both of us.

Refusing an Extra Helping of Food at a Dinner Party—

1. You'd just love me to put on a few pounds of fat!
2. Gee . . . ah . . . Well, since you insist . . . I'll change my mind. Yeah, give me another piece.
3. That food does look good but I don't want any more.

Trying to Get a Group on the Subject After They've Wandered into Tangential Areas—

1. Can't you people get back to work and stop this goofing off?
2. I guess it's just my hang-up. Do you think it'd be OK if we got back to the original subject? I've forgotten it myself (ha ha).
3. What we're talking about is interesting; however, I'm feeling the need to get back to the original subject.

TYPES OF ASSERTION

Basic Assertion

Basic assertion refers to a simple expression of standing up for personal rights, beliefs, feelings, or opinions. It does not involve other

social skills, such as empathy, confrontation, persuasion, etc. Examples of basic assertions are:

When being interrupted—
Excuse me, I'd like to finish what I'm saying.

When being asked an important question for which you are unprepared—
I'd like to have a few minutes to think that over.

When returning an item to a store—
I'd like my money back on this saw.

When refusing a request—
No, this afternoon is not a good time for me to visit with you.

When telling a parent you don't want advice—
I don't want any more advice.

Basic assertion also involves expressing affection and appreciation toward other people:

I like you.
I care for you a lot.
Having a friend like you makes me feel happy.
You're someone special to me.

The following is a particularly touching example of assertively expressing affection:

A father overheard his five-year-old child saying to a playmate: "Are you having a good time?" When the playmate replied "Yes," the child continued, "I am too. I'm so glad that I invited you to come over and play!"

Empathic Assertion

Often people want to do more than simply express their feelings or needs. They may also want to convey some sensitivity to the other person. When this is the goal, the empathic assertion can be used. This type of assertion involves making a statement that conveys recognition of the other person's situation or feelings and is followed by another statement which stands up for the speaker's rights.[1] Examples of empathic assertions are:

When two people are chatting loudly while a meeting is going on—

You may not realize it, but your talking is starting to make it hard for me to hear what's going on in the meeting. Would you keep it down?

When having some furniture delivered—

I know it's hard to say exactly when the truck will come, but I'd like a ball park estimate of the arrival time.

When telling a parent that you don't want advice—

I know that you give me advice because you don't want me to get hurt by mistakes I might make. At this point in my life, I need to learn how to make my own decisions and rely on myself, even if I do make some mistakes. I appreciate the help you've given me in the past and you can help me now by not giving me advice.[1]

There is considerable personal power in the empathic assertion because other people more easily respond to assertion when they have been recognized first. This power, however, should not be used as a manipulation to merely gain one's own ends, without genuine respect for the other person. Repeatedly saying, "I understand how you feel but . . . " can be just "mouthing" understanding and conning other people into believing that their feelings are being taken into account when in fact their feelings are really being discounted. Such behavior does not involve empathic assertion.

Another important benefit of the empathic assertion is that it causes the speaker to take a moment to try to understand the other person's feelings before the speaker reacts. This can help the speaker keep perspective on the situation and thus reduces the likelihood of the speaker's aggressively overreacting when irritated.

Escalating Assertion

According to Rimm and Masters,[5] escalating assertion involves starting with a "minimal" assertive response that can usually accomplish the speaker's goal with a minimum of effort and negative emotion and a small possibility of negative consequences. When the other person fails to respond to the minimal assertion and continues to violate one's rights, the speaker gradually escalates the assertion and becomes increasingly firm. We have observed that often it is not necessary to go beyond the initial minimal assertion; but if it is necessary, the person can become increasingly firm without becoming aggressive. The escalating assertion can occur from a request to a demand, from a preference to an outright refusal, or, as the following example illustrates, from an empathic assertion to a firm basic assertion.

The speaker is in a bar with a woman friend, and a man repeatedly offers to buy them drinks—

That's very nice of you to offer, but we came here to catch up on some news. Thanks, anyway!

No, thank you. We really would rather talk just to each other.

This is the third and last time I am going to tell you that we don't want your company. Please leave![6]

In this example, the final blunt refusal was appropriate because the earlier escalating assertions were ignored. If the woman had started with the highly escalated assertion the first time the man had approached, her response would have been inappropriate. Since assertion involves direct, honest, and *appropriate* expressions of thoughts and feelings, her reaction would be aggressive, rather than assertive. Likewise when a person has not objected to taking the minutes of a meeting, but one day suddenly says, "I'm getting sick and tired of being the secretary just because I'm the only woman in the group," her response would be aggressive, rather than assertive. Only if her comment had been preceded by successively escalated assertions which had been ignored would her comment be appropriate and assertive.

A final point about the escalating assertion is that just before making the final escalated assertion, we suggest that one consider offering a "contract option," in which the other person is informed what the final assertion will be and is given a chance to change behavior before it occurs. For example, when a repair shop repeatedly refuses to settle an unreasonable bill, one may say, "I'm being left with no other alternative than to complain to the Better Business Bureau and your distributor. I'd prefer not to do that but I will if this is the only alternative I'm left with." Often people only recognize that one means business at the contract option point.

Whether the contract option is simply a threat depends on how it is said. If it is said in a menacing tone of voice which relies on emotionality to carry the argument, it is a threat. When the contract option is carried out assertively, it is said in a matter-of-fact tone of voice which simply gives information about the consequences which will occur if the situation is not equitably resolved.

Confrontive Assertion

Confrontive assertion is used when the other person's words contradict his deeds. This type of assertion involves objectively describing what the other person said would be done and what the other actually did do, after which the speaker expresses what he wants.[1] The entire assertion is said in a matter-of-fact, nonevaluative way, as the examples below show:

I was supposed to be consulted before the final proposal was typed. But I see the secretary is typing it right now. Before he finishes it, I want to review the proposal and make whatever corrections I think are needed. In the future, I want to get a chance to review any proposals before they're sent to the secretary.

I thought we'd agreed that you were going to be more considerate toward students. Yet I noticed today that when two students asked for some information you said that you had better things to do than babysit for kids. As we discussed earlier, I see showing more consideration as an important part

of your job. I'd like to figure out what seems to be the problem.

I said it was OK to borrow my records as long as you checked with me first. Now you're playing my classical records without asking. I'd like to know why you did that.

The above are examples of initial confrontive assertive statements. In most cases the ensuing conversation would be an extended interaction between the two people. This is particularly true in the last two examples in which the speaker wanted additional information and the resulting discussions would be problem-solving ones.

In contrast to assertive confrontation, aggressive confrontation involves judging other people—rather than describing their behavior—and trying to make others feel guilty. For example:

Hey, those are my records! Evidently your word means absolutely nothing to you! Just for that I want my records right now and in the future you're going to find them locked up. Then you'll have to ask me first.

SUMMARY

Assertion involves standing up for personal rights and expressing thoughts, feelings, and beliefs in direct, honest, and appropriate ways which respect the rights of other people. In contrast, aggression involves self-expression, which is characterized by violating others' rights and demeaning others in an attempt to achieve one's own objectives. Nonassertion involves behavior which violates one's own self by failing to express honest feelings or thoughts. It may also involve diffident, overly apologetic, or effacing expression of personal rights and preferences.

It is important that assertive skills be used responsibly, that is, used in ways which treat others fairly and help facilitate others becoming more assertive.

Losing others' approval is a major fear which prompts many individuals to act nonassertively. For those who are frequently aggressive, a typical fear concerns their losing control and power over other people. A major reason for acting assertively rather than unassertively is that assertion increases one's own sense of self-respect and personal control.

References

1. Jakubowski, P. (1977). Assertive behavior and clinical problems of women. In E. Rawlings & D. Carter (Eds.), *Psychotherapy for women: Treatment towards equality.* Springfield, IL: Charles C. Thomas.
2. Mehrabian, A. (1972). *Nonverbal communication.* Chicago: Aldine/Atherton.
3. Eisler, R. M., Miller, P. M., & Hersen, M. (1973). Components of assertive behavior. *Journal of Clinical Psychology, 29,* 295–299.
4. Galassi, J. P., Galassi, M. D., & Litz, M. C. (1974). Assertive training in groups using video feedback. *Journal of Counseling Psychology, 21,* 390–394.
5. Rimm, D. C., & Masters, J. C. (1974). *Behavior therapy: Techniques and empirical findings.* New York: Academic Press.
6. Jakubowski, P. (1977). Self-assertion training procedures for women. In E. Rawlings & D. Carter (Eds.), *Psychotherapy for women: Treatment towards equality.* Springfield, IL: Charles C. Thomas.

Follow-Up

1. *Give examples of instances when you acted in these ways: nonassertively, assertively, aggressively (as explained in the article). What is your predominant style of expressing your rights and beliefs? Give a brief explanation supporting your answer.*
2. *Although there is a difference between assertive and aggressive behavior, some see both as pushy. Is this true for you? Explain your response.*
3. *If you have been aggressive in expressing your rights and beliefs, what have been the consequences?*
4. *Choose one or more of the following types of assertion and attempt to be more skillful in expressing them: basic assertion, empathic assertion, escalating assertion, confrontive assertion.*
5. *Assertive behavior is closely related to self-esteem. One approach to enhancing your own esteem level is to become more appropriately assertive. Try some gradual and appropriate risks in assertiveness to see if this is true for you.*
6. *For further reading on this topic go to almost any major bookstore and browse the self-help or psychology sections. One highly recommended practical book on assertiveness is the most recent edition of* Your Perfect Right *by Alberti and Emmons.*

Personal Journaling as a Life Companion

Lou Beeker Schultz

"Question—I'm not presently keeping a diary, but sometimes I do feel the need to sit down and write down my feelings. So I decide I will write a diary; I get everything ready, open the book, and then comes the question: where do I start?

Anais Nin—Put yourself right in the present. This was my principle when I wrote the diary—to write the thing I felt most strongly about that day. Start there and that starts the whole unravelling, because that has roots in the past and it has branches into the future. The main thing is that what you feel strongly about today is where you're at today, and that is what the purpose of the diary is....I chose the event of the day that I felt most strongly about, the most vivid one, the warmest one, the nearest one, the strongest one."

Anais Nin, *A Woman Speaks*, p. 163

The people's faces change from journal class to journal class, but the beginning questions are the same, "How do I begin to keep a journal?" and "What is the purpose and benefit of keeping one?"

This one life activity can be a catalyst to increased productivity, deepening life's meanings, enriching one's creativity, and connecting into the inner wisdom we have.

Many famous people have experienced the benefits from keeping a journal. A few are: George Washington, Leonardo da Vinci, Georgia O'Keeffe, May Sarton, Henry David Thoreau, Thomas Edison, Walt Whitman, Charles Lindbergh, Elizabeth Cady Stanton, Susan B. Anthony, and Ralph Waldo Emerson.

You are about to begin a significant journey with paper and pen friends that can always be with you through the ebbs and flows of your life. A constant companion—*Your Personal Journal.*

WHAT IS JOURNALING?

As we travel through life, we are always with ourselves. The journal can be a steadfast companion through life's journey. It will always be there, receptive of our deepest internal thoughts, feelings, and truths—a written documentation of what is happening in the individual moments of life and how we interpret the experiences.

It is essential to remember that journal writing is not a panacea. It is not a record of our daily activities. However, it is an effective tool to record our honest feelings, thoughts, and beliefs at a specific moment in time. We are photographing, in words, a slice of time. We can release on paper what we believe is within our hearts, even buried within our inner-being. Then later, as we reread our journals, we can let our entries feedback to us of where we have been, what has been accomplished, and let the experience weave into our life.

Journaling provides a place to chart life's progress, record treasured memories, and accept, know, and value oneself. It becomes an oasis to contemplate memorable times, value ordinary moments, and listen to inner hunches.

By developing the regular habit of recording thoughts in a journal, many people have come to see and feel greater ease in effective communication with both oneself and others. Insoluble problems at the time of a writing seem resolved later when reading back through the entries. Over time this notebook can be valued as an abiding and trusting friend.

SPECIALIZED JOURNALS

Blank journals can be customized and tailored to fit individual needs. Workshop participants have claimed the following notebooks earmarked for their special interest have served them well:

Life Goals	Health
Career	Family
Spirituality	Ideas
Counseling	Travel
Gratitude	Diet
Gardening	Exercise
Financial	A Child
Dreams	Transitions
Illness	Simplify Life
Family Entries	Nature
Meditation	Life's Milestones
Feng Shui	Synchronicity

Explore the activities in your life and contemplate the kind of journal most beneficial for you during this season of your life. Some readers may prefer utilizing one notebook with jottings from the above topics. This is appropriate, too.

JOURNALING MUSTS

The mechanics of journal writing are easy. There are two primary guidelines. One, date every journal entry. If there is any cardinal rule, this would be the one. Second, write in the honesty of the moment. Because of these few basic guidelines, the journal provides us with a significant component—its non-judgmental quality.

WRITING TOOLS

Materials for this endeavor are minimal. Peruse through your local bookshop and office supply store and select either a spiral notebook, bound blank book, a three-ring binder with loose leaf paper, artist sketch book, lined or un-lined paper. With over 5,000,000 blank books sold annually, you will find the best one for you.

Experiment with a pen or pencil that fits with ease into your hand. Explore the use of fountain pens, roller balls, ball points, gel-inks, colored pencils, and various point styles of colored markers. Remember to use the style of journal and writing implement appropriate and comfortable for you.

Some journalers prefer using a computer. If this is your preferred method, keep a few things in mind. Utilize your own personal computer and not one that is connected to the work of your professional organization, even if it is password protected. With privacy issues today within a corporate structure, one does not know who may have access to reading what you enter online. Ultimately, a journal is personal and for your eyes only. Sometimes participants will print out a copy of their entry to keep in a notebook, and store the daily entry in their own personal computer disk file. In essence, use what works for your lifestyle.

PRIVACY

Journal privacy is a universal theme. When you are not writing in your journal, keep it in a safe place. Be careful where you leave your journal. This is not the type of leisure reading you want to lie around on the coffee table for family and friends, tempting them to read its pages while visiting. Some journal writers place their notebooks in closets, metal boxes, shoe boxes, suitcases, safes, briefcases, large handbags, trunks or glove compartments, or drawers. There are as many various places to store your writings as there are people. Explore the nooks and crannies in your home and find the best place for your journal.

For some journalers for whom privacy is of extreme importance, consider writing names, phrases, events, and so on in a code.

Remember to translate your code and store it somewhere different from your journal. Over time, as you see the benefits of jounaling your life, you may discover this is not as big of an issue as initially perceived.

If you plan to carry your journal with you, place your name, address, telephone number, and e-mail address on the initial inside page. Consider adding a privacy statement such as "Please respect my privacy and refrain from reading this notebook." Some journal writers will add a subsequent addendum stating, "Financial reward given upon its return."

JOURNAL WRITING GUIDELINES AND EXERCISES

1. At the beginning of each journal I leave a few blank pages. These can be used for volume number, titling, key topics/issues, beginning and ending dates, and disclaimers. In addition, I write on only one side of each page. This provides space on the reverse side for additional notes during the reading back process. At the end, I leave several pages for the writing of the feedback process. This may include additional writings, questions, thoughts, follow-up activities, and informal indexing.

2. Some people prefer writing at the same time each day, either early morning or late evening, in the same location. Set the timer for ten to fifteen minutes. Others may prefer keeping their journals portable, transporting them and writing as the time and urges unfold naturally throughout the day. Still others enjoy a combination of both.

Remember that "waiting times" are an excellent gift of time to write an entry. A few minutes in the post office line, grocery store line, airports, dentist's and doctor's offices can add up to hours of journal writing time.

3. As you transition into this solitude time of writing, be observant of yourself: What am I thinking? What am I feeling? Think of using descriptive words in the journal entry. What are the actions planned or already taken? Include sensory details—the sounds, the tastes, the touches, the sights. If possible, consider the sense of smell; it can be the most powerful. Add adjectives that are descriptive, providing distinctive and clear information. Are there humorous situations? What are the metaphors and similes conveying deeper meanings of an experience?

4. What follows is an exercise applying Carl Jung's concept, "stream of consciousness." It is an intuitive process, encouraging our conscious and subconscious minds to empty out whatever is inside us. As you sit comfortably with your open journal and pen, take three or four deep breaths from the lower part of your abdomen. Relax. Give yourself permission to write whatever comes to you. Place the current date in your notebook then proceed to write quickly for five to ten minutes, continuously. Keep your hand moving. Write your initial thoughts. Write what is coming into your mind, from the depths of your being. The thoughts may appear logical, or they may not. They could be pictures, images, ideas, snippets of songs, movie clips, hunches, and/or insights. There may be negative thoughts; there may be positive thoughts. In the journal there is no wrong. There only *is*. All are welcomed in this open moment. There is no one to be judgmental here of you or your writing. Let yourself be "free in the moment." Write the truth of how you believe, see, feel, think, and/or value today. Surrender to the moment's flow. Write naturally. Be not concerned with misspellings, correct grammar, cross-outs, capital letters, dotting every *i*, and crossing every *t*. The personal journal is not the resident for English Format 101. A free-writing exercise of this type consistently practiced over time can provide us with a myriad of insights, creative ideas, and depth into the truth of our higher self and bring forth our best gifts we have to claim for ourselves, provide to others, and develop for our life's purpose. In essence, be willing to risk on the writing page.

5. A spin-off of this exercise can be "Journaling in the Round." As you read over a stream of consciousness entry, notice the sentence, phrase, or paragraph resonating within you. What is whispering for additional attention? Take this sentence, write it at the top of the next page in your journal and continue writing whatever comes to you. From this second exercise, transfer another line to the next page, continuing with a third entry, then a fourth. Repeat this as often as you desire. This exercise will take you in unexpected and unexplored directions.

The journal can be a source of decision making for multiple opportunities coming simultaneously. Explore the decisions you make daily in your life. At the top of the blank page write the current date. Title the page, "Conscious Choices I Made Today." Underneath, list the deliberate decisions you selected. Expand it to include the various options you had presented before you. At the day's end reflect back over your list and appreciate the conscious choices you made to live your life truest to your authentic internal values and goals.

6. Your notebook can be a place of acceptance and space to vent your feelings and emotions through catharsis writing. A place to write until you are empty. It is a safe and secure haven to release temporary intense feelings of loss and helplessness due to death, job loss, divorce, trauma, or severe illness.

7. Sometimes images are able to deeply express what words cannot. The journal can be a place to doodle, draw, and sketch images you feel within. One does not have to have artistic talent to express the symbols and forms that are within. After a written entry, some journalers on the receptive page will briefly outline or sketch an image symbolizing what is felt inside.

Include photographs in the journal if you desire. With the picture, consider adding a reflective and meaningful commentary to it.

Sometimes the combination of using both written words and visual images, engaging both hemispheres of the brain, can ultimately be a sense of feeling freedom and lightness within.

8. When there are multiple people, ideas, and things competing for attention simultaneously, one tool for realignment and regaining centeredness is to propose two basic questions in the journal:

1. What do I *have* to do today?
2. What do I *want* to do today?

Ensure a combination of both are achieved to foster greater sense of balance and wholeness within.

9. When reading newspapers, magazines, and books, there may be quotes that capture your attention and stay in your thoughts. Seize this writing opportunity. Cut out and insert or tape the clipping in your notebook. Ponder your thoughts and ideas on the journaling page. Write the maxim down, then write what comes to you next. What does this mean to you? Is it motivating you? Is it something you want to live your life by? Write the adage several times. Follow where your consciousness leads you.

10. Sometimes you may sit down at the blank page and wonder what to write or think "I have nothing to write." Following are a few of my favorite prompts to help with this temporary state. Almost immediately upon writing the beginning sentence I am transformed. I begin thinking a plethora of information, details, insights, connections that I had no dream I could have thought of in just the previous moments:

Today I accomplished . . .
Today I had a meaningful conversation with _____. I learned from this encounter . . .
Last night I dreamed . . .
I remember the time . . .
Deep inside my being I hear . . .

JOURNAL FEEDBACK

Over the weeks, months, and years of keeping a journal, perhaps you begin thinking, "What can I do with all these accumulated writings?"

This is part of the feedback process. This can be a significant, productive time of solitude. Begin with an open frame of reference. Anticipate receiving beautiful and meaningful gifts. The book, *Harvesting Your Journals* (Deer/Strickland, 1999), provides numerous ideas. The authors highly recommend using the following stem statements after reading a journal notebook:

"I learned . . .
I relearned . . .
I discovered . . .
I regret . . .
I appreciate . . .
Right now, I feel . . .
I will . . . "

Another exercise while reading the journal is to highlight action words, or *verbs*, used in the journal. Focus on the movement of your life. Recognize, value, and appreciate your accomplishments, growth, and development. If necessary, note the areas where taking action is avoided.

A favorite feedback approach I use is to read a journal entry. Pause. Reflect on the time period I was in and where I am now, gaining a new perspective. On the opposite or reverse page of the initial writing, place the present date of this feedback entry and begin writing in a stream-of-consciousness flow. If applicable, I will write about recognizing specific small action steps taken in moving toward a desired goal, or recall and appreciate a meaningful moment invested with family and friends. As additional observations and insights appear, they are captured in the notebook.

As this article comes to a close, it is your turn to decide what you will do with this information. Will it be just an interesting article and then you move on to the next one? Or will you find a pen and a piece of paper and experiment with one of the various exercises provided?

With the birth of this upcoming hour, may you embark on your own discovery into the creativity awaiting you with your own indispensable journal companion.

References

Adams, K. (1990) *Journal to the Self. Twenty-two Paths to Personal Growth* NY: Warner Books

Adams, K. (1994) *Mightier Than the Sword: The Journal as a Path to Men's Self Discovery.* NY: Warner.

Baldwin, C. (1991) *Life's Companion: Journal Writing as a Spiritual Quest.* NY: Bantam.

Capacchione, L. (1989) *The Creative Journal for Children: A Guide for Parents, Teachers, and Counselors.* Boston: Shambhala.

Heart, Rosalie Deer and Alison Strickland (1999) *Harvesting Your Journals: Writing Tools To Enhance Your Growth And Creativity.* Sanfa Fe, NM: Heart Link Publications.

Klauser, H. (1995) *Put Your Heart on Paper.* NY: Bantam.

Klauser, H. (2000) *Write it Down, Make it Happen.* NY: Scribner.

Progoff, I. (1975) *At a Journal Workshop.* NY: Dialogue House Library.

Rainer, T. (1978) *The New Diary. How to Use a Journal for Self Guidance and Expanded Creativity.* Los Angeles, CA: Tracer, Inc.

Schiwy, M. (1996) *A Voice of Her Own: Women and the Journal Writing Journey.* NY: Fireside Book/Simon & Schuster.

Schiwy, M. (2002) *Simple Days: A Journal on What Really Matters.* Notre Dame, IN: Sorin Books.

Follow-Up

1. *Experiment with keeping a personal journal. Write three to five entries weekly for four weeks. After this experience:*
   - *What are the pluses and/or minuses of this activity for you?*
   - *Is this a worthwhile investment of your time and energy? Explain.*
   - *Is this journal writing experience an activity you will further explore? Why or why not?*
2. *The author recommends several journal writing exercises. Select one and explore it. On a separate sheet of paper write your response to this activity.*
3. *Beeker Schultz implies keeping a journal can be the closest companion one has in life. Write your response to this implication based on your life experiences.*
4. *Select one of the quotes and explore how this maxim translates meaningfully for you. If it does not, write about these thoughts, also.*

Awakening Intuition

Frances Vaughan

Carl Jung has defined intuition as one of four basic psychological functions, the other three being thinking, feeling, and sensation. He characterizes intuition as the function that explores the unknown, and senses possibilities and implications which may not be readily apparent. Intuition perceives what is hidden, and thus enables one to perceive obscure meanings in symbolic imagery, or subconscious motives in oneself and in others. It is also associated with insight, or the ability to understand the dynamics of a personality or situation. Jung distinguished between the introverted intuitive person, whose intuition focuses primarily on the inner world of the psyche, and the extroverted intuitive, whose perceptions of the external world consistently lead to frontiers of exploration. Many successful entrepreneurs who have an uncanny ability to know what will happen next in their businesses are of the latter type.

Intuition is also the psychological function operative in scientific inventions or discoveries. Mathematicians, for instance, readily acknowledge the value of intuition in formulating new hypotheses, and exercise proof and verification as secondary processes. Likewise in physics and other sciences, it is intuition which provides researchers with new possibilities to pursue with the instruments of science. The history of science shows clearly that great breakthroughs in human understanding have been the result of intuitive perceptions that are only later tested and verified.

> This term [intuition] does not denote something contrary to reason, but something outside the province of reason.
>
> —C. G. Jung: *Psychological Types*

Having defined intuition as a mode of knowing and a psychological function which is potentially available to everyone, let us turn our attention to examining the variety of human experiences which are commonly called intuitive. Intuitive experiences include, but are by no means limited to, mystical insights into the nature of reality. Experiences which are commonly called intuitive also include discovery and invention in science, inspiration in art, creative problem solving, perception of patterns and possibilities, extrasensory perception, clairvoyance, telepathy, precognition, retrocognition, feelings of attraction and aversion, picking up "vibes," knowing or perceiving through the body rather than the rational mind, hunches, and premonitions.

Intuition is often associated with having a hunch or a strong feeling of knowing what is going to happen. Often these hunches are vague, and since they are rarely recorded they are seldom verifiable.

At times hunches may seem negative, such as the hunch that you will forget something when you go on a trip. At other times they may be positive, such as the hunch that you will get a job you applied for even though the competition is stiff, or the hunch that you will do well in an exam despite inadequate preparation. What is necessary in the beginning, regardless of whether the hunch is positive, negative, or neutral, is to learn to distinguish genuinely intuitive hunches from those which are simply a product of anxiety or wishful thinking.

The best way to do this is to keep a record of your hunches in a journal or a diary. In this way you can check up on yourself, to see how often your hunches turn out to be accurate. Subjectively you may begin to notice that intuitive hunches feel different from those which turn out to be purely imaginary. The only way you can learn to make the distinction for yourself is to learn by trial and error. At first, when you begin to keep a record of your hunches, you may find a high percentage of errors. As your sensitivity to nonverbal cues, both internal and external, is refined, your record may improve. Don't be discouraged by errors. Every time you make an error you have the opportunity to learn something about yourself. If you are willing to acknowledge yourself as the source of your error—that is, to take responsibility for it rather than blaming it on outside circumstances—you may quickly learn to see how your personal interests distort your perceptions and get in the way of clear intuition.

The conscious mind, or ego, frequently interferes with intuitive perception. The more you want something to happen, the less you are able to sense whether it will happen or not. For example, if you want someone you love to call you, you may think it is him or her every time the phone rings, only to be disappointed each time. On the other hand, someone you hardly know, or whom you have not thought about in weeks, may come into your mind inexplicably, and then, a few minutes later, that person may call. Fear and desire both interfere with intuitive perception. If you are anxious, angry, or emotionally upset, you are not likely to be receptive to the subtle messages which can come into consciousness via intuition.

Lack of acceptance of intuition in the culture at large certainly contributes to its suppression in individuals who do not want to be "different." Many adults in my groups have said that they felt they were more intuitive as children, and that they learned to keep their intuitive perceptions to themselves after encountering skepticism or ridicule from adults.

One woman who attended an intuition workshop recalled an incident in her life when she was about five years old. On a Friday she announced to her mother that Grandmother would not be coming to dinner on Sunday because she had hurt her foot. Her mother did not pay much attention to her remark, as she assumed she was making it up. To her amazement, the following day Grandmother called and said she would not come to dinner the next day because she had sprained her ankle the previous afternoon.

Such incidents may be frightening to adults who do not understand them or consider them paranormal. Parents who are afraid of what seems incomprehensible often respond angrily to intuitive observations by their children. They may attempt to explain them away, or to deny the child's experience, saying something like, "You couldn't possibly know that. Don't lie to me." At best, the child's remarks may be ignored.

Young children learn very quickly that there are some things they are not supposed to talk about. For many this reticence persists into adulthood. Participants in intuition workshops often express appreciation for having the opportunity to talk about experiences which they would ordinarily not discuss for fear of being considered "weird" or "crazy." Children seldom share their inner world of fantasy and perception with adults, because sympathetic, understanding adults are rare.

In general, intuition flourishes only when it is valued, and clearly certain lifestyles and experiences facilitate or nourish it. Inspiration needs space and attention if it is to take shape in a creative endeavor. Attention acts as psychic energy and enhances the process it values. The artist who is highly intuitive in his or her perceptions of reality knows that inspiration always seems to come of its own accord. Effort is invariably involved in the creative process, but flashes of inspiration tend to occur spontaneously. Seeking inspiration requires a receptive mode of consciousness and is comparable to trying to remember something you know but have forgotten. Tarthang Tulku, a Tibetan Lama, writes: "If we wish to regain some memory or insight that is 'there,' but is temporarily elusive, it is often most effective to put aside any grasping or tight achievement-orientation and become passively receptive. By quietly opening the mind, the hidden element is allowed to present itself on its own. In a similar manner, artists seeking inspiration used to go to sleep, hoping for a visit from a muse, who would speak to them—and then through them—in their art. People courting divine intercession have long understood that they must *open* themselves to divine messages and purposes, as in the cases of prayer and oracles. According to all these various orientations, the importance of surrendering the self has been emphasized."

In a sense, everyone is an artist in charge of designing his or her life. If the unexamined life is not worth living, what about the uninspired life? Certainly many, if not most, people in our society would not consider their lives to be particularly inspired. Yet the possibility is there for *everyone* to tap the creative source of inspiration which comes from well-developed intuition.

Perhaps you have had the experience of struggling with a problem or a decision until you were sick of it, and then deciding to forget it for a while. Very often the solution pops into your head when you least expect it. The expression "sleep on it" refers to allowing this intuitive process to be completed during sleep. Many people report finding solutions to apparently insoluble dilemmas through their dreams and daydreams. When you stop trying to make something happen, intuition is allowed to operate.

If you are serious about wanting to fully experience the potential of both the right and left hemispheres of the brain and find a lifestyle that is truly satisfying to you, then you must give yourself the time and space necessary for allowing your intuition to come into conscious awareness. Remember, there is nothing you can do to make intuition happen, but there is much that you can do to allow it to happen. Be gentle. There is no need to force anything.

The regular practice of meditation is the single most powerful means of increasing intuition. Taking time to do the exercises in this book is a good first step, but once you have decided that clear intuition is a valuable asset in your life, you will want to continue to sharpen and expand your awareness of it. The silent mind, cultivated in many different forms of meditation, is the matrix of intuition. When you are in touch with the stillpoint at the center of your being, there is no need to use imagery or verbal exercises to activate intuition. It flows by itself, unimpeded by fears and preoccupations.

The wisdom of intuition does not follow the rules of logic. It will never make rational, discriminating choices for you. It is no substitute for careful research or data gathering. It is a purveyor of possibilities, not an evaluating faculty. Critical judgment may inhibit intuition, yet intuition never becomes a substitute for discrimination. Discriminating judgments are essential to making choices in the world, but let the mind be guided by reason, not bound by it. Your intuition can show you alternatives; it can give you a sense of what is possible for you. It does not tell you what is right or wrong, but it is a reliable indicator of what you need at a particular time. How you feel about trusting your intuition inevitably affects its functioning. If you value it and affirm it, it will flourish. How you think about intuition will determine how you use it, whether you bend it to egotistical purposes, or follow where it leads you. Pure intuition remains unaffected by thoughts and feelings, and will always take you beyond the boundaries of present conscious knowledge.

References

Tulku, T. (1977). *Time, space, and knowledge.* Emeryville, CA: Dharma Publishing.

Von Franz, M. L., & Hillman, J. (1971). *Jung's typology.* New York: Spring Publications.

Weil, A. (1972). *The natural mind.* Boston: Houghton Mifflin.

Follow-Up

1. *Select two statements from Vaughan's article and offer your interpretations.*
2. *Do you value and encourage intuition in your life? Explain your answer.*
3. *Vaughan says that fear and desire interfere with intuitive perception. Have you found this to be true? Why? Explain how you can detect when emotional needs are blocking intuitive reception.*
4. *Vaughan recommends keeping a record of your "hunches" in order to distinguish true intuition from wishful or anxious thinking. Try this and report the results.*

Sensational Living

Nelson Goud

John Muir liked nothing better than to roam the Sierra Nevada mountain range. In December of 1874, he was exploring a Yuba River valley when a howling windstorm moved in. Instead of going to the home of a nearby friend, Muir headed for a forest grove. He thought it would be interesting to be with the trees during the storm. When he arrived at the grove, he could hear the cracking and thumps of trees falling every two to three minutes. Standing on the grove's edge, he saw "delicious sunshine pouring over the hills, lighting the tops of the pines, and setting free a stream of summery fragrance that contrasted strangely with the wild tones of the storm. . . . The force of the gale was such that the most steadfast monarch of them all rocked down to its roots with a motion plainly perceptible when one leaned against it." Hiking from ridge to ridge, Muir could "distinctly hear the varying tones of individual trees—Spruce, and Fir, and Pine, and leafless Oak—and even the infinitely gentle rustle of the withered grasses at my feet— [each] singing its own song." After climbing to the summit of the highest ridge, it occurred to him to experience the storm with a tree. He selected a 100 foot high Douglas Spruce and climbed to its top, where "never before did I enjoy so noble an exhilaration of motion. The slender top fairly flapped and swished in the passionate torrent, bending and swirling backward and forward, round and round, tracing indescribable combinations of vertical and horizontal curves, while I clung with muscles firm braced, like a bobolink on a reed." Muir kept his loft for hours, often closing his eyes to better hear the tree music and smell the scents of resin and pine needles and tinges of the ocean from which the storm originated. Muir concluded that there is a kinship between humans and trees. In their manner, trees could travel while swinging to and fro in the wind. Similarly, "our own little journeys, away and back again, are only little more than tree-wavings, many of them not so much" (Muir, 1997, pp. 467–473).

John Muir could be said to possess a high degree of sensory intelligence. He was at home with his senses and could readily connect with the sensory messages of other living earthly beings. For most, however, there seems to be a gradual loss in our sensory intelligence. Modern living values abstract notions of reality rather than reality itself. We are increasingly becoming detached from direct experience with the world and seem to prefer electronic representations of it. It is not that we have lost our sensory capabilities but instead we tend not to exercise them. Sensory intelligence appears to occupy a low rung on modern life's priority ladder.

David Abram argues that "our bodies have formed themselves in delicate reciprocity with the manifold textures, sounds and shapes of an animate earth. . . . To shut ourselves off from these other voices . . . is to rob our own senses of their integrity. . . . We are human only in contact [with] what is not human" (Abram, 1996, p. 22).

To be fully human means, in part, to realize our human potentialities. Abraham Maslow pointed out that actualizing one's capacities can be an enjoyable growth path. But he also stated that "the unused skill or capacity or organ can become a disease center or atrophy or disappear, thus diminishing the person" (Maslow, 1968, p. 201). Activating our sensory intelligence, then, is as essential to human growth as developing reason and the intellect. Each has its limits as well as its capabilities. Our senses cannot navigate in dimensions beyond our bodies like our intellect can do with its imagination and language abilities. The intellect comes up short in directly experiencing the world and its many offerings, as Kazantzakis illustrates: "You feel hungry, but instead of drinking wine and eating meat and bread, you take a sheet of paper, inscribe the words wine, meat, bread on it, and then eat the paper" (Kazantzakis, 1965, p. 190).

The sensory modes provide immediate, direct connections both with the external world and within ourselves. You do not have to think about or analyze a sound, scent, touch, sight, or taste to have them appear—they are here, now. Why is a face-to-face encounter with another person so different from a cell phone or e-mail communication? Psychologists would say that more nonverbal cues are present in person-to-person communication. These include such things as eye contact, mannerisms, voice inflections, body proximity, facial movements, scent of cologne, moisture on the forehead, and so on. Researchers tell us that two-thirds of our emotional and attitudinal messages are sent and received through nonverbal channels. Reading these nonverbal cues is largely a sensory process. We read nervousness by observing twitching hands or feet and perhaps darting eyes. If someone yells I'M NOT MAD, do you place more meaning on the words or the voice tone? At times, nonverbal modes are the best choices. For example, when attempting to show emotional support during times of grief, we offer light touches or an embrace. These and hundreds more all demonstrate the central role of sensory intelligence in being human.

Our senses are a major source of life's pleasures, delights, and moments of wonder. Imagine your life without tasting favorite foods and beverages, without music, without being able to touch a lover or child or a pet, without the smell of perfume or the spring rain, or without seeing a sunset or flowers or a friend. The senses are not just diversions or entertainers, not servile participants, but are central players in our overall well-being. The significance of a sense sometimes is only noted when it is absent (e.g., a severe head cold temporarily shuts down taste and smell), or when it is enhanced (e.g., obtaining a first pair of glasses or a hearing aid). I often take students on a trust walk, in which they are paired off and one is designated the leader. The other (follower) is blindfolded or shuts his or her eyes. Neither may talk. In a column of twos, we wander the campus under trees, up and down steps, along a narrow ledge at the edge of a fountain, and just explore the surroundings. The pairs must communicate nonverbally. Afterward, we discuss the experience. Many of the responses focus on sensory experiences: "I could smell things that I didn't before like someone's cologne, traces of cigarette smoke on clothes, the damp air;" "I knew something was coming up when I heard the groans and giggles from others in front;" "I was very aware of how my feet and legs adjusted to the different surfaces and elevations;" "My partner had a firmer touch when we were about to encounter an obstacle." Almost all agree that their nonvisual senses became enhanced. A more accurate explanation would be that they experienced an augmented attention to their nonvisual senses. Because sight and language dominate how we navigate through the world, it is instructive to shut these down occasionally to reveal learnings from other modes. Try it—wherever you are, close your eyes and listen quietly to your surroundings for a minute. What is there now that you did not detect with your eyes open? Our sense of touch also includes our internal sense of the body—its location and movement, and each of its components (the kinesthetic and proprioceptive sense). Anyone involved in sports, dance, and other movement domains are usually highly aware of this inner sense. But it is with us everywhere and anytime. How are you breathing right now—with shallow and quick breaths or long, deep ones? Are the muscles in your upper back and neck tight or relaxed? Stand up, close your eyes, and then lift one leg waist high and try to hold it for a few seconds. This will reveal several proprioceptive sensations involved in balancing your body.

Our senses do not operate in isolation from other human dimensions such as language and memory. Scent is often mentioned in triggering sharp and instant memories even if many years have passed. A counselor, also trained in massage therapy techniques, writes about a time when she massaged her mother's back:

> I lingered for just a moment to take in her scent, so reminiscent of my childhood, my mother's fragrance. It is the smell of summer sunshine and good, warm, garden earth. My mother, goddess of summer sun and gardening. My mother's skin emits the mingled aromas of freshly mown grass, sweet potting soil, garden seeds, musky flower bulbs, fresh snapped green beans, polished piano keys, clean clothes hung to dry on the line and gardenias. I want to trap it in a bottle. I want to be able to open that bottle and get a rush of her fragrance when I need comfort or to be transported to a time in my distant past. I want to have it handy for that time when I can no longer burrow my face in her neck and breathe deeply of her sweet, warm essence that nourishes me and makes me feel safe.

> —Emily Runion,
> personal correspondence, 2003

Every sensory experience is multisensory. Although one sense may dominate, others are simultaneously present. Kiss a lover and there is touch, scent, sound, taste, and sight (which may be purposely shut down to accentuate the other senses). Playing my trumpet is not a purely auditory act. The muscles in my left forearm slightly tighten at the weight of the horn and my left hand feels its hard coolness. The first three fingertips on my right hand feel the pressure of the valves and their smooth, marble tops. I can taste the mouthpiece as well as feel it pressing against my lips, particularly the upper one. I smell the valve oil. I see the silver sheen of the horn and the music notes and sometimes other players or an audience in my peripheral vision. If done right, I hear some sweet notes or a piercing high one and when with a band, a blend of instrumental sounds. Every few seconds there are small muscle shifts in my stomach, legs, and shoulders depending on the musical effect I am attempting to produce. Sometimes, and only sometimes, I hear sounds of a good trumpet player and I wonder who is playing.

We blend our sensory experiences so naturally that we experience *synesthesia*—using one sense to describe another (e.g., describing clothing as loud, or perceiving sounds as brittle or soft). In a strong wind you not only feel its force, but also see it in the leaves and on the top of large bodies of water. Jon Kabat-Zinn states that our "senses overlap and blend together, and cross-pollinate. . . . We are not fragmented in our being" (2005, p. 190). In addition to simultaneously experiencing several senses in a single moment, it must be stated that each sense has its own variations. For example, sight involves brightness, movement, size, distance, and color (to name a few dimensions). For a detailed and worthy tour of the senses, consider Diane Ackerman's *A Natural History of the Senses* (1990).

One of the major impediments to using our sensory intelligence is sensory overload. Modern living bombards the senses. A single TV screen image may have up to six pieces of visual information in addition to music and words and constant changes. Our ears are assaulted by the sounds of machines—cars, leaf blowers, construction equipment, cell phone shouters, jets, overlapping conversations, unwanted music blasting from apartments and cars. A robin's chirp goes unheard. This constant bombardment is noted as one of the major sources of stress. Often our only way out of going completely loony is through habituation and desensitization—not paying attention anymore. Some say we are numbing down our senses. A few even buy white noise devices so that they can sleep. The accelerated pace of life causes many to hurriedly multitask and in the process block out sensory experiences. We may, for instance, gulp down a meal at our desks or in the car without a hint of what we are experiencing in our taste and smell dimensions. A restaurant can become so loud that to be heard you have to shout and this triggers more shouting. Getting our sensory attention often means increasing stimulus input, which leads to the overload problem. Increasing our sensory intelligence in these environments means to decrease the intensity and frequency of sensory input.

During the South Asia tsunami disaster of December 2004, over 1,000 persons were killed on a small island south of India. On visiting the site, government officials encountered a few members of the highly secretive Jarawa tribe who choose to remain isolated from civilization. All 250 members of the tribe survived by heading inland before the tidal waves arrived. The officials surmise that their intimate knowledge of the sea, wind, and bird movements alerted them to the danger.

David Abrams contends that we tend to place earth's entities on a hierarchy with inanimate objects at the bottom and then proceed from single cell organisms to the top where humans reside. What if we abandoned the hierarchy and just accepted that non-human beings have gifts that differ from ours? The Jarawa tribe surely does not need this advice. But we do not have to live in an isolated manner in a jungle to do this. What is the voice of the sky, a mountain, a cat, a tree, a river, or the small chickadee flitting about on a cold, snowy day?

Swaying in the top of a Douglas Spruce during a windstorm, John Muir fully activated his sensory being. We can do the same without climbing a tree in the wind. Our sensory intelligences can be quickly enhanced without taking a course, attending a workshop, or logging on to the Internet. All we have to do is pay attention to the body we already have. We can come to our senses.

References

Abram, D. (1996). *The spell of the sensuous.* New York: Vintage Books.

Ackerman, D. (1990). *A natural history of the senses.* New York: Vintage Books.

Kabat-Zinn, J. (2005). *Coming to our senses.* New York: Hyperion.

Kazantzakis, N. (1965). *Report to Greco.* New York: Touchstone.

Maslow, A. (1968). *Toward a psychology of being.* New York: Van Nostrand Reinhold.

Muir, J. (1997). *Muir: Nature writings.* New York: The Library of America.

Follow-Up

1. *Choose two statements from this article and discuss their meanings and applications toward your life.*
2. *Attempt to increase the functioning of any aspect of your sensory intelligence and report the results.*
3. *Observe non-human beings in your environment and attempt to detect any of their messages. Describe your learnings.*

4. *Select an activity that fully activates several senses and describe it. Some common activities include sports, dance, arts, nature experiences, playing with a child, and so on. Explain what you learned.*
5. *Attempt a trust walk (as mentioned in the article) and report your findings. Make sure you are both a leader and a follower sometime in this activity.*
6. *Attempt the Sense Sampler or Trust Feast as instructed in the Applied Activities at the end of this section.*
7. *See related articles in this book—"Mindfulness" (Section One); "A Teacher Hears" (Section Two); "Little Joys" (Section Five); "Teachers in the Forest" (Section Six).*

The Nature and Uses of Dreaming

Ernest Hartmann, M.D.

A 20-year-old college student barely escaped with his life from a fire that killed several members of his family. A few nights later, he had a vivid dream: "I was on a beach when a huge tidal wave came along and engulfed me. I was flipped over and over; there was nothing I could do. I was just about to drown when I woke up." On another night, he also dreamt: "I was swept away in a whirlwind. I was helpless, just blown away." These dreams clearly do not picture the details of what happened to him—the fire. Rather, they picture his emotional state—his feeling of fear, terror, and helplessness.

I have collected and studied many series of dreams after major trauma and repeatedly have come across such dreams as tidal waves, whirlwinds, or being chased by gangs of thugs. I am convinced that these dreams are a sort of paradigm, a place where we can see most clearly what is happening in all dreams. Such dreams are by no means nonsense. They picture the emotional state of our minds.

My collaborators and I have been developing a view of dreams which differs considerably from accepted wisdom on the subject. Nevertheless, it turns out to be very compatible with the commonsense experience of those who remember their dreams and have developed an interest in them.

Over all, dreams have not gotten much respect in the past few decades. There have been two dominant schools of thought. One view championed by some biologists is that dreams basically are random nonsense, the products of a poorly functioning brain during sleep. If there is any meaning to dreams, it is "added on later" as our brains try to "make the best of a bad job." A related view proposed by other biologists is that dreaming may function as an "unlearning" procedure: a dream is garbage being thrown out by a computer to keep itself from being clogged up. In this view, we dream specifically about what we do *not* need to remember.

The other view of dreams, more common among psychoanalysts and therapists, derives broadly from the work of pioneering psychoanalyst Sigmund Freud. He did take dreams seriously in one sense, calling them the "royal road" to the workings of the unconscious. However, Freud felt that his main contribution—his discovery of the secret of dreams—was his finding that, when properly analyzed, every dream turns out to be a fulfillment of a wish. Further, although Freud appears to take dreams much more seriously than the biologists do, he does not place much value on the dream itself, which he calls the "manifest dream." He repeatedly refers to the dream as an irrational mental product, whose value emerges only when one subjects it to a process of free association leading eventually to an underlying "latent dream" containing the underlying wish.

After having spent many years conducting research on the biology of dreaming, I disagree with both these broad views. Indeed, there now is available a tremendous amount of information about the biology of sleep and specifically the biology of REM (rapid eye movement) sleep, the part of sleep in which most of our memorable dreams occur. However, this knowledge of the underlying biology of dreaming does not tell us the true nature or functions of dreaming, and it certainly is not a reason for dismissing the psychological meaning of dreams. Why should the developing understanding of the biology underlying it make dreaming meaningless, any more than the developing understanding of the biology underlying thought makes thought meaningless?

I have spent many years analyzing my own and my patients' dreams in my clinical work. Establishing the necessary climate of safety comes from a sense of alliance between patient and therapist. The patient is allowed to tell his or her story about the trauma or new event over and over again, making connections to other material, gradually seeing it in a new light. I believe this happens in dreaming as well. The safe place is provided by a bed and the muscular inhibition of REM sleep, which assures that the sleeper will lie quietly in bed, rather than running around acting out the dream. Once safety is established, the broad connections gradually are made.

Finally, in addition to the basic function of dreaming, which I believe probably helps us even when we do not remember dreams, there are many ways in which dreams can be useful to us when we do remember them. For example, the women who dreamt some version of "Jim turned into my father" generally found this a useful insight, a new way of looking at things that helped in their relationship. Sometimes, the new and broader connections made by dreaming can be helpful in our work and in artistic and scientific discovery.

A number of creative people have made use of dreams in their discoveries. Some of the best known examples are the French chemist Auguste Kekulé, who saw snakes biting their tails in a dream, which led him to the correct ring structure for the benzene molecule. Inventor Elias Howe attributed the discovery of the sewing machine to a dream in which he was captured by cannibals. He noticed as they danced around him that there were holes at the tips of spears, and he realized this was the design feature he needed to solve his problem. Vladimir Horowitz and several other well-known pianists have described playing piano pieces in their dreams and discovering a new fingering they had not tried previously and which turned out to work perfectly. Robert Louis Stevenson said that his book, *The Strange Case of Dr. Jekyll and Mr. Hyde,* came to him in a dream.

In these cases, I am not saying that all the hard work of discovery happened in the dream. Generally, the artist or scientist made one new connection in a dream and then developed the work in the waking state. Stevenson probably saw a respectable doctor turning into a monster—this is, in fact, quite a typical nightmare image—and then his waking writing skills took over from there. In each case, the dreamers were well-versed in their fields and were worrying hard about a particular problem, which thus had become an emotional concern and was pictured in a dream.

I believe that, by its broader connective features, dreaming has obvious uses of this kind and we probably can make a good deal more of our dreams than we do. For instance, many Native American and South American cultures have adopted a methodology for career choice. In puberty, a young man—or, in some cases, young woman—is sent out into the desert to have a dream or a vision. Often, the young person will return with a powerful dream which, with or without help from the elders, leads to a decision about a future life course.

We might tend to dismiss this as superstition having no relevance to our lives. However, I suggest that we can benefit from the techniques of these cultures. I believe they are making good use of the broader connective powers of dreaming. The young person, who clearly has his future role or "career" in mind as an emotional concern, goes out and has a dream that makes connections more broadly than he does in waking life, which pictures something for him based on his concerns, wishes, or fears, and this often turns out to be very useful to him.

I have known a few people who informally have made use of such a technique. In our culture, we generally ask a young person to consider carefully his or her possible choices for a career, make a list of pros and cons, and so on. There is nothing wrong with this, but I have known several cases in which the decision truly came together or felt right only after a dream.

Sometimes, dreams can be extremely useful in our personal lives, scientific or artistic work, or even something as basic as career choice. I certainly am not suggesting substituting the dream for waking thought, but why leave it out entirely? Dreaming is one end of the continuum, a way of making connections more broadly than our focused waking thought, but guided by what is important to us. Why should we not use everything we have and allow ourselves to notice and employ this additional connecting power?

Follow-Up

1. *Hartmann claims that dreams provide a context for emotional concerns, make new connections among our experiences, and can be helpful in making choices. Explain why you agree or disagree with his ideas.*
2. *How have dreams played a role in your life?*
3. *Select two ideas from this article and offer your interpretations.*
4. *For a related reading, see "Awakening Intuition" by Frances Vaughan in this section.*

Applied Activities for Section Two

LIFESTORIES

This is an open-ended activity best experienced in a relaxed, informal atmosphere with people you already know and trust. Not only will you learn a little more about yourself, but a bit more about the others in your life. Some general guidelines:

- Groups should have two to five members.
- One person chooses and discusses an item from the list below. The other group members just listen and offer comments after the speaker is finished.
- Everyone should get a turn. There is also the option to pass.
- Discuss as many items as you wish (and in any order).

1. Your earliest memory
2. Your first good friend
3. A favorite place in your childhood home
4. A special moment with a parent (guardian)
5. What you did in summers before high school
6. How you are like and unlike one of your parents (guardians)
7. Favorite subjects in school
8. Least favorite subjects in school
9. A favorite teacher
10. A childhood vacation that stands out
11. A major hero as a child or adolescent
12. One of your current favorite sounds or tastes
13. Describe one major success in your life
14. A failure or dead end
15. Two little joys (small pleasures)
16. One of your current favorite places to be
17. One major experience or accomplishment yet to occur which you desire
18. A treasured possession
19. A person (excluding a significant other or family member) you would like to spend time with (can be a historical figure if you choose)
20. Something that inspires you
21. A fear
22. When do you feel lonely?
23. How are you different now compared to age 16? How are you the same?
24. Something you'd like to do for another person
25. Something you want and need further growth in

Editor's Note: An excellent reference for further pursuing this activity is *The Common Ground Book: A Circle of Friends* by Remar Sutton and Mary Abbott Waite. British American Publishing, 1992.

SENDER–RECEIVER EXCHANGE

This activity combines self-disclosure, listening, and self-knowledge. It has the most value when participants have some beginning acquaintance and are willing to disclose new dimensions of themselves. The procedure is as follows:

1. Read the articles on self-disclosure and listening in this book or other resources.
2. Choose a partner (there might be one three-member group).
3. Find a location with a minimum of distractions. It is recommended that sixty minutes be given to this activity (minimum of thirty minutes).
4. The basic task is for each participant to finish the sentences below. Each person is to complete an item before going on to the next. If you are in the sender role, complete the sentence in the most genuine manner possible (which can be the choice of *not* talking). If you are in the receiver role, your mission is to understand but not to offer reactions or interpretations.
5. It is more important to take quality time per item than to race through the list. If you cannot think of an adequate response to an item, skip it and go on to the next (you can always return to the skipped item if you choose).

Sender–Receiver Items

1. The name I'm to be called is _____ .

2. One of the best experiences I had during the past year was _____

    _____ .

3. Two traits or qualities others say I have are _____ and

    _____ .

4. One of my favorite free-time activities or hobbies is _____ .

5. One impression I seem to give to others that isn't totally true is _____

    _____ .

6. If for some reason I could only keep three possessions (excluding houses,

    vehicles, properties), they would be _____ , _____ ,

    and _____ .

7. If given *one* of the following at this time in my life, it would be _____

    _____ because _____ .

    (a) a week alone in a favorite spot
    (b) an activity with excitement, adventure
    (c) a new friend to share experiences with

(d) an answer to what I should be in life

(e) an intimate, loving relationship

(f) accepting myself as I am

(g) a chance to help make a positive change in another's life

(h) to be recognized as being an expert in some field

(i) a deep spiritual/religious experience

(j) learn a new skill or special knowledge

8. Given some time with any person of my choice (current or historical), it would be _____ because _____ .

9. One thing I would like to change about myself is _____ .

10. My age is _____ and how I feel about it is _____ .

11. (a) I *like* being a male/female because _____ .

    (b) I *dislike* being a male/female because _____ .

    (c) One way I interact differently with the opposite sex is _____ _____ .

12. The degree of satisfaction and fulfillment with my occupation or major is _____ .

13. I am fully accepted for who I am (no conditions) by _____ .

14. Compared to age 15, how are you different? _____ .

    The same? _____ .

15. A way I am the *same* as one or both of my parents (guardians) is _____ .

16. For at least two of the following emotional states, explain what normally causes them and how you react:

    Worried-anxious-nervous   Wonder-awe-amazement
    Lonely-not belonging-alienated   Joy-ecstasy
    Angry-frustrated   Loved-intimate-belonging
    Inadequate-inferior-failure   Confident-self respect
    Confused-uncertain-lost   Sense of purpose and direction

17. My spiritual beliefs emphasize _____ .

18. A potential or ability that I have not fully developed, but want to, is _____ .

19. Describe two activities that tend to produce for you a sense of well-being, centeredness, or harmony with life. How often do you experience these activities?

20. Within the next year it will be very important for me to _____

_____ .

Follow-Up

1. In small groups or with the whole class, discuss the following: What ideas in the article on self-disclosure applied to this experience (e.g., trust, over-/under-discloser, appropriate discloser)?
2. Write a brief reaction paper on what you learned from this activity.
3. Try this activity with someone outside of class (if they agree to the conditions).
4. Estimate how one of your significant others would respond to some or all of these items (check it out with their permission).
5. Select one item from the Sender–Receiver list to explore in more depth (either through writing, talking, or reflection).
6. Complete this activity one year from now.

POINT OF VIEW

1. Choose a topic about which you have strong beliefs and feelings—for example, the death penalty; prayer in schools; Republicans; Democrats; assisted suicide; a current crime trial; a current world/national/local issue; a controversial person, movie, or book.
2. Interview others on this topic until you find two persons who essentially have the same views as yours and two persons who have opposing views. Your interview should last at least 4–5 minutes to gather sufficient information.
3. During each interview you are to remain as nonjudgmental as possible. The other person should not know your stance on the topic as you converse. Your sole mission is to find out the other person's thoughts and feelings on the topic. You may ask questions, but only those that are necessary to clarify the other person's views. You could consider yourself a news reporter who is interviewing people for their views on a story. You may have to explain your role to others prior to the interview.

Complete the above actions before continuing to the next steps.

4. Describe your thoughts and feelings while interviewing those who disagreed with you. Do the same for those who agreed.

   • Did you have any interfering listening reactions during the interviews (e.g., strong urges to present your ideas, thinking of other arguments while lis-

tening, impatience, and so on)? If yes, how did this influence your understanding of the other person?
  - How did the others respond when you showed that you understood their positions without a challenge?
  - What have you learned, if anything, from this experience that can be used elsewhere?

(If this activity was difficult to accomplish, consider trying it several times until you have mastered this skill.)

EFFECTIVE COMMUNICATOR CHECKLIST

Sending and listening skills are listed below. Rate your skill at each one, using the code provided. (If you prefer, ask someone else to rate you.)

1 = Very Poor   2 = Poor   3 = Adequate
4 = Good   5 = Excellent

Sending Skills

____ Have something useful to say

____ Have necessary knowledge of the topic

____ Attempt to detect how the message is understood by the receiver(s)

____ If possible, use multiple methods (such as writing, talking, nonverbal expressions)

____ Be aware of the *context* (the time factor, noise level, distractions, and emotional state) of the situation

____ Make your verbal and nonverbal messages match (e.g., do not smile when angry, look concerned if you say you are)

Listening Skills

____ Can understand (or attempt to understand) the speaker from his or her point of view

____ Can focus on the speaker without getting caught up in distracting thoughts or your own ideas

____ Can understand another even when emotions or beliefs are at a high intensity level (especially if you differ)

____ Give verbal and nonverbal feedback to the speaker on how they are being received

____ Can pick out the main idea or feeling without getting distracted by secondary points

Consider choosing at least one sending and one listening skill to further develop. Discuss your learnings.

HE SAID, SHE SAID

Observe several men and women as they communicate. Observe in a variety of formal and informal situations and try to sample from different age categories. Consider pairing with a partner of the opposite gender for an observation session or two. Your own interactions can count. Circle the choice that *most frequently* communicates in the manner indicated.

1. Conversations are about events, issues, things.	Men	Women	Both	Neither
2. Conversations are about people and/or themselves.	Men	Women	Both	Neither
3. Touch the other person while talking.	Men	Women	Both	Neither
4. Establish frequent eye contact, often engage in "facial mirroring."	Men	Women	Both	Neither
5. Smile while talking.	Men	Women	Both	Neither
6. Tend to use sweeping gestures versus smaller, controlled ones.	Men	Women	Both	Neither
7. Prefer to interact face to face.	Men	Women	Both	Neither
8. Prefer to interact side to side.	Men	Women	Both	Neither
9. Tend to lean back when interacting.	Men	Women	Both	Neither
10. Most at ease with self-disclosures.	Men	Women	Both	Neither
11. Often engage in several topics during one interaction.	Men	Women	Both	Neither
12. More often interrupt when interacting with opposite gender.	Men	Women	Both	Neither
13. Use hostile words, profanity.	Men	Women	Both	Neither
14. Use qualifying language (i.e., "If it is okay…"; "What do you think?"; "Maybe…"; end sentences with a questioning tone).	Men	Women	Both	Neither

Follow-Up

1. Discuss your findings with classmates and compare your observations.
2. Discuss or write how these gender communication differences reflect cultural norms for men and women.
3. Rate yourself on the above items and provide a brief interpretation.
4. Consider adding more items from your observations of men and women as they communicate.

A COMMUNICATION MEDLEY

Try one or more of these communication experiences to enhance your sending or listening skills:

1. Watch a few TV talk shows with the intent of observing communication skills, particularly listening. Observe the effects of good and poor sending and listening behaviors (the Effective Communicator Checklist located in this section may be of help here).

2. Watch a dramatic movie or TV program *without* sound. Attempt to understand what is happening by observing only nonverbal actions (gestures, facial expressions, movements). If possible, rerun the program with audio to check your accuracy.

3. Some hints that indicate you need work on sending skills: others often ask you to clarify something you said; you notice others get that glazed look after several minutes of listening to you; others nod politely but find an excuse to leave before you have finished.

4. Approximately two-thirds of our emotions are sent and received through nonverbal channels. If you are experiencing difficulty in having others understand your emotions, try experimenting with nonverbal behaviors. For example, warmth and caring is expressed with a genuine smile, consistent but nonpiercing eye contact, and closer proximity. Enthusiasm is generally expressed with active gestures, vocal variety, and facial vitality. It is also helpful to observe others who are good at showing the particular emotion you want to convey and watch their nonverbal communication.

INTUITION HISTORY

Although the intuitive mode prefers nonverbal forms, there are some "verbal bridges" that get at its meaning and intent. Here are a few phrases often heard when one is describing the intuitive state:

- My instinct tells me . . .
- I have this gut feeling . . .
- The idea just came out of the blue (or nowhere).
- I had this strong hunch . . .
- I followed my heart.
- I can't explain it, I just have this strong attraction to . . .
- I had these powerful stirrings, inner rumblings urging me to . . .
- I don't think about it, I just act.
- There was this instant and uncanny connection.
- Don't ask me how, I just *know*.

List two instances in your life in which your actions were strongly influenced (at least 50%) by intuition. Here are some categories to consider: school/college experiences, relationships (entering or leaving), geographical move, career decisions/choices, non-career interests (hobbies, pursuits), taking a trip/vacation, making a major purchase, changing an aspect of your lifestyle or personality.

1. _____
   _____
2. _____
   _____

Name an instance when you *did not* follow your intuitive urgings and things did not turn out right. _____
_____

Name an instance when you acted *mainly* on intuition and things did not turn out right. _____
_____

Follow-Up

1. Describe your learnings and views about the role of intuition in your life.

INTUITIVE PROBLEM-SOLVING THROUGH GUIDED IMAGERY

Take some time now to think about a problem that you are currently facing. It can be any situation, any unresolved question concerning relationships, work, growth, or anything else that is important to you.

The first step in this exercise is to formulate a question—any question. In formulating the question, make it as clear as possible. What is the question you want to resolve? When you have a question clearly in your mind, write it down so it is clearly stated. The next step in this exercise is to begin your relaxation practice. Focus your awareness on your body. Take your awareness up to the top of your head and move it slowly down over your whole body, penetrating deeply inside your body, as well as moving it over the surface of your skin. Take as long as you want. When you have focused your awareness, and your mind is quiet, remember the question that you posed earlier. There is nothing you have to do about the question; just hold it in your awareness.

Imagine now that you are at the shore of a large body of water. You get into a small boat and settle comfortably down with a blanket. The boat begins to drift away from shore and is carried gently by the current in the water further and further from the shore. Listen to the sound of the water lapping against the sides of the boat and imagine the rocking motion of the gentle current as you drift slowly further and further away. There is no cause for worry or anxiety because the current will carry you where you need to go. After a time you notice that the light is fading and you see that you have drifted into an underground passage. It gets darker and darker but the movement of the water continues and you drift along feeling quiet and peaceful. After some time you see a light in the distance and you realize that your boat is being carried toward the light. The light becomes brighter and brighter as you get closer to it. The intensity is almost unbearable. Finally your boat emerges into brilliant sunshine and you find yourself on a gently moving stream in a beautiful quiet meadow. The boat comes to a stop and you get out on the bank of the stream. In this place someone or something will bring you a message. The message may not seem to answer the question you asked, but don't worry about that. Trust that it will tell you something you need to know for the solution to your problem. Allow yourself to be quiet and still and wait for whatever image or message comes to you. When you have heard or seen whatever it is that is there for you, get back in the boat and turn on the motor. Very quickly you will find yourself back at the shore where you started. You can leave the boat now and bring your awareness back to the present time and place, to your physical body, feeling comfortable and relaxed. Take a few minutes now to write down what happened in the meadow. If there was anything you heard, anything you saw, write it down. It may not make sense at the moment, but something of value to you can emerge from it.

JOURNAL BEGINNINGS

Following are additional prompts to support your journaling goals. Read the prompts and select one that stands out to you. Set the timer for five minutes. Write continuously until the timer rings.

- Three things I plan to accomplish this week are . . .

- The thought that keeps coming to my mind is . . .

- Today's newspaper headlines read . . . my reaction to this is . . .

- A risk I plan to take is. . . . The benefits are. . . . This risk is important to me because . . . I will do this by _____ (date).

- This moment, I am thinking/feeling . . .

- Today, for fun I . . .

- One thing I would genuinely like to change about myself is . . .

- My biggest fear is . . .

- What did I accomplish today?

- Look out your window. Write what you see.

- One thing I want to achieve in my life time is _____ because . . .

SENSE SAMPLER

Name three favorite ways to experience the following senses:

Taste	_____	_____	_____
Touch	_____	_____	_____
Smell	_____	_____	_____
Hear	_____	_____	_____
Sight	_____	_____	_____

1. Attempt to experience at least one activity for each sense during the next week.

2. Combine two or more favorite sensory treats at one time.

3. Add more experiences to your list as you think of them.

Follow-Up

1. Describe what you have learned from this activity and how you could apply it further in your life.

TRUST FEAST

What we think we like to eat and drink is influenced by how it looks (sight) and language. To more directly involve the senses of taste, smell, and to some extent, touch, conduct a trust feast.

1. Groups should have at least two persons (it's better with more).

2. Each person brings small morsels of assorted foods and drinks. A wide variety is helpful—vegetables, fruits, meats, sauces, spices, sweets, and so on. Cover the food and beverages so that others cannot see them.

3. Pair off and decide who will be the first to taste. Also ask if there are any allergies or other restrictions.

4. The feeder then selects small samples of the foods and places them in the mouth of the taster, who has her or his eyes closed. The taster is to guess what the food or beverage is. Be experimental and combine different foods and spices in unusual ways (e.g., put mustard on a piece of chocolate). Often a person will like the taste of an unusual food combination if they are not told what it is.

5. Switch roles, so the feeder can become the taster.

Follow-Up

1. Describe what you have learned from this activity and how you could apply it in your life.

SECTION
THREE

GROWTH
DYNAMICS

Change is inherent in growth. In the accompanying magnolia photo we see this change in the stages of bloom—full, partial, and buds representing potential flowering. Similarly, human potentialities exist in various stages of maturity. Growth psychologists contend that there is a basic underlying force directing growth.

> Whether one calls it a growth tendency, a drive toward self-actualization, or a forward-moving directional tendency, it is the mainspring of life. . . . It is the urge which is evident in all organic and human life—to expand, extend, become autonomous, develop, mature—the tendency to express and activate all the capacities of the organism [and] [t]he actualizing tendency can be thwarted or warped, but it cannot be destroyed without destroying the organism. (Rogers, 1980, p. 118; 1961, p. 35).

> We have, each one of us, an essential inner nature which is instinctoid, intrinsic, given, "natural". . . and which tends strongly to persist. . . . Each person's inner nature has some characteristics which all other selves have (species-wide) and some which are unique to the person (idiosyncratic). . . . This inner core or self grows into adulthood only partly by (objective or subjective) discovery. . . . Partly it is also a creation of the person himself. . . . If this essential core is frustrated, denied or suppressed, sickness results (or one becomes) a "diminished or stunted person" (Maslow, 1968, pp. 190–193).

123

"Magnolia" by Nelson Goud. Copyright © 1996.

Barry Stevens (Rogers & Stevens, 1971) refers to this growth tendency as her "built-in pathfinder" that, if listened to, helps a person to see clearly even in times of turmoil. This growth tendency can be inhibited or enhanced by interactions with the outside world (especially other people), and by individual decisions. A person's growth status is the outcome of the continual interaction of this actualizing tendency and demands from the outside world.

Carl Rogers (1961, 1971; Rogers & Freiberg, 1994) describes some valued directions of persons moving toward greater growth and maturity:

- A movement away from facades, pretenses, defensiveness, and putting up a front.
- A movement away from pleasing others as a goal in itself.
- Being real and genuine is positively valued. A person tends to move toward his or her real self and real feelings.
- Self-direction is positively valued. A person discovers an increasing pride and confidence in making choices and guiding his or her life.
- A person becomes more open to experience, becomes increasingly able to sense inner experience and external reality *as it is,* rather than distorting it to fit a preconceived pattern.

The person can react more readily to new people and situations and tolerate more ambiguity with this kind of perception.

- Being a process is positively valued. A person accepts himself or herself as a stream of becoming, not a finished product. A person prefers the process, both fascinating and uncertain, of being in the midst of constantly developing potentialities.
- Others are increasingly appreciated for what they are, just as the person has come to appreciate his or her being. The person seeks to achieve close and real relationships, including the deeply intimate.

Abraham Maslow (1968, 1970) also found the qualities listed above in his studies of self-actualizing persons. He added the following items to the list of self-actualizing characteristics.

- A problem-centered versus an ego-centered orientation. A person devotes much energy to a life mission, a cause, or a task beyond his or her own existence.
- An ability to appreciate, again and again, basic life experiences with awe, pleasure, and wonder.
- A special kind of creativity evident in a person's attitude and unique ways of doing even everyday things.
- A framework of values, a philosophy to live by.

Factors that impede or promote growth are the focus of the readings in this section.

- What does it mean to realize one's potentialities? Humanist psychologist Abraham Maslow discusses nine features of self-actualization in "Self-Actualizing and Beyond."
- Nelson Goud engages in a one-person dialogue on whether an individual is truly unique in "Uniqueness."
- Harold H. Bloomfield and Robert B. Kory present several practical ideas for overcoming feelings of stagnation and powerlessness in "Getting Unstuck: Joyfully Recreating Your Life."
- Guidelines for finding a passion, modifying life dreams, and furthering your education are central issues for the emerging adult. "The Emerging Adult: Finding a Passion, Modifying Dreams, and Further Education" by Nelson Goud addresses these concerns.
- In "The Unpredictable" Nelson Goud contends that unplanned experiences exert major influences in shaping one's life.
- In "The Lesson of the Cliff" Morton Hunt presents a strategy for working through fears.

- How a street peddler affected lives is the subject of Tom Keating's "Herbie."
- An excessive need for control and perfectionism is discussed by Allan E. Mallinger, M.D. and Jeanette DeWyze in "Too Perfect."
- Thoughts on suicide are offered by Poe Ballantine in "Advice to William Somebody." Jenny Montgomery describes the effects of suicide on the survivors in "Left Behind."
- Kinds of courage are outlined in "Courage" by Rollo May.
- In "Vital Moments" Nelson Goud explains the nature of wonder, peak experiences, flow, and psychological epiphanies.
- The danger of both delaying and speeding up growth choices are highlighted in "The Pace of Growth" by John Knowles, an undergrad student, and Nikos Kazantzakis.
- Negating her poem's title, Daphne Haygood-Benyard describes how she is perfect in "No One's Perfect."

Be sure to check out the Follow-Up questions at the end of each article. Applied Activities are presented at the end of this section.

References

Maslow, A. H. (1968). *Toward a psychology of being.* New York: Van Nostrand Reinhold.

Maslow, A. H. (1970). *Motivation and personality.* New York: Harper & Row.

Rogers, C. R. (1961). *On becoming a person.* Boston: Houghton Mifflin.

Rogers, C. R. (1980). *A way of being.* Boston: Houghton Mifflin.

Rogers, C. R., & Freiberg, H. (1994). *Freedom to learn.* New York: Merrill.

Rogers, C. R., & Stevens, B. (1971). *Person to person: The problem.* New York: Pocket Books.

Self-Actualizing and Beyond

Abraham Maslow

What does one do when he self-actualizes? Does he grit his teeth and squeeze? What does self-actualization mean in terms of actual behavior, actual procedure? I shall describe [nine] ways in which one self-actualizes.

First, self-actualization means experiencing fully, vividly, selflessly, with full concentration and total absorption. It means experiencing without the self-consciousness of the adolescent. At this moment of experiencing, the person is wholly and fully human. This is a self-actualizing moment. This is a moment when the self is actualizing itself. As individuals, we all experience such moments occasionally. As counselors, we can help clients to experience them more often. We can encourage them to become totally absorbed in something and to forget their poses and their defenses and their shyness—to go at it "whole-hog." From the outside, we can see that this can be a very sweet moment. In those youngsters who are trying to be very tough and cynical and sophisticated, we can see the recovery of some of the guilelessness of childhood; some of the innocence and sweetness of the face can come back as they devote themselves fully to a moment and throw themselves fully into the experiencing of it. The key word for this is "selflessly," and our youngsters suffer from too little selflessness and too much self-consciousness, self-awareness.

Second, let us think of life as a process of choices, one after another. At each point there is a progression choice and a regression choice. There may be a movement toward defense, toward safety, toward being afraid; but over on the other side, there is the growth choice.

To make the growth choice instead of the fear choice a dozen times a day is to move a dozen times a day toward self-actualization. *Self-actualization is an ongoing process*; it means making each of the many single choices about whether to lie or be honest, whether to steal or not to steal at a particular point, and it means to make each of these choices as a growth choice. This is movement toward self-actualization.

Third, to talk of self-actualization implies that there is a self to be actualized. A human being is not a *tabula rasa*, not a lump of clay or Plasticine. He is something which is already there, at least a "cartilaginous" structure of some kind. A human being is, at minimum, his temperament, his biochemical balances, and so on. There is a self, and what I have sometimes referred to as "listening to the impulse voices" means letting the self emerge. Most of us, most of the time (and especially does this apply to children, young people), listen not to ourselves but to Mommy's introjected voice or Daddy's voice or to the voice of the Establishment, of the Elders, of authority, or of tradition.

As a simple first step toward self-actualization, I sometimes suggest to my students that when they are given a glass of wine and asked how they like it, they try a different way of responding. First, I suggest that they *not* look at the label on the bottle. Thus they will not use it to get any cue about whether or not they *should* like it. Next, I recommend that they close their eyes if possible and that they "make a hush." Now they are ready to look within themselves and try to shut out the noise of the world so that they may savor the wine on their tongues and look to the "Supreme Court" inside themselves. Then, and only then, they may come out and say, "I like it" or "I don't like it." A statement so arrived at is different from the usual kind of phoniness that we all indulge in. At a party recently, I caught myself looking at the label on a bottle and assuring my hostess that she had indeed selected a very good Scotch. But then I stopped myself: What was I saying? I know little about Scotches. All I knew was what the advertisements said. I had no idea whether this one was good or not; yet this is the kind of thing we all do. Refusing to do it is part of the ongoing process of actualizing oneself. Does *your* belly hurt? Or does it feel good? Does this taste good on *your* tongue? Do *you* like lettuce?

Fourth, when in doubt, be honest rather than not. I am covered by that phrase "when in doubt," so that we need not argue too much about diplomacy. Frequently, when we are in doubt we are not honest. Clients are not honest much of the time. They are playing games and posing. They do not take easily to the suggestion to be honest. Looking within oneself for many of the answers implies taking responsibility. That is in itself a great step toward actualization. This matter of responsibility has been little studied. It doesn't turn up in our textbooks, for who can investigate responsibility in white rats? Yet it is an almost tangible part of psychotherapy. In psychotherapy, one can see it, can feel it, can know the moment of responsibility. Then there is a clear knowing of what it feels like. This is one of the great steps. Each time one takes responsibility, this is an actualizing of the self.

Fifth, we have talked so far of experiencing without self-awareness, of making the growth choice rather than the fear choice, of listening to the impulse voices, and of being honest and taking responsibility. All these are steps toward self-actualization, and all of them guarantee better life choices. A person who does each of these little things each time the choice point comes will find that they add up to better choices about what is constitutionally right for him. He comes to know what his destiny is, who his wife or husband will be, what his mission in life will be. One cannot choose wisely for a life unless he dares to listen to himself, *his own self,* at each moment in life, and to say calmly, "No, I don't like such and such."

The art world, in my opinion, has been captured by a small group of opinion- and taste-makers about whom I feel suspicious. That is an *ad hominem* judgment, but it seems fair enough for people who set themselves up as able to say, "You like what I like or else you are a fool." We must teach people to listen to their own tastes. Most people don't do it. When standing in a gallery before a puzzling painting, one rarely hears, "That is a puzzling painting." We had a dance program at Brandeis University not too long ago—a weird thing altogether, with electronic music, tapes, and people doing surrealistic and Dada things. When the lights went up everybody looked stunned, and nobody knew what to say. In that kind of situation most people will make some smart chatter instead of saying, "I would like to think about this." Making an honest statement involves daring to be different, unpopular, nonconformist. If clients, young or old, cannot be taught about being prepared to be unpopular, counselors might just as well give up right now. To be courageous rather than afraid is another version of the same thing.

Sixth, self-actualization is not only an end state but also the process of actualizing one's potentialities at any time, in any amount. It is, for example, a matter of becoming smarter by studying if one is an intelligent person. Self-actualization means using one's intelligence. It does not mean doing some far-out thing necessarily, but it may mean going through an arduous and demanding period of preparation in order to realize one's possibilities. Self-actualization can consist of finger exercises at a piano keyboard. Self-actualization means working to do well the thing that one wants to do. To become a second-rate physician is not a good path to self-actualization. One wants to be first-rate or as good as he can be.

Seventh, peak experiences are transient moments of self-actualization. They are moments of ecstasy which cannot be bought, cannot be guaranteed, cannot even be sought. One must be, as C. S. Lewis wrote, "surprised by joy." But one can set up the conditions so that peak experiences are more likely, or one can perversely set up the conditions so that they are less likely. Breaking up an illusion, getting rid of a false notion, learning what one is not good at, learning what one's potentialities are *not*—these are also part of discovering what one is in fact.

Practically everyone does have peak experiences, but not everyone knows it. Some people wave these small mystical experiences aside. Helping people to recognize these little moments of ecstasy when they happen is one of the jobs of the counselor or metacounselor. Yet, how does one's psyche, with nothing external in the world to point at—there is no blackboard there—look into another person's secret psyche and then try to communicate? We have to work out a new way of communication. I have tried one. It is described in another appendix in that same book, *Religions, Values, and Peak-Experiences,* under the title "Rhapsodic Communications." I think that kind of communication may be more of a model for teaching, and counseling, for helping adults to become as fully developed as they can be, than the kind we are used to when we see teachers writing on the board. If I love Beethoven and I hear something in a quartet that you don't, how do I teach you to hear? The noises are there, obviously. But I hear something very, very beautiful, and you look blank. You hear the sounds. How do I get you to hear the beauty? That is more our problem in teaching than making you learn the ABC's or demonstrating arithmetic on the board or pointing to a dissection of a frog. These latter things are external to both people; one has a pointer, and both can look at the same time. This kind of teaching is easy; the other kind is much harder, but it is part of the counselor's job. It is metacounseling.

Eighth, finding out who one is, what he is, what he likes, what he doesn't like, what is good for him and what bad, where he is going and what his mission is—opening oneself up to himself—means the exposure of psychopathology. It means identifying defenses, and after defenses have been identified, it means finding the courage to give them up. This is painful because defenses are erected against something which is unpleasant. But giving up the defenses is worthwhile. If the psychoanalytic literature has taught us nothing else, it has taught us that repression is not a good way of solving problems.

Ninth,* in examining self-actualizing people directly, I find that in all cases, at least in our culture, they are dedicated people, devoted to some task "outside themselves," some vocation, or duty, or beloved job. Generally the devotion and dedication is so marked that one can fairly use the old words vocation, calling, or mission to describe their passionate, selfless, and profound feeling for their "work."

Put all these points together, and we see that self-actualization is not a matter of one great moment. It is not true that on Thursday at four o'clock the trumpet blows and one steps into the pantheon forever and altogether. Self-actualization is a matter of degree, or little accessions accumulated one by one. Too often our clients are inclined to wait for some kind of inspiration to strike so that they can say, "At 3:23 on this Thursday I became self-actualized!" People selected as self-actualizing subjects, people who fit the criteria, go about it in these little ways: They listen to their own voices; they take responsibility; they are honest; and they work hard. They find out who they are and what they are, not only in terms of their mission in life, but also in terms of the way their feet hurt when they wear such and

**Editor's Note:* This last dimension appeared in a later work of Maslow's. It is included because Maslow emphasized this quality as an attribute of self-actualization.

such a pair of shoes and whether they do or do not like eggplant or stay up all night if they drink too much beer. All this is what the real self means. They find their own biological natures, their congenital natures, which are irreversible or difficult to change.

Follow-Up

1. *Maslow poses nine dimensions of self-actualization. Describe how your life fulfills (or does not fulfill) four of these dimensions.*
2. *Which self-actualization dimension needs the most development in your life? Discuss how you could act on this improvement at this time.*
3. *Maslow states that self-actualizing persons are devoted to a call or work "larger than themselves." How does this statement apply to your life?*
4. *Select two statements from this article and offer your interpretations.*
5. *For further reading, see Maslow's* The Farther Reaches of Human Nature, *Esalen Books, 1971.*

Uniqueness

Nelson Goud

As a kid I spent many hours daydreaming about what I would be when I grew up. I had this intuition that I had some kind of specialness. The intuition was a faint but persistent voice, somewhat like sensing the dim signals sent by a distant star.

I grew up. I look about me for evidence of what I was destined to uniquely accomplish. Maybe I need help—please let me know if you have spotted it. I am even finding out that my special destiny fantasy is quite common, perhaps you have experienced it also. Even my daydreams aren't original.

Sometimes this special destiny illusion persists and lingers until just the right circumstances arise to release it. Then "if only's" get in the way: "I could be great if only I had more time; if only I had the resources and opportunity; if only others didn't make so many demands; if only the sun wasn't in my eyes; if only the world would adjust itself solely to me." Most of us, though, gradually learn that only a rare few invent a cure for a major disease, create pieces of art and music that express the human soul for millions, or develop a theory that completely changes how people view the world and themselves. How humbling to know whatever your accomplishments, only a few will have intimate knowledge of them. Most of what we do in life has either been done before or is, at best, a new variation of themes others have created. Surprisingly I remain unconvinced by my own arguments. The faint inner voice still says, "You are a unique person." So the dialogue must continue.

One comment that makes us feel unique is "You're one in a million." Then we read that the current U.S. population is around 300 million. This means that there are 300 people in the United States just like you. If extended to the world population, there are 6,000 people just like you. You could form a small town made up of persons exactly like you. You would never need a mirror or snivel that "no one understands me." If we buy the estimate that there are 100 billion planets in our galaxy alone that are capable of supporting life forms, then what are our chances of being special or significant?

I still feel unique. Okay, let's try another angle. We can examine our significance and specialness over time. In *The Dragons of Eden*, Carl Sagan condensed the 15 billion year lifetime of the universe into a single calendar year. Here are a few events in the history of the universe, including your life, if they had occurred in twelve months.

- Big Bang: January 1
- Origin of the Milky Way Galaxy: May 1
- Our solar system: September 9
- Earth appears: September 14
- First life on Earth: September 25
- Invention of sex (by microorganisms): November 1
- Oldest photosynthetic plants: November 12
- First humans: December 31 (10:30 p.m.)
- Invention of agriculture: December 31 (11:59:20 p.m.)
- European Renaissance: December 31 (11:59:59 p.m.)

What we studied in history took place in less than a second. Our current lives would not even merit a rapid eye-blink. We are not even cosmic trifles. We make no difference at all. In a way, after some initial chin dragging, this could be welcome news. No longer do we have to despair at a low grade, or get upset by an unfair supervisor, or losing a lover—what difference do they make anyway?

It seems, you may say, that the arguments here are one-sided. You would be correct. There are some unresolved questions concerning human uniqueness. Why is it, for example, that one of life's most fundamental impulses is to produce such astounding variety? Why are there over 1,000,000 species of bugs? At least 175,000 species of trees? Even the green stuff we see on ponds and the seas, algae, has 25,000 forms. Experts won't even venture a guess at how many species of fish there are. There are so many kinds of living organisms that some scientists devote whole careers trying to classify them. My personal favorite, the one-celled Euglena, is so unique that experts cannot determine whether it is a plant or animal—now that's originality!

We are part of a universal life force that presses toward variation and individuality. It is our first affirmation that we have the potential for uniqueness.

Our bodies show uniqueness. With some exceptions for identical twins, each of us has distinctive cell protein makeup, scents, blood antigen combinations, teeth surface patterns, and fingerprints. Differences become even more pronounced between individual humans when we examine the psychological, social, and various mental behaviors. Even identical twins can show wide variations in the latter areas.

Each minute of existence is a changing combination of sensory inputs, other people, and your inner world of thoughts and feelings. How you make sense of these demands minute-by-minute is a distinctive act. No one experiences the world exactly like you, nor can your experience be duplicated. "Every new mind is a new classification . . . and is new in nature," exclaims Emerson (1951, p. 32). This continuing process of unique experiencing is a fundamental source of original ideas and behavior, and of being in the world.

Pulitzer Prize–winning author Annie Dillard claims that our creative uniqueness helps keep the universe together. According to the law of entropy, things eventually disintegrate. Citing Buckminster Fuller, she says that "by creating things, by thinking up new combinations, we counteract this flow of entropy. We make new structures, new wholenesses, so the universe comes out even. A shepherd on a hilltop who looks at a mess of stars and thinks, 'There's a hunter, a plow, a fish,' is making mental connections that have as much real force in the universe as the very fires in those stars themselves."

This whole discussion is starting to get a bit confusing and contradictory. First we see that attaining cosmic uniqueness and significance is futile. We are told that anything we do is not truly original, but a variation on existing themes. Our "special destiny" is but an illusion. Then we are presented with the view that a basic life force compels variety and individuality in all living organisms, even in a one-celled Euglena. In humans this variation is demonstrated in both bodily and psycho-social traits. How we experience life in each moment is offered as a kind of uniqueness.

There is more. . . . The least discussed kind of uniqueness is our *way of being*. The distinctive manner in which we carry out life's activities, the way we do things—this can be a source of true uniqueness. It is not unique to be a teacher, secretary, executive, friend, lover, or parent. But we have a choice on how to perform these and other major life roles. We can perform them in a standard, conventional manner, or we can choose to have them be mediums of our own individual personality.

Sometimes style is substance. Imagine two of your favorite singers singing the same song. It is the style of each performer which makes the performances unique. John Steinbeck describes a woman who was valued for her unique style of human interaction. "She had a way of laughing appreciatively at everything anyone said, and, to merit this applause, people tried to say funny things when she was about. . . . She made people feel good. No one could ever remember that she said anything, but months after hearing it, they could recall the exact tones of her laughter" (p. 160). We know a person has developed an individuality of style when it is said, "I don't know quite how to explain it, but he has a way about him."

Role models can help us develop a way of being. There comes a point, though, when we have to say that we have learned all we could from them and then venture out to find our own voice. Miles Davis, the pioneering jazz trumpeter, is known for his special tone and phrasing. When asked how he learned this style, Davis said that he did not play in this manner at first. Instead, he started by playing like other jazz trumpeters. Eventually he decided to blend techniques from them with his own "feel" of the music. He concluded that "it takes a long time to play like yourself." Thanks, Miles, for taking that time. It will take some time, some experimenting, but we too can learn to "play like ourselves."

Earlier it was contended that only the "greats" create the ideas and products of the first magnitude, the grand themes. This does not mean that there is no room left for originality in our creations—they are just of another magnitude. As the naturalist John Audubon pointed out, "The fields would be very silent if no birds sang there except those

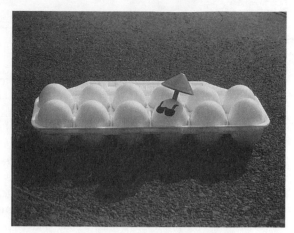

"Unique" by Nelson Goud. Copyright © 1996.

who sang best." What a loss if only the best chirpers sang and they were all in a distant village. What a loss if only the greatest could perform life's tasks—could we exist for long this way? All our voices, especially those that show our special way of being, are needed if life is to function as it is intended.

I've always been a bit puzzled by the philosopher Martin Buber's idea that if there were other persons just like us, then there would be no need for us to be in the world. It is now starting to make sense. Life is *asking us* to share our specialness. This is not a selfish or oddball act. Choosing to share our uniqueness is a profound way to follow a primary life directive and to form a connection with the world. We can contribute a dimension of required newness. It is our choice, though.

So, how are you expressing your specialness?

References

Emerson, R. W. (1951). *Essays by Ralph Waldo Emerson*. New York: Harper & Row.

Steinbeck, J. (1932/1982). *The pastures of heaven*. New York: Penguin Books.

1. *Did you, like the author, have a special destiny intuition as a child? What has happened to it? If it still persists, toward what direction is it pointing?*
2. *It is stated that "Most of what we do in life has either been done before or is, at best, a new variation of themes others have created." Do you agree with this? Explain your answer.*
3. *Relate one or more of the following statements to your life:*
   * *"The distinctive manner in which we carry out life's activities, the way we do things—this can be a source of true uniqueness."*
   * *"It takes a long time to play like yourself." (Miles Davis)*
   * *Choose any other statement that evoked a reaction.*
4. *In what ways are you unique without doing anything but just existing? In what ways do you have to make a conscious choice and effort to develop your uniqueness?*

Getting Unstuck:
Joyfully Recreating Your Life

Harold H. Bloomfield
and Robert B. Kory

I feel trapped. I spend my days wiping runny noses, preparing meals that get cold before they get eaten, doing dishes, clipping supermarket coupons, cleaning house. No matter how hard Jim works, we always seem to be scrimping to get by. This isn't what I had in mind when I said "to have and to hold till death do us part." Some days I get the urge to pack up and leave. Other days I feel depressed, sort of sorry for myself. Most of the time I'm just bored.

These are the words of a young mother, married to a young aerospace engineer. They live in a quiet residential area, have a small house, two cars, and a future that promises them all the comforts of the suburban American lifestyle.

Jim and Barbara love each other, and their marriage has been stable. Neither raves about their sex life, but neither has sought extramarital sexual contact. Casually appraised, they are beneficiaries of the American dream, both college-educated, both products of middle-class families. Nevertheless, Barbara feels she is suffocating; Jim feels too pressured by his work to be of help. Both feel stuck . . . good and stuck.

The "I'm stuck" syndrome, an anhedonic* emotional trap if ever there was one, is reaching epidemic proportions. It's wide-

spread among young marrieds, but the same feelings of depression and resignation are showing up among adults at every stage of life. Perhaps you're feeling stuck in your job. If you're older, you may feel cornered by inflation or illness. Many a mother going back to work soon feels stifled by the limited opportunities. Having played out the singles scene, you may be pessimistic about your chances of finding a lasting relationship that will work. Or you may be twenty years into a bad marriage and unable to get out. The common denominator is the feeling of being caught by a situation beyond your control, it leaves you depressed about the present and resigned to the future.

If you've been bitten hard by the "I'm stuck" bug, you can marshal any number of reasons to justify your frustrations. You may get angry at the company that doesn't recognize your ability and give you the promotion you feel you deserve. You may complain about the government, which mishandles the economy and allows inflation and taxes to keep rising through the roof. If you're a woman, a black, a Chicano, or a member of any other group that has suffered discrimination, you can blame the system that denied you your opportunities. Spouses make excellent targets to blame for your distress.

The frustrations of the "I'm stuck" syndrome may be more or less legitimate: you are facing a very difficult and perhaps oppressive situation. But that insight doesn't accomplish very much other than to justify indulging in self-pity. The important questions are: Why

Editor's Note: Anhedonic is a word derived from the Greek an- (not) and hedone (pleasure) and refers to the inability to experience pleasure. Anhedonic means inhibiting pleasure or interfering with pleasure. For more about anhedonia and anhedonic things, see their book Inner Joy from which this reading was condensed.

do you let difficult situations make you feel powerless? What can you do to start molding your life to suit your desires?

PUTTING IT OFF

Some people get themselves stuck with what may seem to be the best of intentions. They don't want to make trouble for others, or don't want to risk losing what they have in order to create something better. Rather than take control of their lives and accept the risks of growth, they choose to put up with stifling jobs, lingering health problems, collapsing marriages, or destructive habits. It's an anhedonic trap. The longer they procrastinate, the more difficult change becomes, and the more desperate they are likely to feel.

John, a college student, complains, "I can count the number of dates I've had on one hand and not run out of fingers." He's obviously got a sense of humor, but he is afraid to be himself around women. "I'm shy," he says. "That's my nature." John recalls his mother telling people that he was "the shy one." He never realized that his mother had an emotional investment in keeping him tied to her apron strings. John spent his childhood and adolescence living up to the family label of "the shy one." No doubt he had a tendency to be shy as a little boy, but with their labeling, his parents helped him develop that tendency into a full-blown personality characteristic. The question is whether John is going to continue justifying his fears of women with the rationale: "Shyness is my nature." Whenever you resort to a label to explain a negative personality characteristic, you're only making excuses for avoiding the challenge of growth.

Gloria is twenty-six and overweight. She has tried every imaginable diet, managed on several occasions to lose over thirty pounds, but always put the weight back on. She says she wants to shed her excess poundage forever, but in the same breath she reveals why she has always been unsuccessful in her attempts up to now. "I've always had a weight problem, ever since I was a little girl. I must have too many fat cells or a low metabolism or something." Gloria keeps herself stuck with the classic recall to her physiology. What she doesn't see is the hidden payoff. As long as she is fat she has a built-in excuse for feeling lonely and unattractive. Terrified by the prospect of rejection, she avoids it by rejecting herself, then hiding her self-rejection ("I've always been that way"). You may be tall, short, fat, thin, big-bosomed or small-breasted, bushy-headed or bald as a snowball. None of these physiological characteristics is justification for keeping yourself stuck and unhappy. They just aren't that important. Far more significant is your vitality, your friendliness, your self-confidence, your inner joy. These are the qualities you can choose to make outstanding in your life.

Vanessa at twenty-eight has been offered a major promotion at work. A vice-president has asked her to become his administrative assistant. The new job requires that Vanessa polish up on her basic math. Vanessa wants the job, but she is afraid to take it because she has always had difficulty with math. "I barely passed math in high school," she says. "Numbers make me nervous. I can't even balance my checkbook." For sixteen years Vanessa used this "I've always been" to avoid the extra effort required for her to become proficient in basic math. Now she has a choice. She can continue to use her "I've always been that way" as an excuse, or she can decide to focus whatever energy it takes for her to develop her math skills. The first choice is guaranteed to keep her stuck; the second opens broad new possibilities for success. Who knows why she has had difficulty with math in the past? It really doesn't matter, because she has the intelligence to acquire the skills the new job demands. All she needs now is the courage to challenge her "I've always been."

Tim is known for a short temper and frequent angry outbursts. His boss has told him that if he wants to make any kind of progress with the company he will have to learn to control his temper and develop his interpersonal skills. Tim's response has been consistent, "Sure, I have a short temper! I'm Irish." Ever since Tim got into fights on the school playground, his parents indulged his temper with this excuse. Now Tim sits at his desk in a sullen rage; his boss has told him that due to economic pressures on the company, Tim will be out of a job. His boss did not hide the fact that Tim, of all the junior executives, was dismissed because senior management found him hard to work with. This blow was finally enough for Tim to realize he had to make some changes. The alternative was to get stuck not only emotionally, but also economically. Having put all his excuses aside, Tim is now working on developing the emotional skills he needs to be a better manager.

SOME STEPS TOWARD SELF-DIRECTION

Once you have decided to take control, you *have* the power to create your own life according to your personal vision. You *can* establish your own values based on your own experience. To get unstuck, you need to seize this power to break free from your past and transform your intuitions into realities. The decision to take control of your life is a first step. Transforming that decision into action is the real test. Here are some suggestions that you may find useful:

Stop thinking of yourself as fragile.

Behind every anhedonic choice that keeps you stuck is the belief that you (or your life) will fall apart if you challenge the rules. This is a powerful myth! It can keep you absolutely paralyzed! The only way to rid yourself of it is to put your psychological strengths to the test. Few people realize how strong they really are until they stop putting up with the problems in their lives and take some steps toward change. It won't be easy. You may get knocked down a few times, but you won't fall apart. On the contrary, the more you assert your ability to take control over your life, the stronger you'll become. Developing psycho-

logical strengths is just like developing physical abilities. The more you exercise, the stronger you become.

Once and for all, you must eliminate the words wish, hope, and maybe from your vocabulary.

These are sedatives you administer to yourself to numb your sensitivity to your emotional realities. Like any narcotic, wishing and hoping weaken your power to take control of your life. In place of wishing and hoping, you have to substitute a new confidence in your willpower.

Substitute *"I will make it happen"* for "I hope things get better."

Substitute *"I am going to do x, y, z, so I'll feel better"* for "I wish things were better."

Substitute *"I will make my marriage work"* for "Maybe my marriage will still work out."

Start considering yourself too important to put up with anxiety about the obstacles in you life.

The best antidote for anxiety is action. Instead of bemoaning your problems or worrying about the long way to a major goal, take the first step. If your job is suffocating you, stop complaining and put together your résumé. Get any assistance you need to make certain it's the best résumé you can possibly write. If you're in a relationship that is faltering, gather up the courage to have a long talk about your future with your lover. Don't put it off until tomorrow. Do it today! Action, even one small step, breaks the illusion that makes personal problems seem insurmountable. You can only solve your problems one step at a time. Taking the first step has the amazing effect of reducing any problem to life size.

Choose one of your bigger dreams and start making it a reality.

One of my clients had always dreamed of exploring the Inca ruins in Peru. She had never been out of the United States and, as a secretary, didn't earn a large income. Nevertheless, this was the dream she chose. I suggested she contact travel agencies, museums, and local universities to explore all possibilities for her trip. The cost of a commercial tour was out of her reach, but she did discover that she could for a modest cost join an archaeological expedition from a local museum. She paid for some of her expenses and joined in the work as a volunteer. The result was the most rewarding vacation of her life. More: by actualizing just one of her dreams, she broke the cycle of defeatism that was keeping her stuck. Now at twenty-seven she is back at school to study archaeology. Fulfilling a dream is an exercise in discovering personal power. It can turn your life around.

Stop feeling you always have to have a plan.

Plans have their place, but planning involves only half of your brain, the verbal, analytic hemisphere. There is a huge silent dimension of your personality, the intuitive dimension, and you're probably not using it. Scientific research on creativity shows indisputably that the creative process depends just as much on the right brain functions (intuition) as on the left brain operations (analysis and language). If you insist on always having a plan, you cut yourself off from your intuitive self and the inner joy it provides. To break planning addiction, indulge in one freedom. Decide to spend a day exploring a park or a neighborhood with curiosity as your sole guide. Enroll in a local university and take a course that strikes your interest. You never know, it may lead you into a new occupation. The next time you feel attracted to someone you don't know, and want to introduce yourself, go ahead. You're likely to make a new friend. By giving yourself freedom to follow your hunches, even in small ways, you develop your sensitivity to your inner voice. You learn to hear the quiet messages that can make your life an adventure.

CREATE AN INTEGRATED SUCCESS PROFILE

Here are some techniques to help you reshape your success profile.

Begin by giving yourself full permission to succeed.

Most people are held back by the fear that they don't have what it takes. While they may pay lip service to believing in themselves, they turn right around and complain about all the obstacles that stand in the way: the boss, the company, too much work, too little work, too many "bad breaks." The fact is that many successful people do not have exceptional ability and many have limited education. They didn't score at the top in IQ tests, nor did they go to the best schools or get the best grades. Many come from humble backgrounds and have had bad breaks. The common denominator among all successful and happy people is desire, determination, and confidence. Your chance of success and fulfillment is just as good as anyone else's, and probably much better than you think. Only when you understand this key fact can you plunge ahead with enthusiasm and start functioning at your full potential.

Think of success as a process, not a final destination.

Highly successful people don't set out to achieve one grand goal and, on achieving it, pronounce themselves successful. They view their lives as an adventure and themselves as the heroic players. Perhaps this seems a little grandiose to you, but it's far better to think of yourself as a hero and play life to the fullest than to minimize your abilities and never give yourself a chance to exercise all your talents. You are the creator of your life; why not create it heroically? It doesn't matter how old you are or where you may be on the success ladder. You have the power to create a life that will exceed your highest expectations. All you have to do is learn how to use it.

Beware of any lingering fears of success.

It may surprise you to hear that many people block their success by fear, but the facts are there to be examined. Success implies change—in responsibility, life-style, relationships, and many other aspects of life—and for most people change is frightening. They're reluctant to surrender the safety of the routine and the familiar. Except in rare individuals, the instinct to resist change, do nothing, and accept the mediocre is measurably stronger than the desire to succeed.

People undermine their success in subtle ways. They choose wrong jobs, submit to employers who use them, behave in ways that undermine their chances of promotion, rely on weakness out of habit, and ignore strengths out of ignorance. To create a success profile of maximum opportunity you have to put an end to any lingering fears of success. You must be determined to discover your strengths and cultivate your talents; you must learn to relish your own growth.

Set attainable goals and learn to enjoy each small step of progress.

One of the most common ways people sabotage themselves is by trying to achieve too much too fast. There is a Wall Street saying that warns against this folly: "Bulls make money, bears make money, hogs never make money." While learning to take risks is important, foolish risks are nothing other than foolish.

Don't overschedule.

Most people have a tendency to assume they can accomplish more in a given period than they actually can. The problem arises from planning a project without allowing enough extra time for things to go wrong (as they always do). Deadlines are valuable, because most people are more efficient and creative when they accomplish a task within a given period. However, you would be wise in setting your deadlines to allow an extra 20 percent for things to go wrong. When deadlines are so short that they cause anxiety and a last-minute rush, you and your work suffer unnecessarily.

Insulate yourself as much as possible from interruption.

Nothing is more jarring to the nervous system than repeated interruptions when you're in the midst of concentrating on an important problem. One of the worst mistakes is to get into the habit of taking every phone call no matter what you're doing. A good way to handle the telephone is to concentrate your calls in one time segment, say between nine and ten in the morning or four and five in the afternoon. During that time you take all calls, and call people back who called you. You aren't being rude to refuse a call because you are busy. You are being wise. If you are a victim of the telephone, telephone screening can change your work life.

Consciously project ease and enjoyment.

For example, when you're at a meeting, sit back and relax. This is far more effective for listening than sitting on the edge of your chair. When you wish to speak, your movement forward will draw attention and quiet the group. Above all, don't hurry your speech. When you have something important to contribute, there is no rush! Your *words* are going to have an impact on your listeners. Take your time, be brief, and speak clearly. Intersperse pauses after key points. The value of silence is too often ignored. Be sure to enjoy yourself. That way you project maximum power and make others feel most comfortable. It's always a pleasure to listen to someone who is calm, speaks clearly, and projects a natural enthusiasm.

Become aware of your natural optimum work/play cycles.

Just as you have a unique personality, you have an optimum work cycle that is likely to be different than anyone else's. Some people do their best work in the morning, others have an intense burst of concentration toward the end of the day. There are also people who have concentration bursts for brief intervals throughout the day. We call these periods of maximum alertness "prime time." Once you understand your prime time, you can schedule your activities so that you'll tackle the important and challenging ones at your peak creative periods and relegate mundane activities to your low points. Substantial evidence indicates that your prime time and optimum work cycle are biologically or even genetically determined. Trying to force yourself into in unnatural pattern (such as doing your most difficult work in the morning when you concentrate best in the afternoon) is a big mistake. You will cause needless tension, your work will suffer, and you will cheat yourself out of the most important thing of all—enjoying what you're doing.

Identify the conditions that help you get into a "state of flow."

Almost everyone has had the experience of starting work on a project and getting so im- mersed that they completely forget time, fatigue, even where they are. Many hours later, when the task is complete, they become aware that they've been functioning at a unique, high level where creative energies pour out effortlessly. Psychologists call this a state of flow. This wonderful and productive state is not arbitrary. You can learn how to create it and then use it at will to accomplish a great deal of work in the shortest time. The key is learning what conditions trigger the inner shift from ordinary functioning to flow. For some people, quiet is necessary. Most people must be well rested. Time of day is almost always a key factor. Flow is much more likely during your prime time than during a low period. Perhaps you need to be working at a particular desk or computer for flow to happen. There could be any number of critical conditions. Once you have learned what they are, you have made a major discovery. Flow is one of the basic means of "doing less and accomplishing more." It is also a natural state of inner joy, even ecstasy.

Follow-Up

1. *Describe a "stuck" time in your life, indicating how you got stuck and how you got yourself unstuck (or are trying).*
2. *Review the steps toward self-direction in this article. Choose one or more to apply to your life if you are stuck in your growth.*
3. *Select and apply one or more of the ideas mentioned in the section "Create an Integrated Success Profile."*

The Emerging Adult: Finding a Passion, Modifying Dreams, and Furthering Education

Nelson Goud

"Follow your bliss" was the advice mythologist Joseph Campbell gave when asked how to live a fulfilling life. Many twentysomethings would agree with Campbell, but are still seeking what is blissful for them. Here are some guides as offered by Alexandra Robbins in *Conquering Your Quarterlife Crisis* (2004):

> The passion test: "see whether I become oblivious to the world when immersed in that activity" (p. 17)

> Cultivating passion: "Live. A passion is something you discover in your lifetime. It's not gift wrapped up in a pretty package, and it's different from something you're just good at doing. A passion is a sacrifice; you may even say you earn it . . . it comes with a price, but a passion is part of you. There's no sure path to it. You just know you have it. . . . It gets stronger with challenge. It's your lifeblood. It's what's in your spirit." (p. 23)

MODIFYING YOUR LIFE DREAM

If you have been pursuing a life dream or passion but have not attained it, should you let it go or keep plugging at it? According to Robbins, this question is a common dilemma for twentysomethings. The main guideline here is to re-examine your dream and possibly create new approaches. She outlines a four-step process for re-evaluating a life dream.

Dissect Your Dream

Let's say you dream of becoming an actor. You might be convinced that you won't be fulfilling your dream unless you land a full-time acting role on Broadway or in Hollywood. When you're ready to move into the next phase, you could dissect your dream by analyzing which parts of the dream you truly need. Is it the actual acting—the inhabiting of other characters and personalities? The rush of performing in front of other people? Or would you never be satisfied unless you achieved the rank of superstardom?

Gauge What's Realistic

After you've dissected your dream and isolated the part of it that you believe you truly need, it's a good time to work out which aspects of it are realistic versus those that are likely unattainable at this point in your life. This process requires as much objectivity as you can muster and can be a difficult step to work through. If you have credit card debt out the wazoo because you can't support yourself while pursuing an aspect of your dream full time, it's not realistic to think you could continue pursuing it in the same way at this time.

Let Your Heart Soar but Keep Your Head Grounded

Once you have figured out which parts of your dream *are* realistic for now, you can either pursue them full time or chase them part time while working on something else on a parallel track. If your dream doesn't pay the bills, do what you need to do to pay the bills and pursue your dream when you're not at work. It's not all or nothing. You can always, *always* pursue parts of your dream on a smaller, modified scale. If the dream is too far fetched, modify it. Can't be a movie star? Join a local theater troupe or teach acting classes. Can't write for the *New York Times*? Write for a small local paper. You never know where the connections will ultimately lead you; in fact, you could end up on a track that ends up plunking you right where you wanted to be.

As Wanda Lessing, a 28-year-old lawyer, says, "You should never let go of a dream, but it's important to realize that you have to get a job and pay bills, and that's just reality. Somewhere along the line you have to figure out that your dream may not come in the form of your full-time job." Wanda says her work is interesting but unfulfilling. But during her off-hours, she has become heavily involved in her community and in local politics. Last year she was unanimously nominated to run as a candidate for probate judge in her hometown. "Granted, I lost, but I had a good showing, and I found something I'm passionate about: politics and giving back," she says. "I'm still very involved in politics, and I have a lot of fun with it. And, hopefully, at some point in my life, my 'hobby' and my 'career' will intersect."

Consider Other Options

Here's another thought. If you haven't yet been able to achieve your dream, how do you know it's precisely the right path for you? You won't know, of course, until you get there or are on your way. Keeping this in mind, you should remain open to the idea that there may be other ways to get at your dream and other, less obvious paths that might be even more suitable for you and relevant to your passions. (pp. 36–37)

SHOULD I ENROLL IN COLLEGE OR GRAD SCHOOL?

Pursuing life dreams and passions or attempting to become unstuck often involves the issue of continuing one's education. Robbins asked a number of twentysomethings for their advice, and they essentially agreed on the following suggestion:

> Think about your reasons to go back to school and make sure you're doing it for the right ones, *not* because what you're doing now isn't working out and grad school seems like a good alternative. (p. 123)

> If you are considering going to grad school as a stall tactic, simply because you don't know what else to do, then don't. At the very least, find a job, however menial, in the field you would study before you go ahead and apply. . . . You should go to graduate school when you have a plan for exactly what you want to get out of it. (p. 126)

Follow-Up

1. *Select one or more of the themes discussed above and explain how it applies to your life.*

The Unpredictable

Nelson Goud

"No origin is like where it leads to . . . the grape doesn't look like the vine . . . a blossom does not look like seed," observed Rumi, the Persian poet. so it is with who we have become.

Last week I was hiking through Fort Harrison (Indiana) where I was stationed as an Army captain 30 years ago. At the end of the old parade field was a touring replica of the Vietnam Veterans Memorial Wall. I had seen it before but never stopped. This time it beckoned. I knew the reason for the force pulling me toward the Wall. I was assigned to this fort immediately after my graduate studies. It was 1967 and the Vietnam War was in full battle. In January of 1968 the Tet offensive resulted in several hundred American deaths on the first day alone. One of these was a 19-year-old warrior from Indianapolis. I was ordered to be the Survivor Assistance Officer which meant that I was the Army Liaison and responsible for funeral and burial arrangements. As I headed for the Wall, I remember some details of that duty: waiting three weeks for the body to arrive from Vietnam, having to convince family not to open the casket (he was killed by an artillery blast), listening to the honor guard fire off three rounds followed by a bugler playing Taps, trying to remain composed as the mother cradled a U.S. flag.

Strolling along the Wall, I searched for a hint of his name among the 58,191 listed there. Placed against the Wall were flowers, stuffed animals, and photos of those killed. A few persons stood silently gazing at a spot on the Wall. The Wall emits a force field which compels one to respond to it. I was surprised at my own emotional reaction from just walking slowly by the panels. The most intimate act is touching a name on the Wall. You can sense a surge, not unlike a benign electrical current, flowing from the Wall to the one reaching out toward it.

I have yet to find his name. A sign says that the volunteer tent has a name locator. Entering the tent, I notice it has several Vietnam War displays. There is also a table covered with roses and accompanying notes. One said, "Mac, I drop by each time the Wall is in town to see how you're doing.—Love, Ann."—My emotional lid was loosening, and I walked to the locator table.

"I believe his last name is R___." I stated. "It has been over 30 years and that is all I recall."

The volunteer opened a larger folder and asked, "Was his first name David?"

The lid came off for a couple of seconds, and I could not answer. My son's name is David. I put on my sunglasses and responded. "I don't know his first name, but if he is the only R___ from Indianapolis, killed in January of 1968, then that would be him." I was given a one-page printout of his military history—all of 10 months. His name was inscribed on section 36E of the black granite Wall. Afterwards I realized he was only five years younger than me. If he had lived, he would be in his 50's and probably griping about the heat on this July 4th weekend and wondering how many hot dogs to get for the family reunion tonight. But this did not happen, and all that is there is his name in white letters on a slab of polished stone. He does not know the impact of the man now looking at his name.

Within a week after his burial, I was asked, on the spot, to explain to a new class of lieutenants what it was like to be a Survivor

Assistance Officer. When I finished, the instructor of the course thanked me and then asked, "Have you considered becoming a full-time instructor here? I'll recommend you." I found the idea appealing. There was an opening that month and I was accepted. Four months later, I was also teaching psychology two nights a week at a nearby university. At the end of my tour of duty, the university asked if I would like to join them as an assistant professor. Becoming a university professor was not among my career choices when I began an Army tour. But now it was the most preferred choice and that is how I became a professor.

Rumi was right, life outcomes often do not resemble their origins. In my case . . . becoming a professor, writing/editing a book, playing trumpet in several countries with volunteer bands, starting an alternative school, meeting almost all of my friends and non-family significant others . . . these and many other life outcomes all had their starts from unlikely (and usually unanticipated) origins. Try it yourself: trace the steps of one of your life outcomes to its beginnings. How did you choose a major, get a job, meet your lover/spouse or pursue a special interest or hobby?

Life paths depend as much on the unpredictable as the predictable. Compare yourself now to the person and life circumstances of ten years ago. How many events since then could you have accurately predicted? Our lives are continually shaped by the unexpected and the unplanned. Destinations are greatly influenced by random encounters, chance readings, fortune and misfortune, serendipities, epiphanies, and synchronicities (meaningful coincidences). Even your origin was a chance event—if the sperm swimming right next to yours had been a jot faster, someone else would be here now.

Embracing both the predictable and unpredictable is essential in the art of good living. Sometimes purposeful efforts permit one to reap the benefits of the unplanned. "Chance favors only the prepared mind," argued Louis Pastuer. My decision to become a professor was a combination of the unexpected (the chain of events triggered by a soldier's burial) and planned experiences (primary university studies). Pasteur's observation, though, omits another truth, that is, an *overprepared* mind may be unresponsive to the gifts of unexpected occurances. It is possible to arrange a life completely dominated by schedules, clocks, and crammed daily planners. Life then becomes a giant Things To Do list requiring one to scurry about like the Roadrunner saturated with triple espressos. Even the Bluebird of Happiness could land on one's shoulders only to be swatted away because its chirping interferred with multi-tasking.

Pasteur's quote must be amended to include—"Chance ignores the cluttered mind." A prepared mind possesses not only relevant skills and knowledge, but also is primed to detect offerings from unpredictable sources. It means respecting the boundaries of what can be known, controlled, or mapped out. It means being mindful to the possibilities on the periphery. It means trusting one's capabilities to adapt to the unanticipated.

We seek opposites. We are drawn to the known and predictable for their safety and security. Many like to know where they are going and precisely how to get there. But as John Steinbeck expressed it, "I know people who are so immersed in road maps that they don't see the countryside they pass through." We also possess the opposing attraction for the unknown as it is the source of the basic human yearnings for wonder, mystery, and curiosity. The opposing attractions of these two forces is demonstrated in this scenario, you are presented with a detailed life calendar of your future—How much of it would you need?

Not long ago I was attempting, without success, to photograph some California quail in a national part. These fleet birds were camera shy and dashed into brush cover each time I raised my camera. Finally one came out in the open. Just as I was ready to take a shot, my peripheral vision registered movement in shrubbery and saw the head of a bobcat peering out at me. I did not know that bobcats lived here, but I did know photographing a bobcat in its natural surroundings was a rare opportunity. The bobcat started to walk away and then turned its head back to me as if to say, "I'll stop here for a second or two for your photos, but then leave me alone." I intended to photograph the common quail and instead obtained two nice photos of a bobcat. There seemed to be some lessons here. Plan for what you can foresee. Start walking. Travel with a mind that can see bobcats in the periphery.

Follow-Up

1. *The author asks you to compare yourself to the person you were ten years ago and then estimate how many events since then you could have accurately predicted. He contends that a good portion of your experiences in the past decade were unplanned and unexpected. Is this true for you? Explain the consequences of this idea if it is true for you.*
2. *Choose at least one statement from the article and offer a personalized commentary.*

The Lesson of the Cliff

Morton Hunt

It was a sweltering July day in Philadelphia—I can feel it still, 56 years later. The five boys I was with had grown tired of playing marbles and burning holes in dry leaves with a lens and were casting about for something else.

"Hey!" said freckle-faced little Ned. "I got an idea. We haven't climbed the cliff for a long while."

"Let's go!" said someone else. And off they went, trotting and panting like a pack of stray dogs.

I hesitated. I longed to be brave and active, like them, but I'd been a sickly child most of my eight years and had taken to heart my mother's admonitions to remember that I wasn't as strong as other boys and not to take chances.

"Come on!" called Jerry, my best friend. "Just because you've been sick is no reason to be a sissy." "I'm *coming!*" I yelled, and ran along after them.

Through the park and into the woods we went, finally emerging in a clearing. At the far side, 40 to 50 feet away, loomed the cliff, a bristling, near-vertical wall of jutting rocks, earth slides, scraggly bushes and ailanthus saplings. From the tumbled rocks at its base to the fringe of sod at its top, it was only about 60 feet high, but to me it looked like the very embodiment of the Forbidden and Impossible.

One by one, the other boys scrabbled upward, finding handholds and toeholds on rocky outcrops and earthen ledges. I hung back until the others were partway up; then, trembling and sweating, I began to climb. A hand here, a foot there, my heart thumping in my skinny chest, I made my way up and up.

At some point, I looked back—and was horrified. The ground at the base of the cliff seemed very far below; one slip and I would fall, bouncing off the cliff face and ending on the rocks. There, shattered and strangling on my own blood, I would gurgle, twitch a few times, and then expire, like the cat I had seen run over a few days earlier.

But the boys were chattering above me on an earthen ledge two-thirds of the way to the top. It was 5 to 6 feet deep and some 15 feet long. I clawed my way up to them; then I crawled as far back on the ledge as I could, huddling against the rock face. The other boys stood close to the edge and boldly urinated into space; the sight made me so queasy that I surreptitiously clutched at the rocks behind me.

In a few minutes, they started up to the top.

"Hey, wait," I croaked.

"So long! See you in the funny papers," one of them said, and the others laughed.

"But I can't . . . I . . . " That spurred them on: jeering and catcalling back to me, they wriggled their way to the top, from where they would walk home by a roundabout route. Before they left, they peered down at me.

"You can stay if you want to," mocked Ned. "It's all yours." Jerry looked concerned, but he went with the others.

I looked down and was overcome by dizziness; a nameless force seemed to be impelling me to fall off. I lay clinging to a rock as the world spun around. I could never climb back down. It was much too far to go, too hazardous; partway, I would grow feeble or faint, lose my grip, fall and die. But the way up to the top was even worse—higher, steeper, more treacherous; I would never make it. I heard someone sobbing and moaning; I wondered who it was and realized that it was I.

Time passed. The shadows gradually lengthened, the sun disappeared from the treetops beyond the clearing below, dusk began to gather. Silent now, I lay on my stomach as if in a trance, stupefied by fear and fatigue, unable to move or even to think of how to get back down to safety and home.

January 1945, Watton Air Base, East Anglia. This morning I found my name posted on the blackboard: Tomorrow I fly another weather reconnaissance mission over enemy territory. All day my mind was whirling; at dinner I felt as if I might throw up at any moment.

I knew that I needed a good night's sleep, so I took a pill and went to bed early, but I could not make myself stop imagining the endless flight in which I, as pilot, and my navigator would venture in our unarmed twin-engine Mosquito far into German-held territory.

Hour after hour I thrashed around in bed; from time to time I would drift off, only to wake with a dreadful start, gasping for breath, my heart flopping like a beached fish as I imagined the shellburst in the cockpit, the blood and the sickening white-hot pain, the fire, smoke and spurting oil, the Mozzie winging over into a spin while I, shattered and half-conscious, am too weak either to fight the controls or pull myself up and out the escape hatch as the plane screams down and down.

Next morning, in the locker room, as I get into my flight outfit, it is clear to me that I simply can't do it. The mission is a 1000-mile trip, three hours of it over German-held territory and Germany itself—too deep in to go unnoticed. I can't possibly strap myself into that defenseless little plane and, with my own hands and feet, make it climb 5 miles high,

guide it out over the winter sea and into a Europe bristling with Nazi anti-aircraft batteries, radar stations and fighter planes, and finally make it back to safety.

Even as I zip up my boots and pull on my helmet, I know I can't. I will get in the plane, warm up and check out the engines, but at the runway my hands will freeze on the controls, and I will be unable to make the plane move.

January 1957, New York. I'm delirious with joy.

I've always felt that if I didn't write a book by the time I was 40, I'd never do so. With only three years to go, I've been offered a book contract—by the most distinguished of American publishers. Alfred Knopf himself, after reading an article of mine, had written to invite me to submit a proposal. After months of hard work, I had turned in an outline and sample chapter. Now Knopf and his editors have said yes.

But, later in the day, I begin to fear that I have made a terrible mistake. I've suggested a history of love, tracing its evolution from the time of the early Greeks to the present—a vast project, but fun to think about and to sketch in outline form. Yet now that the moment of truth has come, I see how rash I've been. Having spent months researching and writing the sample chapter, I can look ahead—and what I see is frightening.

How could I have imagined I'd ever be able to learn what love meant to the ancient Greeks, to the imperial Romans, to the ascetic early Christians, to the knights and ladies of the Middle Ages, to—? Enough! It's hopeless, impossible, more than any one person can do.

Or, at least, more than I can do. Even if I found everything I needed in the library and took reams of notes, how could I ever make sense of it all? Or organize it? Or write about it entertainingly, sentence after sentence, page after page, chapter after chapter? Only now,

"Coming to a Roadblock" by tom mcCain. Copyright © 1996.

when a contract is being offered me, can I see clearly what I will have to do—and realize that I cannot.

June 1963, New York. I am lying in bed, sleepless, although it is 2 a.m.; I suspect that she, quiet in the dark next to me, is awake too. Tonight we agreed that it was useless to go on and that I should move out as soon as I can.

But I feel as if the ground is giving way beneath me, as if I am falling through space. How can we ever decide how to divide our possessions and our savings? How will we work out my rights as an absentee father? Will I be able to find a place for myself and, without help, make it homelike? I have never lived alone, how will I feel when I close the door at night and am imprisoned in my solitude?

What will I tell my family, and how will they take it? Will my married friends shun me? What can I say to my 8-year-old son, and what will happen to his feelings about me? Where will I meet single friends? Whom will I talk to, eat with, share my life with? I haven't the least idea how to start; I haven't been single since my 20s.

Yet what if, somehow, after a while, I were to meet the right woman and feel desire stirring in me? But here my mind goes blank. I haven't been to bed with another woman in over 17 years; how should I behave, what should I do? What if my hesitant actions are scorned? What if I seem clumsy, gross, nervous, foolish?

And even if all goes well, how will I know whether what I feel is love or only lust? Can I trust myself to love again—or trust anyone else to love me? Will anyone, could anyone, ever do so? Will I ever want to marry again? There is so much to be said, learned, worked out first; so many hints, allusions, promises, bargains, plans; so many beliefs and tastes to be exchanged and harmonized—no, it is too hard a road to travel, too remote a goal. I can't do it.

Twilight, a first star in the sky, the ground below the cliff growing dim. But now in the woods the beam of a flashlight dances about and I hear the voices of Jerry and my father. My father! But what can he do? Middle-aged and portly, he cannot climb up here. Even if he could, what good would that do?

Staying well back from the foot of the cliff so that he can see me, he points the beam up and calls to me. "Come on down, now," he says in a perfectly normal, comforting tone. "Dinner's ready."

"I can't!" I wail. "I'll fall, I'll die!"

"You got up," he says. "You can get down the same way. I'll light the way."

"No, I can't!" I howl. "It's too far, it's too hard, I can't do it."

"Listen to me," my father says. "Don't think about how far it is, how hard it is. All you have to think about is taking one little step. You can do that. Look where I'm shining the light. Do you see that rock?" The beam bounces around on a jutting outcrop just below the ledge. "See it?" he calls up.

I inch over. "Yes," I say.

"Good," he says. "Now just turn around so you can put your left foot on that rock. That's all you have to do. It's just a little way below you. You can do that. Don't worry about what comes next, and don't look down any farther than that first step. Trust me."

It seems possible. I inch backward, gingerly feel for the rock with my left foot and

find it. "That's good," my father calls. "Now, a little bit to the right and a few inches lower, there's another foothold. Move your right foot down there very slowly—that's all you have to do. Just think about that next step, nothing else." I do so. "Good," he says. "Now let go of whatever you're holding onto with your left hand and reach back and grab that skinny tree just at the edge, where my light is. That's all you have to do." Again, I do so.

That's how it goes. One step at a time, one handhold at a time, he talks me down the cliff, stressing that I have only to make one simple move each time, never letting me stop to think of the long way down, always telling me that the next thing I have to do is something I *can* do.

Suddenly I take the last step down onto the tumbled rocks at the bottom and into my father's strong arms, sobbing a little, and then, surprisingly, feeling a sense of immense accomplishment and something like pride.

January 1945. I taxi out onto the runway and firmly shove the throttles forward. I remember at last that I *know* how to do what I must. All I have to do is take off and climb to 25,000 feet, heading eastward over East Anglia; that's all I need think about right now. I can do that.

Later: The North Sea is just ahead. All I have to do, I tell myself, is stay on this heading for about 20 minutes, until we have crossed over Schouwen Island in the Netherlands. That's all; I can do it.

Over Schouwen Island, my navigator tells me to turn to a heading of 125 degrees and hold it for 10 minutes, until we reach our next checkpoint. Good; that's not so hard; I can do that.

That's how it goes. I drive the roaring little plane across Holland and Germany, high over fields and woods, cities, rivers and mountain ranges, never envisioning the whole trip but only the leg we are flying, never thinking of the hours ahead but concentrating on getting through each brief segment of time, each measured span of miles, until at last sunlight dazzles off the wrinkled sea ahead of us and in a few minutes we are out of enemy territory, safe and still alive.

January 1957. After tossing about much of the night, thinking about the impossibly ambitious book I had said I could write, I remember the old lesson once again: Though I know what the goal is, I can avoid panic and vertigo if I look only at the next step.

I'll keep my gaze on the first chapter. All I have to do is read whatever I can find in the library about love among the Greeks; that isn't impossibly hard. Then I'll tell myself that all I have to do is sort out my notes, dividing the chapter into a number of sections; I can do that. Then I'll make myself look no further ahead than writing the first section. And with that thought, I heave a great sigh and fall asleep.

And that's the way I spend more than two and a half years. Then, one exhilarating afternoon, the last of 653 pages emerges from my typewriter and, like a boy, I turn somersaults on the living room floor in sheer joy. Some months later, I hold in my hands the first copy of my book, *The Natural History of Love*—already chosen by the Book of the Month Club—and a few weeks after that I read my first major review, praising the book, in the *New York Times Book Review.* For a while, I occasionally leaf through the book, marveling that I could ever have done all this—and knowing that I learned how, long ago, in the dusk on the face of a small cliff.

September 1963. I unlock the door of my tiny apartment, carry my bags in and close the door behind me. I have taken one step; it wasn't so hard. I had remembered the lesson that I have applied again and again throughout my life; one step at a time, one step that I can manage.

The first was to find an apartment; I looked no further into the future until I had done that. Then I went about furnishing my two rooms, I looked no further ahead until that was done. Today, I am moving in; I have made my own little nest, and it looks pleasant. I unpack, make a few phone calls, fix lunch, feel at home. Good; I've taken that step.

By the next year, I have constructed a new life, gotten my final divorce decree, acquired the social and emotional skills that I need as a middle-aged single man (I would remain one for five years), and even have become a passable bachelor cook. And discovered once more, to my surprise, that I do know how to make my way toward a distant, difficult goal.

I have realized with the same surprise, time and again throughout my life, that, having looked at a far and frightening prospect and been dismayed, I can cope with it after all by remembering the simple lesson I learned so long ago. I remind myself to look not at the rocks far below but at the first small and relatively easy step and, having taken it, to take the next one, feeling a sense of accomplishment with each move, until I have done what I wanted to do, gotten where I wanted to be, and can look back, amazed and proud of the distance I have come.

Follow-Up

1. *Describe a problem that overwhelmed you, but which you might have dealt with successfully by working on it one step at a time.*
2. *Describe a problem that you dealt with successfully by working on it one step at a time.*
3. *Describe a formidable problem or task that you now face in your life. What is the first step that you might take toward its mastery?*

Herbie

Tom Keating

If you have lived between 16th Street and Broad Ripple in the last 25 years you probably have seen him a dozen times and likely bought his goods.

He is a little old fellow, slightly stooped. He walks with a shuffle and always carries two shopping bags. And he always smiles.

His name is Herbert Wirth. Most people call him Herbie. He is 72 and has made his living since 1944 selling dishrags and wash cloths door to door.

He has never owned a car. He calculates he has walked more than 50,000 miles since he began his selling career at the age of 57 after losing his job at a dry goods company.

He works 9 a.m. to 6 p.m. six days a week and doesn't stop for lunch.

But, he doesn't just pick a street at random and start selling.

"Everything I do has been worked out systematically over the years through trial and error," he explained.

"I start at 46th Street and Winthrop Avenue and in one day will work up the east side of Winthrop to the canal in Broad Ripple. Then the next day I'll work the west side of Winthrop all the way to the canal again. After that I just keep moving over a street every day working from 46th to the canal until I reach Boulevard Place.

"After that I start again at 46th and Winthrop and this time work down to Fall Creek. Again I work one street at a time until I get to Pennsylvania Street. Every day I cover at least one whole side of a street, catching the side streets as I go along.

"It takes me about four months to complete the whole circuit. Then I start all over again. This way I get around to my customers three times a year.

"The reason I don't bother with lunch is because I found out that it takes me almost exactly nine hours to cover one street, and if I stop to eat it throws my schedule off. I do stop for a glass of water several times during the day. People are real nice about that."

Wirth starts each day with two large shopping bags filled to the brim with the six items he sells—dishrags, wash cloths, pot scrapers, large red handkerchiefs, two sizes of ladies hankies and black, brown and white shoelaces.

"I sometimes think the weight of the bags (25 pounds each at the start) acts as an incentive for me to sell.

"My feet never bother me. I guess once you get used to walking a lot, your feet get tough. It varies how much I sell each day. I usually average around 40 dishrags, 35 wash cloths and 25 pot scrapers. They all sell for a quarter."

"I use psychology in my work. There is a great art to selling. I try not to make a pest of myself. If people want my products, fine. If not, I thank them and be on my way. I don't try to play on people's sympathy. I don't want them to buy anything they can't use just because they feel sorry for me.

"I know many housewives are afraid of door-to-door salesmen, but by now most everyone knows me so I have somewhat of an advantage in this respect. I even have people who call me at home now to order articles.

"The Northside has changed a lot in the last 25 years, but the people have stayed about the same. Most are basically good. I get a door slammed in my face once in a while, but only once or twice a year.

"And regardless of what a lot of people say about youngsters, they are every bit as nice today as they were in the 1940s and 1950s.

"I get along with kids and dogs real well. I've always heard that postmen have trouble with dogs. I've never been able to figure that out. I guess some people just don't understand dogs."

Born in Lake Forest, Ill., Wirth moved here at the age of 13. He lives in a small house almost in the middle of his territory.

"When you get to be 72 you find yourself looking back and wondering what would have happened to your life if you had done this or that at a certain time. But, it's too late at my age to do anything but wonder. I guess that is the worst thing about growing old.

"I don't see any reason I can't keep working for many years. I feel great and I think I'd go out of my mind if I had to sit around and loaf every day.

"I've always taken life very seriously— probably too seriously. I've never had the time for many hobbies. In my free time about all I do is watch TV and read. I made the mistake of never getting married when I was young and now I don't have any close family. I live by myself and it's not too much fun.

"I know that selling dishrags is not the most important job in the world. I sometimes have envied men who are doing exciting and glamorous things.

"There won't be much of a dent in the world when I die, but at least I can say I made an honest to God try to do what I did as a nice man."

[One year later.] Despite the fact he was well known, he had no relatives so he lived alone for the last 20 years or so and worked at his job with few complaints and few fears.

But, he was afraid of one thing—that he wouldn't have anyone at his funeral.

He explained two years ago that he didn't mind living alone, except maybe at Christmas, but he didn't like the idea of dying without someone taking the time to say a few prayers for him and remember that he had "tried to be a good man."

Saturday, Herbert Wirth died of a heart attack in a Northside supermarket. There was some concern for a while because no relatives could be found to handle the funeral arrangements.

But Herbie had known that this would be the case and on March 5, 1968, he had paid cash to the Flanner and Buchanan Mortuaries for a complete funeral and burial.

He requested that there be no service in the funeral home nor in a church. All he wanted was a graveside service.

And that some people be there.

Something kind of strange and warm and you might even say wonderful happened in Indianapolis yesterday.

More than 1,000 persons showed up for the funeral of a 73-year-old man who sold dishrags door to door.

Not a tycoon nor a big politician nor a sports idol—just a little old fellow who lived alone and peddled odds and ends on the Northside for 25 years and never did anything special except be himself.

His name was Herbie Wirth and he said a couple of years ago that he didn't want to be buried without someone there to say a prayer or two for him.

A newspaper story Tuesday mentioned this wish and everyone thought maybe 10 or 20 or even 30 people might show up for the graveside services at Crown Hill Cemetery.

But shortly before 10 a.m. a huge bell in the cemetery gate tower began ringing for the first time in more than 40 years and when the services started there were more people present than have attended a graveside funeral in this city in possibly 20 years, according to cemetery officials.

The people who were there were white and black, old and young, rich and poor.

They were soldiers in uniform, flower children with long flowing hair, businessmen in suits and overcoats, women carrying babies, truck drivers, elderly people who had to be helped up the icy hill to the grave, and teenagers cutting school.

Wives and husbands who hadn't told each other of their plans, met unexpectedly at the grave.

Many of these people said they didn't even know Herbie. Many others did. For whatever reason they came, not one stood to gain a thing, not even gratitude.

Coming to this funeral was not a casual stop. Many had to park their cars at least a mile from the grave and walk over hills in a snowstorm in 20-degree weather.

Why did so many come?

Well, you think it might have something to do with the almost universal fear of being alone, of having no one. You think it might also be because Herbie was well-liked and the simplicity of his life was what was being honored.

But when a thousand people stand in freezing weather to pay homage to a little man who was neither rich nor famous, you have to think above all that it is simply because a lot of people do care about others.

Someone brought a large guest book to the grave and most of the people present signed it before leaving.

Because Herbie had no relatives, the book was placed in the casket with him.

It was a very full book.

Follow-Up

1. *What are your feelings and thoughts about Herbie's story?*
2. *Tom Keating gave his conclusions on why so many people attended Herbie's funeral at the end of the article. Comment on his interpretations and possibly add your own if different from Keating's.*
3. *Did Herbie live a life in a healthy, responsible manner according to the concepts mentioned in the earlier articles by Goud, Arkoff, and the psychologists cited in the introduction?*

Too Perfect

*Allan E. Mallinger, M.D.,
and Jeanette DeWyze*

This is . . . about people who are too perfect for their own good.

You know them. You may be one of them. And if you are, you have much to be proud of. You're one of the solid, good people of the world: honest, reliable, hardworking, responsible, exacting, self-controlled.

But for many people there is also a dark side to this perfection. The very traits that bring them success, respect, and trust can also cause them serious problems. These people aren't fully able to savor relationships with others and with the world at large, nor are they at ease with themselves in their universe. Consider:

- The person so driven to meet professional and personal goals that she can't abandon herself to a few hours of undirected leisure without feeling guilty or undisciplined.
- The person so preoccupied with *making the right choice* that he has difficulty making even relatively simple decisions usually regarded as pleasurable: buying a new stereo; choosing where to go on vacation.
- The person so finicky that his pleasure is spoiled if everything isn't "just so."
- The "thinkaholic" whose keen, hyperactive mind all too often bogs her down in painful worry and rumination.
- The perfectionist, whose need to improve and polish every piece of work chronically causes her to devote much more time than necessary to even inconsequential assignments.

- The person so intent upon finding the ultimate romantic mate that he seems unable to commit to *any* long-term relationship.
- The person so acclimated to working long hours that she can't bring herself to cut back, even when confronted with evidence that the overwork is ruining her health or her family relationships.
- The procrastinator who feels angry at his "laziness"—unaware that the real reason he is unable to undertake tasks is that his need to do them flawlessly makes them loom impossibly large. . . .

If there is a single quality that characterizes obsessive people it is a powerful, unconscious need to feel in control—of themselves, of others, and of life's risks. One of the primary ways in which this need manifests itself is perfectionism. A whole family of personality traits is rooted in these two needs—to be in control and to be "perfect." These include:

- a fear of making errors
- a fear of making a wrong decision or choice
- a strong devotion to work
- a need for order or firmly established routine
- frugality
- a need to know and follow the rules
- emotional guardedness
- a tendency to be stubborn or oppositional
- a heightened sensitivity to being pressured or controlled by others

- an inclination to worry, ruminate, or doubt
- a need to be above criticism—moral, professional, or personal
- cautiousness
- a chronic inner pressure to use every minute productively . . .

A SELF TEST

The first step is recognizing and understanding the cluster of traits that constitute the obsessive personality. To help you determine if you (or a loved one) are obsessive, I've prepared the following questionnaire, intended as a further clarification of the family of obsessive traits.

1. Do you get caught up in details, whether you're preparing a report for work or cleaning out the garage at home?
2. Is it hard for you to let go of a work project until it's just right—even if it takes much longer than it should?
3. Have you often been called picky or critical? Or do you feel you are?
4. Is it important to you that your child, spouse, or subordinates at work perform certain tasks in a certain specific manner?
5. Do you have trouble making decisions? (For example, do you go back and forth before making a purchase, planning a vacation, or choosing what to order from a menu?)
6. After you do make a decision, do you find yourself second-guessing or doubting your choice?
7. Do you find it embarrassing to "lose control" and be emotional (e.g., to look nervous, weep, or raise your voice in anger)?
8. At the same time, do you sometimes find yourself wishing it were easier for you to show your feelings?
9. Do you have a particularly strong conscience, or do you often feel guilty?
10. Is self-discipline important to you?
11. Are you especially wary of being controlled, manipulated, overpowered, or "steam-rollered" by others?
12. Is it important for you to get a "good deal" in your financial transactions, or are you often suspicious of being "taken"?
13. Do you think you're more guarded than most people about sharing your possessions, time, or money?
14. Do you tend to be secretive? That is, are you reluctant to reveal your motives or feelings?
15. Is it hard for you to let yourself be dependent on others, rather than self-reliant? (For instance, are you uneasy about delegating tasks at work or hiring help with taxes or home repairs?)
16. Do you have trouble putting a problem out of your mind until it's resolved, even when you're doing other things?
17. In thinking about some future event, such as a vacation, a dinner party, or a job report, do you dwell upon the things that might go wrong?
18. Do you worry more than most people?
19. Do you derive a great deal of your sense of worth from being able to perform your job flawlessly?
20. Do you get extremely upset when someone is unhappy with or critical of a piece of work you have done, even when the criticism is mild or valid?
21. Do you feel that your family life, social life, or leisure-time enjoyment is being damaged or compromised by the amount of worry, time, or energy you put into work?
22. Do you feel guilty when you aren't getting something done, even in your time off (no matter how hard you've worked all week)?
23. Do you make lists of things you "should" do, even in your spare time?
24. Do even occasional "white lies" bother you?
25. Do you find it hard to trust that things will probably turn out for the best?

INTERPRETING YOUR RESPONSES

If you find yourself answering "yes" to more than just a few of these questions, you (or your loved one) are probably at least somewhat obsessive. Now look once again at the questions to which you answered "yes," and for each one, answer a second question: Does this characteristic cause difficulties in relationships, work, or leisure activities, or does it interfere with your ability to enjoy life in general? If you answer "yes" to this *even once,* you will benefit from learning more about obsessiveness and about the possibility for change.

Before beginning, however, I offer this cautionary note: If you are strongly obsessive, you're a careful person who finds security in sameness and predictability. You're more wary of change and newness than the average person—and changing isn't easy for anyone!

But change is always possible. It may involve time and struggle. It may occasionally be painful. But it can be a journey toward a happier, more relaxed and fulfilling life. . . .

Thinking in Extremes

These examples point up an important characteristic of many obsessives: their tendency to think in extremes. To yield to another person, for example, may be felt as a humiliating total capitulation. Similarly, to tell one lie, break one appointment, tolerate a spouse's criticism just once, or shed a single tear is to set a frightening precedent. One patient told me she hated to miss even a single workout because it made her feel she couldn't trust herself, and that frightened her.

This all-or-nothing thinking occurs partly because obsessives rarely live in the present. They think in terms of trends stretching into the future. *No* action is an isolated event; each is merely a part of something bigger, so every false step has major ramifications.

Such distorted thinking can cause a host of problems. I've known obsessives, for instance, who had trouble relaxing and enjoying first dates because they were so preoccupied with the possible remote consequences of such occasions. ("Would I want to marry this person?") In all-or-nothing thinking, one's perspective is badly distorted; there's a failure to step back and remind oneself that going out with someone *doesn't* commit one to any long-term romance.

Another consequence of such thinking is that it aggravates the pain of worry and rumination. Obsessives tend to envision the worst possible outcome of a scenario and then worry as if such a scenario had in fact come to pass. Or they will mentally magnify small personal gaffes into something far more serious. Some of my patients have had trouble sleeping after briefly losing their composure in a therapy group, assuming that the others had judged this "emotional lapse" as harshly as they themselves did. . . .

The Cosmic Scorekeeper

Many obsessives quell their anxiety about life's possible catastrophes in still another way. At an unconscious level they convince themselves that terrible things will not happen to them simply because *life is fair.*

This conviction, though deeply buried and therefore unspoken, is crucial to obsessives. They can't bear to face the reality that they are at least somewhat at the mercy of such haphazard or uncontrollable forces as accidents, illness, and the peculiarities of others. Facing this fact would be terrifying because to the obsessive's all-or-nothing way of thinking, imperfect protection is the same as *no* protection at all.

Their "fairness doctrine" helps them to hold on to the illusion of control. And intertwined with the conviction of cosmic justice, most obsessives hold a belief, also unconscious, in what I call the Cosmic Scorekeeper. The Scorekeeper may dovetail with a belief in an established religion, but I've also seen plenty of atheists with the unconscious faith that an omnipresent, omnipotent force assesses and reconciles the score, thus ensuring that people get what they deserve. This notion enables obsessives to believe that they can control their destiny by being good or bad.

They can guarantee themselves safe passage by making the Scorekeeper *owe* it to them. They do this by piling up a track record of self-denial, sacrifice, industry, diligence, honesty, and loyalty rivaling that of a saint. They try to avoid behaviors, feelings, even thoughts that will subtract points from their stockpile of sacrifices. They avoid selfishness, lust, dishonesty, laziness, hedonism. Even enjoying themselves costs them points!

Before doing something "selfish," they may need to earn it by performing some distasteful (but noble) duty. They might put in extra overtime at work, or undertake an unpleasant home-repair project. Such sacrifices increase the debt owed them by the Scorekeeper., With a huge positive balance, they might even be able to take a vacation or spend money on a personal indulgence without bankrupting their account. . . .

RISING ABOVE PERFECTIONISM

The ultimate irony —and tragedy—of perfectionism is that *it simply doesn't work*. It's supposed to earn you rave reviews and exempt you from criticism. Instead it damages both your work and your relationships, and puts you under an unrelenting pressure. If you've concluded that your perfectionism is hurting you, you *can* make changes.

Perfectly Human

Part of the Perfectionist's Credo is the notion that other people won't like you as well if you make a mistake, or you don't know things, or you allow your faults to show through. In fact, the opposite is true. Your need to be right all the time often repels friends and associates.

Nobody will ever feel empathy for you, love you, or enjoy being close to you simply because you are right or because you hardly ever make mistakes. It's true that people may admire your abilities or knowledge. Being competent, circumspect,

and smart is a plus, but these qualities alone will never win you love.

So try this: next time you are asked a question and don't know the answer, say so. Just say, "I don't know." Don't fudge; don't reel off a dozen possibilities to avoid admitting ignorance; don't offer something you do know but that doesn't answer the question. Just "I don't know." Then keep track of how many friends you lose. See how much less. loved you are. Note particularly how much less respect you get.

And the next time you're wrong about something, just admit it. Don't explain why you made the mistake. Don't show how anyone could have made that mistake under the circumstances. Don't insist that your answer actually *was* correct but was misunderstood.

Just confess, "I was wrong about that." Then start counting the people who shrink away from you. I'm exaggerating, of course. But when you start letting your fallibility show, when you let go of your need to know everything and to show how smart you are, you'll feel a burden being lifted. You'll feel more relaxed. It will be easier to smile. You'll be free! And these changes will occur *the very first time* you suppress your perfectionistic need to be infallible.

Confronting Your Inner Saboteurs

Whether you're writing a paper, painting a living room, or preparing a dinner for guests, if you're a perfectionist you tend to be haunted by such unconscious assumptions as:

- "I couldn't stand it if my work wasn't as good as X's."
- "It's got to be great!"
- "It would be intolerable for them to see me make a mistake."

You may be entirely unaware you're saying such things to yourself; they may sound completely foreign. But from their silent place within, such enduring, submerged beliefs govern many people's more visible behaviors and conscious concerns.

If you're such a person, what you need to know right now is:

- You are *choosing* to think these thoughts.
- They are obliterating your chances at happiness.
- You can start making significant chances right this minute

For example, let's say you're writing a report or a paper. Maybe you've always thought that a good written report includes every possible angle on the subject, answers every conceivable question, and reflects as much research as is humanly possible.

Well, that's wrong. And it's just that kind of thinking that will prevent you from reaching your creative and productive potential.

In most situations, the best report is the one that's done as well as possible *within the given time limits.*

Getting Your Work Done

If getting work done in a timely manner invariably proves to be difficult or painful, you've got to recognize that *your* way (perfection) isn't working. So try this: every time one of those irrational beliefs ("It's got to be done flawlessly!") starts pushing in on you, push back. Tell yourself, "No, it's got to be *completed!*" and keep moving. Focus on how good it feels to make progress on the task. Refuse to judge whether or not you are doing a terrific piece of work. The beauty of finishing on time (or even ahead of schedule) is that you can go back and fine-tune later. Think in terms of movement.

Give serious attention not just to doing the work but scheduling it *realistically.* Perfectionists tend to schedule their time as if they will perform ideally and can anticipate perfect conditions. They assume, for example, that nothing will interrupt them, that fatigue won't hamper their efficiency, that they'll be able to move along at top speed. Instead of blindly making such assumptions, set up realistic checkpoints for achieving certain tasks, even if

the work is less than perfect. If you slip behind in one phase, just accept this and get rolling; tighten up a succeeding phase. Accept that your project won't be, *cannot be,* as "perfect" as it could be if you had no deadline and no other responsibilities. Time constraints do shape most things!

Each time you find yourself getting sidetracked by details, or images of how the project will be evaluated, slam your palm down on the desk or your thigh and say "Move!" Take a deep breath, refocus on the goal, and continue on.

Imagine yourself swimming down a river, with the current, toward a goal. You have to arrive there before dark, or it will be too late. Whenever you get sidetracked by details or fine points, envision your self losing the current and drifting slowly out of the main river into a stream, and from there into a never-ending maze of smaller and smaller streams. They are seductive and interesting, but you lose momentum when you investigate them. Get back into the main river and move into the central current again!

Do the finest piece of work you can, given the limitations of deadlines and the legitimate requirements of your health, family, social life, and leisure pursuits. Remember that all of these dimensions are crucial to your enjoyment of life.

Cutting The Clutter

Streamline your life, from your verbal style to your physical surroundings. If you know you have a tendency to present too much information verbally, take a step toward correcting that! If you know you'll be in a situation where you'll be tempted to give too many details, prepare in advance by writing down (or at least outlining) what you'd like to cover. Then practice, timing the material as you deliver it. If you run over, edit yourself ruthlessly. Work at it until you can deliver it in *less* than the time allowed. The irrational worries we mentioned earlier will keep trying to assert themselves.

They are habits. Don't let them in. Imagine them pulling you away from the current and, just as in completing a task, slap your hand on your desk, say "Move!" take a deep, breath, relax, and refocus, then get going. . . .

DEMAND-SENSITIVITY

Obsessives tend to be especially sensitive to demands, either real or imagined, that are placed upon them. One aspect of demand-sensitivity is the tendency to "hear" demands or expectations in an exaggerated way. When the boss says he'd like to have something on his desk by Wednesday, the obsessive person often feels the expectation more acutely than others. In fact he often hears more of an imperative than the boss intended.

The obsessive person also exaggerates more subtle or inferred demands. Suppose, for instance, I've drafted a letter to the editor of the local newspaper and have given it to you, saying, "If you have a chance, let me know what you think of it." If you're a demand-sensitive obsessive, you'll feel a pressure not only to look over the piece, but to offer helpful suggestions and return the material to me as soon as possible. While you may not actually

do these things, you'll probably perceive my request as much more of a demand than it was, and even resent me for placing such a burden on you! . . .

The Angst of All-or-Nothing

The familiar force of all-or-nothing thinking also shapes the work-heavy lifestyles of many obsessives. They seem to feel as if cutting back on their work hours even slightly will lead them to cut back more and ever more, eventually bringing them to a horrifying state of indolence.

Many find it hard to start certain projects, knowing that once they start they'll have trouble stopping before the task is completed (and perfectly, at that). Their reluctance to interrupt the work, in turn, comes partly from their knowledge that if they lose their momentum it will be hard to start up again. . . .

Remember, the Perfectionists Credo that I outlined at the beginning . . . is based on inaccurate assumptions. Flawless living is not necessary or possible, or even desirable. You don't have to know everything or perform according to some mythical specifications in order to be worthwhile, loved, or happy.

Follow-Up

1. *Take the self-test in this article and comment on the results.*
2. *Choose two statements from this article and apply them to your life.*
3. *Attempt at least one change to make your life less perfectionistic and report on the results.*

Advice to William Somebody

Poe Ballantine for Donna Brown

I can't count the number of times I have officially assembled the equipment to take my life: a knife, a handgun, a plastic bag, a bottle of codeine and a fifth of vodka. My motivations are never quite clear: perception of failure, futility, a sense of irremediable isolation, MTV—nothing everyone else hasn't suffered through. Yet I tend to magnify my gloomy outlook into a drive-in picture of the end of the world. I can't seem to remember that despair is a temporary state, a dark storm along the highway; that if I can just stick it out, keep the wipers going and my foot on the gas, I will make it through to the other side.

Once, while driving across the country writing suicide notes in my head for no good reason at all, I pulled off for gas in Las Vegas, New Mexico. I remember it exactly: a Phillips 66, pump number seven, $1.09 a gallon. When I went inside to pay, everyone in the store was speaking Spanish. I paid and asked the skinny Mexican kid behind the register where the coffee was. He pointed to the back. I used the restroom, then went over and got the coffee. I had decided to drive on through to Phoenix, approximately one million miles.

The store was big and new and sterile and hopeless, like the blossoming commercialism of everything. I set the large cup of coffee on the counter.

"Anything else?" asked the kid.

"Pack of Newport 100s."

He slid the cigarettes across, looking at me.

"How much?" I said.

"Two-fourteen," he said.

The price seemed too low. "For both?" I asked.

"Coffee's on me," he said.

I didn't ask him why. Maybe he was quitting after this shift. Maybe it was store policy: free coffee with every fill-up. Maybe he recognized my turmoil and understood the power of kindness from a stranger. Or maybe he represented the invisible divinity that runs through all humanity like an old FDR radio speech and appears only when you need it the most. Whatever the case, I drove on through to Phoenix without another thought of my demise.

Another time, in the other Las Vegas, where I couldn't get a job and was already five hundred in the hole and the air stank with shallow unfriendliness and mistrust, I was riding my bicycle down to the union office to see if they had found me a job. I had paid them two hundred dollars a month ago, and they still hadn't gotten me any work. (The union never did find me a job. I finally broke one of their picket lines—you know, I'm sorry, but I was five hundred in the hole and my rent was coming up.) That day, I was riding along in the hot June sun, secretly thinking about throwing myself in front of a truck, when I coasted by a garage across from Bob Stupak's Vegas World (a now defunct hotel and casino), and a black mechanic sitting on a tire in the dark, cool interior smiled at me and put up his thumb. I don't think he understood how important that single gesture was, what it meant to me.

I am ashamed to admit that I think so much about taking my life. I have no right. I am fit. I am independent. I am a member of a privileged society. A billion Third World people would give their left lung to be in my position. They would probably work hard and shut up for a minute and appreciate their lives.

But I, like so many members of my generation, am overwhelmed by a certain modern black plague—call it depression, if you like.

I have known a dozen people who have taken their lives, all of them young, none of them, in my opinion, justified. I remember the girl in Number 1, who killed herself the day after I moved into a dilapidated, nearly empty apartment complex in Niagara Falls, New York. Though I'd spoken to her only once, I was horrified, struck hollow by the act. I met her father and brother that day on the stairs. They'd come to retrieve her belongings. They were haggard and gray with grief and reached out to me for some explanation, as if I could offer one. I grew angry with the girl and her thoughtless infliction of pain on the people who loved her. She had quit the game in the middle; like a spoiled child, she had thrown all her unopened Christmas packages out into the snow.

Or I'll be leafing through a newspaper in a laundromat and see that William Somebody has died of a self-inflicted gunshot wound at the age of thirty-eight, and I'll wonder, with a little rip in my stomach: Why couldn't he make it? Why couldn't he see the absolute permanence of his mistake? Why didn't he talk to someone? Why didn't he talk to *me?* I could've told him: Life is sacred. Suicide is wrong. You're going to die someday anyway; why speed the inevitable?

But when *my* unendurable dread descends, I don't remember my indignation at the selfishness of the girl in Number 1 or my cleareyed missionary advice to William Somebody. All I want is out.

The fact that I am still alive amazes me every morning. I wish I had a psychological formula, a rescue kit to hand out to my fellow melancholics. I wish I could say, *This is what saved me.* But each time it's something different: Kindness from a stranger. Lack of courage. Obligation to parents. Inability to write a good note. The possibility that I will have to start over again as a one-legged beggar in Tijuana or a housefly hatching out of a Dairy Queen swirl of yellow poodle droppings. Or I'll imagine the appearance of my corpse, its state of decomposition by the time I am found, which always makes me think of the Jonestown mass suicides and how silly those people looked, all swollen in polyester heaps and black at the fingertips—the ultimate in bad fashion.

Recently, I took the worst trip of my life. It started out fairly well on a sunny, early-spring day in El Paso. I got on a Greyhound bus headed north. By the time I'd reached Colorado, I was consumed in the flames of a strep infection, my back was out, and snow was falling by the foot. I got stuck in South Dakota for three days. I began to miss all the appointments I had made with friends along the way. I ended up in New York City, not once, but twice in a period of twenty-four hours, both times against my will, the second time hobbling in a pointless, amoral fever around the labyrinth of the Port Authority Bus Terminal, talking to myself and smashing my fist into my face as hard as I could. I was trying to break teeth, draw blood, damage brains and vertebrae. People were staring at me, even the New Yorkers, who are accustomed to the insane. All the destinations looked the same to me. All the buses were the same. I stopped a woman with a clipboard whose job it was to rescue idiot travelers lost in the Port Authority.

"Can you tell me when the next bus leaves?" I said.

"Which bus?" she said.

"It doesn't matter," I said.

She seemed shocked, this woman who worked in the bowels of New York City, insane asylum of the world.

"How about LA?" I said.

She looked at her sheet. "Four o'clock," she said. "Three hours."

"What about Washington, D.C.?"

"Half an hour," she said, squinting at me, then glancing at her clipboard. "Gate 82. That's the Richmond bus."

I got on the Richmond bus, and all the way down to D.C., I plotted my demise as the

CARRYING TOO MANY BURDENS

"Carrying Too Many Burdens" by tom mcCain

snow flowed starlike across the glass. I wondered what everyone would think when they heard the news. I wondered how my meager possessions would be distributed. I wondered who would care, who would laugh, who would secretly rejoice. I wondered if anyone would feel sorry for me, if anyone would miss me.

We were soon approaching D.C., and I had done nothing but daydream about my end. My neck was sore, my tooth was chipped, and my cheek was swollen to the eye.

God, please, just let me die.

Then three kids boarded the bus, ball caps on sideways. They swaggered down the aisle. Each wore a new snow white down jacket. I caught the dull nickel gleam of a gun handle in a waistband. Two of the kids dropped into the seats directly behind me. They spoke loudly for everyone's benefit.

"What'chu lookin' at?"

"Lemme see that *gun.*"

"You ain't afraid to *show* it.' "

"Lookit. I got a straight bead on the driver."

The woman next to me blanched and flattened against her seat. I felt my bladder float up into my chest cavity. Time stopped and draped itself like a braided pearl net across the aisle. One of the kids stood up. I saw the driver's eyes freeze in the mirror. I pictured the massacre photos in the next day's paper, my name misspelled, page four. Life was suddenly sweet. I prayed with a coward's softness. The snow flew past the windows.

Follow-Up

1. *Select two statements by Ballantine and offer your interpretations.*
2. *How do you respond when in a state of despair and gloom? What seems to (a) prolong and (b) get you out of this state? What have you found to be helpful for another person in a state of despair?*
3. *Ballantine writes about the power of kindness from a stranger. Describe a time when you were the recipient of such a kindness. A giver? How can you enhance this quality in your life?*
4. *For a related reading see "Left Behind" and the Applied Activity entitled "Depression Checklist" (in this section).*

Left Behind

Jenny Montgomery

On Sept. 13, more than 100 people gathered to pay respect to a man who had ended his own life just five days earlier. Warm embraces and comforting words were exchanged throughout the evening as people struggled to understand why Merle, 27, could not express his pain. His diminutive father sat solemnly in the same seat for hours, staring at the table as if he were looking for some meaning. No one knows exactly what he was feeling.

A good friend, during the informal memorial service, read Merle's explanatory note with great fortitude. Some were touched to hear that Merle looked forward to meeting his long-deceased mother in the afterlife, and that he had wanted to "go out on my own terms." But the most shocking news was that he had been considering suicide for awhile, yet he never asked for help.

He asked that his friends feel no responsibility for his decision, but, nevertheless, inner voices prompted many to ask themselves why they weren't more perceptive. Unfortunately, the only person who could have changed his ultimate decision was Merle.

Those who commit suicide never see the hollow eyes of the people they leave behind. They never hear the soft cries, humorous stories and cherished memories swirling like smoke through a room as loved ones huddle together for support.

They never see how people who shared only moments of their lives come to say goodbye, anyway.

These are the repercussions of suicide. And while it was obvious that each person was coping with the loss in a different way, those who knew Merle had lost a little part of themselves when he pulled the trigger. We wondered if he realized just how much he meant to so many people— maybe he just could not care.

As the evening grew long, old grudges were laid to rest, and estranged friends vowed to rekindle what they had lost. Many of us vowed to be better listeners and more supportive in our friendships. Most importantly, we swore that we would never cause anyone to feel what we were feeling then.

One of Merle's closest friends constructed a website, dedicated to his memory, complete with a guest book. One woman wrote, "Merle was truly a kind, funny man, and I can't stop thinking about how his life ended. Please, if anyone gets to this point, talk to your friends and find another way out."

Follow-Up

1. *What are your thoughts and feelings concerning this article?*

Courage

Rollo May

[*Editor's Note:* In his book *The Courage To Create*, Rollo May expresses his belief that we are between eras and that this involves radical changes in how we choose to live. We can respond with apathy, paralysis, or as May hopes, with courage. May discusses four kinds of courage.]

1. *Physical courage.* This is different from the kind of physical courage which stresses power over people. May proposes a new form which develops the "capacity to listen with the body . . . a learning to think with the body. It will be a valuing of the body as the means of empathy with others, as expression of the self as a thing of beauty and as a rich source of pleasure. . . . I propose the use of the body not for the development of musclemen, but for the development of sensitivity" (p. 6).

[*Editor's Note*: Physical courage also refers to times when one purposely, but not foolishly, places oneself in situations in which the body is potentially at risk.]

2. *Moral courage.* "Moral courage has its source in identification through one's own sensitivity with the suffering of one's fellow human beings . . . it depends on one's capacity to *perceive*, to let one's self see the suffering of other people. If we let ourselves experience the evil, we will be forced to do something about it. . . . The most prevalent form of cowardice in our day hides behind the statement 'I did not want to become involved' " (pp. 8–9).

[*Editor's Note*: Although not explicitly stated by May, moral courage may also include acting on principle, or taking a stand on what you believe is right in the face of opposition.]

3. *Social courage.* "The courage to relate to other human beings, the capacity to risk one's self in the hope of achieving meaningful intimacy . . . to invest one's self over a period of time in a relationship that will demand an increasing openness. . . . Intimacy requires courage because risk is inescapable" (p. 9).

   The primary risks in entering or not enterimg an intimate relationship, according to May, are (a) we will change in some way, (b) facing the fear that one may lose a sense of individuality, and (c) facing the fear of being abandoned.

4. *Creative courage.* This is the courage to introduce new forms, symbols, or patterns within a society. Among these are original ideas that

emanate from your deepest centers. Not having creative courage, May contends, results in a betrayal of yourself and your community. In addition, "By the creative act, we are able to reach beyond our own death. . . . Creativity is a yearning for immortality . . ." (pp. 19, 27).

May discusses the paradox of courage: "We must be fully committed, but we must also be aware at the same time that we might possibly be wrong" (pp. 12–13). He contends that those who are convinced that their way is the only right way leads to dogmatism and fanaticism. Doubt is required to be open to new truths. "Commitment is healthiest," says May, "when it is not without doubt, but in spite of doubt" (p. 14).

May concludes that "in human beings courage is necessary to make being and becoming possible. An assertion of the self, a commitment, is essential if the self is to have any reality . . . a man or woman becomes fully human only by his or her choices and his or her commitment to them. People attain worth and dignity by the multitude of decisions they make from day to day. These decisions require courage" (pp. 4–5).

Follow-Up

1. *Describe an instance in your life when you demonstrated one or more kinds of courage as stated by Rollo May.*
2. *Describe a current situation in your life that is demanding one or more kinds of courage. Explain how you are behaving in this situation.*
3. *Describe at least one person who has consistently demonstrated one of the kinds of courage May outlines. How has this person influenced you?*
4. *Discuss or write a reaction to one or more statements from this article.*

Vital Moments

Nelson Goud

Humans have the capacity to experience intense and vitalizing moments of joy, wonder, illumination, serenity, mastery, and ecstasy. These experiences can be collectively characterized as *vital moments*. Vital moments are instances of pure being when one feels completely and fully alive. In these moments a person becomes totally absorbed in the present and often feels connected to fundamental life sources and energies. Emerson (in Whelan, 1991) said that "there is a depth in those brief moments which constrain us to ascribe more reality to them than to all other experiences" (p. 64).

Vital moments serve many functions including making life choices and decisions; providing therapeutic effects such as symptom removal, creativity, tolerance and acceptance; and philosophical shifts. Among their most basic value is to affirm the value of life. Maslow (1970), in his studies of peak experiences, stated that "they give meaning to life itself . . . it proves to the experiencer that there are things or objects or experiences to yearn for which are worthwhile in themselves" (pp. 62–63). For more extensive reading in this area see Goud (1995).

Vital moments appear under several guises. Some of the most commonly experienced moments are described next.

PEAK EXPERIENCES

Here one may experience an immense infusion of joy and happiness or an immersion in great serenity. Often one believes that life can be viewed as it is, and has a sense that everything is connected. Some examples:

• "I always wondered how you know when you are truly in love. And then I found

out it is something that can hardly be described with words. We had shared a wonderful weekend trip and I just wanted to hug the world on the drive home. I felt like I would explode with happiness and delight. I knew I loved him within weeks after meeting him but this was new. I wanted to share my life with him and the parts of me that I don't share with anyone. I wanted to run and laugh and yell and tell him I knew for sure that I was truly, madly and deeply in love with him. I wanted to tell everyone and I wanted to tell no one. I wanted to share this incredible feeling of completeness but I didn't want to share something so incredibly personal and real. I felt like I was in a whirlwind and I felt all of this while sitting quietly next to him during the car ride home. I still have fleeting moments of those feelings, although not as intensely as that particular day. I feel much more content and whole having experienced such joy and utter ecstasy from simply knowing another human being." (M. Laski, 1961, p. 205)

• It was happening again. My mind was being invaded by a rushing torrent of insights, a volcanic explosion of truths. I had no choice but to just let it happen. I was caught in another "idea storm." Images, answers, questions, and insights were bombarding me with unusual ferocity and clarity. Puzzles that months of serious thinking couldn't unravel were solved for me. New associations were exploding all around. Glimpses of exciting new paths to explore were unveiled right before my eyes. It was like being in the midst of a forest where the trees had just shed rainbows of newly fallen leaves. Then suddenly a strong gust of wind would swoop in, encircling me with thousands of swirling leaves. To my wonderment each leaf had an idea on it. All I had to do was pluck one from mid-air and record its message. In a frenzy, I started to scribble a word or two from each leaf I grabbed. Each leaf lost in the wind was possibly an idea I wouldn't see again. I was missing as many as I caught. Ecstasy and frustration somehow coexisted in the same moment but there was no time to fully experience either one. Even though I only captured a small portion of this amazing shower of ideas, I have plenty to savor for months to come. I'm left with a nice blend of peaceful exhaustion, awe, and wonder. (N. Goud)

• "One day when I was four, I found myself standing at the beach, alone. The sea touched the sky. Breathing with the waves, I entered their rhythm. Suddenly there was a channeling of energy: the sun, the wind, the sea were going right through me. A door opened, and I became the sun, the wind, and the sea. There was no 'I' anymore. I had merged with everything else. . . . Sound, smell, taste, touch, shape—all melted into a brilliant light. The pulsating energy went right through me, and I was part of this energy." (E. Hoffman, 1992, p. 38)

• "When I am at my best, as a group facilitator or as a therapist . . . when I am closest to my inner, intuitive, self . . . then whatever I do seems to be full of healing. Then, simply my presence is releasing and helpful. . . . It seems that my inner spirit has reached out and touched the inner spirit of the other. Our relationship transcends itself and becomes a part of something larger. Profound growth and healing and energy are present." (C. Rogers, 1980, p. 129)

WONDER

Here one experiences complete awe and astonishment in the presence of some form of newness and mystery. Some examples:

• "Once it chanced that I stood in the abutment of a rainbow's arch, which filled the lower stratum of the atmosphere, tingeing the grass and leaves around, and dazzling me as I looked through colored crystal. It was a lake of rainbow light, in which, for a short while, I lived like a dolphin." (H. Thoreau, 1962, p. 255)

• When I was a second-grader, the teacher gave a homework assignment introducing the concept of zero. . . . Most of my classmates regarded this as simply another of the innumerable rules to be memorized. . . . But I sat alone in my room that night and stared with tears at the seemingly senseless problems. I wondered, 'How could I add something to a number and yet the number remain unchanged?' Suddenly, I understood—the immensity of the concept of nothingness overwhelmed me. I was awed that mathematicians were brilliant enough to capture this immensity in a little symbol . . . and decided to become a mathematician." (E. Hoffman, 1992, p. 39)

• I first saw you in the newborn nursery. There was this large window and a couple rows of babies behind it—just like the movies. I was determined not to look like a goony father and to maintain my cool. A nurse came in and bent over this crib and picked up this tiny human organism and walked over the window and held you up to my face. You were a bit tired. Then you opened your eyes and we made a connection. There is nothing like it. An unseen current locked us in and I was so damn happy and proud that I pointed you out to everyone exclaiming all your virtues and potential greatness. Since the nurse was the only one there, I lost my cool status. But I was too absorbed and overwhelmed with your existence to even notice anything but you and me. (N. Goud)

PSYCHOLOGICAL EPIPHANY

This is a sudden revelation about one's identity or view of life. Some examples:

• "With dinner concluded, the waiter set the check down in the middle of the table. That's when it happened. My father did not reach for the check . . . my father did nothing. Finally, it dawned on me. Me! I was supposed to pick up the check. I whipped out my American Express Card. My view of myself was suddenly altered. With a stroke of a pen, I was suddenly an adult." (R. Cohen)

• "I was a workaholic, a crazy, crazy woman. I was on a plane four times a week. I just wanted to get to the top. One morning at home I opened the bathroom cabinet and counted 150 shampoo bottles brought back from these trips. All of a sudden, I realized that I was reaching that goal but wasn't happy. A year would go by and I wouldn't know what had happened. I left that work and eventually bought a small, neighborhood grocery store and am liking life again." (J. Castro, 1993)

FLOW

This is an extended state of pleasure gained through mastery. It is a time when one is fully functioning in an activity (for further reading see Csikszentmihalyi, 1990, 1997). Some examples:

• "You get it rolling, and all of a sudden, you just start clicking, and the basket seems to be as big as the ocean. It seems like the whole game, everything, is in slow motion, but you're going regular speed. . . . You can't force it. You have to let it flow, let it ride." (Bill Walton, after making 21 of 22 shots in a UCLA game.)

• "I used to fight and argue about practicing the piano. Then one day I was by myself and it came out just right, more than perfect. It was as though I hadn't played it but something in the world had played that piano just right . . . it was a mystery. After that, I played the piano my same old way, but I didn't argue about it anymore. I just wondered if it would ever happen again." (I. Progoff, 1992, p. 264)

• "The only way I can describe what happens is that when I have a clear and powerful insight, and I am writing with attention to I, the words fairly dance on the page before me. I say things I am not conscious of ever having thought before, in ways that surprise me." (A. Greeley, 1974, p. 52)

APPLICATIONS

There are ways to arrange a life to invite or inhibit vital moments from occurring. Contacting triggers is the main path for experiencing vital moments. *Triggers* are the stimuli which produce moments (e.g., nature, the arts, love, sex, mastery, contemplation, beauty, special places). Triggers alone are not sufficient, though. *How* one experiences a trigger is just as significant. Encountering loud and distracting behaviors while walking through a forest grove would be an example of an anti-trigger. Other anti-triggers include treating everything as a means and not as an end in itself; an over-scheduled and excessively busy life; anything that inhibits full absorption and being-in-the-moment.

Many find it difficult to express the feelings and meaning of vital moments. Unless you have the skill and a willing receiver, it may be best *not* to communicate a vital moment. An inadequate expression tends to diminish or lessen the experience. For some, journaling or other creative modes may be helpful. We may find, like Thoreau, that "the facts most astounding and most real are never communicated."

Vital moments are times when we experience life's ultimates—what we live for. They can also show us our true paths, paths that have the most likelihood of meaning and even bliss. One way to test this conclusion is to construct your own history of vital moments. What is it that has and still provides wonder, flow, or peak experiences? What have been your life-changing epiphanies? Constructing such a history is therapeutic in itself—you may even re-experience parts of these moments while recalling them.

• "Outside he stood for a while on the sidewalk, just breathing deeply and feeling the pleasure of being alive. . . . A sharp breeze tingled his flesh and made his eyes get a little watery, and when he blinked and opened them, it seemed for a moment as if everything was bathed in a soft gold light. . . . It was just for a moment but it gave Sonny a sudden sense of joy that seemed to spread through his whole being. He had known these moments before, in different times and places, and they had seemed so intense and so real that everything else was like sleep. Such moments made you feel completely alive, reminded you of being alive, and Sonny wondered if perhaps that's what 'real life' was after all—those moments." (D. Wakefield, 1970, p. 319)

References

Castro, J. (1993). The Simple Life. In A. Arkoff (Ed.), *Psychology and personal growth* (4th ed.). Boston: Allyn & Bacon.

Cohen, R. (1998). Suddenly I'm the Adult? In *Psychology and personal growth* (5th ed.). Boston: Allyn & Bacon.

Csikszentmihalyi, M. (1990). *The psychology of optimal experience.* New York: Harper & Row.

Csikszentmihalyi, M. (1997). *Finding flow.* New York: Basic Books.

Goud, N. (1995). Vital moments. *Journal of Humanistic Education and Development, 34,* 25–33.

Greeley, A. (1974). *Ecstasy: A way of knowing.* Englewood Cliffs, NJ: Prentice-Hall.

Hoffman, E. (1992). *Visions of innocence: Spiritual and inspirations experiences of childhood.* Boston: Shambhala.

Laski, M. (1961). *Ecstasy in secular and religious experiences.* Los Angeles: Jeremy P. Tarcher.

Maslow, A. (1970). *Religions, values, and peak-experiences.* New York: Viking Compass.

Progoff, I. (1992). *At a journal workshop.* New York: Jeremy P. Tarcher/ Perigee Books.

Rogers, C. (1980). *A way of being.* Boston: Houghton Mifflin.

Thoreau, H. (1854/1962). In J. Krutch (Ed.), *Thoreau: Walden and other writings.* New York: Bantam Books.

Wakefield, D. (1970). *Going all the way.* Bloomington: Indiana University Press.

Whelan, R. (1991). *Self-reliance: The wisdom of Ralph Waldo Emerson.* New York: Bell Tower.

Follow-Up

1. *Describe two vital moments from your life and their effects.*
2. *Attempt a Vital Moment History as described at the end of the article. Discuss your learnings.*
3. *The author says that contacting a* trigger *is the main path for experiencing vital moments. What are some of your triggers that often lead to vital moments? Are you experiencing these triggers on a consistent basis? Discuss your answers.*
4. *Provide and discuss examples of anti-triggers as described in the article.*
5. *For a related reading see "Little Joys" by Abe Arkoff in the Emotions and Feelings Section (Section Five).*

The Pace of Growth

Below are excerpts from two novelists and an undergraduate student.

INDIAN SUMMER

"His goal was simply to be a full human man, making the best of himself. He was disgusted and fearful of what failure to do that had done to many people, to most people he knew. He did not want to be . . . twisted by subservience . . . ground down by poverty . . . slowly poisoned by contempt for (him)self. . . . Most of all, he did not want to be defeated as most people in the world were, that is, simply by not really living, eaten by the termites of a half life semilived.

All the same there was one wonderfully encouraging fact, which he kept the firmest possible grip on at all times. He actually knew one or two people who had broken past all these blocks and became real, true, full human beings.

Very soon now he was going to have to put a stop to this downward path he had let himself be persuaded to set out upon; he was going to have to halt this descent very soon or else, he sensed, it would be too late because he would have lost the power to escape. . . . If he took one gram too much of humiliation here, then the fuel of self-liking necessary to carry him away might be gone, and like so many . . . he would turn from a venturer into a clinger, caution would move one degree higher on the scale than ambition and so dominate it and finally crush it, doubt would inch ahead of certainty, fear would crowd out confidence, and his life would in all essentials be finished and its great issue lost.

We're out of phase with life; we live our lives out of season . . . [we] begin to fall behind too, like everybody else, into an Indian summer of brief, too late, doomed flowering."

—John Knowles

LEARNING THE WRONG THINGS

"I'm confused and frustrated. Humans are very adaptable to situations. We do learn from everything we do. What happens when you learn what you don't want to learn, but as a result of that exposure it becomes a part of you anyway? You should be very aware of the learning environments you find yourself in. If you're not, then in subtle ways you are going to become what you do. If you're in an environment you disagree with, you'd better do something before it changes you."

—An undergraduate student

THE BUTTERFLY

"I remembered one morning when I discovered a cocoon in the bark of a tree, just as the butterfly was making a hole in its case and preparing to come out. I waited a while, but it was too long appearing and I was impatient. I bent over it and breathed on it to warm it. I warmed it as quickly as I could and the miracle began to happen before my eyes, faster than life. The case opened, the butterfly started slowly crawling out and I shall never forget my horror when I saw how its wings were folded back and crumpled; the wretched butterfly tried with its whole trembling body to unfold them. Bending over it, I tried to help it with my breath. In vain. It needed to be hatched out patiently and the unfolding of the wings should be a gradual process in the sun. Now it was too late. My breath had forced the butterfly to appear, all crumpled, before its time. It struggled desperately and, a few seconds later, died in the palm of my hand.

That little body is, I do believe, the greatest weight I have on my conscience. For I realize today that it is a mortal sin to violate the great laws of nature. We should not hurry, we should not be impatient, but we should confidently obey the eternal rhythm. . . . Ah, if only that little butterfly could always flutter before me to show me the way."

—Nikos Kazantzakis

Follow-Up

1. *The first two authors warn against staying too long in an environment that stunts growth. Can you think of an example where this happened to you or someone you know? Is it happening to you now?*
2. *Kazantzakis's excerpt provides a warning for pushing growth too quickly—forcing something before its time. Has this ever happened to you in some aspect of your life? How about now?*
3. *Do you tend to err in lingering too long or pushing too hard in your own personal growth? What are some specific steps you could take to create the best pace or tempo for your growth?*
4. *John Knowles's character mentions that he knew one or two people who were "real, true, full human beings." How many do you know (if any)? What makes them this way?*
5. *Discuss and/or write a reaction paper to one or more of these questions.*

No One's Perfect

Daphne Haygood-Benyard

No one's perfect . . . they say
Well I disagree!
I happen to be a perfect example of a perfect person
I'm perfectly good in my goodness
Perfect at being angry when I'm mad
I'm perfectly disagreeable when I argue
And make perfect mistakes in my errors
I develop a perfectly negative attitude when moody
I'm perfectly happy in my happiness
And will cry perfectly when sad
I'm perfectly calm in my coolness
Fall perfectly short in my shortcomings
And when I make a mess . . . it's a perfect wreck
I pout . . . shout . . . and strike out perfectly
In the insanity of living in this perfectly imperfect world.
So no one's perfect?
WELL!! PERFECTLY, I DISAGREE!

Applied Activities for Section Three

EVOLUTION OF A PERSON #1

1. **Lifeline.** List the events and people that have significantly influenced your life development. These are the events and people that have made a difference in determining your self-image, interests, and skills; how you relate to other people; your career and school choices; and your values. As you examine your life, past and present, what have been some turning points? Perhaps a path you did not take but wonder about now? Or a decision that turned out right? What are some untried dreams or goals? Place these persons and events along a line starting with your birth and ending with the current date.

2. **Symbolic drawing.** On a single piece of paper draw a shape that symbolically represents your life from birth to the present. This drawing does not have to look artistic. Use shapes, lines, or even shadings and colors. Sometimes you have to think about your whole life in a gentle, reflective manner for a few minutes and wait for an image to appear. If an image does not immediately appear, do not force it. Wait a few hours or a day or two and probably one will emerge. A single drawing will be easier to remember and will tend to capture the emotional tones better than words.

3. In your lifeline and symbolic drawing, make sure to include all major influences, whether positive or negative. If you do not want anyone to see your work, disguise an event by using your own symbols (for example, you could use a number to represent a particular traumatic event).

4. Discuss what you have learned with classmates, or write a reaction paper. Remember that you need only share what you are comfortable disclosing.

5. An extension of this activity will be explored later in an Applied Activity appropriately called Evolution of A Person #2. (See Section Six, A Quality Life.)

STRETCHING LIMITS

Knowing personal limits is necessary for making wise life choices. Often, however, a person creates internal boundaries that are too constricting. Certain qualities are not expressed because opportunities to draw them out are not taken. Fears, a few failures, or plain inexperience restrain what we think we can do. Only when individuals do something they "are not capable of" are the internal boundaries challenged and usually expanded. When boundaries are extended, life is experienced more fully.

There are two ways to check whether your inner limits are too restrictive: (1) attempt to take a current strength to a higher or deeper level, or (2) attempt a task that taps an undeveloped capacity—one you believe you have but have given little chance to develop.

The key is to design activities that challenge you to think and act at higher levels. In short, you are to set up realistic but challenging goals. For example, let's say that you have always wanted to try a few original ideas in your work but have not done so. You would then select the "best chance" new idea and design an action plan to try it out. You might consider telling a trusted other of your plan in order to develop a support person. Report what you learned about stretching your limits.

TRAIT EXAGGERATION

If you desire to strengthen a quality in your natural repertoire, you may have to *over*practice it for awhile (like learning an athletic or musical technique). For example, let's say you want to become a better listener. For two weeks, saturate yourself in learning and practicing listening—watch good listeners, read about listening, purposely emphasize listening in your normal interactions. This same approach can be used for almost any interpersonal or emotional quality. Describe your activities, results, and what you learned.

STRENGTHS RECOGNITION

A healthy self-perception depends in part on an awareness of personal strengths. In general, the more genuine strengths a person recognizes and values, the higher the level of self-esteem. It is not a common experience, though, to talk about your strengths without it being classified as bragging. However, it is socially acceptable to have someone else recognize and mention your strengths. It is important to talk about strengths, because this is a major way to maintain strength awareness. The following activities are two methods for recognizing strengths in others. You may be surprised how others react to these acknowledgments.

1. A strength is excellence in any skill, knowledge, or personal quality. In a proper time and context, directly tell three or more people what you believe to be one of their strengths. It is also helpful to provide an example of this strength. Note the immediate verbal and nonverbal reactions of those being acknowledged. Did they accept the recognition, or tend to sidestep or downplay it? Did they feel compelled to say something complimentary back to you?
2. If you have been part of an ongoing small group, in or outside of class, consider this activity. Tape a blank sheet of paper on the back of each group member. Distribute packets of Post-it notes. Then each person thinks of two strengths of every other group member. These are written on separate Post-it notes. After everyone has had time to finish writing, meander around and place your strengths notes on the back of the appropriate person. You may want to share your impressions and thoughts with the group after viewing your strengths notes.
3. Discuss or write about what you learned from one or both of these strengths recognition activities.

FIRST TIMES

One way to chart your life journey is to remember "first times." Each first time becomes a small or even a major threshold of your personal development. Try to list as many first times as you can. Here are some examples taken from several adults.

I'll never forget the first time I . . .

Rode a bike on my own	Had a period
Drew an original picture	Flew on an airplane
Went to school	Went to a prom
Could read something	Got my driver's license
Flunked a test	Voted
Saw my baby sister	Got drunk
Bought a new baseball glove	Made a stand
Played a song on my trumpet	Was totally out of line
Kissed a boy	Went to a funeral
Played in a recital	Visited a foreign country
Had a child	

Now it's your turn. Write as many as you can on a separate piece of paper.

I'll never forget the first time I . . .

Follow-Up

1. Discuss one or more first times with someone.
2. Write a reaction paper on what these first times meant to you.
3. For further reading on this topic, see Robert Fulghum's *From Beginning To End: The Rituals of Our Lives* (1995).

DEPRESSION CHECKLIST

Depression is linked with suicide, substance abuse, and several mental disorders. Clinical depression is a major health problem. It is an illness, not a character flaw or personality weakness. It is not the same as having a short-term case of the blues or the blahs. Below is a checklist of commonly noted signs of depression. It can be used for examining yourself or for someone you know. A key point in marking any item is to determine whether it has persisted for at least two weeks.

Body signs

_____ Major change in sleep patterns (less or more)

_____ Major change in appetite/weight

_____ Pronounced loss of energy

_____ Drug/chemical abuse

Emotional signs

_____ Deep sadness

_____ Intense feelings of hopelessness, worthlessness

_____ Pervasive loss of interest in everything (even former favorite activities)

_____ Irritableness and anger

_____ Continual thoughts/statements of death and/or suicide

_____ Frequent crying spells

Cognitive signs

_____ Inability to concentrate

_____ Inability to make decisions

_____ Constant confusion

Interpersonal signs

_____ Social withdrawal ("I want to be alone.")

_____ No one cares or needs me

If you or someone you know has consistently shown one or more of these indicators for over a two week period, then professional help may be needed. Keep in mind that a depressed person often has little energy or desire to seek help; someone else may have to initiate this step. Professional help is necessary for successful treatment. Below are some resources to consider for depression information treatment interventions:

Local medical doctors and counseling services (in emergencies call 911 or your local suicide/crisis hotline number)

SOS: Signs of Suicide (1-800-973-2211) A phone site designed to teach people how to recognize someone who may be at risk for taking his/her life. This information is also available on the Web at www.mentalhealthscreening.org/parade.

Depression and Bipolar Support Alliance (1-800-826-3632) Besides current screening information, this organization can also provide contacts for support groups. This information is available on the Web at www.dbsalliance.org.

Depression Awareness, Recognition, and Treatment (D/ART)
National Institute of Mental Health
Room 10-85
5600 Fishers Lane
Rockville, MD 20857
(Call 1-800-421-4211 for a free brochure.)

SECTION
FOUR

HUMAN RELATIONSHIPS

O ne of the best ways to learn the function of anything is to do without it. An injury to any part of your body readily shows its taken-for-granted purpose. A power outage highlights our pervasive dependence on electricity. Imagine a life without other people. Sometimes we may want such a thing, but only when we choose it. What we consider to be typical human behavior would not be possible without constant interaction with many persons in our lives. Observations of persons raised in isolation from an early age show great deficits in language, emotional expression, and a marked incapacity for a mature, sustained human interaction.

Most of us cannot escape the influence of our fellow humans even when we are alone—we think of them, we wonder what they are doing, we wonder if they miss us, we may even get mad at them, we might feel lonely. We are so enmeshed in our significant relationships that their influence permeates our existence even after their deaths.

Our human interactions differ according to their type, intensity, frequency, and duration. You can visually capture these dimensions by making a human web. Place a dot in the middle of a blank piece of paper—this dot represents you. Draw lines from the dot to circles with these labels: relatives, friends, colleagues, teachers, professional relationships, authority figures, social groups, neighbors, acquaintances, heroes, mentors, role models, romantic encounters, disliked persons, and any other relationship categories. When you place names by each of these circles, you begin to see how much of your life is spent in human interactions. You, too, are a member of many other webs.

Embedded deep within the human is the need to love and belong, in the dual sense of giving and receiving. Much of our lives is spent in attempting to fulfill these two needs. Abraham Maslow (1968) said that "no psychological health is possible unless the person is fundamentally accepted, loved and respected by others" (p. 196).

The reading selections in this section represent some of our most significant human relationships.

- In "Shoulders" Nelson Goud explains how we rely on a vast network of shoulders to be the persons we are.
- Models of pairing (or nonpairing) are outlined in "Intimate Relationship Choices" by Abe Arkoff.
- The dynamics of effective and ineffective marriages are the topic of "Making Marriage Work" by John Gottman and Nan Silver.
- A day of joining and parting is described by Tom Keating in "Sometimes it Rains."
- Handling money conflicts in relationships is the theme of Dianne Hales' "Are Money Fights Ruining Your Marriage?" Even nonmarried couples will find this piece of interest.
- In "Thoughts on Intimacy" Nelson Goud summarizes ideas on superrelationships, sex, and cyberaffairs.
- The excitement and difficulties of e-mail relationships are detailed in "Internet Romance" by Meghan Daum.
- Judith Viorst writes about six "Kinds of Friends."
- Mark Murrmann talks about past friends in "Lamenting the Fading of Friendships."
- Findings on same-sex and opposite-sex friends are described in Nelson Goud's "Thoughts on Friends."
- The struggle to become independent from parents and to accept them as distinct persons is the thesis of "Parents" by Martin Shepard.
- Young adult issues of finding friends, living alone, and living with parents are discussed in "The Emerging Adult: Finding Friends, Living Alone, and Living with Parents" by Nelson Goud.
- The role of siblings in human development is summarized in "Thoughts on Siblings" by Nelson Goud.
- Characteristics of effective mentoring are outlined in "Thoughts on Mentoring" by Nelson Goud.

- Ideas and strategies for "Resolving Interpersonal Conflicts" are explained by David W. Johnson.
- Guidelines for making apologies are described by Nelson Goud in "Making an Apology."
- A teacher who cared is featured in "The Missing Halloween" by Nelson Goud.

Reference

Maslow, A. H. (1968). *Toward a psychology of being.* New York: Van Nostrand Reinhold Co.

Shoulders

Nelson Goud

I was about six years old when my parents took me to a parade. Standing there in a crowd of giants all I could see were knees and belt buckles. The bands, floats, and zany clowns passed by unseen. "I can't see! I want to see!" I yelled. Within a couple seconds two strong arms lifted me up high above the crowd. I had the best seat in the house up there on my father's shoulders. He didn't seem to mind at all that he was half strangled each time I got excited.

Two weeks ago I took some college students through a modified Outward Bound initiatives course. One task was to figure out how to get over a sheer 13-foot wall using only their minds and bodies. Gradually they decided to place a couple of people at the base of the wall. Sandy was elected to climb up on their shoulders. Sandy stretched and still was six inches from reaching the upper ledge. The two classmates she was standing on then pushed her up until she caught hold of the ledge and scrambled over. The rest of the class cheered Sandy. No one gave a hand to the two below with dirty shirts and sore shoulders.

It took actual shoulders to see the parade and climb the wall. Shoulders come in many other forms—teachings, models and mentors, others' past efforts. Our most accomplished persons readily acknowledged shoulders. "Many times a day I realize how much my life is built upon the labors of my fellow men, both living and dead," said Einstein. Eddie Robinson, immediately before the game that made him college football's winningest coach, said to his players—"It's a record made up of men like you for the last 40 years."

Why is it, then, that most of us, most of the time, forget that we stand on shoulders? It appears that once our foundations are established, they are dropped from waking consciousness. Our attention becomes fully focused on current struggles, unattained goals, and ungratified needs. Successes are seen as the result of personal resourcefulness, perseverance, and possibly a few breaks. Occasionally we might throw in a plaudit for those we stand on, but it generally rings of the obligatory. I was reminded of this when someone asked me how I achieved a certain style of trumpet playing. My response centered on individual effort and practice. Later reflection revealed gaping holes in this answer. I forgot my shoulders. Any current trumpeting skill would have to be traced to my mom's encouragement while hearing me butcher pieces like "The Carnival of Venice" in the back room; and to Hendrik Buytendorp, the music teacher who made it clear that trumpet scales were just as important as Little League baseball practice; and to Ferguson, Severinsen, Hirt, Mangione. An honest and true answer would have to acknowledge all these influences. Try it yourself—just attempt to fully explain how you are able to do something well. The answer will unveil a vast network of shoulders.

Forgetting shoulders may be linked to distorted notions of self-sufficiency. We value and reward self-direction, individual initiative, and taking responsibility. A healthy person possesses these qualities. It is when these traits are exaggerated out of proportion that problems begin. Healthy autonomy turns into neurotic self-reliance. A person gradually begins to believe he or she can master life's challenges by relying solely on personal resources, and that to even acknowledge the help of others is a "weakness." It may even work for awhile. Then prices must be paid—some develop illusions of omnipotence or step into the trap Karen Horney called the pseudosolution of mastery. This "I don't need anybody, never had, never will" orientation propels one to the outpost of alienation.

One does not lose uniqueness by tracing an accomplishment or ability to the influence of others. The actual idea and action is an individual one; it has your stamp. That is what shoulders are for, they permit a stretching of the limits of what has gone on before. By remembering shoulders while perched up there, you get the bonus of a profound sense of belonging. One may even realize Thoreau's advice—"If I devote myself to pursuits and contemplations, I must first see, at least, that I do not pursue them sitting upon another man's shoulders. I must get off him first, that he may pursue his contemplations too."

Sometimes I realize my part in this shoulders network in simple ways. I am watching the Indianapolis 500 parade with 250,000 other giants. The bands, floats, and clowns pass by and I hear my four-year-old son hollering, "I can't see! I want to see!" I hoist him up on my shoulders and he half strangles me.

Follow-Up

1. *The author maintains that we often forget the contributions of others toward our accomplishments. Discuss whether this is true in your life and in the lives of others.*
2. *Some people feel that acknowledging help from others is a form of weakness. Offer your thoughts on this idea.*
3. *Thoreau was quoted on the observation that at times a person must "get off another's shoulders" so that the latter person can freely pursue a life. Discuss your views on this idea.*
4. *The author suggested thinking of one of your skills or accomplishments and then tracing it back to its origins. Try this and report on the role of others in this history.*

Intimate Relationship Choices

Abe Arkoff

Below are brief descriptions of five models of pairing or, in one case, nonpairing. Read each description, and complete the incomplete statements following it by giving as many reasons as you can. If a model is generally unattractive to you, try to find something about it that you like. If a model is generally attractive to you, try to find something about it that you *don't* like.

1. The traditional model: One partner is primarily the breadwinner while the other partner is primarily the homemaker.

   This model is attractive to me because

   This model is unattractive to me because

2. The shared-roles model: The parties share equally in the bread-winning and homemaking activities.

   This model is attractive to me because

   This model is unattractive to me because

3. The reversed-roles model: Partners reverse the breadwinner and homemaker roles.

   This model is attractive to me because

   This model is unattractive to me because

4. The living-together model: The parties live together without being formally married and possibly with no intention to have children or permanency.

   This model is attractive to me because

   This model is unattractive to me because

5. The singlehood model: The person lives alone.

   This model is attractive to me because

   This model is unattractive to me because

Identify the pairing model that you prefer for yourself and explain in detail why it is your preference.

Making Marriage Work

John Gottman
and Nan Silver

The chance of a first marriage ending in divorce over a forty-year period is 67 percent. Half of all divorces will occur in the first seven years. Some studies find the divorce rate for second marriages is as much as 10 percent higher than for first-timers. The chance of getting divorced remains so high that it makes sense for all married couples—including those who are currently satisfied with their relationship—to put extra effort into their marriages to keep them strong.

One of the saddest reasons a marriage dies is that neither spouse recognizes its value until it is too late. Only after the papers have been signed, the furniture divided, and separate apartments rented do the exes realize how much they really gave up when they gave up on each other. Too often a good marriage is taken for granted rather than given the nurturing and respect it deserves and desperately needs.

FRIENDSHIP VERSUS FIGHTING

At the heart of my program is the simple truth that happy marriages are based on a deep friendship. By this I mean a mutual respect for and enjoyment of each other's company. These couples tend to know each other intimately— they are well versed in each other's likes, dislikes, personality quirks, hopes, and dreams. They have an abiding regard for each other and express this fondness not just in the big ways but in little ways day in and out.

Take the case of hardworking Nathaniel, who runs his own import business and works very long hours. In another marriage, his schedule might be a major liability. But he and his wife Olivia have found ways to stay connected. They talk frequently on the phone during the day. When she has a doctor's appointment, he remembers to call to see how it went. When he has a meeting with an important client, she'll check in to see how it fared. When they have chicken for dinner, she gives him both drumsticks because she knows he likes them best. When he makes blueberry pancakes for the kids Saturday morning, he'll leave the blueberries out of hers because he knows she doesn't like them. Although he's not religious, he accompanies her to church each Sunday because it's important to her. And although she's not crazy about spending a lot of time with their relatives, she has pursued a friendship with Nathaniel's mother and sisters because family matters so much to him.

If all of this sounds humdrum and unromantic, it's anything but. Through small but important ways Olivia and Nathaniel are maintaining the friendship that is the foundation of their love. As a result they have a marriage that is far more passionate than do couples who punctuate their lives together with romantic vacations and lavish anniversary gifts but have fallen out of touch in their daily lives.

Friendship fuels the flames of romance because it offers the best protection against feeling adversarial toward your spouse. Because Nathaniel and Olivia have kept their friendship strong despite the inevitable disagreements and irritations of married life, they are experiencing what is known technically as "positive sentiment override." This means that their positive thoughts about each other and their marriage are so pervasive that they tend to supersede their negative feelings. It takes a much more significant conflict for them to lose their equilibrium as a couple than it would otherwise. Their positivity causes them to feel optimistic about each other and their marriage, to assume positive things about their lives together, and to give each other the benefit of the doubt.

Rediscovering or reinvigorating friendship doesn't prevent couples from arguing. Instead, it gives them a secret weapon that prevents quarrels from getting out of hand. For example, here's what happens when Olivia and Nathaniel argue. As they plan to move from the city to the suburbs, tensions between them are high. Although they see eye to eye on which house to buy and how to decorate it, they are locking horns over buying a new car. Olivia thinks they should join the suburban masses and get a minivan. To Nathaniel nothing could be drearier—he wants a Jeep. The more they talk about it, the higher the decibel level gets. If you were a fly on the wall of their bedroom, you would have serious doubts about their future together. Then all of a sudden, Olivia puts her hands on her hips and, in perfect imitation of their four-year-old son, sticks out her tongue. Since Nathaniel knows that she's about to do this, he sticks out his tongue first. Then they both start laughing. As always, this silly contest defuses the tension between them.

In our research we actually have a technical name for what Olivia and Nathaniel did. Probably unwittingly, they used a *repair attempt*. This name refers to any statement or action—silly or otherwise—that prevents negativity from escalating out of control. Repair attempts are the secret weapon of emotionally intelligent couples—even though many of these couples aren't aware that they are doing something so powerful. When a couple have a strong friendship, they naturally become experts at sending each other repair attempts and at correctly reading those sent their way. But when couples are in negative override, even a repair statement as blunt as "Hey, I'm sorry" will have a low success rate.

The success or failure of a couple's repair attempts is one of the primary factors in whether their marriage flourishes or flounders. And again, what determines the success of their repair attempts is the strength of their marital friendship. If this sounds simplistic or obvious, you'll find in the pages ahead that it is not. Strengthening your marital friendship isn't as basic as just being "nice." Even if you feel that your friendship is already quite solid, you may be surprised to find there is room to strengthen it all the more. Most of the couples who take our workshop are relieved to hear that almost everybody messes up during marital conflict. What matters is whether the repairs are successful.

In the strongest marriages, husband and wife share a deep sense of meaning. They don't just "get along"—they also support each other's hopes and aspirations and build a sense of purpose into their lives together. That is really what I mean when I talk about honoring and respecting each other.

Very often a marriage's failure to do this is what causes husband and wife to find themselves in endless, useless rounds of argument or to feel isolated and lonely in their marriage. After watching countless videotapes of couples fighting, I can guarantee you that most quarrels are really not about whether the toilet lid is up or down or whose turn it is to take out the trash. There are deeper, hidden issues that fuel these superficial conflicts and make them far more intense and hurtful than they would otherwise be.

Once you understand this, you will be ready to accept one of the most surprising truths about marriage: *Most marital arguments cannot be resolved.* Couples spend year after year trying to change each other's mind—but it can't be done. This is because most of their disagreements are rooted in fundamental differences of lifestyle, personality, or values. By fighting over these differences, all they succeed in doing is wasting their time and harming their marriage.

This doesn't mean there's nothing you can do if your relationship has been overrun by conflict. But it does mean that the typical conflict-resolution advice won't help. Instead, you need to understand the bottom-line difference that is causing the conflict between you—and to learn how to live with it by honoring and respecting each other. Only then will you be able to build shared meaning and a sense of purpose into your marriage.

HARSH STARTUP

When a discussion leads off this way—with criticism and/or sarcasm, a form of contempt—it has begun with a "harsh startup." Although Dara talks to Oliver in a very soft, quiet voice, there's a load of negative power in her words. After hearing the first minute or so of their conversation, it's no surprise to me that by the end Dara and Oliver haven't resolved their differences at all. The research shows that if your discussion begins with a harsh startup, it will inevitably end on a negative note, even if there are a lot of attempts to "make nice" in between. Statistics tell the story: 96 percent of the time you can predict the outcome of a conversation based on the *first three minutes* of the fifteen-minute interaction! A harsh startup simply dooms you to failure. So if you begin a discussion that way, you might as well pull the plug, take a breather, and start over.

THE FOUR HORSEMEN

Certain kinds of negativity, if allowed to run rampant, are so lethal to a relationship that I call them the Four Horsemen of the Apocalypse. Usually these four horsemen clip-clop into the heart of a marriage in the following order: criticism, contempt, defensiveness, and stonewalling.

Horseman 1: Criticism

You will always have some complaints about the person you live with. But there's a world of difference between a complaint and a criticism. A complaint only addresses the specific action at which your spouse failed. A criticism is more global—it adds on some negative words about your mate's character or personality. "I'm really angry that you didn't sweep the kitchen floor last night. We agreed that we'd take turns doing it" is a complaint. "Why are you so forgetful? I hate having to always sweep the kitchen floor when it's your turn. You just don't care" is a criticism. A complaint focuses on a specific behavior, but a criticism ups the ante by throwing in blame and general character assassination. Here's a recipe: To turn any complaint into a criticism, just add my favorite line: "What is wrong with you?"

Horseman 2: Contempt

Dara doesn't stop at criticizing Oliver. Soon she's literally sneering. When he suggests that they keep a list of his chores on the refrigerator to help him remember, she says, "Do you think you work really well with lists?" Next, Oliver tells her that he needs fifteen minutes to relax when he gets home before starting to do chores. "So if I leave you alone for fifteen minutes, then you think you'll be motivated to jump up and do something?" she asks him.

"Maybe. We haven't tried it, have we?" Oliver asks.

Dara has an opportunity here to soften up, but instead she comes back with sarcasm. "I think you do a pretty good job of coming home and lying around or disappearing into the bathroom," she says. And then she adds challengingly, "So you think that's the cure-all, to give you fifteen minutes?"

This sarcasm and cynicism are types of contempt. So are name-calling, eye-rolling, sneering, mockery, and hostile humor. In whatever form, contempt—the worst of the four horsemen—is poisonous to a relationship because it conveys disgust. It's virtually impossible to resolve a problem when your partner is getting the message you're disgusted with him or her. Inevitably, contempt leads to more conflict rather than to reconciliation.

Contempt is fueled by long-simmering negative thoughts about the partner. You're more likely to have such thoughts if your differences are not resolved. No doubt, the first time Peter and Cynthia argued about money, he wasn't so disrespectful. He probably offered a simple complaint like "I think you should wash your own car. It costs too much to always have someone else wash it." But as they kept disagreeing about this, his complaints turned to global criticisms, such as: "You always spend too much money." And when the conflict continued, he felt more and more disgusted and fed up with Cynthia, a change that affected what he said when they argued.

Belligerence, a close cousin to contempt, is just as deadly to a relationship. It is a form of aggressive anger because it contains a threat or provocation. When a wife complains that her husband doesn't come home from work in time for dinner, a belligerent response would be "Well, what are you going to do about it?" When Peter says to Cynthia, "What are you going to do, sue me?" he thinks he's making a joke, but he's really being belligerent.

Horseman 3: Defensiveness

It's no surprise, considering how nasty her husband is being, that Cynthia defends herself. She points out that she doesn't get her car washed as often as he thinks. She explains that it's more difficult physically for her to wash her car herself than it is for him to wash his truck.

Although it's understandable that Cynthia would defend herself, research shows that this approach rarely has the desired effect. The attacking spouse does not back down or apologize. This is because defensiveness is really a way of blaming your partner. You're saying, in effect, "The problem isn't *me*, it's *you*." Defensiveness just escalates the conflict, which is why it's so deadly. When Cynthia tells Peter how hard it is for her to wash her car, he doesn't say, "Oh, now I understand." He ignores her excuse—he doesn't even acknowledge what she's said. He climbs farther up his high moral ground, telling her how well he takes care of his vehicle and implying that she's spoiled for not doing the same. Cynthia can't win—and neither can their marriage.

Criticism, Contempt, and Defensiveness don't always gallop into a home in strict order. They function more like a relay match—handing the baton off to each other over and over again, if the couple can't put a stop to it. You can see this happening as Oliver and Dara continue their discussion about cleaning their house. Although they seem to be seeking a solution, Dara becomes increasingly contemptuous—mocking Oliver in the guise of questioning him and tearing down every plan he devises. The more defensive he becomes, the more she attacks him. Her body language signals condescension. She speaks softly, her elbows resting on the table, her intertwined fingers cradling her chin. Like a law professor or a judge, she peppers him with questions just to see him squirm.

Horseman 4: Stonewalling

In marriages like Dara and Oliver's, where discussions begin with a harsh startup, where criticism and contempt lead to defensiveness, which leads to more contempt and more defensiveness, eventually one partner tunes out. This heralds the arrival of the fourth horseman.

Think of the husband who comes home from work, gets met with a barrage of criticism from his wife, and hides behind the newspaper. The less responsive he is, the more she yells. Eventually he gets up and leaves the room. Rather than confronting his wife, he disengages. By turning away from her, he is avoiding a fight, but he is also avoiding his marriage. He has become a stonewaller. Although both husbands and wives can be stonewallers, this behavior is far more common among men, for reasons we'll see later.

During a typical conversation between two people, the listener gives all kinds of cues to the speaker that he's paying attention. He may use eye contact, nod his head, say something like "Yeah" or "Uh-huh." But a stonewaller doesn't give you this sort of casual feedback. He tends to look away or down without uttering a sound. He sits like an impassive stone wall. The stonewaller acts as though he couldn't care less about what you're saying, if he even hears it.

Stonewalling usually arrives later in the course of a marriage than the other three horsemen. That's why it's less common among newlywed husbands such as Oliver than among couples who have been in a negative spiral for a while. It takes time for the negativity created by the first three horsemen to become overwhelming enough that stonewalling becomes an understandable "out." That's the stance that Mack takes when he and his wife Rita argue about each other's behavior at parties. She says the problem is that he drinks too much. He thinks the bigger problem is her reaction: She embarrasses him by yelling at him in front of his friends. Here they are, already in the middle of an argument:

RITA: Now I've become the problem, again. I started off with the complaint, but now I am the problem. That always seems to happen.

MACK: Yeah, I do that, I know. *(Pause.)* But your tantrums and childishness are an embarrassment to me and my friends.

RITA: If you would control your drinking at parties, puleese . . .

MACK: *(Looks down, avoids eye contact, says nothing—he's stonewalling.)*

RITA: Because I think *(laughs)* for the most part, we get along pretty well, really *(laughs).*

MACK: *(Continues to stonewall. Remains silent, makes no eye contact, head nods, facial movements, or vocalizations.)*

RITA: Don't you think?

MACK: *(No response.)*

RITA: Mack? Hello?

It may seem to Rita that her complaints have no effect on Mack. But nothing could be further from the truth. Usually people stonewall as a protection against feeling *flooded.* Flooding means that your spouse's negativity—whether in the guise of criticism or contempt or even defensiveness—is so overwhelming, and so sudden, that it leaves you shell-shocked. You feel so defenseless against this sniper attack that you learn to do anything to avoid a replay. The more often you feel flooded by your spouse's criticism or contempt, the more hypervigilant you are for cues that your spouse is about to "blow" again. All you can think about is protecting yourself from the turbulence your spouse's onslaught causes. And the way to do that is to disengage emotionally from the relationship. No wonder Mack and Rita are now divorced.

Another husband, Paul, was quite up front about why he stonewalls when his wife, Amy, gets negative. In the following discussion he articulates what all stonewallers are feeling.

AMY: When I get mad, that's when you should step in and try to make it better. But when you just stop talking, it means, 'I no longer care about how you feel.' That just makes me feel one inch tall. Like my opinion or feelings have absolutely no bearing on you. And that's not the way a marriage should be.

PAUL: What I'm saying is, if you wanna have a serious conversation, you're gonna do it without yelling and screaming all the time. You start saying things that are hurtful.

AMY: Well, when I'm hurt, mad, and I wanna hurt you, I start saying things. And that's when we should both stop. I should say, "I'm sorry." And you should say, "I know that you wanna talk about this. And I really should make an effort to talk instead of just ignoring you."

PAUL: I'll talk when—

AMY: It fits your purpose.

PAUL: No, when you're not yelling and screaming and jumping up and down stomping.

Amy kept telling Paul how it made her feel when he shut down. But she did not seem to hear him tell her *why* he shuts down: He can't handle her hostility. This couple later divorced.

A marriage's meltdown can be predicted, then, by habitual harsh startup and frequent flooding brought on by the relentless presence of the four horsemen during disagreements. Although each of these factors alone can predict a divorce, they usually coexist in an unhappy marriage.

Just because your marriage follows this pattern, it's not a given that a divorce is in the offing. In fact, you'll find examples of all four horsemen and even occasional flooding in stable marriages. But when the four horsemen take up *permanent* residence, when either partner begins to feel flooded routinely, the relationship is in serious trouble. Frequently feeling flooded leads almost inevitably to distancing yourself from your spouse. That in turn leads you to feel lonely. Without help, the couple will end up divorced or living in a dead marriage, in which they maintain separate, parallel lives in the same home. They may go through the motions of togetherness—attending their children's plays, hosting dinner parties, taking family vacations. But emotionally they no longer feel connected to each other. They have given up.

REPAIR ATTEMPTS

It takes time for the four horsemen and the flooding that comes in their wake to overrun a marriage. And yet divorce can so often be predicted by listening to a single conversation between newlyweds. How can this be? The answer is that by analyzing any disagreement a couple has, you get a good sense of the pattern they tend to follow. A crucial part of that pattern is whether their repair attempts succeed or fail. Repair attempts... are efforts the couple makes ("Let's take a break," "Wait, I need to calm down") to deescalate the tension during a touchy discussion—to put on the brakes so flooding is prevented.

Repair attempts save marriages not just because they decrease emotional tension between spouses, but because by lowering the stress level they also prevent your heart from racing and making you feel flooded. When the four horsemen rule a couple's communication, repair attempts often don't even get noticed. Especially when you're feeling flooded, you're not able to hear a verbal white flag.

In unhappy marriages a feedback loop develops between the four horsemen and the failure of repair attempts. The more contemptuous and defensive the couple is with each other, the more flooding occurs, and the harder it is to hear and respond to a repair. And since the repair is not heard, the contempt and defensiveness just get heightened, making flooding more pronounced, which makes it more difficult to hear the next repair attempt, until finally one partner withdraws.

In emotionally intelligent marriages I hear a wide range of successful repair attempts. Each person has his or her own approach. Olivia and Nathaniel stick out their tongues; other couples laugh or smile or say they're sorry. Even an irritated "Hey, stop yelling at me," or "You're getting off the topic" can defuse a tense situation. All such repair attempts keep a marriage stable because they prevent the four horsemen from moving in for good.

SHARED MEANINGS

But it is also true that a rewarding marriage is about more than sidestepping conflict. The more you can agree about the fundamentals in life, the richer, more meaningful, and in a sense easier your marriage is likely to be. You certainly can't force yourselves to have the same deeply held views. But some coming together on these issues is likely to occur naturally if you are open to each other's perspectives. *A crucial goal of any marriage, therefore, is to create an atmosphere that encour-* *ages each person to talk honestly about his or her convictions.* The more you speak candidly and respectfully with each other, the more likely there is to be a blending of your sense of meaning.

Follow-Up

1. *Select two ideas from this article and comment on their meaning and application.*
2. *Choose one of the negative relationship factors and attempt to decrease it in an ongoing relationship.*
3. *Try to apply the concept of "repair attempts" in an ongoing relationship and report the results.*
4. *Complete the "Love Maps" Applied Activity at the end of this section and comment on your learnings.*
5. *For more detail on the ideas in this article, see* The Seven Principles for Making Marriage Work *by John Gottman and Nan Silver (Three Rivers Press, 1999).*

Sometimes It Rains

Tom Keating

The rain was coming down in solid sheets, but the young man and woman holding hands as they ducked into the revolving door at the Delaware Street entrance to the City-County Building didn't notice at all.

Storms, even tornadoes, are relative on your wedding day.

Shaking the rain out of their hair and laughing, they bounced along the main floor of the building and grinned at each other steadily as they stepped onto the escalator to the basement.

The young man was 20. The girl was 18.

They looked very much like any other young couple except that they were dressed in their best clothes and looked like they had just discovered one of the world's top secrets.

In the basement they met another young man and woman who were even more exuberant. The men shook hands while the girls exchanged hugs and brief kisses on the cheek.

After a minute of excited talk, they all gathered in the chambers of the Center Township justice of the peace for the ceremony.

Six floors up a woman with a streaked red face and tired eyes was standing across a courtroom from a hefty man who minutes before had been her husband. They were listening intently as the judge read the final divorce decree.

The judge explained the particulars of the separate existence they would be living from now on.

He repeated how and when the couple's three children would be shifted about and how much money would exchange hands on what dates and who would get to keep which of the possessions that had accumulated in nine years of marriage.

The man was 30. She was 28.

During the divorce proceedings the wife had charged mental cruelty and infidelity. The husband had not challenged the charges or made any of his own, but he said privately that he felt she was to blame for the breakup.

Both the man and the woman felt a vague embarrassment at airing their most personal failings in public. So the divorce had been handled with little emotion.

As the judge concluded, the man glanced at his wife. He tried to sneer but it came off instead as a look of boredom. The woman alternated between paying polite attention to the judge and searching her husband's face as if to see if he would have a last-minute change of heart.

When the court proceedings were finished, the couple stood separately in the wide hallway, each talking quietly with their respective attorneys. After a few minutes, the woman approached the man who was now her ex-husband.

"Well, good-by," she said. "I hope you'll be happy."

"I will, don't worry," he returned.

After a pause, however, he thought better of what he had said and added, "Well, I hope you're happy too. I don't know what happened, but I guess we'll both be better off."

"Sure, I agree, sure," she said, straining to smile.

With that the man turned and walked across the hallway to a bench where a young woman in a bright blue dress was waiting. They talked together in whispers for a moment and then disappeared into an elevator. The girl was smiling. The man was not.

The ex-wife watched them go and then sighed deeply, shrugged her shoulders and got onto another elevator alone.

On the main floor, the newly married couple was staring out the high glass doors at the rain with the perspective that only comes when you are young and everything is yet to happen.

"I love storms," the girl said. "Don't you?"

"Let's go then," her husband said. Grabbing her around the waist. They raced down the sidewalk for a few feet and then stopped and leaned against a pole in a tangle, oblivious to the fact they were getting drenched.

A few moments later, the divorced woman peered out the same glass doors.

"This is the lousiest weather I've ever seen in my life," she said. "But, what the hell, maybe I'll catch a cold."

She passed the young couple on the sidewalk but didn't notice them. Her head was down and she was looking for puddles.

Follow-Up

1. *The newly divorced man says to his now former wife, "I don't know what happened, but I guess we'll both be better off." They were married nine years. How could the relationship disintegrate without them knowing what happened? Would you guess that the newly divorced couple were like the newly married couple nine years ago? Offer your views on these questions.*
2. *Write about or discuss any other thought that this article evokes.*

Are Money Fights Ruining Your Marriage?

Dianne Hales

Whether couples are rich, poor or somewhere in between, whether they have two steady incomes or one that's erratic, most fight about money. And as money gets tight—which is increasingly common these days—battles over the budget increase.

"When couples are forced to set priorities, someone has to give up something—and that's when the fights begin," explains Victoria Felton-Collins, author of *Couples and Money: Why Money Interferes with Love and What to Do About It.* Once money spats flare up, they can turn ugly. "Money is a magnet that draws in all the frustrations in our lives," she observes.

It doesn't have to be this way, but you do have to delve beyond the dollars-and-cents dilemmas before you can stop the fights. Says Felton-Collins: "Money is a metaphor for power, freedom, self-esteem and love. You must understand how you and your spouse view and use money if you're going to stop fighting about it."

Consider how some real couples—who asked that their names be changed—handled these typical situations:

"WHAT AM I WORTH IF I LOSE MY JOB?"

Despite 15 years' seniority, Ned was fired when his company was sold. At first, he and his wife were thankful they had Pam's salary. But after months of fruitless job hunting, Ned started making snide remarks. "I can't spend a dime without getting her highness's approval," he complained. And Pam grew resentful. "I'm working extra hours just to pay our mortgage, utility and food bills," she said. "When I get home at night, I'd like to feel appreciated."

Losing a job is a blow to ego as well as to income—especially for men, who define manhood in terms of money, sex and power. When Ned lost his job, he—like many men—pulled away from his family. Pam didn't know what to say to make him feel better. Ned interpreted her silence as criticism. When they started sniping at each other, both realized something was wrong.

"Men never talk about it," says Felton-Collins, "but when their wives make more money than they do, they worry about being needed. If his family doesn't need him as a provider, a man wonders if they need him at all."

Pam finally took the initiative. "I told Ned that I felt we were both tiptoeing around on eggshells because money had become such a sensitive issue," she explains. "It took a lot of encouragement, but Ned gradually began to open up. He felt he wasn't contributing to the family anymore, so I told him all the things I'd assumed he knew—like how much we all love him, what a wonderful husband and father he is. I also described my own feelings about being the primary breadwinner. He'd thought I enjoyed having the upper hand, when I really hated it."

Pam and Ned also talked about practical matters. After losing his job, Ned stopped paying the bills. That made Pam feel that all their financial problems had been dumped on her. Once Ned resumed an active role in managing their money, both felt better. He also volunteered to help with school sports and other activities. "He saw how much the kids loved having time with him, and that made a difference too," says Pam. "And now that everything is out in the open, we all have the sense that we'll get through these tough times together."

"WHOSE MONEY IS IT ANYWAY?"

Before his marriage last year, Jake never thought twice about spending money. "Why not have fun when I'm young?" he said. Now, whenever Jake spends $50 on a night out with the guys, his wife, Lucy, gets angry. "How can you be so selfish?" she asks. "We could use that money for a down payment on a house."

"Why should you tell me how to spend my money?" Jake counters.

In more than half of all marriages today, both spouses work. Yet many enter marriage with very different notions about what's his, hers and theirs. Jake, for instance, simply assumed he could spend "his" money as he chose; Lucy thought his earnings were "theirs."

Lucy and Jake finally had an overdue talk about their goals and priorities. "We both want to buy a house before starting a family," says Jake. "To me, that's down the road a bit. But Lucy thinks we have to start saving now or we'll never make it. She spent her childhood moving from one military post to another with her dad. To her, having a house is the dream of a lifetime. When she explained that, I understood why she'd gotten so upset."

Talking, though, is just the first step. According to Alexis Mitchell, a certified financial planner and vice president of Fidelity Investments in Sacramento: "Two people have to negotiate until they reach a decision—and then make a commitment to stick to their agreement."

For Jake, the bottom line was having some money to spend as he pleased. Lucy, on the other hand, wanted a real commitment to shared goals. Their solution involved three separate bank accounts—an individual account for each, plus a joint account. Jake can spend his money without answering to Lucy. She can do the same. But both deposit 75 percent of their take-home pay into the joint account to cover expenses and start saving toward their own home.

"WHY DOES HE KEEP OVERDRAWING OUR CHECKING ACCOUNT?

Allison meticulously records every check she writes. Steve often forgets to make a deposit or record a withdrawal. When their telephone was cut off after yet another check bounced, Allison was furious. "How can you be so irresponsible?" she demanded.

"I work hard; I've got other things on my mind. Give me a break," Steve said.

Allison and Steve are a financial "odd couple," with her playing finicky Felix to his disorganized Oscar. To break out of their checkbook checkmates, they decided Allison would be responsible for the family's paperwork. All Steve had to do was put all his receipts in a shoe box. Every week Allison unfolded these crumbled papers and recorded them.

The system worked: No more checks bounced. But Steve began to wonder where the money was going. "I felt I had no control," he explained. "Whenever I asked Allison about our balance, she got defensive."

Allison explains why: "Here I was, cleaning up his chaos, and he was second-guessing me."

To stop this new round of spats, they talked about money in terms of control and security. For Allison, keeping tabs on every dime made her feel in control. Steve didn't care about every dime or dollar, but he needed a sense of the big financial picture. Both would feel more comfortable, they decided, with a weekly conference.

Allison now fills Steve in on their bank account balances every Sunday. Together they decide which bills to pay. When they have extra savings, Steve, who enjoys reading the financial pages, looks into possible investments. "I do what I do best, and Steve does what he

HOW TO AVOID MONEY CONFLICTS

Many money fights can be avoided by taking these practical steps in advance:

- *Don't let a lack of information create misunderstandings.* Go over your finances together. Prepare a simple financial worth statement so you're both aware of debts, assets, investments and obligations.
- *Discuss your feelings about money.* Does having it make you feel independent, secure, successful, loved, powerful? How do you feel when you spend money on yourself or give it to others? What worries you the most?
- *Tackle one financial chore at a time.* Don't try to establish a budget and make investment decisions all at once.
- *Recognize the value of unpaid work.* A husband in school or a wife raising children at home should feel that these contributions are just as vital as a salary.
- *Set financial goals and discuss how you'll meet them.* "Management by objective is always preferable to management by accident," notes financial planner Victoria Felton-Collins.
- *Make sure each partner has money to spend without answering to the other.* Even $10 a week can ease tensions.
- *Take your time on major decisions.* "A truly wonderful opportunity," says psychotherapist Arlene Modica Matthews, "should stand up to scrutiny. Do not bend to pressure to act hastily."
- *Consider "what-if" scenarios.* What would you do if you lost your job? If a family member had enormous medical bills? If the stock market crashed? By planning ahead, you'll feel less anxious.
- *Ask each other how you'd feel if you got what you want* (more money, more spending freedom or whatever). "Most people say, 'I'd feel loved,' or 'I'd feel respected' or 'I'd feel secure,' " observes therapist Suzanne Pope. "That feeling can help pinpoint what money fights are really about."

---

likes best," says Allison. "We work together rather than harping at each other."

"WHY SHOULD I HAVE TO BEG FOR MONEY?"

Jennie worked from the time she graduated from high school until her first child was born. Now a full-time mother of three, she feels she has to plead for money. "If I ask Greg for $20, he wants to know what I'm going to spend it on," she says. "He even checks the receipts to make sure I really did buy diapers."

Greg, a salesman whose commissions have fallen off, feels he's simply being responsible. "Jennie used to blow $20 on makeup every week," he says in self-defense. "We can't afford that kind of spending with three kids."

Babies invariably change the emotional and economic dynamics of a relationship. "A lot of working couples live like financial roommates until they have a child," notes psychologist Arlene Modica Matthews, author of *If I Think about Money So Much, Why Can't I Figure It Out?* "Parenthood makes them feel more bonded to each other."

"Couples who have been very modern and businesslike in handling money may return to old family patterns once they become parents," Mitchell observes. "The husband may have thought in terms of *his* money and *her* money. When her money stops coming in, he's still thinking it's all *his* money—and he resents spending some of it on her needs."

Mitchell urges new parents to talk about their feelings. Jennie, for example, told Greg that his failure to discuss money matters made her feel that she didn't count anymore. When she accused him of treating her "like a child," Greg remembered that his own father had handled the family finances by controlling every penny. "When I became a father, I guess I thought that was how I had to act," he admitted.

Jennie and Greg decided that both needed to keep track of their money. For three months, they recorded every dollar that came in and how it was spent. That gave them a clear idea of their cash flow. They discussed ways to supplement their income if Greg's commissions continued to drop. For example, Jennie might take care of neighborhood children. They also agreed on a weekly amount for Jennie to receive to cover household expenses.

"HOW CAN YOU TAKE SUCH RISKS WITH OUR MONEY?"

When Andy won $10 on a $2 lottery ticket, he bet on a horse and won $20. He thought his wife would be thrilled. Lisa was annoyed. "How can you gamble when we can't even afford new tires for the car?" she asked. But when Lisa suggested shifting their savings into high-yield stocks, Andy got angry. "We can't afford to play the stock market," he said. "You're the real gambler in the family."

Risks are always relative. Andy, who follows horse racing, thinks he knows a safe bet when he sees one. But he doesn't know a blue chip from a poker chip, so the stock market seems far more treacherous to him than the track. Lisa, on the other hand, works for an investment firm and sees that money put into good stocks grows a lot faster than it does in a savings account.

To stop their arguments, Andy and Lisa took the advice of experts in her firm: They discussed their financial objectives, considered various ways to reach them and tried to antici-

pate what could go wrong with each approach. "We realized that, in a sense, Andy was right: I *am* more of gambler," says Lisa. "He doesn't mind blowing a few bucks on a horse, but when it comes to serious money, he's very cautious."

Ultimately, they decided to diversify—to invest a limited portion of the money they're saving for their children's college education in high-yield bonds. They kept another portion in insured certificates of deposit and put the rest into mutual funds.

"Couples should realize that risk-taking doesn't have to be an all-or-nothing venture," says Mitchell. "They need to be conservative about money saved for emergencies, but should agree on a certain percentage—say 10 to 25 percent—that they'll wager for greater rewards."

"WHY CAN'T WE GET OUT OF DEBT?"

Jason and Molly aren't quite broke, but they owe thousands of dollars on their credit cards. Despite promises to stop spending, both continue to find—and charge—items they can't resist. "How could you spend so much on a tennis racquet?" Molly cries when she sees the bills. "Well, look at how much you spent on clothes!" counters Jason.

Jason and Molly are out-of-control spenders. "They're like kids in a candy store," says Mitchell, who finds that such couples often need professional help. Molly and Jason consulted a therapist with experience in solving money problems. As a first step, she advised leaving their credit cards at home.

Each calculated how much cash was needed each day and carried only that amount. "At first, I was crushed when I'd see great earrings and not be able to buy them," says Molly, "but when I went back to the store later they didn't have the same appeal. I began to see that I bought a lot of things simply to make me feel better." Jason came to a similar realization: He spent money impulsively when he felt unsure of himself. He'd buy a sports jacket, for instance, before calling on a new client.

Jason and Molly also made a list of all their assets and liabilities. They agreed to allocate $300 a month to paying off their credit cards before making any new purchases. Then they came up with alternative ways to boost their spirits: weekend drives in the country, free concerts in the park, dinners at inexpensive restaurants. "We also learned how to express our feelings directly," says Molly "Now if I get angry, I tell Jason how I feel rather than heading for the mall to shop."

"HOW CAN WE STOP FIGHTING?"

Bill and Jeanne had bickered about their budget for years, but their arguments grew more fierce after they retired. Jeanne claims that Bill turns every conversation into a money fight. "If I say it's raining, he'll say he hopes the roof doesn't leak because we can't afford to fix it when I spend so much on the grandchildren," she complains. "Money is all he thinks about." Bill's usual response: "Well, someone has to think about it."

When arguments are repetitive, more than dollars and cents is at stake. Bill was used to calling the shots in his own appliance-repair firm. To him, keeping a keen eye on finances was simply good business. After retirement, he shifted his focus from office to home—and the sudden intensity of his involvement was bewildering to Jeanne.

Underlying Bill's penny-pinching was anxiety about the future. Had he saved enough for their golden years? What if one of them developed a serious illness? What if something happened to their investments? Were they in danger of losing all they'd worked for?

Jeanne finally asked Bill why he was so concerned about every penny. When he spoke vaguely about their fixed income, she asked for details. Then, seeing Bill's anxiety, she suggested they talk to a financial adviser. At first Bill balked at revealing details of their finances to a stranger. But after meeting with the adviser, he felt less anxious.

The money fights eased for a while. But each minor crisis caused the squabbling to resume. One day Jeanne borrowed her granddaughter's tape recorder and turned it on as another battle erupted. The next day she played it back. Both had to smile as they listened to their familiar attacks and counterattacks. "Now what was that really all about?" Jeanne asked. It turned out that Bill was worried about his health, but found it easier to focus on money.

For Bill and Jeanne—as well as other couples torn by money conflicts—finding solutions isn't easy but can result in unexpected dividends. "If couples learn to deal with money, they can tackle other issues—such as success, independence, trust, commitment, power," says Rodney Shapiro, Ph.D., director of family therapy at California Pacific Medical Center in San Francisco. "Once they've worked out their money problems, they have more confidence in their problem-solving skills and more trust in each other. If they can stop fighting about money, they think they can handle anything. They may be right."

Follow-Up

1. *Select one of the situations described as causing conflict and apply it to your life. What are some possible actions that could help in this situation?*
2. *Apply one or more of the suggestions in the section "How to Avoid Money Conflicts" and report on the results.*
3. *Select two statements or ideas from the article and apply them to your life. Discuss your thoughts.*
4. *For a related reading, see "Personality and Money Orientations" in Section Six (A Quality Life).*

Thoughts on Intimacy

Nelson Goud

EXPECTATIONS

What do we expect from an intimate relationship? Security? Sex? Companionship? Friendship? A soulmate? Many people seem to want all of these, most of the time. Gone seem to be the times when economic security, companionship, and an occasional spark of romance were good enough.

Craig Cox argues that many people now want a "superrelationship" based on extremely heightened expectations of what an intimate connection should be. Beyond love, sex, and communication is the search for a mate who deeply intuits his or her partner's nature—who "gets" them. Well, who wouldn't want that? Often overlooked is the price demanded for such superrelationships.

> "What's really demanding about the building of a superrelationship is the level of maintenance it requires to run smoothly. . . . Because couples in these types of marriages expect an uncommon level of emotional intimacy—the closeness of soulmates —they must constantly strive to maintain a high level of trust and loyalty." Cox contends that this makes a superrelationship more demanding and fragile than 'good enough' relationships. (*Utne*, Nov–Dec 2004, p. 54)

Author Erica Jong supports this line of thinking:

> The problem with Americans is that . . . we want all our emotional eggs in one basket. We crave passion, sex, friendship and children all with the same partner. Can such miracles occur? And if they occur, how long can they last? . . . The glue that holds couples together consists of many things: laughter, companionship, tenderness—and sex. The busyness of marriage is real, but we also use it to protect us from raw intimacy, from having to be too open too much of the time. (*Newsweek*, June 30, 2003, p. 48).

In her lyrical book *Gift from the Sea*, Anne Lindbergh places the questions in another framework. She views an intimate relationship much like the ebb and flows of the tides.

> When you love someone you do not love them all the time, in exactly the same way, from moment to moment. It is an impossibility. It is even a lie to pretend to. And yet this is exactly what most of us demand. We have so little faith in the ebb and flow of life, of love, of relationships. We leap at the flow of the tide and resist in terror its ebb. We are afraid it will never return. We insist on permanency, on duration, on continuity; when the only continuity possible, in life as in love, is in growth, in fluidity—in freedom, in the sense that the

dancers are free, barely touching as they pass, but partners in the same pattern. The only real security is not in owning or possessing, not in demanding or expecting, not in hoping, even. Security in a relationship lies neither in looking back to what it was in nostalgia, nor forward to what it might be in dread or anticipation, but living in the present relationship and accepting it as it is now. For relationships, too, must be like islands. One must accept them for what they are here and now, within their limits—islands, surrounded and interrupted by the sea, continually visited and abandoned by the tides. One must accept the security of the winged life, of ebb and flow, of intermittency.

Lindbergh says that intermittency is a given of our emotional and interpersonal life. A constant state of soulmate immediacy is not of our nature. One must learn to not to only go with the flow, but also accept the ebbtides of intimacy.

Follow-Up

1. *Explain why you agree or disagree with the excessive expectations and demands of a superrelationship.*
2. *What is your idea of a deep, intimate relationship? Could this ideal inhibit seeing the actual nature of another person?*

SEX ON THE THIRD

It is increasingly mentioned that the new rule of thumb for first-time sex is the third date. Sex before the third date signals that you are promiscuous or, at best, madly in love at first sight. If there is no sex on the third date, then this is an indication that the relationship is going nowhere. For those who buy into this norm, there are several consequences:

1. Expecting sex on the third date leads to intense pressures during the first two, thereby warping the natural flow.
2. Not having sex on the third date and ending the relationship may mean prematurely closing off a potentially good relationship given a little more time.
3. Having sex on the third date may mean an over investment into a relationship that has just started.

Follow-Up

1. *What are your thoughts and evaluation of the sex on the third date?*

CYBERAFFAIRS

Whether through dating sites, chat rooms, personals, message boards, or e-mail, finding romance online is becoming a major means of "hooking up." Meghan Daum's article "Internet Romance" highlights the benefits and drawbacks of online communication for single persons. A new dimension enters the scene when a person in a committed relationship pursues online intimacy. Is a cyberaffair of the same magnitude as an in-person one? As in online communication, there are several advantages for the users: anonymity and a borrowed identity; less inhibition and little to fear; a high degree of control of how and when to respond; the excitement and anticipation of the next message. Whether the cyberaffair involves exchanging sexual fantasies with one another, is it an act of infidelity? Or emotional cheating? Psychologists who work with couples with relationship difficulties argue that online affairs cause as much emotional disruption as in-person ones, if discovered. They also recommend that if the couple is not already in counseling, a cyberaffair is a good reason to initiate a change in the relationship and probably begin therapy. Both must agree to the therapy for it to be effective.

Follow-Up

1. *Is a cyberaffair as significant as a face-to-face affair? Why?*
2. *What is the difference between the fantasy of an online affair and having one in your daydreams?*
3. *Are there good reasons to have cyberaffairs? Why?*

Internet Romance

Meghan Daum

One morning I logged on to my America Online account to find a message under the heading "is this the real meghan daum?" It came from someone with the screen name PFSlider. The body of the message consisted of five sentences, entirely in lowercase letters, of perfectly turned flattery, something about PFSlider's admiration of some newspaper and magazine articles I had published over the last year and a half, something else about his resulting infatuation with me, and something about his being a sportswriter in California.

I was charmed for a moment or so, engaged for the thirty seconds it took me to read the message and fashion a reply. Though it felt strange to be in the position of confirming that I was indeed "the real meghan daum," I managed to say "Yes, it's me. Thank you for writing." I clicked the Send Now icon and shot my words into the void, where I forgot about PFSlider until the next day, when I received another message, this one labeled "eureka." "wow, it is you," he wrote, still in lowercase. He chronicled the various conditions under which he'd read my few and far between articles: a boardwalk in Laguna Beach, the spring training press room for the baseball team he covered for a Los Angeles newspaper. He confessed to having a "crazy crush" on me. He referred to me as "princess daum." He said he wanted to propose marriage or at least have lunch with me during one of his two annual trips to New York. He managed to do all of this without sounding like a schmuck. As I read the note I smiled the kind of smile one tries to suppress, the kind of smile that arises during a sappy movie one never even admits to seeing. The letter was outrageous and endearingly pathetic, possibly the practical joke of a friend trying to rouse me out of a temporary writer's block. But the kindness pouring forth from my computer screen was unprecedented, bizarrely exhilarating, and I logged off and thought about it for a few hours before writing back to express how flattered and touched—it was probably the first time I had ever used "touched" in earnest—I was by his message. . . .

PFSlider and I tossed a few innocuous, smart-assed notes back and forth over the week following his first message. His name was Pete. He was twenty-nine and single. I revealed very little about myself, relying instead on the ironic commentary and forced witticisms that are the conceit of most e-mail messages. But I quickly developed an oblique affection for PFSlider. I was excited when there was a message from him, mildly depressed when there wasn't. After a few weeks he gave me his phone number. I did not give him mine, but he looked me up anyway and called me one Friday night. I was home. I picked up the phone. His voice was jarring yet not unpleasant. He held up more than his end of the conversation for an hour. . . .

Pete, as I was forced to call him on the phone—I never could wrap my mind around his actual name, privately referring to him as PFSlider, "e-mail guy," or even "baseball boy"—began calling me two or three times a week. He asked if he could meet me in person and I said that would be okay. Christmas was a few weeks away, and he would be returning east to see his family. From there, he would take the short flight to New York and have lunch with me. "It is my off-season mission to meet you," he said. "There will probably be a snowstorm," I said. "I'll bring a team of sled dogs," he answered. . . .

Other times we would find each other logged on to America Online at the same time and type back and forth for hours. For me, this was far superior to the phone. Through typos and misspellings, he flirted maniacally. "I have an absurd crush on you," he said. "If I like you in person you must promise to marry me." I was coy and conceited, telling him to get a life, baiting him into complimenting me further, teasing him in a way I would never have dared in the real world or even on the phone. I would stay up until 3:00 A.M. typing with him, smiling at the screen, getting so giddy that I couldn't fall asleep. I was having difficulty recalling what I used to do at night. My phone was tied up for hours at a time. No one in the real world could reach me, and I didn't really care. . . .

My interaction with PFSlider was more human than much of what I experienced in the daylight realm of live beings. I was certainly putting more energy into the relationship than I had put into any before, giving him attention that was by definition undivided, relishing the safety of the distance by opting to be truthful rather than doling out the white lies that have become the staple of real life. The outside world, the place where I walked around on the concrete, avoiding people I didn't want to deal with, peppering the ground with half-truths, and applying my motto of "let the machine take it" to almost any scenario, was sliding into the periphery of my mind. I was a better person with PFSlider. I was someone I could live with.

This borrowed identity is, of course, the primary convention of Internet relationships. The false comfort of the cyberspace persona has been identified as one of the maladies of our time, another avenue for the remoteness that so famously plagues contemporary life. But the better person that I was to PFSlider was not a result of being a different person to him. It was simply that I was a desired person, the object of a blind man's gaze. I may not have known my suitor, but for the first time in my life I knew the deal. I knew when I'd hear from him and how I'd hear from him. I knew he wanted me because he said he wanted me, because the distance and facelessness and lack of gravity of it all allowed him to be sweeter to me than most real-life people had ever managed. For the first time in my life, I was involved in an actual courtship ritual. Never before had I realized how much that kind of structure was missing from my everyday life.

And so PFSlider became my everyday life. . . .

Since graduating from college, I had spent three years in a serious relationship and two years in a state of neither looking for a boyfriend nor particularly avoiding one. I had had the requisite number of false starts and five-night stands, dates that I weren't sure were dates, emphatically casual affairs that buckled under their own inertia even before dawn broke through the iron-guarded windows of stale, one-room city apartments. Even though I was heading into my late twenties I was still a child, ignorant of dance steps or health insurance, a prisoner of credit card debt and student loans and the nagging feeling that I didn't want anyone to find me until I had pulled myself into some semblance of a grownup. I was a true believer in the urban dream, in years of struggle succumbing to brilliant success, in getting a break, in making it. Like most of my friends, I was selfish by design. To want was more virtuous than to need. I wanted someone to love me, but I certainly didn't need it. I didn't want to be alone, but as long as I was I had no choice but to wear my solitude as though it were haute couture. . . .

My addiction to PFSlider's messages indicated a monstrous narcissism. But it also revealed a subtler desire that I didn't fully understand at the time. My need to experience an old-fashioned kind of courtship was stronger than I had ever imagined. . . .

For the first time in my life, I was not involved in a protracted "hang out" that would lead to a quasi-romance. I was involved in a well-defined structure, a neat little space in which we were both safe to express the panic and intrigue of our mutual affection. Our interaction was refreshingly orderly, noble in its vigor, dignified despite its shamelessness. We had an intimacy that seemed custom made for our strange, lonely times. It seemed custom made for me.

The day of our date was frigid and sunny. Pete was sitting at the bar of the restaurant when I arrived. We shook hands. For a split second he leaned toward me with his chin as if to kiss me. . . .

He talked and I heard nothing he said. He talked and talked and talked. I stared at his profile and tried to figure out if I liked him. He seemed to be saying nothing in particular, though it went on forever. Later we went to the Museum of Natural History and watched a science film about storms. We walked around looking for the dinosaurs, and he talked so much that I wanted to cry. Outside, walking along Central Park West at dusk, through the leaves, past the horse-drawn carriages and yellow cabs and splendid lights of Manhattan at Christmas, he grabbed my hand to kiss me and I didn't let him. I felt as if my brain had been stuffed with cotton. Then for some reason I invited him back to my apartment, gave him a few beers, and finally let him kiss me on the lumpy futon in my bedroom. The radiator clanked. The phone rang and the machine picked up. A car alarm blared outside. A key turned in the door as one of my roommates came home. I had no sensation at all, only the dull déjà vu of being back in some college dorm room, making out in a generic fashion on an Indian throw rug while Cat Stevens's *Greatest Hits* played on the portable stereo. I wanted Pete out of my apartment. I wanted to hand him his coat, close the door behind him, and fight the ensuing emptiness by turning on the computer and taking comfort in PFSlider.

When Pete finally did leave I sulked. The ax had fallen. He'd talked way too much. He was hyper. He hadn't let me talk, although I hadn't tried very hard. I berated myself from every angle, for not kissing him on Central Park West, for letting him kiss me at all, for not liking him, for wanting to like him more than I had wanted anything in such a long time. I was horrified by the realization that I had invested so heavily in a made-up character, a character in whose creation I'd had a greater hand than even Pete himself. How could I, a person so self-congratulatingly reasonable, have gotten sucked into a scenario that was more like a television talk show than the relatively full and sophisticated life I was so convinced I lead? How could I have received a fan letter and allowed it go this far? Then a huge bouquet of FTD flowers arrived from him. No one had ever sent me flowers before. I was sick with sadness. I hated either the world or myself, and probably both. . . .

As human beings with actual flesh and hand gestures and Gap clothing, Pete and I were utterly incompatible, but I pretended otherwise. . . .

Unlike most cyber romances, which seem to come fully equipped with the inevitable set of misrepresentations and false expectations, PFSlider and I had played it fairly straight. Neither of us had lied. We'd done the best we could. We were dead from natural causes rather than virtual ones. . . .

At least seven people confessed to me the vagaries of their own e-mail affairs. The topic arose, unprompted, over the course of normal conversation. Four of these people had gotten on planes and met their correspondents, traveling from New Haven to Baltimore, New York to Montana, Texas to Virginia, and New York to Johannesburg. These were normal people, writers and lawyers and scientists I knew from the real world. They were all smart, attractive, and more than a little sheepish about admitting just how deep they had been sucked in. Very few had met in chat rooms. Instead, the messages had started after chance meetings at parties and on planes; some, like me, had received notes in response to things they'd written on-line or elsewhere. Two of these people had fallen in love, the others chalked it up to strange, uniquely postmodern experience. . . .

If Pete and I had met at a party, we probably wouldn't have spoken to each other for more than ten minutes, and that would have made life easier but also less interesting. At the same time, it terrifies me to admit a firsthand understanding of the way the heart and the ego are snarled and entwined.

Follow-Up

1. *Describe the advantages and disadvantages of e-mail romances.*
2. *According to Daum, online encounters allow you to portray another identity, or to express an aspect of yourself that is normally hidden in face-to-face encounters. Is this true in your online encounters? What are the advantages and disadvantages of this portrayal?*
3. *E-mail exchanges cannot reveal one's nonverbal behaviors such as gestures, frowns or smirks, voice tone, eye contact, and so on. Studies show that the majority of emotional messages are conveyed through nonverbal means. Discuss the effects of the absence of nonverbal behaviors in e-mail exchanges.*
4. *Starting a relationship through e-mail exchanges often results in a flurry of intense correspondence. This raises expectations. Upon meeting your cyberpartner in person, you are disappointed. Comment on this phenomena.*
5. *The author discovered that she wanted an "old-fashioned courtship" after several exchanges with her Internet partner. Why do you think this intimacy need had gone undetected? Is this unusual or typical in our society today? Offer your thoughts.*
6. *Choose any two statements or ideas from this article and offer your commentary.*

Kinds of Friends

Judith Viorst

In her book *Necessary Losses,* Judith Viorst discusses how we form different categories of friendships. A brief description of each kind of friendship is given below:

1. *Convenience Friends*—Persons with whom we exchange small favors; a friendly, but limited, intimacy relationship.
2. *Special Interest Friends*—Persons with whom we share common interests and activities; regular involvement, but not deep intimacy.
3. *Historical Friends*—Persons who were friends in our past but who we do not see often; there may be little in common now, but there is an intimacy that derives from being able to say, "I knew you when. . . ."
4. *Crossroads Friends*—Significant friends at a special time of our lives (e.g., college, former roommate, military service); little current contact, but the specialness can be quickly regenerated if there is an interaction.
5. *Cross-Generational Friends*—The older–younger relationships that have influence and intimacy. It may be a relationship of a mentor, or a cherished non-family friendship in which the older persons are valued for their counsel and acceptance and the younger persons for their liveliness and eagerness to learn.
6. *Close Friends*—Persons who hear our deeper disclosures; those whom we can trust and with whom we can just "be."

Follow-Up

1. *Do your friends generally fall into the categories listed above? If not, what other friend category(ies) would you add?*
2. *Viorst says we have ambivalent feelings toward close friends. There may be envy and competition, as well as affection and love. We generally are more aware of the positive feelings. Is this true for you?*
3. *How would you (or do you) feel about being classified into these categories by your friends?*
4. *Discuss and/or write about your reactions.*

Lamenting the Fading of Friendships

Mark Murrmann

People change.

I know I'm a different person, in some aspects, than I was just six months ago.

It's hard to deal with people changing, especially when those people are, or used to be, your friends.

Of my good friends in high school, I am still close with exactly none of them. Some of them I see once in a while, and we still get along well. Others I see maybe once a year, passing each other by chance on the street. We haven't got much to say, though.

Most of my old friends and I haven't really got much in common anymore. Thus, our conversations are limited to what we've been doing with our lives, what we plan on doing with our lives and what others are doing with their lives.

That is a boring, tired conversation. I may as well be talking to a stranger.

I am at fault for not seeing many of my old friends, and that makes me mad at myself. One of my best friends in high school lived one block away for the past year. I saw him only a few times—the times he came to my house.

Now that he's moved, I feel dumb for never stopping by.

SHARED PAST NOT ENOUGH

Other friends I have shut out of my life on purpose. We were once friends, and now we're not. We once had a lot in common; now we have little. All we have in common is a part of our past.

It's hard to have a relationship with someone based solely on the past. There is only so much you can reminisce over.

But I'm not going to take full blame for the friends with whom I've lost touch.

People change, but I'm not the only one.

It's sad sometimes, thinking of all the great plans we had for the future, all the "forevers, alwayses, nevers."

Then we drifted apart, for one reason or another. And now sometimes when I see an old friend approaching on the street, I almost wish I could turn invisible.

There are other times when I'd like nothing more than to call an old friend, if nothing else, just to say hello.

But I've lost contact.

Now I have more acquaintances, but fewer friends. And while sometimes I miss my old friends, my new friends are great. Really good friends are hard to come by, and it's sad that so many of mine have been swallowed by shadows.

People change, and so do I.

Follow-Up

Mark Murrmann discusses how he and his former high school friends now have little in common.

1. *Do you feel some sense of guilt when former friendships are not maintained?*
2. *What seems to be the norm for changing friends?*
3. *How should we act when it is time for a friendship to change?*

Thoughts on Friends

Nelson Goud

SAME-SEX FRIENDS

Most of the studies on friendships and gender seem to agree that

1. Women's friendships emphasize shared feelings, self-disclosure, nurturance, and emotional support.
2. Men's friendships emphasize shared activities, and conversation generally tends to be about things and events (with the exception of crisis time disclosures).

In her book *Just Friends*, Lillian Rubin notes further differences between male and female friendships:

- Three-fourths of single women could identify a best friend, whereas only one-third of single men could do so.
- Of the single men who could name a best friend, the friend was most likely a woman.
- Most men do not feel comfortable sharing their personal lives with other men because of a hesitancy in revealing weakness or vulnerability.
- The shared intimacy between female friends is different from their family relationships.
- Men often have strong bonds with other men because of intense shared experiences (e.g., war, sports), but do not feel the need to verbally acknowledge these feelings.

It should be added that part of men's difficulty in expressing emotions is due to the lack of experience and encouragement for doing so while growing up (when compared to women).

Follow-Up

1. *Does your experience as a man or woman reflect these findings?*
2. *If you have close same-sex friends, explain what they provide in your life.*

OPPOSITE-SEX FRIENDS

The trend of having close friends of the opposite sex has increased over the past two decades. Part of the reason is the increased frequency of contact between the sexes while growing up (e.g., sports, communications technology, coed dorms) and more male–female working relationships. Here are some findings from those who write about opposite-sex friendships:

- Among 25–34 year olds, about one in ten said their best friend is of the opposite sex (American Demographics Synovate 2002 survey). Many of these friendships remain even if one gets married.
- Women find that men are not as emotionally nurturing and disclosing, but they still value male friends for their differing points of view.
- The different communication styles of men and women create both positive and negative consequences in an opposite-sex friendship. The aspect each values in the other sex is also the source for frustration. Lillian Rubin explains this ambivalence in *Just Friends:*

> Both men and women, then, find their differences bind them while they also separate them. The "hard edge" men present makes it easier for a woman to deal more directly with a male friend, while it also frustrates her. The concern that women display for process that can be so irritating to a man also underlies the nurturance for which he turns to her so eagerly. They each maintain a love-hate ambivalence toward the other's different intellectual and emotional styles, both getting something they want or need from the other's mode, while also feeling it alien and oppressive at times. (p. 164)

See also Deborah Tannen's article in Section Two for descriptions of male–female differences in communication.

One woman says "With a woman, there's always something to chew on. . . . Something's brought up and we dissect it and look at it from all angles for hours. With a man, he goes for the solution, and that's not always what you want" (Rubin, 1985, p. 160). But, as Rubin adds, many women look forward to a male friend's interaction for an alternative perspective not probable from a female friend.

One man says "All that talk just to get where I was hours ago" (p. 161). Men, however, do treasure the nurturance and safe disclosures not generally present with male friends.

Whether acted on or not, sexual attraction or tension is usually present in opposite sex friendships. Studies have pointed to mixed findings regarding friends and sexuality.

- Most believe that sexual relations complicate the friendship. "I don't think sex just inhibits friendships; it overpowers it and pushes out." (Rubin, p. 151)
- Initial sexual attraction tends to fade over time. If there is sexual contact it tends to be at the beginning of the friendship (although one study showed that at the two-year mark some

platonic friendships reconsider the romantic and sexual dimension).

• Some heterosexual opposite-sex friendships feel that the sexual charge, if not acted on, added some zest that other same-sex friends could not provide. This zest comes in the form of mild flirtations and validations of physical attractiveness.

In one study, over half of gay men had at least one close female friend, most often a straight woman. About one-fifth of lesbian women report a close male friend, most frequently a gay man. Lesbians tend to report that they have more in common with straight women than with either gay or straight men. Friendships between straight women and gay men show that they converse in similar ways and on similar topics, compared to straight women–straight men friendships. (Rubin, pp. 170–172).

Other readings on this topic include *Women and Men as Friends: Relationships across the Lifespan in the 21st Century,* by Michael Monsour (Lawrence Erlbaum, 2002) and *We're Just Good Friends: Women and Men in Nonromantic Relationships,* Kathy Werking (Guilford, 2003).

Reference
Rubin, L. B. (1985). *Just friends.* New York: Harper & Row.

Follow-Up

1. *Choose two statements about opposite sex friendships and offer your analysis and point of view.*
2. *If you have opposite sex friendships, which of the statements reflect your experience (or not)? Discuss your positions.*

Parents

Martin Shepard

Learning to accept your parents as people in their own right—different and distinct from you—is a task that poses difficulties for quite a large number of people. There should be nothing surprising in all of this. For we all have one very good historical reason—our childhoods.

The infant is born into a world in which he is, literally, *part* of his mother. Without her to comfort, clothe, feed and shelter him, he could not survive. During childhood our little girl and boy still depend greatly on their parents. They have not yet acquired the skills necessary to provide for and sustain themselves. This is a time one learns certain "do's" and "don'ts." You learn how to count and how to read, how to cook and how to sew, how to hammer and how to saw. And you learn *not* to swallow iodine, *not* to put a fork in the electrical outlet, and *not* to cross a street unless you look to make sure there is no traffic approaching.

Typically the child's contract with the parent is one in which he accepts the dependent role in return for the favors/protection/guidance/and support he receives from them. There are, of course, dissatisfactions. He prefers taking things out to play with more than he does putting them away. He wants to do and try things he sees grown-ups doing and resents it when they say "No." He may want to come and go more freely than they are ready to allow. And he'd rather watch television than do his homework or practice the piano.

Adolescence marks the years during which relatively accepting and "sweet" children become adults in their own right. Following the sexual maturation of puberty, adolescents typically reject the dependent contracts that as children they had with their parents. It is a period of much storm and strife, both in the inner life of the adolescents and in their relationships to their parents. Opposition/confrontation/argumentation are a natural part of the process as the adolescent seeks to break away and find his or her own adulthood. If it is accomplished smoothly, and the adolescent truly feels adult, he comes to accept his parents as he would other adults. If they share common interests and *if* the parents accept him as an adult (not only as their child), they remain close. If their interests are not similar and/or if the parents cannot transcend their *roles* as parents, there is a polite distance—as any adult would have with people who are on different wavelengths. This second alternative is a more common outcome of maturation.

What I have described thus far is "normal" maturation. Many individuals, no matter how old they are, never make it, psychologically speaking, past either childhood or adolescence when it comes to relating to their parents. Those stuck in the childhood phase remain overly docile and dependent. Those stuck in adolescence relate to their parents in a perpetually rebellious and ill-tempered way.

Given the cultural roles males and females are assigned (males presumably being "aggressive" and females "passive"), one might expect that women are more likely to become stuck in the childhood state and men in the adolescent one. And—although there are many reversals to this expectation—such is usually the case.

Louise is a good example of such a child/woman. In her childhood and adolescence, her parents were perpetually available to her.

They were quick to comfort and pamper her. They always soothed her hurts, took her side, indulged her fancies. She, in turn, pampered their egos by letting them know how exceptional they were, how they were the only people who understood her, how much wisdom and sage advice they had, and how appreciative she was.

At twenty-two she married for the first time. Her husband, Greg, was an insurance salesman and just out of college. He was a decent, responsible, upright young man, who looked forward to supporting Louise and raising a family. But it never worked out that way.

Louise was incapable of accommodating herself to the rigors of a more spartan and independent existence. She consulted her mother daily, both to ask for advice on simple housekeeping chores and for consolation over any minor inconveniences she was having with Greg. She was incapable of sticking to a budget and so, behind Greg's back, ran to her physician father for extra funds to pay her charge-account bills and indulge her passion for clothes, cars (which she insisted on changing yearly), and innumerable redecoration schemes.

When her first and only child was born, her parents hired a maid for her. And Mother came over daily for several months to help out and give advice.

After three years of marriage, Louise left Greg. Marriage didn't conform to her picture of "picket fences and lace curtains." She was interested in playing more and working less. Her parents were sympathetic. They agreed with Louise that Greg was "cheap," "selfish," and that he "always got his way." Besides which, Mother was willing to raise Louise's daughter while Louise went back to school and tried to find a new man.

Now thirty-nine years old and on her fifth husband, Louise lives in another city. But she still phones her family a few times each week.

Sam, who is twenty-eight, is the sort of person who typifies adolescent "stuckness." For he remains continuously close to, yet antagonistic toward, his parents.

While attending a local college, he, like many other students, began smoking marijuana. Not content to do it privately, he naturally let his parents know of his activities. They were frightened, shocked, and strongly disapproving. Sam, rather than dropping the subject, continued to let them know of his usage by smoking at home. Quarrels/insults/door-slamming occurred frequently on both sides.

Dinner conversations to this day are reminiscent of the popular television series *All in the Family*—with Sam typically attacking his father's political and social points of view and Mother acting as a harassed peacemaker.

Four years ago Sam moved out of his parents' home but continued to bring home his laundry for his mother to wash. His attitude was sullen. If his mother inquired about his life he would give her flippant answers or accuse her of trying to hold on to him. Yet he made it a point to inform his parents of many of his activities that he knew they objected to—his dating a woman of another religion, his intention of quitting a promising job, his experimentation with LSD.

Every now and then he would ask his father for a loan or the use of the family car. He felt it was coming to him. On those occasions when his father refused him, he always had some unkind words for the old man.

Two years ago he married. He made it a point to tell his mother not to interfere when she offered to help care for Suzy, Sam's daughter, who was born eight months ago. But whenever Sam and his wife, Brenda, have a party to attend, Sam calls up his mother, expecting her to be always available for babysitting. When she is not, he accuses her of being a hypocrite for having offered to help out earlier.

How can you tell if you are *stuck,* in any respect, regarding your parents? One way is to see if they embarrass you. Perhaps you don't want your parents to meet your friends because you fear they will act in a way that will humiliate you; that they will treat you as their little girl or boy, correct you, or behave "coarsely" in front of your friends.

Such embarrassment is often related to your still feeling yourself a *part* of—an extension of—your parents. You fail to realize that if your parents do react absurdly, it is *they* who will be laughed at, not you. Unless, of course, you take it as personally as a thirteen-year-old who brings her first date over to the house.

Other indications of dependency are the making of routine daily or weekly telephone calls to your parents, wanting their approval constantly, or finding that there is "no other person as good, wise, and kind to me as my mother (or father)."

Signs of rebelliousness are so self-evident, emotionally, to the sufferer, that they need no further elaboration.

There is a certain validity to a child's blaming a parent when things don't work out to his satisfaction. After all, the parent *is* in charge. If a meal doesn't taste good, the child can't very well cook his own. If the family moves and the child must give up his neighborhood friends, that is the parents' responsibility, not his. *But once you pass the age of eighteen,* those conditions no longer hold true. There is no further need to depend upon your parents.

The task of both the *child-stuck* and *adolescent-stuck* person is to get *un-stuck,* by learning to do things on your own and, in doing so, becoming a more self-sufficient human being. You can't have a very good self-concept—can't very well consider yourself any person's equal—if you remain a child-at-heart in relationship to your parents. Whatever *advantages* there are in taking things from your parents by continuing the "child" or "adolescent" integrations are more than offset by the loss of basic self-esteem that results from staying in that role.

The "child" is reluctant to go *through* the adolescent, rebellious, phase. The "adolescent" is reluctant to achieve total self-sufficiency. He wants all of the advantages of both childhood *and* adulthood, but none of the disadvantages

of either. "Adolescents" are too embarrassed to admit how much they still *want* their parents, and how much they might even love them.

Both groups ask for their parents' support and approval (albeit in different ways) long after they are capable of managing their own lives. Not only does this interfere with their lives in general (witness Louise and Sam), but it certainly prevents the possibility of their establishing a realistic present-day relationship with their parents.

I've talked frequently in this book* about living in the *here and now,* and how emotions, people, and relationships change. One of the things that can certainly be said of people who have trouble dealing with their parents is that they are usually reacting to *memories* of both their parents and themselves—as they all were ten, fifteen, or twenty years ago—and *not* in terms of the realities of all of them now. This is always due to the *holding back* of the maturational process.

We are left, therefore, with many adults who still *blame* their parents for the way they have treated them. As if their parents had chosen to make the child's life miserable.

Yet there are very few parents who *intentionally* act cruelly. Every set of parents, if they could choose, would elect to be the world's best parents.

Of course, lack of "intent" does not mean that parents don't occasionally act cruelly. Why shouldn't they? They are primarily *people* before they are parents. All of us are capable of cruelty. Besides, they had parents who "misunderstood" them, too. Parents, like all people, can be tight-fisted, generous, disappointing, helpful, indifferent, funny, tender, or short-tempered.

When I was twenty-five and a student in medical school, I was still reacting to my parents as an adolescent. I resented having to go visit them each week. I felt they were still

Editor's Note: Martin Shepard is referring to his book *The Do-It-Yourself Psychotherapy Book.*

trying to control me. When I was questioned by my analyst whether the situation might not be reversed—whether I might not be trying to control *them*—I realized that I made my weekly sojourns to pick up a weekly allotment that they were generous enough to offer me. And that I could possibly manage to get by with a much lower amount. And that I needn't show up weekly to "pay my dues" for their generosity—that they gave it out of kindness and not for my weekly shows of obeisance. With that realization I stopped my mechanical visits, cut down on what I was receiving and began to relate to them more adultly.

A therapist friend of mine was treating a young man who constantly fought with his mother. He wanted her approval, but she was constantly critical. Mother was an exceptionally irrational woman and never saw how much her son wanted her blessings. He, in turn, could not accept her irrationality.

My friend asked his patient the following question: "If you passed by a mental institution and saw your mother looking through the barred windows on one of the floors, and she was screaming the same things at you, as you passed by, that she now screams at you at home, would it still trouble you?"

"No," said the young man. "I'd discount it, because I'd know she was crazy."

"From now on, then, every time your mother gets on your nerves, I want you to recall that picture of her shouting from that hospital window."

His patient did just that and found his aggravation and frustration subsiding.

A device such as this is I think, a useful tool for people who find themselves continuously fighting with a non-accepting parent.

A rule to bear in mind that will help you to see your parents more realistically, is:

Grown-ups are merely children in aging skin.

When you get to feeling overwhelmed by your parents' (or parent substitutes—such as bosses or teachers) "wisdom" or resentful over their "shortcomings," try to see the child that is hiding and acting inside of them.

I have purposely avoided writing a chapter on *being a parent*—on dealing more effectively with your children—for a number of reasons. One is that there is no way to be a *parent*. You can only be *yourself*. And if you become a mentally healthy adult (as, I'm sure, all of the readers of this book are trying to become), you will do all right both as *yourself* and as a parent.

As a psychiatrist, I have seen hundreds upon hundreds of people complaining about their parents. If they were given a great deal of material advantages, they would complain that "my parents bought me things as a substitute for love." If they were given few things, the complaint was "my parents were cheapskates and didn't love me enough." If they were given a great deal of freedom by their parents, they would lament that their "parents weren't interested in me or what I did." But if they were closely supervised, it was because "my parents were too strict."

Naturally it helps to be kind, tolerant, and understanding of your children. Remembering your own childhood helps. But sometimes a spanking or some punishment may well be in order.

So there are no suggestions I have to offer you as a parent, except to bear in mind that *whatever you do, it is likely to be wrong in your child's eyes.* But when and if your child grows to maturity—if he or she doesn't get stuck in child-like or adolescent behavior—your child will come to appreciate that you did the best that you could.

And further—it is your *child's* responsibility to grow up, to mature—not yours to do it for him. Just as you must realize that you are no longer part of your parents—that things aren't *their fault* —your child has to learn the same things about you.

The exercises that follow attempt to help you continue your own maturational process vis-à-vis your parents. You may need *repeated* work on the exercises in order to abandon your unrealistic views of both yourself and your parents. For you must, eventually, learn to let go of them, give up your demands that they be different than they are, forgive them their faults (and all of the things that they "should" have done, did do, and didn't do)—and come to realize that your parents couldn't possibly have been anything other than what they were and what they are.

SHEPARD'S EXERCISES

1. Work with two empty chairs. Put your father in one and tell him all of the negative things you've held back from him—your resentments, frustrations, hatreds. Be as specific as you can. Then, switch seats, be him, and respond to "you." Say how you feel hearing all of these negative things. Keep the dialogue going by changing chairs once more and telling your father what you needed, now need, wanted, and now want from him. Have him respond by saying what he needs and wants from you (past and present). See whether or not you can achieve any greater understanding of one another's positions, as you keep the dialogue going, as opposed to finding yourselves simply *arguing*.
2. Repeat exercise 1, substituting your mother for your father.
3. Pretend you are your father and write a short composition about "The Difficulties I Had in Raising My Child."
4. Repeat exercise 3, but now write as your mother instead of your father.
5. Place your father back in the empty chair. Tell him all of the things you've appreciated or loved about him. Switch seats and, as your father, say what you *feel* about your child's telling you such nice things. Keep the dialogue going.
6. Repeat exercise 5 with your mother.
7. Be your father and tell your child all the things you've loved and appreciated about her (or him). Switch chairs, be yourself, and say how you feel about hearing these things. Be your father again and respond.

8. Repeat exercise 7 with your mother.
9. List all of the secrets concerning your private life that you would never tell your parents. Place each of your parents in an empty chair in front of you and tell each one, in turn, these secrets. Be your parents and react. Again, keep switching chairs and get a dialogue going. See whether you can move toward mutual understanding rather than conflict and confrontation.
10. If your relationship with either parent is characterized by dependent routines, daily or weekly phone calls or visits (if you are living away from home), take a month's vacation from these activities. Don't call. Don't visit. Politely tell your parents that you simply want to see what it's like to live without such regular contact with them. And stick to your word.

    If you are over twenty-one and still live with your parents spend the next month living elsewhere, giving the same reasons. Move in with a friend or series of friends, into a Y, a hotel room, with a sibling, or with a different relative. Better still, try all of these different arrangements for a few nights each so that you might see what it is like to live in different spaces.
11. If your relationship with either parent is characterized by aloofness or grumpiness, or if you have not had much contact with them in some time, see what it is like to try to get closer.

    Make a date to meet them somewhere and treat them to a dinner. Give them a small gift—a token of your "appreciation" (whether it is felt or not). Ask them details about their lives. Tell them whatever things you appreciate or like about them—and work hard at avoiding unkind words during this experience.

    A day later, write about your experience. Describe what it meant to you and what you learned from it.

    If either of your parents is dead, do the above exercise in fantasy for the one (or ones) you can't bring along in reality.

Follow-Up

1. *In what major ways are you like and unlike each of your parents/guardians? How much choice do you have in keeping or changing these qualities?*
2. *If you are a parent of adolescent or adult children, explain why you agree or disagree with some of Shepard's ideas.*
3. *Write about or discuss any other main point of this article.*
4. *Attempt one or more of the exercises listed at the end of the article and report what you learned.*

The Emerging Adult: Finding Friends, Living Alone, and Living with Parents

Nelson Goud

NEW SOCIAL NETWORKS

One of the major adjustments twentysomethings face is finding new friends and social networks. If they have just graduated from college, most of their friends disperse, and frequent opportunities for meeting others also vanish. Some may move to a location where they have no friends. Work colleagues often have other agendas other than becoming friends. In *Conquering Your Quarterlife Crisis*, Alexandra Robbins found that establishing new social networks is a gradual process that takes time and effort. Following are a few suggestions she offers:

1. Wean yourself from watching TV and from indirect communication modes (e.g., IMing people) and engage in more direct contact.
2. Find an event and invite people to it (going to a local food-tasting, festival, etc.). Encourage those who want to go to invite another person or two.
3. Do not rush the process of developing friendship—it has its own pace.
4. The best single approach is to join groups that involve one of your interests (e.g., sports, books, volunteer service, bike clubs). If one group does not pan out, try another.

The key to developing new social networks is act instead of waiting for things to happen to you. Initiate rather than react.

LIVING ALONE

Living alone is a first-time experience for some emerging adults, and it can be a lonely one:

> I come home at night, and I'm all by myself. There's no one to share my home with or to share my accomplishments during the day or my bad moments with. I don't someone home for me to talk to . . . to share meals with. . . . I have too much time to think. . . . It feels kind of empty, very quiet. (Robbins, 2004, p. 129)

Emerging adults who have lived alone advise the following:

1. Remind yourself that living alone does not reflect any personal shortcoming.

2. This may be your first experience in living without others. Learn to like your own company.
3. Make your place your own—decorate and furnish your place so that it reflects your personality. Put your stamp on where you live, and it will feel more like a home instead of a place where you go to sleep and eat.

LIVING WITH PARENTS

The most recent census shows that about 14 percent of young adults ages 18 to 34 live with their parents. (Between 1970 and 2000, the percentage of 24 to 34 year olds living with parents or grandparents increased by 50 percent.) Robbins (2004) claims that approximately half of recent college graduates between the ages of 21 and 31 will live with their parents at some time. The reasons for living with parents vary: financial relief, psychological support, a means to enjoy life without full responsibility (loaf), having a temporary retreat during a storm. Although it is more prevalent now than at any other time, living with parents still carries negative connotations for many emerging adults. Some feel like they are failures or immature; some find it difficult to act like an adult when in their parents' home; some feel they have to explain themselves to peers. Self-sufficiency is a primary characteristic of adulthood in our culture. Robbins offers one main guide for those living with parents:

> Whether you live rent free or contribute to the household . . . you don't have to feel like you're muddling through your 20's alone if you're living with people who care about your well-being. The caveat is that while it's normal to temporarily depend on your parents as a safety net, it's not fair to them or to you to use them as a crutch. If you use a rent-free life as an excuse to loaf rather than sincerely trying to figure out how to support yourself, then you're not helping anyone. You want your parents to be assured that they're helping you learn to stand on your own, not delaying your self-sufficiency. (p. 167)

Another factor that enters the situation is that the parents' options are limited when a young adult returns home. Plans to sell a home, to move, or to retire may have to be delayed.

Reference
Robbins, A. (2004). *Conquering your quarterlife crisis.* New York: Perigee.

Follow-Up

1. *Discuss the ideas provided for finding new social networks, living alone, and/or living with parents.*
2. *Apply one or more of the suggestions and report on the results.*

Thoughts on Siblings

Nelson Goud

Over 80 percent of Americans have at least one, they outlast parents and marriages, and they know you in ways no other human can, whether you like it or not. They are siblings—our brothers and sisters.

Freud said "A small child does not necessarily love his brothers and sisters" (cited in Viorst, 1986, p. 97). Some young children greet a newborn sibling by asking the parents whether the baby is staying. Some wonder about their own status, as shown in the following poem (Viorst, 1986, p. 97):

> My mom says I'm her sugarplum.
> My mom says I'm her lamb.
> My mom says I'm completely perfect.
> Just the way I am.
> My mom says I'm a super-special wonderful terrific little guy.
> My mom just had another baby.
> Why?

Following are some selected findings from studies on siblings:

• Rivalry between brothers and sisters is natural. It takes the form of degrees of competition, jealously, territoriality, or resentment. Sibling rivalry is minimized by proper parenting actions such as encouraging older siblings to help care for younger ones, talking about feelings of envy and anger, giving special quality time (but not excessive) to the older sibling when a new one arrives, and not favoring any sibling.

Sibling rivalry tends to decrease throughout childhood; it is most intense in the first two years. Although some sibling rivalry may occasionally erupt, most sibling research points to more positive, prosocial interactions between siblings as they get older. Some of these prosocial interactions include teaching, protection, caregiving, playing, social competence, problem solving, and modeling. Some siblings have stronger attachments with each other than with their parents (especially under conditions of divorce, remarriage, etc.).

• Each child experiences the family in a different manner. Your brother or sister functions in a unique micro-environment within the family. Studies show that siblings are only slightly more similar than they are to non-family peers, hence the oft-asked question "How did such different kids come from the same family?"

• *Lifespan changes.* In childhood, siblings are in daily contact. In young adulthood, there tends to be limited contact as each pursues paths of work and family. Siblings tend to increase their contact in middle adulthood for several reasons: children are leaving home, divorce, illness, or parental caregiving. In middle and older adulthood, the sister–sister relationship is the closest of the sibling bonds (followed by sister–brother, and brother–brother).

Five types of relationships among older adult siblings have been studied by Kail and Cavanaugh (2004).

Intimate (14%)—high levels of closeness and low levels of envy and resentment

Congenial (30%)—high levels of closeness, moderate contact, low envy and resentment

Loyal (34%)—average closeness and contact, low level of envy and resentment

Apathetic (11%)—low levels of closeness, contact, envy and resentment

Hostile (11%)—high level of involvement and resentment, low level of intimacy

Note that about two-thirds have a congenial or loyal relationship with siblings.

• *Birth order.* Research is mixed on the effects of birth order on achievement, social skills, personality traits, and so on. Many of the effects are influenced by the number of siblings in the family, the age gaps between siblings, and family social class, to name a few.

• Close sibling support is highest among those who live in close proximity. Siblings from larger families are more likely to give support than those from small families.

• *Only children.* Reviews of dozens of studies have found that only children are generally high on measures of self-esteem and achievement motivation, are more obedient and slightly more scholastically competent than those with siblings, and are likely to establish good peer relations. (Shaffer, 1996)

A brother or sister has a life-long connection with your personal and family history. In the web of human relationships, a brother or sister holds a distinct position in our lives.

Other readings on this topic include "The Secret World of Siblings" by Erica Good (*U.S. News & World Report,* January 10, 1994); *The Lifespan* by Guy Lefrancois (Wadsworth, 1999); and *Human Development* by James Vander Zanden (McGraw Hill, 2000).

References

Kail, R., & Cavanaugh, J. (2004). *Human development.* Belmont, CA: Thomson/Wadsworth.

Shaffer, D. (1996). *Developmental psychology.* Pacific Grove, CA: Brooks/Cole.

Viorst, J. (1986). *Necessary losses.* New York: Fawcett.

1. *If you have brothers or sisters, how are you alike and different from them? Why do you think this is?*
2. *Describe how your relationship with a sibling has evolved in your lifetime and offer a commentary.*
3. *If you are the parent of two or more children, comment on two statements in this article.*
4. *How have your sibling relationships influenced your personal development?*
5. *If you are an only child, what do you believe has been different compared to those with siblings (if anything)?*
6. *Select two statements from the article and offer an analysis.*

Thoughts on Mentoring

Nelson Goud

A mentor is an older, experienced person who facilitates another's progress (usually in a work or professional setting). Studies show that having an effective mentor makes a difference in the progress of attaining full-functioning competency in an organization. This does not mean that career achievement is not likely if you do not have a mentor. Many women, for example, have a smaller pool of female mentors to guide them (male mentors may be effective if the sexual overtones are worked out). Carl Rogers, the eminent psychologist, said he did not have a mentor.

A true mentor performs many functions: model, sponsor, evaluator, teacher, and work friend. A mentor may explain to a protégé that although he or she is performing well in X tasks, the Y tasks are more important for future progress. As a guide, the mentor outlines possible paths, shows how to avoid trouble spots and people, makes sure the protégé is noticed for his or her work, and demonstrates concern for the protégé's psychosocial life.

A complete mentoring relationship usually develops through four stages: initiation, cultivation, separation (when mentors and protégés spend less time together), and a redefinition (the relationship either ends or changes into another kind of relationship). Sometimes the ending is negative (e.g., the protégé begins to disagree with the mentor and goes his or her own way). Whether positive or negative, most male protégés end the mentor–protégé tie in order to, as Daniel Levenson states it, "become one's own man."

Mentors, too, benefit from the process by being able to share experiences and learnings. Mentors help provide a sense of continuity within an organization, and they are often the recipient of expressions of gratitude.

Some organizations attempt to provide systematic mentoring. It is crucial to point out that research shows that having a poor mentor is *worse* than having no mentor at all (see Kail & Cavanaugh, 2004).

Reference

Kail, R., & Cavanaugh, J. (2004). *Human Development*. Belmont, CA: Thomson/Wadsworth.

Follow-Up

1. *If you had (or have) a mentor, analyze this experience using the ideas presented above. If you did not (or do not) have a mentor, evaluate whether it has made a difference in your work.*
2. *If you are (or were) a mentor, analyze this experience using the ideas presented above.*

Resolving Interpersonal Conflicts

David W. Johnson

When you become engaged in a conflict, two major concerns you have to take into account are

1. Achieving your goals. Each person has personal goals that he or she wishes to achieve. You are in conflict because your goals conflict with another person's goals. Your goal may be placed on a continuum from being of little importance to you to being highly important.

2. Maintaining a good relationship with the other person(s). Some relationships are temporary, and some are long-term. Some long-term relationships are vital and others are peripheral. Your relationship with the other person may be placed on a continuum from being of little importance to you to being highly important.

How important your personal goals are to you and how important the relationship is perceived to be determine how you act in a conflict. Given these two concerns within a relationship, there are five basic strategies that may be used to manage conflicts:

1. The Turtle (Withdrawing). If you act like a turtle, you give up both your goals and the relationship, and, therefore, you avoid the other person and the issue. Avoiding a hostile stranger may be the best thing to do. Or you may wish to withdraw from a conflict until you and the other person have calmed down and are in control of your feelings.

2. The Shark (Forcing). If you act like a shark, you try to achieve your goals at all costs, demanding that the other person let you have your way, no matter how much it hurts the relationship. When the goal is very important but the relationship is not, such as when you are buying a used car, you may want to act like a shark and use force. Never use force with someone you will have to relate to again soon.

3. The Teddy Bear (Smoothing). If you act like a teddy bear, you give up your goals in order to maintain the relationship at the highest level possible. When the goal is of no importance to you but the relationship is of high importance, you may want to act like a teddy bear and smooth. When a colleague feels strongly about something, and you couldn't care less, smoothing is a good idea. When you are smoothing, do so with good humor. Be pleasant about it. At times, to smooth you may need to apologize. Saying "I'm sorry" does not mean "I'm wrong." "I'm sorry" lets the other person know that you are sorry about the situation. When you think the other person's interests are much stronger or more important than yours, smooth and give the other person his or her way.

4. The Fox (Compromising). If you act like a fox, you give up part of your goals and sacrifice part of the relationship in order to reach an agreement. When both the goal and the relationship are moderately important to you and it appears that both you and the other person cannot get what you want, you may want to negotiate like a fox. When there is a limited amount of money, and both you and a fellow employee want a large raise, for example, negotiating a compromise may be the best way to resolve the conflict. You can meet in the middle, each taking half, or flip a coin and let chance decide who will get his or her way.

5. The Owl (Problem Solving/Negotiating). If you act like an owl, you initiate negotiations aimed at ensuring that you and the other person both fully meet your goals and maintain the relationship at the highest level possible. An agreement is sought that satisfies both you and the other person and resolves any tensions and negative feelings between the two of you. When both the goal and the relationship are highly important to you, you may want to act like an owl. Face the conflict. Negotiate to solve the problem. Think of solutions that will give both you and the other person what you want and will keep the relationship positive.

Each conflict strategy has its place. You need to be able to use any one of the five, depending on your goals and the relationship (see Figure 4.1). In deciding which of the five strategies to use within any one conflict, there are six rules to consider (Johnson & Johnson, 1995a, 1995b):

1. Do not withdraw from or ignore conflicts. When the goal is not important and you do not need to keep a relationship with the other person, withdrawing from the conflict may be appropriate. If the relationship is going to continue, however, ignoring a conflict keeps emotional energy tied up in resentment, hostility, or fear. In the long run, it is almost always easier to face a conflict in an ongoing relationship.

2. Do not engage in win-lose negotiations. When the goal is very important to you but the relationship is unimportant, forcing the other person to give in may be appropriate. In an ongoing relationship, however, you almost never go for the win because the loser may be resentful and want revenge. In the long run, it is almost always easier to ensure

High Importance

Low Importance   **High Importance**

Figure 4.1   Conflict Strategies

that the other person is satisfied and happy with the resolution of the conflict.

3. Assess for smoothing. When the goal is unimportant to you (or far more important to the other person than to you) and the relationship is very important, smoothing may be appropriate. Giving up your needs for the needs of another person only works in the long run if the other person reciprocates. It is a mistake, however, to smooth if in fact the goal is very important to you.

4. Compromise when time is short. When the goal and the relationship are of moderate importance to you, you may wish to compromise. Usually, compromising is used only when there is not enough time to solve the problem.

5. Initiate problem-solving negotiations. When both the goal and the relationship are important to you, you initiate negotiations to solve the problem. You ask the other person to join with you in problem solving negotiations if he or she is rational and able to do so. The best time to problem solve is when the issue is small, concrete, and immediate. This way issues are dealt with when they are most easily resolved.

6. Use your sense of humor. Humor is very helpful in keeping conflicts constructive. Laughter usually does a great deal to resolve the tension in conflicts and helps disputants think more creatively about how to solve the problem.

In following those rules there are a number of guidelines to keep in mind. First, to be competent in managing conflicts, you must be able to engage competently in each of the five strategies. Each strategy is appropriate in certain circumstances, and you need to be good at all of them. Second, some of the strategies require the participation of the other disputant, and some may be enacted by yourself alone. You can withdraw or smooth alone, but you have to have the cooperation of the other person to force, compromise, or problem solve.

Third, the strategies tend to be somewhat incompatible in the sense that choosing one of them makes choosing the others less likely. Forcing is not typically followed by smoothing. Fourth, certain strategies may deteriorate into other strategies. When you try to withdraw and the other person corners you, you are likely to respond with forcing. When you attempt to smooth, and the other person responds with forcing and anger, you may withdraw. Then you may force if the other person continues to be angry and competitive. Forcing creates counterforcing. Even negotiations may deteriorate into forcing when (a) the timing is wrong and the other person does not respond constructively or (b) the person negotiating lacks the skills necessary to keep the management of the conflict constructive. When time is short, negotiating sometimes deteriorates into compromise.

Fifth, in ranking the strategies from the one you use most frequently to the one you use least frequently, you need to be aware of your second as well as your first strategy. When you become very angry and upset, you will tend to regress to your backup strategy. You need to be sensitive to your backup strategy as well as your dominant one. Finally, the most competent business executives tend to be very relationship-oriented and primarily use smoothing and problem solving while the least competent business executives tend to be very goal-oriented and primarily use forcing and withdrawing. Competent people tend to be highly relationship-oriented, negotiating when the goals and needs involved in the conflict are important to them and smoothing when they are not. In ongoing relationships, even if you do not like the other person, it is usually a good idea to smooth or problem solve.

In some ways the five strategies present a simplified view of how most conflicts are managed. The complexities of the interaction between two individuals far exceed their initial approaches to the conflict. Conflicts can deteriorate. Within most conflicts there are initial strategies followed by backup strategies followed by other strategies that are based on what the other person is doing. You may wish to negotiate but when faced with a colleague who is forcing, you may force back.

Follow-Up

1. *Which of the five conflict strategies do you tend to use repeatedly? Are these effective in (1) achieving your goals and (2) maintaining good relationships? Provide examples and commentary.*
2. *Johnson recommends selecting a primary strategy and a back-up one in case the primary does not fit. Attempt this idea in a current conflict situation and report the results.*
3. *Choose any statement or idea and discuss how it applies to your conflict-resolution experiences.*

Making an Apology

Nelson Goud

After spending seventeen years in prison for a rape conviction, Brandon M_____ is standing in another courtroom. A district attorney faces him and says that new DNA testing proved that Brandon was innocent and that he would be released immediately. The attorney added "I know we can't give you back your years and for that I'm extremely sorry." Brandon responded by saying "I accept your apology."

British historian Thomas Carlyle spent several intense months hand writing a history of the French revolution, and he gave it to his friend John Stuart Mill to review. Somehow during the weeks Mill had it, he placed it in a pile a maid used for burning material. The whole manuscript was burned. Mill profusely apologized to Carlyle and showed genuine grief and self-recrimination. Mill gave Carlyle enough money to meet a year's needs, as partial restitution. Carlyle wrote Mill a letter that said, "You left me last night with a look which I shall not soon forget. Is there anything that I could do or suffer or say to alleviate you? For I feel that your sorrow must be far sharper than mine."

Apologies may not erase offenses, but they are often essential in healing the rifts caused by injury, belittlement, being ignored or betrayed, or by causing a loss. This does not mean that an apology excuses the offense or must even be accepted. But for a restoration or a relationship to occur, an apology is a necessary part of the process. Those who work in the areas of apology and forgiveness offer these guidelines:

1. An apology must be genuinely felt. A forced apology, or one that does not take responsibility for the offensive act, does little to repair a rift. The main intent of an apology is to salvage or restore a relationship. The offender must be credible.

2. For an apology to be effective, the offender must attempt to show that he or she is the one who should be diminished or shamed, or who is wrong, insensitive, mistaken, or just plain dumb. It is an attempt to relieve the hurt or shame of the offended person.

3. There are three components of a successful apology: (1) name and take responsibility for the offense (show that you know what the offense was and the impact it had), (2) explain why you committed the offense and, if it is true, why this is not your normal way of acting (this reveals that you are interested in maintaining a relationship and that future acts like this are unlikely), and (3) demonstrate true remorse.

4. Along with a verbal message, other reparations may be helpful. These can take the form of financial compensation, a gift, or a favor or two.

5. The *timing* of an apology is important. Some apologies should be given immediately (e.g., embarrassing someone or spilling liquid on their clothes); major offenses may require extended time—possibly weeks or months—to initiate the proper apology process.

6. Nathaniel Wade and Everett Worthington (2003) make a distinction between the states of forgiveness and unforgiveness. Forgiveness means to give up hatred, shame, revenge, punishment, and demands of restitution. Unforgiveness refers to the feelings of resentment, hostility, or bitterness that result from interpersonal transgressions. They point out that it is possible to reduce feelings of unforgiveness without attaining forgiveness. Many find some offenses too severe to completely forgive, but desire to get beyond the damaging emotions of unforgiveness. Some of the ways to reduce unforgiveness include: seeking restitution, reframing the events and circumstances, seeking legal justice, stress management, and accepting the hurt.

Aaron Lazare (1995) summarized the dynamics of an apology as follows:

> Far and away the biggest stumbling block to apologizing is our belief that apologizing is a sign of weakness and an admission of guilt . . . we deny our offenses and hope that no one notices. In fact, the apology is a show of strength. It is an act of honesty because we admit we did wrong; an act of generosity, because it restores the self-concept of those we offended. It offers hope for a renewed relationship. (p. 78)

References

Lazare, A. (1995). "Go ahead, say you're sorry," *Psychology Today*, January/ February, 40–43, 76, 78

Layton, M. (1999). "Apology not accepted," *Utne Reader, 92,* March–April, 45–50.

Wade, N. G., & Worthington, E. L. "Overcoming interpersonal offenses: Is forgiveness the only way to deal with unforgiveness?" *Journal of Counseling and Development, 81,* Summer 2003, 342–252.

Follow-Up

1. *Select one of the main points and discuss your thoughts.*
2. *Name and discuss the effects of someone apologizing to you.*
   Name and discuss the effects of you apologizing to someone.
3. *Apply one or more ideas above and report on its results.*

The Missing Halloween

Nelson Goud

When you are ten years old, Halloween takes a good four weeks to plan if you want to do it right. For one, you want to make sure your costume is different from the others, and this requires some checking around. Then there is the challenge of planning the route—a route that hits the big givers first before they run out of the good stuff. This means several sprints from one neighborhood to the next, swooping in on the target homes, and then hustling back to get the homes you skipped. It is also crucial to play along with the crazy adults. Adults like Mr. and Mrs. Parish who dress up in monster costumes and try to scare the kids by jumping out from behind furniture—if you scream real loud it is good for at least a Snickers bar. And when you have all the rounds made you and your friends make sure to knock on Mr. Warren's door. We know he is in there, but he will not come to the door, and one of us stands guard while the others soap a few of his windows. After all there is a "trick" in trick-or-treat. And along the way it is mandatory to hide behind a large tree until your sister and her friends come along, and then leap out in the midst of screeches that will echo the nights until December. Advanced Halloween veterans remember their sacrificing parents and share some of the booty with them—things like apples, walnuts, and other assorted items you don't like.

Everything went as planned that Halloween except that I did not get to go. A sore throat and a stiff neck kept me out of school three days before Halloween. The town Doc came over—they did that back then—and checked me over and told my folks "He has polio." I was whisked off to a big hospital in Kalamazoo and spent Halloween looking out a window at the wall of another building.

A ten-year-old does not get depressed about things like this, unlike older persons. Confused and worried, but not bummed out. For one, the pain was not too bad and everyone paid me a lot of attention. Nurses told jokes as they placed steaming hot packs on my back and legs. The doctors just asked me to do simple things like touching my toes, and when I could not do that they said it was okay anyway. My parents came by often and brought a radio, my favorite foods, and acted very normal in the way only parents can when they are afraid but cannot let their children know it. And there were cards, candy, and comic books coming in on a steady basis. In a way I became a small celebrity.

After a week or so I was taken out of isolation and placed in a large room with five other guys who had polio also. Some seemed to have it worse. Johnny had braces and could not walk so I had to drag his bed next to mine to play cards. Then there was Mike, about six, who never had a visitor. He whined and cried a lot at night and we eventually had to tell him to shut up but he kept crying anyway.

The World Health Organization is predicting that polio will be eliminated from the Western Hemisphere. It was reading this news release that released my memories. I was one of the fortunate ones who eventually fully recovered. Johnny remained permanently impaired. I do not know what happened to the six-year-old who cried at night. I do know that the year of the missing Halloween was the one Jonas Salk first introduced the polio vaccine. Bad timing for some of us. But Halloween and polio are only background for my real story.

Each day in the hospital I received at least two cards from classmates. There was always one card that had a puzzle and the next day would bring a card with the answer and a new puzzle. Normal fifth-graders do not send cards this reliably. But the 10-year-olds in Mrs. Pollack's fifth grade class did.

Mrs. Pollack was a charter member from the traditional school of thought and looked about 90 years old. Adverbs, fractions, and proper punctuation were ecstatic expressions to Mrs. Pollack. No one dared question these life verities. Her face was stern and could contort in a way that even made Max Thundermouth cringe when he got the urge to express his inner being. Even her generous acts had a price. If your birthday fell on a schoolday, Mrs. Pollack would give the lucky student a dime and everyone would get a treat. Then the celebrant would have to walk a gauntlet of classmates for a good ol' birthday spanking and she got in the last lick for good luck. Mrs. Pollack lived in a house on a hill surrounded by trees and no one knew anything about her. I must have thought, back then, that six weeks away from Mrs. Pollack was like an excused vacation. Now I wonder "Why did my classmates send those cards to me?"

Then there was Miss G. Miss G. was our music teacher. Almost all of us liked music until she came along. Other music teachers let us sing like we were spring meadowlarks, like music was to be a joyous occasion and a celestial right of being human. But Miss G. had standards. We were to be the midwest version of the Mormon Tabernacle Choir. I was having problems with Miss G. because of my low voice—I was a baritone at the time. Because I

was a short male, Miss G. felt that I should have a higher voice and told me to sing higher. I tried but could only sing louder. I was faking, she said. We argued a lot. I received my first S− from Miss G. Miss G. even gave me an S− during the time I had polio and wasn't in school. I discovered then that teachers, too, had personalities. Some, like Miss G., were awful. Mrs. Pollack was awful tough, but not awful.

Two weeks after I returned from the hospital, I was still at home trying to regain muscle strength. My mother said I should put on my regular clothes and get into the living room.

"Why?" I asked.

"Because," she said, "there is a school bus in front of our house and your whole fifth grade class is coming to the door."

I threw off my pajamas and put on a shirt and pants and tried to run to the living room but my muscles were too weak and I fell down. I got up and made it to the couch just as Mrs. Pollack knocked on the door.

"Mrs. Goud," she asked. "Is it all right if we visit Nelson for a few minutes?"

"Of course, Mrs. Pollack," said my mother. Mrs. Pollack led the troops into the house and asked how I was doing as she gave me a small gift. All I could muster was an "Okay . . . uh . . . thank you, Mrs. Pollack."

My classmates also gave me several presents and we goofed around for a while and then they left.

Each year there are studies which try to define "the good teacher." I will now suggest they add Mrs. Pollack to the list.

Follow-Up

1. *Think of your favorite teachers from elementary school to the present. What qualities made them so special? Have you ever let them know what they meant to you? (If not, when will you?)*
2. *What effect have teachers, good and bad, had on your development?*

Applied Activities for Section Four

SIGNIFICANT OTHER PERCEPTION INVENTORY

Significant others are persons who influence how you perceive yourself. Some significant other categories include family members, lovers, spouses, friends, colleagues, teachers, supervisors, mentors. Each person determines who is a significant other to them.

This activity asks your significant others to offer their perceptions of you. One of the strengths of significant others is that they can often see things we are not aware of or that we believe are hidden. They can often provide some helpful hints on how to approach life. Look at the sample Significant Other Perception Inventory at the end of this activity.

If you choose to try this activity, follow these guidelines:

1. Try to get at least seven significant other responses. This is necessary to get a minimum number of reactions for analysis and interpretation.
2. Make sure that the significant other is comfortable in filling out the inventory—this helps to attain genuine responses. Sometimes a significant other is not willing to complete the inventory for a number of reasons (it may lead to awkward conversations, they place too much pressure on themselves to please you). You may be asked to complete an inventory on them. Do *not* require the significant other to discuss their responses—only do so if they seem willing.
3. Allow sufficient time for significant others to respond to the activity (sometime these are mailed). If necessary, provide a stamped envelope addressed to you or the instructor. E-mail is another option.
4. Complete a Significant Other Perception Inventory on yourself from your point of view.
5. Analysis and interpretation suggestions:
   a. After all the inventories have been collected, list all responses to each item.
   b. Examine each list for patterns and common responses. Note these themes. Circle any response or theme that has impact for you in any way (positive or negative).
   c. Attempt to really "listen" to your significant others. Try not to dismiss a response if it bothers you or if you disagree with it. Be open to any message before judging or criticizing it.
   d. How did your inventory compare with those of your significant others? Which (if any) responses surprised you or were unexpected? Are there any observations that need further exploration on your part? Are any specific action steps indicated?
6. Discuss or write about what you learned.

Perception Inventory

You have been selected by _____ as having an important influence on his or her life. As part of a group activity, this person has been asked to obtain *your personal perceptions* of him or her as indicated by your completion of this inventory. Your observations and comments will be valuable and appreciated. You do *not* have to sign your name to this inventory.

Your comments will *not* be used in determining any type of grade for this person or as a personal reference. Try to be as open and genuine as you can in answering each item. Also, answer according to *your* point of view, *not* according to the way you think others see this person.

You can return the inventory in one of two ways:

1. Complete it and return it directly to the person or by e-mail.
2. Type your responses and do not write your name on the inventory. Send the completed form by mail to the group facilitator. (The person who asked you to complete the inventory has provided you with an addressed, stamped envelope.) The facilitator will then give your inventory to the appropriate person without revealing the source.

Directions

Keeping the afore-named person in mind, complete each of the following unfinished sentences as honestly as you can. If you cannot think of an appropriate completion or if you choose not to complete an item, do not write anything in the blank provided.

1. *Three adjectives* (traits) that immediately come to mind when I think of this person are

2. At least *three* strengths consistently manifested by this person are

3. a. A potential or ability that this person possesses, but has *not* fully developed yet

   b. One way to further develop this ability would be to

4. a. One obstacle (originating either from outside or from within the person) to this person's realization of full personal growth is

   b. One way to overcome this obstacle would be to

5. Within the next year I believe that it will be very important for this person to

6. If I could give this person a gift (either tangible or intangible) that would make a difference in his or her life right now, it would be

   Thank you for your efforts and cooperation.

LOVE MAPS

Editor's Note: Gottman and Silver believe that emotionally intelligent couples are intimately familiar with each other's world. They remember the major events in each other's history, and keep updating this information. They call this a love map. Couples with detailed love maps are better prepared to cope with stressors and to create shared meanings.

Directions: With your intimate significant other, attempt to answer the following items about the other person. The more items answered accurately, the more extensive the love map.

1. Names of two closest friends
2. A favorite hobby or leisure activity
3. Birthplace
4. A favorite relative
5. A favorite meal
6. A current stress or challenge
7. A fear
8. An unrealized dream or aspiration
9. Favorite time for lovemaking
10. Greatest source of support (other than yourself)
11. Nature of an upcoming event and feelings about it
12. Philosophy of life/religious beliefs

13. Beliefs about money
14. Favorite musician or entertainer
15. Health or medical concerns
16. Favorite holiday and why
17. Ideal job or vacation
18. A regret or failure
19. A major accomplishment or success
20. Favorite activity together (besides sex)

Follow-Up

1. Describe what you learned from attempting this activity.

SEXUALITY QUIZ

Directions: Complete the quiz individually before checking the answers (you could also discuss your answers with a small group prior to checking the answers).

1. What is the age of first sexual intercourse for the average American?

    (a) 11–12   (b) 13–14   (c) 16–17   (d) 18–19

2. How many sex partners, on average, do American *males* report during their lifetimes?

    (a) 3   (b) 6   (c) 12   (d) 19

3. How many sex partners, on average, do American *females* report during their lifetimes?

    (a) 2   (b) 4   (c) 5   (d) 8

4. Which category below reports the lowest incidence of sexual intercourse?

    (a) married couples   (b) single persons   (c) unmarried couples who live together   (d) professors

5. The approximate percentage of *men* who claim to be virgins at the time of marriage (as of 1995)

    (a) 10%   (b) 20%   (c) 30%   (d) 40%

6. The approximate percentage of *women* who claim to be virgins at the time of marriage (as of 1995)

    (a) 15%   (b) 25%   (c) 35%   (d) 45%

7. Which category is most responsive to cultural shifts in sexual attitudes and practices over several decades?

   (a) unmarried females   (b) unmarried males   (c) married couples
   (d) neurotic rabbits

8. Both males and females experience a four-stage sexual response during intercourse. Out of order these stages are: resolution, plateau, excitement, and orgasm. What is the correct order?

9. Which of the following contraceptive techniques has the *lowest* failure rate (i.e., is most reliable)?

   (a) condom   (b) diaphragm with spermicide   (c) combined oral contraceptive pills   (d) spermicidal foam   (e) coitus interruptus

10. Using lubricants such as petroleum jelly enhances the effectiveness of a condom or diaphragm.

    True   False

11. Which group is statistically more likely to contract an STD (sexually transmitted disease) after a single act of intercourse with an infected person?

    Males   Females

12. The most common STD in the United States is

    (a) gonorrhea   (b) chlamydia   (c) acquired immune deficiency syndrome   (d) syphilis   (e) genital herpes

13. A woman or teenage girl can get pregnant during her menstrual flow.

    True   False

14. Menopause causes the majority of women to lose interest in sex.

    True   False

15. Erection problems are most often started by *physical* factors.

    True   False

16. Approximately what percent of persons in their 60s are sexually active?

    (a) 15%   (b) 25%   (c) 40%   (d) 80%

17. Most women prefer a partner with a larger-than-average penis.

    True   False

18. Below are common sexual fantasies. Try to identify the top three fantasies for males and females. Place M's beside your choices for men and W's beside your choices for women.

(a) _____ having sex with a complete stranger (by choice)

(b) _____ being forced to have sex with a chosen partner

(c) _____ group sex

(d) _____ sex with a celebrity

(e) _____ sex in front of an audience

(f) _____ oral sex

(g) _____ sex with a friend's spouse

(h) _____ sex with a person of the same gender

(i) _____ watching two members of the opposite gender have sex

Answers to Sexuality Quiz

1. c

2. b

3. a

4. b

5. a

6. b

7. a. Studies show that unmarried females are the most responsive to shifts in cultural sexual attitudes and practices.

8. Excitement, plateau, orgasm, and resolution

9. c. Here are the failure rates for selected contraceptive techniques:

Method	Failure Rate
Tubal sterilization	0.4%
Vasectomy	0.4%
Combined oral Pill	0.5%
Progestin-only Pill	1.0%
Condom	2.0%
Diaphragm with spermicide	2.0%
Spermicidal foam/cream	3.0–5.0%
Coitus interruptus	16%

10. False. Lubricants erode a condom or diaphragm, allowing STD organisms to pass through.

11. Females

12. b.   Chlamydia is a bacterial disease transmitted during intercourse. It often goes unnoticed. Experts estimate that as many as 10% of sexually active women have chlamydia. It is effectively treated with antibiotics.

13. True

14. False.   Some women report a lowered sex drive, but this can be treated with hormone replacement therapy.

15. True.   Physical factors include disease (e.g., diabetes), drug or alcohol abuse, and medications. Most erections problems can be successfully treated.

16. d.   Additionally, approximately two out of three women and four out of five men are sexually active in their 70s.

17. False.   Most surveys show that women are not as concerned with penis size as are men. Some women even consider a larger-than-average penis to be a problem.

18. The top three *male* fantasies are b, c, and i. The top three *female* sexual fantasies are a, d, and g. If you do not agree, then list your own!

References

Items 1, 9, 10, 11, 13, 14, 15, and 17 are from Reinisch, J. (1990). *The Kinsey Institute new report on sex*. New York: St. Martin's Press.

Items 2, 3, 4, 5, 6, 8, 12, and 16 are from Lefrancois, G. (1996). *The lifespan*. Belmont, CA: Wadsworth.

Item 7 is from Brehm, S. (1992). *Intimate relationships*. New York: McGraw-Hill.

Item 18 is from Walker, R. (1996). *The family guide to sex and relationships*. New York: Macmillan.

HEROES, HEROINES, AND ROLE MODELS

A person who has attained the highest human possibilities we value is our hero or heroine. These persons serve as ultimate guides and inspirations for our own strivings. Our heroes or heroines may even have a flaw or two, but this can make them even more powerful to us because we, too, have flaws. A hero or heroine has qualities that often transcend a particular discipline. One of my heroes is Maynard Ferguson, a jazz trumpeter. Although he does inspire my trumpet-playing, he has an enduring exuberance and commitment that I admire and that I try to emulate in my work as a professor. Our heroes and heroines provide clear standards and ways of being for our lives.

Role models demonstrate highly valued skills and personal qualities in a specific life role. More often than not, we know them. They are the people we strive to be like in our careers, as parents, or as citizens. Like heroes and heroines, role models are inspirational, but their influence may or may not extend beyond a specific role.

Our heroes and heroines and role models help define us as people and shape our values. Try the following activities to see their effects on your life:

1. Briefly list the heroes and heroines from your early childhood until now. These may have been fictional as well as real-life persons. They may have been historical figures or contemporary persons. Who inspired you in ways you admired and imitated?

2. Examine your list. What qualities do these heroes and heroines represent? How do your current heroes and heroines influence your life?

3. Imagine that one of your heroes or heroines talked with you for five minutes. What do you think they would say to you?

4. Identify some of your role models. Which of their qualities do you have? Which qualities do you need to work on?

5. Discuss or write about your responses and what you learned.

EMOTIONS AND FEELINGS

From the list below, place a check by the five feeling states that you most like to experience:

___	1. Excited	___	16. Angry
___	2. Afraid	___	17. Proud
___	3. Confident	___	18. Embarrassed
___	4. Ashamed	___	19. Brave
___	5. Tranquil	___	20. Hurt
___	6. Despairing	___	21. Marveling
___	7. Joyous	___	22. Rejected
___	8. Lonely	___	23. Trusting
___	9. Loving	___	24. Nervous
___	10. Jealous	___	25. Inspired
___	11. Surprised	___	26. Hopeless
___	12. Guilty	___	27. Spontaneous
___	13. Friendly	___	28. Resentful
___	14. Disgusted	___	29. Admiring
___	15. Reflective	___	30. Confused

Review your choices—there is a high probability that the majority are odd-numbered items. These are some of the positive emotions we experience. The even-numbered feeling states are those that most humans do not desire to experience. The listed feeling states are only a small sample of what a human is capable of experiencing. Like colors, emotions can blend to form an almost infinite range of feeling tones. For example, if you are happy, you may be either pleased, cheerful, or ecstatic. If you are angry, your range of anger can extend from annoyance to rage.

To be human means to experience a rich and complex world of emotions. Almost everyone has an approach–avoidance relationship with emotions. We welcome some emotions, but resist or even deny others. We easily reveal some emotions, but we have trouble expressing others. Sometimes we even try to conceal how we feel, only to be betrayed by a tapping foot or quivering lips. Occasionally, humans use one emotion to mask another (e.g., we feel rejected but we show anger, or we feel attracted to another but we look unconcerned, aloof). We know that many of our "disliked" emotions, such as anxiety, are sending us helpful warnings, but often we don't like the message and we blame the messenger.

If our thoughts are like books on library shelves, then our emotions are like wildlife creatures wandering through the library—some playful and curious, some quiet and timid, some sitting sullenly in corners, and some snarling and prowling about when the lights are out. Our rational thoughts can be overpowered by emotion. Carl Jung said that rational discussion only has success if the emotionality of a situation does not exceed a certain critical degree. In short, sometimes we have to put a lid on our emotions.

Sometimes emotions are *required* to fully experience a life event. Victoria Lincoln explains why in a passage from a short story she wrote over 50 years ago in *The New Yorker* (Sept. 28, 1946):

Why are we never prepared, why do all the books and all the wisdom of our friends avail us nothing in the final event? How many deathbed scenes we have read, how many stories of young love, or marital infidelity, of cherished ambition, fulfilled or defeated. There is nothing that can happen to us that has not happened again and again, that we have not read over a thousand times, closely, carefully, accurately recorded; before we are fully launched on life, the story of the human heart has been opened for us again and again with all the patience and skill of the human mind. But the event, when it comes, is never anything like the description; it is strange, infinitely strange and new, and we stand helpless before it and realize that the words of another convey nothing, nothing.

What good are emotions? Probably the best way to answer this query is to imagine a life without them. Do you love someone and are you loved? Do you anticipate with great joy an upcoming concert or athletic event? Have you found that anxiety, guilt, anger, or envy have actually helped you to function better at times? Think of any event or time that is a milestone in your life. Would it be a milestone without emotion? "Nothing great was ever achieved without enthusiasm," said Emerson. It's the emotions that provide our lives with a sense of aliveness and mystery. Emotions alone would lead to a chaotic existence. But thoughts alone would lead to an arid, stale existence. The best balance we can hope for is a good thought propelled by sound emotion.

Selections in this section include:

- In "What's Your Emotional IQ?" Daniel Goleman contends that emotional intelligence is a requirement for a successful life.
- How your complaints reveal your well-being is the focus of "Grumbles" by Nelson Goud.
- Wayne Dyer says that worrying is unnecessary in "Worry."
- Daniel A. Sugarman and Lucy Freeman explain how anxiety can be a positive source for growth in "The Positive Face of Anxiety."
- Five dimensions of loneliness are discussed by William A. Sadler, Jr. in "The Causes of Loneliness."
- Abe Arkoff introduces a powerful and simple way to experience happiness in "Little Joys."
- "Anger" by Wayne Dyer explores both causes and strategies for handling anger.
- Are abstract principles sound guides for living a life? This question is discussed by Nelson Goud in "A Matter of Principle."
- The merits and drawbacks of optimism and pessimism are the themes of Abe Arkoff's "Optimism and Pessimism."
- The negative influences of "Sarcasm and Apathy" are highlighted with a personal touch by an anonymous mother and a teacher.
- In "My Tyrant" Tom Peyton reveals a self-imposed burden.
- A first-person account "On the Death of a Father" is expressed by Sanford Colley.
- A detailed discussion on three phases of "Loss and Mourning" is written by Judith Viorst.

See the Follow-Up questions and Applied Activities at the end of this section for further applications of these topics.

What's Your Emotional I.Q.?

Daniel Goleman

It was a steamy afternoon in New York City, the kind of day that makes people sullen with discomfort. I was heading to my hotel, and as I stepped onto a bus, I was greeted by the driver, a middle-aged man with an enthusiastic smile.

"Hi! How're you doing?" he said. He greeted each rider in the same way.

As the bus crawled uptown through gridlocked traffic, the driver gave a lively commentary: there was a terrific sale at that store . . . a wonderful exhibit at this museum . . . had we heard about the movie that just opened down the block? By the time people got off, they had shaken off their sullen shells. When the driver called out, "So long, have a great day!" each of us gave a smiling response.

That memory has stayed with me for close to 20 years. I consider the bus driver a man who was truly successful at what he did.

Contrast him with Jason, a straight-A student at a Florida high school who was fixated on getting into Harvard Medical School. When a physics teacher gave Jason an 80 on a quiz, the boy believed his dream was in jeopardy. He took a butcher knife to school, and in a struggle the teacher was stabbed in the collarbone.

How could someone of obvious intelligence do something so irrational? The answer is that high I.Q. does not necessarily predict who will succeed in life. Psychologists agree that I.Q. contributes only about 20 percent of the factors that determine success. A full 80 percent comes from other factors, including what I call *emotional intelligence.*

Following are some of the major qualities that make up emotional intelligence, and how they can be developed:

1. Self-awareness. The ability to recognize a feeling as it happens is the keystone of emotional intelligence. People with greater certainty about their emotions are better pilots of their lives.

Developing self-awareness requires tuning in to what neurologist Antonio Damasio, in his book *Descartes' Error,* calls "somatic markers"—literally, gut feelings. Gut feelings can occur without a person being consciously aware of them. For example, when people who fear snakes are shown a picture of a snake, sensors on their skin will detect sweat, a sign of anxiety, even though the people say they do not feel fear. The sweat shows up even when a picture is presented so rapidly that the subject has no conscious awareness of seeing it.

Through deliberate effort we can become more aware of our gut feelings. Take someone who is annoyed by a rude encounter for hours after it occurred. He may be oblivious to his irritability and surprised when someone calls attention to it. But if he evaluates his feelings, he can change them.

Emotional self-awareness is the building block of the next fundamental of emotional intelligence: being able to shake off a bad mood.

2. Mood Management. Bad as well as good moods spice life and build character. The key is balance.

We often have little control over *when* we are swept by emotion. But we can have some say in *how long* that emotion will last. Psychologist Dianne Tice of Case Western Reserve University asked more than 400 men and women about their strategies for escaping foul moods. Her research, along with that of other psychologists, provides valuable information on how to change a bad mood.

Of all the moods that people want to escape, rage seems to be the hardest to deal with. When someone in another car cuts you off on the highway, your reflexive thought may be, *That jerk! He could have hit me! I can't let him get away with that!* The more you stew, the angrier you get. Such is the stuff of hypertension and reckless driving.

What should you do to relieve rage? One myth is that ventilating will make you feel better. In fact, researchers have found that's one of the worst strategies. Outbursts of rage pump up the brain's arousal system, leaving you more angry, not less.

A more effective technique is "reframing," which means consciously reinterpreting a situation in a more positive light. In the case of the driver who cuts you off, you might tell yourself: *Maybe he had some emergency.* This is one of the most potent ways, Tice found, to put anger to rest.

Going off alone to cool down is also an effective way to defuse anger, especially if you can't think clearly. Tice found that a large proportion of men cool down by going for a drive—a finding that inspired her to drive more defensively. A safer alternative is exercise, such as taking a long walk. Whatever you do, don't waste the time pursuing your train of angry thoughts. Your aim should be to distract yourself.

The techniques of reframing and distraction can alleviate depression and anxiety as well as anger. Add to them such relaxation techniques as deep breathing and meditation and you have an arsenal of weapons against bad moods. "Praying," Dianne Tice also says, "works for all moods."

3. Self-motivation. Positive motivation—the marshaling of feelings of enthusiasm, zeal and confidence—is paramount for achievement. Studies of Olympic athletes, world-class musicians and chess grandmasters show that their common trait is the ability to motivate themselves to pursue relentless training routines.

To motivate yourself for any achievement requires clear goals and an optimistic, can-do attitude. Psychologist Martin Seligman of the University of Pennsylvania advised the MetLife insurance company to hire a special group of job applicants who tested high on optimism, although they had failed the normal aptitude test. Compared with salesmen who passed the aptitude test but scored high in pessimism, this group made 21 percent more sales in their first year and 57 percent more in their second.

A pessimist is likely to interpret rejection as meaning *I'm a failure, I'll never make a sale.* Optimists tell themselves, *I'm using the wrong approach,* or *That customer was in a bad mood.* By blaming failure on the situation, not themselves, optimists are motivated to make that next call.

Your predisposition to a positive or negative outlook may be inborn, but with effort and practice, pessimists can learn to think more hopefully. Psychologists have documented that if you can catch negative, self-defeating thoughts as they occur, you can reframe the situation in less catastrophic terms.

4. Impulse Control. The essence of emotional self-regulation is the ability to delay impulse in the service of a goal. The importance of this trait to success was shown in an experiment begun in the 1960s by psychologist Walter Mischel at a preschool on the Stanford University campus.

Children were told that they could have a single treat, such as a marshmallow, right now. However, if they would wait while the experimenter ran an errand, they could have two marshmallows. Some preschoolers grabbed the marshmallow immediately, but others were able to wait what, for them, must have seemed an endless 20 minutes. To sustain themselves in their struggle, they covered their eyes so they wouldn't see the temptation, rested their heads on their arms, talked to themselves, sang, even tried to sleep. These plucky kids got the two-marshmallow reward.

The interesting part of this experiment came in the follow-up. The children who as four-year-olds had been able to wait for the two marshmallows were, as adolescents, still able to delay gratification in pursuing their goals. They were more socially competent and self-assertive, and better able to cope with life's frustrations. In contrast, the kids who grabbed the one marshmallow were, as adolescents, more likely to be stubborn, indecisive and stressed.

The ability to resist impulse can be developed through practice. When you're faced with an immediate temptation, remind yourself of your long-term goals—whether they be losing weight or getting a medical degree. You'll find it easier, then, to keep from settling for the single marshmallow.

5. People Skills. The capacity to know how another feels is important on the job, in romance and friendship, and in the family. We transmit and catch moods from each other on a subtle, almost imperceptible level. The way someone says thank you, for instance, can leave us feeling dismissed, patronized or genuinely appreciated. The more adroit we are at discerning the feelings behind other people's signals, the better we control the signals we send.

The importance of good interpersonal skills was demonstrated by psychologists Robert Kelley of Carnegie-Mellon University and Janet Caplan in a study at Bell Labs in Naperville, Ill. The labs are staffed by engineers and scientists who are all at the apex of academic I.Q. tests. But some still emerged as stars, while others languished.

What accounted for the difference? The standout performers had a network with a wide range of people. When a non-star encountered a technical problem, Kelley observed, "he called various technical gurus and then waited, wasting time while his calls went unreturned. Star performers rarely faced such situations because they built reliable networks *before* they needed them. So when the stars called someone, they almost always got a faster answer."

No matter what their I.Q., once again it was emotional intelligence that separated the stars from the average performers.

Follow-Up

1. *Rate yourself, or have someone you know well rate you, on the five major qualities of emotional intelligence.*

    1 = Very low   2 = Low   3 = Average
    4 = High   5 = Exceptionally high

1. *Self-awareness*	1	2	3	4	5
2. *Mood management*	1	2	3	4	5
3. *Self-motivation*	1	2	3	4	5
4. *Impulse control*	1	2	3	4	5
5. *People skills*	1	2	3	4	5

2. *Choose one or more of the five factors of emotional intelligence to further develop in yourself and report your actions.*

3. *Observe persons who are very skillful in one or more of the five areas of emotional intelligence and report what you learned.*
4. *One of the more powerful techniques for managing moods is "reframing"— how to reinterpret a situation. Try this idea in your life and report on the results.*
5. *Discuss or write about your reactions to Goleman's contention "that I.Q. contributes only about 20 percent of the factors that determine success."*

Grumbles

Nelson Goud

A good amount of our conversations is devoted to complaints, problems, gripes, snivels, rants, and an occasional conniption. A recent survey named the four top causes of discontent in the United States: telephone solicitors, other drivers, home/car repair, and waiting in line or online. Perhaps you do not agree. What would you add?

According to Abraham Maslow, a given of the human condition is to be in a constant state of grumbles. We grumble because we always have some needs that remain unsatisfied. Maslow found that grumbles are useful indicators of one's well-being. He proposed that there is a hierarchy of grumbles that correspond to a hierarchy of needs. He said "to complain about your rose garden means that your belly is full, that you have a good roof over your head . . . that you're not afraid of bubonic plague" (p. 240).

Grumble theory points to several practical applications:

• *Grumble level.* Grumbles may be categorized from small to large depending on their effect on one's well-being. Although waiting in line at the grocery store is aggravating, it would fall into the small category. Not having enough money to buy food in the first place would be a large grumble (as would things like major health problems, job loss, threats to one's safety, etc.). Poor drivers could fall into all categories depending on the degree of danger encountered. A windy day can mess up your hair (small grumble) or fan the flames of a fire in the woods next to your home (large grumble). Seen in this manner, grumbles are a gauge to how well your life is going.

Small grumbles can be a case for joy as well as mutterings.

• *Grumble response.* How one *responds* to a grumble is as significant as the grumble itself. The key is proportionality—that is, the smaller the grumble, the less life energy allotted to it. Discovering that your favorite herbal mint tea is not available is not a stimulus for a nostril-flaring snit at a coffee shop. One can also respond with insufficient intensity when experiencing a large grumble (e.g., denying an addiction). Small grumbles, minor reactions; medium grumbles, moderate reactions; large grumbles, major reactions.

It is very possible that a small grumble may become a larger one due to overreaction. A student may spend endless hours trying to get a grade changed from an A– to an A and develop headaches, hives, and a sour disposition (even if the grade change has no bearing on further schooling or employment). Then there is the wife who became irritated at her husband's habit of biting his knuckles. Reaching a breaking point she slapped him and he slapped back. It escalated to the point that a major fight resulted in the husband's leg being broken. Both ended up in therapy (true case).

• *Grumble perspective.* There is a tendency to judge one's overall well-being based only on immediate circumstances. At work you may be grumbling about too many meetings, poor parking, ugly carpeting, being left out of a memo, and having to talk face to face with a colleague who always eats an onion-laden lunch. Perhaps, though, a few years ago you were worried whether you would even get this job and if you were qualified for it. These earlier and larger grumbles have disappeared from your radar screen. Present day grumbles then become magnified in significance and exist isolated from a larger historical context. This kind of thinking often leads to the error of overreaction (e.g., you leave the job). The key is to examine your current grumbles in an historical context that, in the above case, shows you have progressed from large to small grumbles.

Groups, organizations, or even societies can use the grumble history strategy. For instance, today about 40 percent of sixteen- to nineteen-year-olds have part-time jobs (primarily for pocket money). A century ago most teenagers were employed full-time in order to help their families make a standard living.

• *Grumble comparison.* Another perspective strategy is to compare your grumbles with others. Your boss has bad breath, her boss is known for firing employees for no discernible reason. He gripes about his Mercedes car payments and you have to take a bus to work. I scowl and growl at telephone solicitors. Then I read a story about one solicitor who had to sit in a desk-crammed room making dozens of calls daily reading an eight-page script. Many of the people this solicitor called wanted to have him read all eight pages—they were isolated persons who were lonely and just wanted to hear a live voice.

The comparison approach has a potential pitfall. You can always find someone who has it worse and this may inhibit a full recognition of your grumble or even cause guilt. The point of comparison is to aid in determining where a grumble falls on the grumble hierarchy. Seeing that someone has it worse may lead to empathy or compassion. But adding guilt is unnecessary. A physician addressed this issue in the following manner.

> As a family doctor, I have learned to accept suffering on the sufferer's terms. When an athlete comes to me with knee pain, I don't tell him that he has no right to cry because cancer patients bear burdens far greater. I can't tell a depressed person that she has no right to sorrow because others' sorrows are worse. I don't mock an obese patient's weakness of resolve, and I certainly don't shame him because others are staring. (*Harper's Magazine,* Jan., 1999)

No one has yet discovered how to have all their needs gratified. Grumbles will never cease. Maslow said that "people can live a high life or a low life, they can live barely at the level of survival in the jungle, or they can live in a society with good fortune and with all the basic needs taken care of so that they can live . . . and think about the nature of poetry or mathematics or that kind of thing" (1965, p. 236)

What do your grumbles tell you about your life now?

Reference
Maslow, A. H. (1965). *Eupsychian management.* Homewood, IL: Richard Irwin, Inc. and The Dorsey Press.

Follow-Up

1. *Discuss your reply to the final sentence of this piece.*
2. *Choose two statements from this article and explain how they relate to your experiences.*

Worry

Wayne Dyer

THE PSYCHOLOGICAL PAYOFFS FOR CHOOSING WORRY

• Worry is a present-moment activity. Thus, by using your current life being immobilized over a future time in your life, you are able to escape the now and whatever it is in the now that threatens you. For example, I spent the summer of 1974 in Karamursel, Turkey, teaching and writing a book on counseling. My seven-year-old daughter was back in the United States with her mother. While I love writing, I also find it an intensely lonely, difficult chore which requires a great deal of self-discipline. I would sit down at my typewriter with paper in place and the margins set, and all of a sudden my thoughts would be back on little Tracy Lynn. What if she rides her bicycle into the street and doesn't look? I hope she's being watched at the swimming pool, because she has a tendency to be careless. Before I knew it, an hour had elapsed, and I had spent it worrying. This was all in vain of course. But, was it? As long as I could use up my present moments worrying I didn't have to struggle with the difficulty of writing. A terrific payoff indeed.

• You can avoid having to take risks by using your worry as the reason for immobility. How could you possibly act if you are preoccupied with your present-moment worry? "I can't do a thing, I'm just too worried about _____." This is a common lament, and one with a payoff that keeps you standing still and avoiding the risk of action.

• You can label yourself as a *caring person* by worrying. Worry proves that you are a good parent, good spouse or good whatever. A handsome dividend, although lacking in logical healthy thinking.

• Worry is a handy justification for certain self-defeating behavior. If you're overweight, you undoubtedly eat more when you worry, hence you have a sensational reason for hanging on to the worry behavior. Similarly, you find yourself smoking more in worrisome situations, and can use the worry to avoid giving up smoking. This same neurotic reward system applies to areas including marriage, money, health and the like. The worry helps you to avoid changing. It is easier to worry about chest pains than to take the risk of finding out the truth, and then have to deal forthrightly with yourself.

• Your worry keeps you from living. A worrier sits around and thinks about things, while a doer must be up and about. Worry is a clever device to keep you inactive, and clearly it is easier, if less rewarding, to worry, than to be an active, involved person.

• Worry can bring ulcers, hypertension, cramps, tension headaches, backaches and the like. While these may not seem to be payoffs, they do result in considerable attention from others and justify much self-pity as well, and some people would rather be pitied than fulfilled.

Now that you understand the psychological support system for your worry, you can begin to devise some strategic efforts for getting rid of the troublesome worry bugs that breed in this erroneous zone.

SOME STRATEGIES FOR ELIMINATING WORRY

• Begin to view your present moments as times to live, rather than to obsess about the future. When you catch yourself worrying, ask yourself, "What am I avoiding now by using up this moment with worry?" Then begin to attack whatever it is you're avoiding. The best antidote to worry is action. A client of mine, formerly prone to worry, told me of a recent triumph over it. At a vacation resort he wandered into the sauna one afternoon. There he met a man who couldn't take a holiday from his worries. The other man elaborated all of the things my client should be worrying about. He mentioned the stock market, but said not to worry about short-range fluctuations. In six months there would be a virtual collapse, and that was the thing to really worry about. My client made sure of all the things he should worry about, and then left. He played a one-hour game of tennis, enjoyed a touch football game with some young children, participated with his wife in a Ping-Pong match which they thoroughly enjoyed, and finally, some three hours later, returned for a shower/sauna. His new friend was still there worrying, and began once again to chronicle more things to worry about. Meantime, my client had spent his present moments excitedly alive, while the other man had consumed his in worry. And neither man's behavior had any effect on the stock market.

• Recognize the preposterousness of worry. Ask yourself over and over, "Is there anything that will ever change as a result of my worrying about it?"

• Give yourself shorter and shorter periods of "worry-time." Designate ten minutes in the morning and afternoon as your worry segments. Use these periods to fret about every potential disaster you can get into the time slot. Then, using your ability to control your own thoughts, postpone any further worry until your next designated "worry-time." You'll soon see the folly of using any time in this wasteful fashion, and will eventually eliminate your worry zone completely.

• Make a worry list of everything you worried about yesterday, last week and even last year. See if any of your worry did anything productive for you. Assess also how many of the things you worried about ever materialized at all. You'll soon see that the worry is really a doubly wasteful activity. It does nothing

to alter the future. And the projected catastrophe often turns out to be minor, or even a blessing when it arrives.

• *Just Worry!* See if it is something that you can demonstrate when you are tempted to worry. That is, stop and turn to someone and say, "Watch me—I'm about to worry." They'll be confounded since you probably won't even know how to demonstrate the thing you do so well, so often.

• Ask yourself this worry-eradicating question, "What's the worst thing that could happen to me (or them) and what is the likelihood of it occurring?" You'll discover the absurdity of worry in this way.

• Deliberately choose to act in some manner that is in direct conflict with your usual areas of worry. If you compulsively save for the future, always worried about having enough money for another day, begin to use your money today. Be like the rich uncle who put in his will, "Being of sound mind, I spent all my money while I was alive."

• Begin to face the fears you possess with productive thought and behavior. A friend of mine recently spent a week on an island off the coast of Connecticut. The woman enjoys taking long walks, and soon discovered that the island was populated by many dogs who were allowed to run wild. She decided to fight her fear and worry that they might somehow bite her or even tear her limb from limb—the ultimate calamity. She carried a rock in her hand (insurance) and decided to show no sign of fear as the dogs approached. She even refused to slow down when the dogs growled and came running toward her. As the dogs charged forward and encountered someone who refused to back down, they gave up and ran away. While I am not advocating dangerous behavior, I do believe that an effective challenge to a fear or worry is the most productive way to eradicate it from your life.

These are some techniques for eliminating worry in your life. But the most effective weapon you have for wiping out worry is your own determination to banish this neurotic behavior from your life.

Follow-Up

1. *Which of the psychological payoffs of worrying most apply to you? Discuss your answer.*
2. *Attempt one or more strategies for eliminating worry and report on the outcomes.*
3. *Select two statements or ideas from this article and offer your interpretations.*
4. *For further information, see Wayne Dyer's* Your Erroneous Zones *(1976, New York: Avon Books).*

The Positive Face of Anxiety

Daniel A. Sugarman
and Lucy Freeman

Anxiety is the most painful of all emotions, and many people will do anything to avoid direct confrontation with it. Like a child terrified of going to the dentist, they permit anxiety to fester and cause psychic decay. They refuse to submit to the direct confrontation which removes the decay and the chronic pain. Some use so much energy defending themselves against anxiety that there is little left for the enjoyment of living.

We are learning that it is not anxiety itself, but the way we handle anxiety, that makes the difference between emotional sickness and health. A refusal to acknowledge the anxiety within us prevents the possibility of greater personality growth.

The widespread use of tranquilizers has helped—and hindered. On one hand, millions have obtained sufficient relief from anxiety to cope with daily difficulties; but the indiscriminate use of these powerful medications has prevented many from coming to terms with their conflicts. If they were just a little more desperate, they might seek psychological help and get at the source of the anxiety.

THE GIFT OF ANXIETY

In our hedonistic society, it is difficult for many to believe that anything which stings a bit can be of value. Nevertheless, in spite of our love of the sun, rainy days are important in the total scheme of things. Without any anxiety, we would become like vegetables, unable to sense the passing danger that threatens us from every side. The hyper-vigilance anxiety brings makes it easier for us to detect danger and take appropriate measures against it.

One mother described to me how, in putting her eight-month-old baby to bed one night, she felt suddenly anxious about his health. It seemed he did not look healthy, as though he were coming down with a cold; nor did she like the way he sounded when he cried. With these thoughts in mind, when she went to bed, she had difficulty sleeping. About two in the morning, she became aware of wheezing noises from the child's bedroom. Dashing to his side, she found him in the midst of a severe attack of the croup. Hardly breathing, the child was rushed to the emergency room of a hospital where his life was saved. In this case, as in others, without anxiety on the part of the mother, there might have been a tragedy.

A patient of mine, made anxious one evening by a television program warning against breast cancer, decided to examine her breasts. To her horror, she noted a small lump. Prompt biopsy, performed forty-eight hours later, revealed the lump to be malignant. Although she lost a breast, she is now, five years later, very much alive and well. Without her anxiety, the outcome probably would have been different.

Too often we are ashamed to admit anxiety. Nourished by an emotional diet of heroes, we inflict unreasonable expectations upon ourselves. A deer or rabbit, unencumbered by the pretense of courage, will take to its heels at the first sign of danger and, by doing so, ensure its survival.

Anxiety is the force behind much learning. A student under the pressure of a final examination in physics may be motivated to pick up the book, burn the midnight oil, and cram. As a result, he may find that, not only has he passed the test, but learned a bit of physics. His more carefree classmate, not anxious enough to study, may find his academic career prematurely terminated as a result of flunking the exam.

Anxiety may also prepare us for a stressful future situation. A man who has to give an important speech can be goaded by anxiety to rehearse not only his speech but the fear he may feel on the podium. As he faces this fear in anticipation of the event, there is a better chance that on the day of the speech he will be less afraid.

THE PRICE OF GROWTH

As we move through life, the stability of our personality is not always the same. There are times our defenses work well and life proceeds with little anxiety; but there are other times when defenses fail and we feel less stable or more anxious. Sometimes we experience anxiety when underlying growth is taking place. There has been little awareness that hardly any personality growth occurs without some anxiety.

Many positive steps in our life are accompanied by anxiety. Each time we extend ourselves further, accept new responsibility, or affirm our independence, we may also feel a measure of anxiety.

Once while traveling on a train in September, I sat next to a young girl who, pale and tense, sat with her teeth clenched, obviously very anxious. We began to talk; she told me she was on her way to college and that this was the first time she had ever been away from her family. As she spoke of leaving home, she plainly revealed both the anxiety she felt and her determination to become independent.

She described how she had always been overprotected by her mother and three older brothers and said that although it was hard for her to do, she had decided it would be the best thing for her to go to college in a distant city.

After she got off at her destination, I thought about her and the fact that she would have been relatively free of anxiety had she decided to remain at home. She was not going to let a little anxiety stop her from developing into an independent young woman. Some others, afraid of the anxiety of separation, have remained home, tied to mother and hearth forever.

Observation of children shows that they will attack again and again a fear situation until it no longer causes anxiety. Once they have mastered it, they are ready to move on to the next fearful situation. Almost every sign of growth and independence contains some seeds of anxiety. The first day at kindergarten, the first night of sleeping at a friend's house, the first time on a bicycle—all produce anxiety. The child who has learned early not to shrink in the face of anxiety, but to move through it, will have that sense of increasing mastery which sets the foundation for a healthy personality.

THE WILLINGNESS TO BE HUMAN

To some extent I have stressed the anxiety that results from conflict and from crisis. There is, however, the anxiety that comes from being alive, for, to be human is to be finite and limited, and to be finite and limited is to be anxious.

In some dark, deep recess of our minds, in spite of the din of music and noise and friends and work and travel and sports and food, we never lose the awareness that some day we will die. When we feel alive, we are using our full potential and the thought of death drifts into the shadows.

The knowledge of our finiteness can help us to savor the moments we live, to help us use our limited time in a useful, enjoyable manner. That knowledge can also help keep us appropriately humble in the face of the forces of nature, can make us give pause and consider our little vanities. The knowledge that we are temporary visitors on this planet can put petty quarrels into proper perspective. Temporary frustrations can be seen as part of reality. We can live more in the present and stop pursuing a vain, relentless search for security. Once we accept a certain basic anxiety, we can begin to live more fully.

The willingness to recognize the reality of anxiety indicates an ability to recognize all of reality. Most of us are all too eager to deny that we are anxious. When we do, we gain momentary relief, but pay a high price. We keep out of touch with our real feelings. Our chances of facing our conflicts and easing our anxiety are lessened. We find that we are more alienated than ever, both from our feelings and other people.

If one is able to acknowledge anxiety and battle it, healing forces are frequently set in motion. Dr. Paul Tillich once spoke of the necessity of having the "courage to be," which includes the acceptance and facing of anxiety.

Paradoxically, true courage seems to begin with the admission of anxiety, just as the possibility of true living begins when we do not deny the possibility of death.

If someone looks on anxiety as an enemy, a "disease," the therapeutic way is likely to be rougher and longer. But if he views anxiety as an opportunity to look within, as a mandate for further development, not only will the psychic way be easier, but his anxiety will also lessen that more swiftly. Anxiety is a feeling to become aware of, to be faced, to be understood, and then, almost automatically, it is present only when we realistically need it.

Follow-Up

1. *Respond to the authors' argument that anxiety is a gift. Provide examples from your life.*
2. *How has anxiety presented itself during periods in your life? Discuss the ways you handled it.*
3. *The authors propose that by accepting and trying to understand anxiety, we can learn what is needed and the anxiety will decrease. Explain an instance where this has happened to you, or possibly apply this idea to your current situation.*
4. *Choose any other idea from the article to write about or discuss.*

The Causes of Loneliness

William A. Sadler, Jr.

About a year ago, I had an interview with a reporter that illustrates one of the paradoxes associated with loneliness. She called to ask about my work on the subject, hoping to get help with an article. After giving her some information, I suggested she get in touch with the department of urban studies at a university in the city where she worked. I felt certain that its in-depth, long-range study of a large urban area would yield some insights into loneliness that would be relevant to her article and her newspaper's readers.

Several weeks later, the reporter called back to say that she had been turned away at the university. She was told by the department's assistant director that loneliness was not a social problem worth studying, that no data on loneliness were available, and that none was expected from their study program. Yet during the reporter's visits to mental health clinics and counselors in that area she was told that breakdowns, divorces, alcohol and drug addiction, and suicide were markedly increasing, and that problems such as these were related to chronic loneliness.

That's the paradox. Loneliness is so often dismissed by experts studying modern life, while at the same time it is reported to be an increasingly significant problem in individual and social being.

How can we account for the fact that loneliness, which I find to be a serious problem for many persons in modern America, is virtually ignored by the social sciences? I think there are two basic reasons. The first is theoretical. Until recently we lacked the clear concepts that would allow investigators and counselors to define loneliness and to understand it in a reliable way. The second reason is personal and has to do with the general attitude of the public toward loneliness, which sees it merely as a symptom of a weak character. The result is that one tends to downplay the impact it has in one's life, or even to deny that it has any significance at all. A common response given to persons who admit being lonely is: "Well, what's wrong with you? You don't need to be lonely. Go out and get busy. Join a club. Do something." Frequently through workshops, interviews, and articles I have found the response to be even more negative than this.

Investigations done in the last few years have permitted us to be more precise in defining loneliness. The conceptual understanding of loneliness, which will be presented in this article, shows why the accusatory response misses the mark. Many people in our society are lonely, not because of personality defects, but because there are factors "out there" that cause them to be lonely. Hopefully, this attitude will do more than resolve the paradox. It will help us all understand loneliness more intelligently and sympathetically, and provide a few realistic ideas about how to cope with it productively.

What is meant by *loneliness?* People use the term in different ways. Often loneliness is confused with merely being alone or with isolation. Your own experience should tell you that these are not identical. You can be alone and not lonely. People locked in solitary confinement do not always experience loneliness, at least not to any severe degree. To concentrate on isolation as much as social science has done when it has tried to get at loneliness is to miss the obvious. Some of the most painful, lonely feelings arise in the midst of a relationship or a group. Dr. Carl Jung suggested that "loneliness does not come from having no people about one, but from holding certain views that others find inadmissible." Adolescents, for example, frequently complain of the loneliness they experience in their homes, when they sense a generation gap. Adults they love simply do not understand them.

For this reason I suggest that loneliness is not just a physical condition. It is primarily an *experience*. Furthermore, it is probably unique to mankind. In his study on "the biology of loneliness" the late Dr. Ralph Audy Ph.D., M.D., of the U.C.L.A. Medical Center in San Francisco came to the conclusion that although there are analogies to it in the animal world, only human beings really know loneliness. Animals certainly manifest discomfort from prolonged separation. Ethologists and animal psychologists suggest that there is a basic animal need for attachment and that problems arise when that need is frustrated. It seems likely that humans have a similar need. But the kind of loneliness that I think is particularly troublesome in modern society is more complicated than mere frustration of this need for attachment.

In studying countless expressions of loneliness, both of modern Americans and from other times and places, I have found some common elements. The first and most outstanding feature of loneliness is a painful feeling, sometimes experienced as a sharp ache, as in moments of grief or separation; but it can also be a dull lingering form of stress that seems to tear a person down. Sometimes lonely feelings produce the "blues" of depression; but again, there is a difference between loneliness and depression. In the latter case, when a person is really "feeling down," he does not want to do anything. Depression corrodes motivational resources. Loneliness, by contrast, has a driving power. It sets people in motion—to go out, turn on TV, write a letter, make a phone call, or even get married.

There is another important aspect to this feeling. It is a significant signal coming from within ourselves that something is missing from our lives. Isolation does not imply any special type of awareness; loneliness does. A chief element of loneliness is a painful feeling that tells us something unpleasantly important about ourselves. All types of loneliness that I have studied have this element of painful self-awareness.

Loneliness also speaks of relationship, or rather, the absence or weakness of relationship. There are many different forms of relationship that can produce loneliness. One can be lonely for another person, a group, a home, a homeland, a tradition, a type of activity, and even a sense of meaning, or God.

A notable factor in much modern American loneliness is the quality of surprise. Loneliness so often strikes us unexpectedly. If you plan a trip by yourself, you prepare for lonely moments along the way. When they occur, you can handle them. When loneliness happens where you least expect it, such as in the home, at work, or among friends, it has a tremendous impact. We often do not know how to cope. It can make us confused, distraught, depressed, frightened, and even outraged.

Loneliness that frustrates our expectations is particularly hard to manage. It is this kind that so frequently disturbs people today. In nomadic and hunting societies persons were reared to expect long periods of aloneness. Facing loneliness was once a mark of manhood in American civilization. In an earlier era, Americans were reared to face life on their own in the struggle to achieve success through work. In that sense, being alone was part of the definition of successful living.

In this century the emphasis has been different. "Making it" has come to include "getting along with others." Learning to "fit in" is stressed at home, in school, in churches, and even in sports. Growing up in America often means developing expectations of involvement, popularity, and numerous attachments.

Today, as we tend to evaluate our personal success in terms of being liked, loneliness strikes with a force that is hard to handle. It suggests failure or at least a frightening vulnerability.

One reason loneliness hangs on is because people are either not fully aware of it or not prepared for it. They push it out of their consciousness. They try to find some remedy in drugs, in "busyness," in overly dependent relationships, or by increasing their memberships. I am convinced that much of the fear associated with loneliness, as well as many behavioral problems that arise from too much of it, are unnecessary. We will continue to misunderstand the pain and the problem associated with loneliness until we recognize how complex its multiple causes or sources can be.

I have chosen to refer to these different sources and types of loneliness in terms of *dimensions*. After studying a variety of expressions of lonely people in different contexts, I now classify these expressions according to the object that a person feels is missing or from which he or she feels separated. The dimension aspect refers to the area of relationship a person perceives to be the source of his suffering. There seem to be *five* fairly distinct dimensions. I have labeled them: *interpersonal, social, cultural, cosmic,* and *psychological.* The term dimension suggests that the loneliness has a particular source and also constitutes a distinct type. However, there are few pure types. Sometimes people may experience several of these dimensions at once, often without being fully aware of it. More importantly, they indicate the extent of distress that lonely people may experience. For example, when individuals experience loneliness in four or five dimensions simultaneously and over a long period of time, they can find the stress intolerable and eventually break down.

Of the five the *interpersonal dimension* is generally the most familiar type. In this situation one person misses another. Often it is most intense when a very special person is missed. For example, one English study done by the Women's Group on Public Welfare, a social action organization, suggested that in this context the worst loneliness is a communication gap, such as one preceding the dissolution of a marriage:

"Perhaps there is no greater loneliness than that suffered when a marriage breaks down, particularly in a situation where partnership has so far foundered that communications between the two have become impossible," the study stated. "The divorced and widowed are often more lonely than those who have never been married. This deeper loneliness could be due not only to the loss of a close companion but also where, having married young they have never learned to live with or face up to loneliness in earlier life."

The *social dimension* of loneliness is another familiar type. Here the individual feels cut off from a group that he or she considers important. Here it is a social relationship rather than an interpersonal one that is felt to be ruptured or lacking. Terms such as *ostracism, exile, rejection, blackballed, fired, discrimination,* and *expelled,* to mention only a few, resonate with the sense of this particular kind of loneliness. Often one gets an important sense of self-worth through membership and participation in a particular social environment. Once that membership is denied and participation is no longer possible, a person feels not just cut off but lacking in self-esteem. Not surprisingly a person who feels this social isolation often develops a low self-image and feels impotent to change this unsatisfactory relationship. Literature of minority groups, deviants, and more recently both the youth and the elderly is filled with lamentation and outrage at this kind of loneliness that is unwittingly imposed by society.

When these two forms of loneliness occur in the same individual simultaneously over a prolonged period of time, the result can be unfortunate in growth as well as behavior. Dr. Gisela Konopka, professor of social work at the University of Minnesota, found, for example, that complex, chronic loneliness was a primary factor contributing to the delinquency of adolescent girls. They were unwanted at home, often had no close friends, and were rejected at school and by clubs. Without any meaningful social role in which to demonstrate their worth and have it approved, as well as being without intimate communication, they acted out their feelings of lonely worthlessness in destructive acts of crime. The same applies to boys. The black Puerto Rican author, Piri Thomas, in his autobiography *Down These Mean Streets*, traces back the violent behavior, which led to his imprisonment, to an agonizing loneliness that stemmed from two sources: a lack of communication in his family, and ostracism by a white society because of his dark skin.

Retired persons may also experience an unexpected frustration associated with job severance. These people feel cut off, not merely from work, but from a network of relationships that had provided them with companionship and meaningful support. Housewives, too, have complained of similar combinations of lonely feelings, especially after several moves which leave them cut off from old friends, neighborhoods, and favorite groups.

My own research suggests that there may be a connection between rage and unmitigated complex loneliness. I have found that as you press people with questions on their loneliness they get very violent. In one group I had there was a divorced woman who felt extremely hostile toward her husband. She had lost her father at an early age and looked to her husband as a kind of father figure. He was a failure in every conceivable way and as a result she had bottled up this frustrated rage toward him. One day I threw a pillow down on the floor and said "There's your husband. Do to it what you would do to him." She killed him. Stomped him to death.

I believe that further investigation will bear out this tentative conclusion: very lonely people, who get angry rather than get depressed, will be prone to express their lonely frustration in destructive ways. I do not think it is mere coincidence that we are witnessing an unequalled rise in violence at the same time loneliness is so pervasive and intense. Personal accounts like that of Piri Thomas and studies of the Watts riots have shown that loneliness can be linked with violence when it is combined with a deep sense of frustration, especially in the economic and political realms.

The *cultural dimension* of loneliness refers to an experience some people have who feel themselves separated from a traditional system of meanings and a way of life. Immigrants and people who are continually mobile often experience this in the form of homesickness. People in America can sense this kind of loneliness if they feel the American heritage to be disintegrating. The term alienation may point to this form of loneliness, when it refers to a particular perception. Alienated people often feel that they are strangers in their own land. Members of American minority groups are particularly prone to this kind of loneliness. Even with close family relations they sometimes suffer from lingering loneliness, of being unable to identify with the American cultural heritage.

The feelings linked with cultural dislocation and culture shock likewise indicate a distinct form of loneliness, a sense of being uprooted and out of place. The nostalgia for those "good old days" when there was predictable order and cohesiveness also suggests this form of loneliness. In some cases loneliness may merely be a part of alienation; but in others, where there is a definite awareness of being separated from a meaningful tradition, I think the term loneliness is more accurate.

The *cosmic dimension* of loneliness may take a variety of forms, but essentially it refers to an experience in which a person feels out of touch with an ultimate source of life and meaning. Often it takes a religious form. Religious persons sometimes lament a felt absence of God. The Bible is filled with expressions of lonely persons longing for God. Much contemporary religion also answers to this need of loneliness, promising people a sense of presence and communion in their condition of existential estrangement or loneliness.

In workshops I have had persons express this cosmic loneliness in various ways. One middle-aged man confessed that a constant source of frustration came in the form of "missing God." Earlier he had been a strong believer, but now was an agnostic. He missed the sense of relatedness his youthful faith had given him. Religious persons who have been divorced have found themselves excluded from their religious community and they too have felt the anguish of this kind of loneliness. Some people have expressed a cosmic loneliness in their perception of the apparent absurdity of life. Erich Fromm suggested in *Escape from Freedom* that the experience of being morally and cosmically lonely is characteristic of persons who have realized the implications of autonomy in the modern world. Flight into conformity, becoming overly dependent on others, obsessive concern with others, a compulsive drive for achievement and recognition are some of the unproductive attempts of people to escape this dimension of loneliness.

The *psychological dimension* refers both to the experience a person has of being separate from himself as well as to the personal impact of the other four causes. A student who was in one of my courses made an observation that I have found many respond to: "I am loneliest when I am out of touch with myself." William James and C. J. Jung suggested the experience of a divided self is the root of modern man's search for a deeply personal religion or self-actualization or both. Much success of the Human Potential movement is related to the resolving of loneliness within one's self as well as that which comes from the lack of any intimate relationships with others. The perception of one's self as divided is a distinct form of "suffering self-recognition of separateness."

Here again one usually stumbles into this perception unawares so that this loneliness is aggravated by a clash of expectations.

The psychological dimension indicates a distinctly internal source of loneliness, whereas the other four dimensions specifically refer to external sources. Some aspects of loneliness can be traced to personality features that possibly stand in the way of self-actualization. Shyness, fear of loving and being loved, self-pity, and the development of a schizoid personality are examples of traits that can contribute to loneliness. But one point I emphasize as a sociologist is that *personal troubles often come from outside*, even though the individual experiences them as very private and intimately his own. This sociological analysis helps to get us beyond a narrow psychological and everyday notion that somehow an individual is at fault when he is feeling lonely. On the contrary, if an individual has lost a parent, a friend, or child in death, has moved from home, has changed or lost his job, is rejected by his group, and has lost his religious faith, is confused by his ambiguous American heritage, and does not feel deep, abiding loneliness, then I suspect that something drastic is lacking within him. Much loneliness that I have examined is a normal response to breaks in an individual's important relationships.

In all five dimensions there is the element of a suffering self-recognition of separateness from something, though each general type can be distinguished from the others. In each situation there are different kinds of relationships lacking. Consequently, there are different needs to be met. Recognizing specific needs proper to different dimensions is extremely important when someone is trying to cope with loneliness. For example, a person who sorely misses a special other person will not have the need satisfied by joining a group. Yet in spite of an impressive history of failure, we continue to encourage widows to compensate by joining organizations. That is, we tell them to look to the social dimension to satisfy an interpersonal need. We offer hand-holding to members of minority groups who suffer from a sense of exclusion, instead of creating a place for them to experience participation. Many attempts to cope with loneliness are unsuccessful because the need of a particular type of loneliness has not been met. The conventional wisdom that recommends lonely people keep busy does not confront the problem of loneliness. It dodges it and instead applies compulsive activity like a narcotic. I have been told by countless widows that they have tried this formula only to find that they return home to an empty house exhausted and all the more vulnerable to the painful void of their lives.

If we recognize loneliness as a significant form of self-perception, consider its context, and identify the dimensions involved, then we will be better prepared to face it realistically and positively. We need to get away from the simplistic notion that for loneliness "all you need is love." Love is often not enough. Social action is sometimes necessary and individual preparation for loneliness is essential.

If more than just an interpersonal dimension is present, then a more complex form of response will be needed. For example, persons suffering from both interpersonal and social loneliness are more prone to low self-esteem. The latter can jeopardize close, interpersonal relationships and discourage persons from taking an active role in a group. Meaningful participation in a group and developing some social role of importance can help combat the troubles stemming from the societal dimension of loneliness. It also can improve self-esteem, and prepare a person to become more ready for mature friendships and love.

If we are to meet the needs of lonely people effectively, we must get at the sources of their loneliness. Too often we treat loneliness merely as a symptom; that's one reason it keeps recurring. To confront loneliness in the modern world, our response will have to be a multi-level one. This concept of the five dimensions of loneliness can be helpful to social scientists, counselors, and anyone in detecting intelligently the types of loneliness we may encounter in the course of our lives. It also suggests the various sources from which it arises, and the multi-dimensional approach needed to cope adequately with the complex problem of loneliness.

Follow-Up

1. *Sadler describes five distinct dimensions of loneliness: interpersonal, social, cultural, cosmic, and psychological. Explain how you have experienced each of these dimensions, or as many as you can; how you handled the particular type of loneliness; and its consequences for you.*
2. *Sadler states that loneliness often strikes us unexpectedly. Not being prepared for it, we become confused, frightened, depressed, or find ways to avoid it. Discuss or write about your reactions to his argument.*
3. *Choose any other aspect of this article and write about or discuss your response.*

"HIDEWAYS"

1

IF I SHUT THE DOOR TO
MY HOUSE, YOU CAN'T
COME INSIDE...

2

& EVERYTHING'S FINE
BECAUSE I DON'T
THINK ABOUT YOU....

3

EXCEPT SOMETIMES &
THOSE TIMES I LOCK
MYSELF IN MY ROOM...

4

BECAUSE NOTHING THERE
REMINDS ME
OF YOU...

5

BUT SOMETIMES SOMETHING
DOES & I HIDE IN A
BOX THE TV CAME IN...

6

& THAT KEEPS
YOU AWAY
FROM ME...

7

MOST OF THE TIME... BUT
WHEN IT DOESN'T, I CRAWL
INTO A SHOE BOX
I KEEP IN THE TV BOX....

8

WHERE NOTHING YOU
DID OR SAID
CAN REACH ME...

9

EXCEPT SOMETIMES SO
THEN I CLIMB INTO
A PRESCRIPTION BOTTLE
INSIDE THE SHOE BOX...

10

& IT
HIDES ME FROM
YOU...

11

& IF IT DOESN'T, I ROLL
UP INTO A BALL
BECAUSE I DON'T HAVE
ANYTHING SMALLER TO GET INTO...

12

I WISH I HAD
A THIMBLE...

tom mcCain

"Hideways" by tom mcCain. Copyright © 1996.

Little Joys

Abe Arkoff

When Salman Rushdie was sentenced to death by the Ayatollah Khomeini for writing "The Satanic Verses," he went into hiding. Reminiscing about the life he left behind, he said, "What I miss is ordinary life: walking down the street, browsing in a bookshop, going to a grocery store, going to a movie. I've always been a big movie addict, and I haven't been in a cinema for a year."

"I haven't driven a car for a year," Rushdie continued. "I really love driving, and suddenly I have to sit in the back seat all the time. What I miss is just that, these tiny little things."

The value of little things was what playwright Thornton Wilder had in mind when he wrote *Our Town*, which proved to be his most famous work. The play was, he said, "an attempt to find a value above all price for the smallest events in our daily life." In this simple but moving drama, he eloquently shows what is extraordinary about the most ordinary and commonplace.

In *Our Town*, Emily, who has died in early adulthood, finds she can return to relive a day of her life. When she returns to relive her twelfth birthday, she finds her experience—from the vantage point of death—too poignant and in too great a contrast to the living who move matter-of-factly through the day. Overcome, she returns to death saying:

> Good-by, good-by, world. Good-by Grover's Corners . . . Mama and Papa. Good-by to clocks ticking . . . and Mama's sunflowers. And food and coffee. And new-ironed dresses and hot baths . . . and sleeping and waking up. Oh, earth you're too wonderful for anybody to realize you . . . Do any human beings realize life while they live it?—every, every minute?

My favorite essay on joy is a brief paper by Hermann Hesse. Although written almost 100 years ago, it sounds remarkably up-to-date as it laments the speed of "modern life," with the feverish pursuit of entertainment and ironically less and less joy. Hesse reminds the reader of the little joys available in daily rounds if one will only take a moment for them. He concludes his essay, "It is the small joys first of all that are granted to us for recreation, for daily relief and disburdenment, not the great ones."

Some recent research suggests that Hesse's advice is good psychology. Seek out as many as possible of the small joys each day. Studying both college-age and older persons, Professor Ed Diener of the University of Illinois has found that it is frequent little joys rather than an occasional big joy that make for a general sense of well-being. While less intense positive emotions are common, intense positive emotions are infrequent; furthermore, such intense events are often purchased at the price of past unhappy events and can serve to diminish the sensation of future positive events. Diener found happiness to be associated with those persons who frequently experience positive emotions rather than those whose positive experiences are intense. Thus, Diener and Hesse agree that the key to well-being is to fill one's days with little joys.

More evidence concerning the limited value of big joy was found by a research team who compared the levels of happiness in 22 major lottery winners with the levels of a control group similar in other respects. Each group indicated how happy they were at present, had been earlier (for the winners, before winning, for the controls, 6 months earlier), and expected to be in a couple of years. Significant differences between winners and controls in previous, present, or anticipated levels of happiness: none.

Even more striking results were found when both groups were asked how pleasant they currently found seven activities: eating breakfast, reading a magazine, watching television, talking with a friend, hearing a funny joke, getting a compliment, and buying clothes. Compared to controls, the winners found significantly less pleasure in these activities. Although the emotional big high of winning had not brought a significant, lasting increase in happiness, seemingly, by comparison, everyday little highs had paled.

The Chinese philosopher Lin Yutang passionately described the little pleasures that made his own life joyful. Indeed there were many, and in his enthusiasm, he gave a number of them first place. For example, he wrote, "If there is a greater happiness than lying in the sun, I'd like to be told." But then he noted, "If a man will be sensible and . . . count on his fingers how many things give him enjoyment, invariably he will find food is the first one." Still, later, seemingly to settle the matter, he set down the final truth: "If one's bowels move, one is happy, and if they don't move one is unhappy. That is all there is to it."

There is much in our day we think of as routine that could become little joys if approached in another way. Rushdie noted that he missed things he once thought completely unimportant—even chores—such as shopping for groceries. What once were tasks now were seen as privileges.

George Leonard recommends the Zen strategy of finding joy in the commonplace. What this requires is not a change of activity but rather a change of attitude. Leonard writes, "You might think that the value of Zen practice lies in the unwavering apprehension of the present moment while sitting motionless. But a visit to a Zen retreat quickly reveals that potentially, *everything* is meditation—

building a stone wall, eating, walking from one place to another, sweeping a hallway."

Psychologist Frank Dougherty has made an important distinction between the pursuit of relief and the pursuit of delight. Some of us who (perhaps without knowing it) have spent our lives pursuing relief, wonder why we never feel delight, but no amount of relief can produce delight. People whose minds are set on relief work to make sure that everything is taken care of and under control. There will be time for delight, they think, when things settle down, but of course, things never do.

To pursue delight requires a different mindset, and we can pursue delight even though everything isn't in order. We don't let the work waiting on Monday morning interfere with our enjoyment of the picnic this lovely Sunday afternoon.

Sir Alexander Korda recalled talking with Winston Churchill during the war when some bad news arrived. Churchill glanced at his watch and announced he was due back at 10 Downing Street. "It will all look different after a good lunch, a cigar, and a nap," he said. "Besides, Marshall Stalin has sent us some excellent caviar by courier, and it would be a shame not to enjoy it."

Often, the event that produces relief for one person delivers delight to another who approaches it in a very different way. In this connection, one of my students recalled a backpack trip he had been on with a group of others. Each day, the same person was first to reach their destination. One evening, the group was sharing the memories of the day's beautiful vistas, and this person finally spoke and said, "I guess all I really saw today was the top of my shoes."

Years ago, Sol Gordon wrote a brief set of instructions on how to be happy in an unhappy world. It was simply "to be able to enjoy at least the number of things equal to our age." Gordon was 51 years old at the time, and he wrote out the 51 things he enjoyed. The list included bittersweet stories and chocolate, uninterrupted classical music, reading slowly the good novelists, being warm and intimate with people he really cared about, and fantasizing that one of his still unpublished books was number one or number two on the *New York Times* best-sellers list.

Following Gordon's advice, my students and I make up our own lists of little joys when we are on the topic of happiness. I have found that just making up a list and sharing it with others makes one feel good.

As director of a freshman seminar program and coordinator of a program for older persons, I have taught some of the youngest and oldest students on my campus. The older students seem to compose their long lists of joys as easily as the youngest students do their much shorter ones.

My oldest student (and the one most full of fun and joy) was 91 years old when she made out her list and had no trouble in arriving at 91 items. Now 95, she is recovering from open-heart surgery and writes that she is enjoying in anticipation her next trip to Hawaii.*

After my students compose their little joy lists, I ask them to go back and put a star or asterisk by each item they have actually enjoyed in the past 30 days. What good is something

*Since I wrote this, she has made the trip to Hawaii, and we celebrated her 96th birthday together; she is as full of fun and joy as ever.

that can bring joy if one doesn't take time to enjoy it? I enjoy reading my students' lists as much as my own. Most of the items cost very little or nothing at all. One of the most common items, of course, is chocolate. It appears on Sol Gordon's list and, I confess, my own. However, other common items are calorie-free, such as music, reading, nature, movies, a favorite TV program or comic strip.

The most uncommon joy producer that I have seen on any list is "Standing in the barn loft—after feeding hay to about 100 cattle—and listening to them crunch or munch the hay." It was on the list of one of my older students—a 64-year-old man from Tennessee. His whole list was quite special and not only because it didn't mention chocolate even once. Other items on his list included giving a flower to a lovely lady and watching her eyes light up; sitting on the patio and watching the fields and valleys and mountains change with the shadows as the sun moves across the sky; looking at—and feeling proud of—the many afghans and quilts his mother made and gave to him; driving a good, responsive car on a curvy mountain road; and after a hard, tiring day outside, a drink of good straight sour mash whiskey, mixed with a little 7-Up and cranberry juice.

Make up your list of little joys today, and make sure that in 30 days, each has a star by it.

Follow-Up

1. *Make a list of all the things you are able to deeply enjoy, and include as many items as you are years old. Put a star or asterisk in front of each item you have actually enjoyed in the past 30 days. Then write an account of your thoughts and feelings as you worked on and read over your list.*
2. *Live an ordinary day as you usually would, except be especially aware of everything in the day that brings you joy. Before you go to sleep, write an account of this experience.*
3. *Live an ordinary day as you usually would, except make the most of each joyful moment or each opportunity for one. Before you go to sleep, write an account of this experience.*
4. *How much is your life a pursuit of relief, and how much a pursuit of delight? Discuss this aspect of your life.*

Anger

Wayne Dyer

SOME COMMON CAUSES OF ANGER

You can see anger in operation all the time. Examples of people experiencing varying degrees of immobility, from mild upset to blind rage, are everywhere. It is the cancer, albeit a learned one, that permeates human interactions. Below are some of the more common instances in which people choose anger.

• Anger in the automobile. Drivers scream at other motorists for virtually everything. Pulse-racing behavior results when someone else is going too slow, too fast, doesn't signal, signals improperly, changes lanes or any number of mistakes. As a driver, you may experience a great deal of anger and emotional immobility because of the things you tell yourself about the ways others should be driving. Similarly, traffic jams are key signals for attacks of anger and hostility. Drivers yell at passengers and swear at the cause of the delay. All this behavior is the result of a single thought, "This shouldn't be happening, and because it is, I'm going to be upset and help others to choose unhappiness as well."

• Anger in competitive games. Bridge, tennis, pinochle, poker and a variety of other games are excellent anger inducers. People get angry at partners or opponents for not doing it right or for infractions of the rules. They may throw things like a tennis racket because they made an error. While stomping and throwing equipment are healthier than hitting or screaming at others, they are still barriers to present-moment fulfillment.

• Anger at the out of place. Many people feel rage at an individual or event which they consider out of place. For example, a driver in traffic may decide the cyclist or pedestrian shouldn't be there and try to drive him off the road. This kind of anger can be extremely dangerous. Many so-called accidents are actually the result of just such incidents in which uncontrolled rage has serious results.

• Anger about taxes. No amount of anger will ever change the tax laws of our country, but people rage just the same because taxes aren't what they would like them to be.

• Anger over the tardiness of others. If you expect others to function on your timetable, you will choose anger when they do not and justify your immobilization with, "I have a right to be angry. He kept me waiting half an hour."

• Anger at the disorganization or sloppiness of others. Despite the fact that your rage will probably encourage others to continue to behave in the same manner, you may persist in choosing anger.

• Anger at inanimate objects. If you hit your shin bone or hammer your thumb, reacting with a scream can be therapeutic, but feeling real rage and doing something about it such as driving your fist through a wall is not only futile, but painful as well.

• Anger over the loss of objects. No amount of rage will turn up a lost key or wallet and will probably prevent you from launching an effective search.

• Anger over world events beyond your control. You may not approve of politics, foreign relations, or the economy, but your anger and subsequent immobilization aren't going to change anything.

THE MANY FACES OF ANGER

Now that we've seen some of the occasions on which you might choose anger, let's look at some forms anger takes.

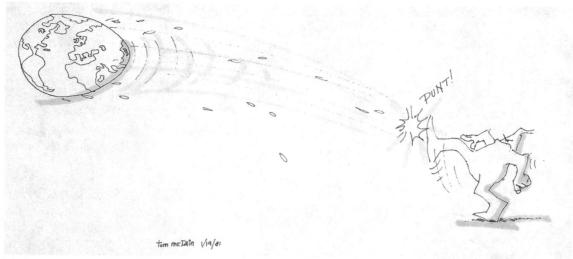

"Anger" by tom mcCain. Copyright © 1996.

• Being verbally abusive or ridiculing a spouse, children, or loved ones, or friends.

• Physical violence—hitting, kicking, slamming—objects or people. Carried to extremes, this behavior leads to crimes of violence which are almost always committed under the influence of immobilizing anger. Murder and assaults don't occur unless emotions are out of control and anger has led to temporary insanity. Believing that anger is normal or subscribing to the psychological schools that encourage you to get in touch with your anger and let it out can be potentially dangerous. Similarly, television, movies and books which popularize anger and violence and present them as normal undermine both the individual and society.

• Saying things like, "He infuriates me," or "You really aggravate me." In these cases you are choosing to let someone else's behavior make you unhappy.

• Using phrases like, "kill him," "clobber them," or "destroy the opposition." You may think they're only expressions, but they encourage anger and violence and make it acceptable even in friendly competition.

• Temper tantrums. Not only is this a common expression of anger, it frequently serves to get the tantrum thrower exactly what he wants.

• Sarcasm, ridicule and the silent treatment. These expressions of anger can be just as damaging as physical violence.

THE REWARD SYSTEM THAT YOU'VE CONSTRUCTED FOR CHOOSING ANGER

Getting a grip on lengthening your fuse will most effectively start with some insight into the reasons for using it in the first place. Here are some of the psychological motives for keeping that fuse as short as it is.

• Whenever you find it difficult to handle yourself, feel frustrated or defeated, you can use anger to direct the responsibility for how you feel to the person or event itself, rather than taking charge of your own feelings.

• You can use your anger to manipulate those who fear you. This is particularly effective in getting those who are younger, or physically or psychologically smaller, in line.

• Anger draws attention and thus you can feel important and powerful.

• Anger is a handy excuse. You can go insane—temporarily—and then excuse yourself by saying, "I couldn't help myself." Thus you can exonerate your behavior with out-of-control logic.

• You can get your way because others would rather placate you than have to put up with the angry exhibition.

• If you are afraid of intimacy or love, you can get angry over something, and thus avoid the risky business of sharing yourself affectionately.

• You can manipulate others with guilt by having them wonder "Where did I go wrong to make him so angry?" When they feel guilty, you are powerful.

• You can break down communication in which you feel threatened because someone else is more skillful. You simply use anger to avoid the risk of looking bad.

• You don't have to work on yourself when you are angry. Therefore you can use up your present moments in the easy business of being fierce and avoid doing whatever it might take to improve yourself. Thus you can use anger to take the heat off yourself.

• You can indulge in self-pity after you've had an attack of anger and feel sorry for yourself because nobody understands you.

• You can avoid thinking clearly, simply by getting angry. Everyone knows that you can't think straight at these times, so why not haul out the old anger when you want to avoid any of the hard straight-thinking.

• You can excuse losing or poor performance with a simple fit of temper. Maybe you can even get others to stop winning, because they fear your anger so much.

• You can excuse anger by saying you need it to help you carry out some task, but in fact anger is immobilizing and never improves performance.

• By saying it's human to be angry, you have a ready justification for yourself. "I'm human, and that's what humans do."

SOME DESIGNS FOR REPLACING ANGER

Anger can be eliminated. It will require a great deal of new thinking and it can be done only one present moment at a time. When confronted with people or events which provoke you to choose anger, become aware of what you are telling yourself, and then work at new sentences which will create new feelings and more productive behavior. Here are some specific strategies for attacking anger.

• First and most important, get in touch with your thoughts at the time of your anger, and remind yourself that you don't have to think that way, simply because you've always done so in the past. Awareness is paramount.

• Try postponing anger. If you typically react with anger in a particular circumstance, postpone the anger for fifteen seconds, and then explode in your typical fashion. Next try thirty seconds, and keep lengthening the intervals. Once you begin to see that you can put anger off, you'll have learned control. Postponing is control, and with lots of practice, you'll eventually eliminate it totally.

• When trying to use anger constructively to teach a child something, try faking the anger. Raise your voice and look stern, but don't experience all of the physical and psychological pain that goes with anger.

• Don't try to delude yourself into believing that you enjoy something that you find distasteful. You can dislike something and still not have to be angry about it.

• Remind yourself at the moment of anger that everyone has a right to be what he chooses and that your demanding that anyone be different will simply prolong your anger. Work at allowing others to choose just as you insist on your own right to do the same.

• Ask someone that you trust to help. Have them tell you when they see your anger, either verbally or with an agreed signal. When you get the signal, think about what you're doing and then try the postponing strategy.

• Keep an anger journal, and record the exact time, place and incident in which you chose to be angry. Be religious about the entries, force yourself to record all angry behavior. You'll soon find, if you are persistent, that the very act of having to write the incident down will persuade you to choose anger less often.

• Announce after you have had an angry outburst that you've just slipped and that one of your goals is to think differently so that you don't experience this anger. The verbal announcement will put you in touch with what you've done, and will demonstrate that you are truly working on yourself.

• Try being physically close to someone that you love at the moment of your anger. One way to neutralize your hostility is to hold hands, despite your inclination not to, and keep holding hands until you've expressed how you feel and dissipated your anger.

• Talk with those who are the most frequent recipients of your anger at a time when you are not angry. Share with each other the most anger-provoking activities in the other, and devise a way of communicating your feelings without debilitating anger. Perhaps a written note, or a messenger, or a cooling-off walk can be mutually agreed upon, so that you don't continue abusing each other with senseless anger. After several cooling-off walks, you'll begin to see the folly of striking out.

• Defuse your anger for the first few seconds by labeling how you feel, and how you believe your partner feels as well. The first ten seconds are the most crucial. Once you've passed these, your anger will often have subsided.

• Keep in mind all the things you believe will be met with disapproval by fifty percent of the folks, fifty percent of the time. Once you expect others to disagree, you will not choose to feel angry. Instead, you'll say to yourself that the world is straight since people aren't agreeing with everything I say, think, feel and do.

• Keep in mind that while the expression of anger is a healthy alternative to storing it up, not having it at all is the healthiest choice of all. Once you stop viewing anger as natural or only human, you'll have an internal rationale for going to work at eliminating it.

• Get rid of the expectations you have for others. When the expectations go away, so will the anger.

• Remind yourself that children will always be active and loud and getting angry about it won't do any good. While you can help children to make constructive choices in other areas, you will never be able to alter their basic nature.

• Love yourself. If you do, you won't ever burden yourself with that self-destructive anger.

• In a traffic jam, time yourself. See how long you can go without exploding. Work at the control aspect. Instead of hollering at a passenger, ask him a civil question. Use the time creatively to write a letter, or a song, or to devise ways out of the traffic jam, or relive the most exciting sexual experience of your life, or better yet, plan to improve on it.

• Instead of being an emotional slave to every frustrating circumstance, use the situation as a challenge to change it, and you'll have no present moment time for the anger.

Anger gets in the way. It is good for nothing. Like all erroneous zones, anger is a means of using things outside yourself to explain how you feel. Forget others. Make your own choices—and don't let them be angry ones.

Follow-Up

1. *Discuss your most common causes of anger, the faces your anger shows, and the rewards for being angry as described by Dyer.*
2. *Select two strategies for replacing anger and try them out. Report your results.*
3. *Choose any two statements or ideas in this article and offer your commentary.*
4. *For further information, see Wayne Dyer's* Your Erroneous Zones.
5. *See also the Anger Management Applied Activity.*

A Matter of Principle

Nelson Goud

Principle: It is wrong to cheat in school.

Practice: The scene: I am in a senior high school English class. We are taking the weekly grammar quiz: *Do you lie/lay the book down? Is Lansing the capital or the capitol? Define a gerund.* I have seen many of these questions since the fourth grade, but still have problems with the lie/lay thing. The teacher has left the room to attend to her part-time librarian duties. My classmates quickly huddle in small groups to complete the quiz. Most get 95 to 100 percent, even Fred who once, when asked to define an adverb, said "It's when you have to add a verb to a sentence." Judy, my main competitor for a college scholarship, is in one of the groups and gets a perfect score. I missed two and score 90 percent. The next week the same thing happens, and so on for four weeks. My average is declining. During the next quiz the teacher leaves as usual. I walked over to one of the few classmates not in a quiz group. We decided to work together on the quiz, he was a whiz at the lie/lay rule and I was an expert on the there/their distinction. I did not want to cheat, but I really wanted that scholarship—and besides, the other students were cheating all the time. But there were three new pimples on my forehead that night. I had abandoned my principle of never cheating.

Principle: I no longer will attend funerals (a matter of individual freedom of choice in how to grieve). I attended my mother's funeral, and it was a very difficult experience for me. At my father's funeral I greeted each visitor at the funeral home, but when the funeral began I drove out to a nearby lake and looked out over the water for an hour. Afterward I vowed not to attend any more funerals. I just cannot stand the ritual. If I did not attend my own father's funeral, why should I attend anyone else's?

Practice: Four years later, I have attended five wakes and three funerals. I went to support friends and family members. Another principle vanishes into the atmosphere.

Principle: If you marry, then it is forever.

Practice: Forever became defined as sixteen years.

I am learning that abstract, predetermined principles are unreliable predictors of behavior. It takes real life experiences to discover your true values and priorities.

Social psychology abounds with studies demonstrating the discrepancies between moral knowledge and moral action. In one classic study, seminary students volunteered to give brief oral presentations. Half of them were to speak on the topic of vocational options in the ministry, the other to expound on the meaning of the parable of the Good Samaritan. Each seminarian had to walk to a nearby building to give their presentation. On their way, each had to pass a shabbily dressed person slumped by the sidewalk with his eyes closed who was groaning quietly. In short, a real life Good Samaritan encounter. Results showed no significant difference in helping the victim between the two groups. Thinking and preparing lessons based on the Good Samaritan parable had little bearing on actual behavior. Interestingly, another variable made a difference in helping behavior: The seminarians were divided into low, intermediate, and high hurry groups (determined by how much time they were given to walk to the nearby building). The less the degree of hurry, the more help they provided. Being on time trumped helping a someone in need.

Principle: If I am to be a full-time writer, then I cannot have children.

Practice: An author recently interviewed on National Public Radio explained this principle by saying that writing required intense concentration and solitude, both of which are not possible with young children around. He did, however, volunteer to teach a creative writing class to juvenile offenders in a correctional facility. His friends said that this would solidify his decision to not have children because of what he would encounter in these youth. After a few weeks the author surprisingly discovered he had strong emotional ties to some of these offenders. It awakened the parental archetype. He and his wife had a child shortly thereafter. His writing became more enjoyable. This same author also had another guiding principle: "I will never change diapers." Guess what happened to this core belief?

An abstract principle is an inadequate guide in real-life encounters for several reasons. One, actual experiences involve other potent factors besides abstract principles. I have met very few adults who have not cheated in some way in their schooling. I have also found that most felt it was wrong but still felt compelled to cheat. You might cheat because a poor grade would mean becoming ineligible for a sport, losing an allowance, diminishing the chance of a scholarship, ruining a GPA, or losing the regard of those important to you. Real-life encounters are infused not only with principles but also with fears, needs, and powerful social demands.

Second, real life dilemmas often entail competing principles. Not going to funerals would follow my principle of freedom of choice, but violate the principles of love and loyalty to friends and family in times of need. Take a case of teachers in a local school system who have to decide whether to follow a strike decision because of unfair working conditions. Here each teacher is faced with an array of difficult and conflicting principles (e.g., loyalty to the association and colleagues versus loyalty to students, etc.).

Knowing how you or another person followed a principle in one real-life context may not predict actions in similar future situations. Some of the teachers in the above strike, for instance, made decisions that reversed their stance in a previous strike. One may act "for the principle of the thing" during one time or context, but not in another because of the consequences endured in the prior stance. Or one may have a new ordering of what is significant.

Finally, at times it requires a real-life experience to even identify a principle. Experiences reveal values, but are also interpreted by them. The author who taught the juvenile offenders is one such illustration.

So, do we abandon principles as life guides if they are so unreliable in predicting our actions? There are some other points to consider.

- Abstract principles do provide an *initial* sense of direction for navigating life's dilemmas. They also function as a countering force to momentary impulse, social approval, and situational pressures. Further, Maslow contends that "the human being needs a framework of values . . . in about the same sense that he needs sunlight, calcium or love" (1968, p. 206).

- For principles to function as worthy life guides, they must be learned and developed in real-life contexts whenever possible. Moral education research points to the feebleness of reciting codes and responding to hypothetical problems in learning moral behavior. It is through real-life encounters that one faces multiple and often competing demands. Life's real challenges also tend to tease out deeper and even unknown priorities. If discussion-oriented sessions on principles are used, they should approximate actual life contexts of the participants.

• Finally, attempting to live by experience-based principles is a useful path for developing human capacities. Trying not to cheat, for example, leaves you with the options of studying, research, practice—in short, building new skills and knowledge along with fortitude and responsibility.

Aristotle believed that virtue is not inborn but developed by practice and habit. "It is by doing just acts that we become just . . . by doing courageous acts that we become courageous," he writes in *The Nicomachean Ethics* (p. 43). So here we have the basic plan. Aristotle added one other consideration: "It is not easy."

References

Aristotle (trans. 1987). *The Nicomachean ethics* (J. E. C. Welldon, Trans.). Amherst, NJ: Prometheus Books.

Maslow, A. H. (1968). *Toward a psychology of being.* New York: Van Nostrand Reinhold.

Follow-Up

1. *Explain why you agree or disagree with the author's statement "I am learning that abstract, predetermined principles are unreliable predictors of behavior."*
2. *Describe two of your experiences that relate to abstract principles and your actual behavior. What did you learn?*
3. *Choose one statement from this article and apply it to your life experience.*

Optimism and Pessimism

Abe Arkoff

Research suggests that optimists tend to do better and behave differently than pessimists in stressful situations. Optimists are more likely to remain focused on the problem, try different strategies, and seek the help of others. Pessimists are more likely to disengage themselves from the goal and focus on the emotion that has been aroused (Scheier & Carver, 1985; Scheier, Weintraub, & Carver, 1986).

From his review of hundreds of studies, Seligman (1991) found that, compared to pessimists, optimists are happier, healthier, and may even live longer. Optimists are superior in school and college and also at work and on the playing field. Optimists exceed what might be predicted from their aptitude scores, and when they run for office, they are more likely to win. Seligman concludes, "There can be no doubt about it: Optimism is good for us" (p. 291). And, as Seligman notes, it is more fun.

Summing up the evidence against pessimism, Seligman (1991) offers these generalizations:

1. Pessimists tend to make gloomy prophecies of failure that are self-fulfilling.
2. Pessimists tend to give up or withdraw in the face of setbacks.
3. Pessimists tend to feel bad (blue, worried) regardless of the circumstance—whether they're right and things turn out wrong or they're wrong and things turn out right.
4. Pessimists are prone to depression and poor physical health.

Seligman finds that being a pessimist is not all pits; there are some cherries. Depressed persons—most of whom are pessimists—are more realistic than are nondepressed persons—most of whom are optimists. In various laboratory situations depressed and pessimistic persons prove to be better judges of reality; for example, they are better judges of the amount of control they have over various laboratory processes and the amount of skill they demonstrate on them. Pessimists also are less likely to interpret information in self-protective ways; therefore, they are better monitors and perhaps quicker to take the measures required by a situation (Cantor & Norem, 1989). They are more likely to see their dentists every six months, watch their blood pressure, and get their mammograms on schedule. They expect the worst and prepare for it; they are not likely to be overconfident and more likely to be ready should things go wrong.

Flexible Optimism. On Seligman's balance sheet, full-blown pessimism gets no respect, and the merits of the everyday, garden variety lag behind those of optimism. However, he notes that there are times when a bit of watch-out pessimism is necessary to damp all-out optimism; there can be a useful dynamic tension between the two, with each continually correcting the other. Optimism helps us dream and carry on, while a touch of pessimism keeps us from being rash and foolhardy.

When is it good to use optimism as a strategy? When should optimism be avoided? According to Seligman, we should mainly consider the cost of failure in a given instance. If the cost is high, optimism is wrong. Examples of the wrong times to be optimistic: a motorist deciding whether his failing brakes will last a little longer or whether he needs to buckle up for just a short ride or whether he can drive home after a stop at a bar. Good times to be optimistic: a shy person deciding to

ARE YOU AN OPTIMIST?

Indicate the strength of your agreement or disagreement with each of the items below by placing a check in the appropriate column.

	Strongly agree	Agree	Neutral	Disagree	Strongly disagree
1. In uncertain times, I usually expect the best.	____	____	____	____	____
2. If something can go wrong for me, it will.	____	____	____	____	____
3. I always look on the bright side of things.	____	____	____	____	____
4. I'm always optimistic about my future.	____	____	____	____	____
5. I hardly ever expect things to go my way.	____	____	____	____	____
6. Things never work out the way I want them to.	____	____	____	____	____
7. I'm a believer in the idea that "every cloud has a silver lining."	____	____	____	____	____
8. I rarely count on good things happening to me.	____	____	____	____	____

The preceding items have been included in a research instrument (the Life Orientation Test) to measure the extent to which persons are optimistic or expect favorable outcomes. Agreement with Items 1, 3, 4, and 7 and disagreement with the remaining items are indicative of optimism. Disagreement with Items 1, 3, 4, and 7 and agreement with the remaining items are indicative of pessimism (Scheier & Carver, 1985). These items, as they are presented here, cannot be considered a definitive test of your degree of optimism or pessimism, but they can help you think about this aspect of your orientation to life.

start a conversation, a salesperson deciding on one more call, a passed-over-for-promotion executive deciding to put out some job feelers. In addition to the matter of cost, here are three situations in which to use optimism and three in which to avoid it, according to Seligman:

- If you are in an achievement situation (getting a promotion, selling a product, writing a difficult report, winning a game), use optimism.

- If you are concerned about how you feel (fighting off depression, keeping up your morale), use optimism. . . .
- If you want to lead, if you want to inspire others, if you want people to vote for you, use optimism. . . .
- If your goal is to plan for a risky and uncertain future, do not use optimism.
- If your goal is to counsel others whose future is dim, do not use optimism initially.

- If you want to appear sympathetic to the troubles of others, do not begin with optimism, although using it later, once confidence and empathy are established, may help. (pp. 208–209)

Learning Optimism. We can increase our optimism by modifying our explanatory style or the way we habitually account for the events in our lives.

Pessimists, depressed persons, and those who give up easily tend to believe that their bad events have a *permanence*—that these events will persist, never go away, always affect their lives. Optimists, nondepressed persons, and those who resist helplessness believe the causes of such events to be temporary. For example: The pessimist fails at a task and says, "I'll never be able to do this." The optimist might say, "I'm a bit tired," leaving the door open to success after a bit of rest. Further example after a bad day in Las Vegas: The pessimist says, "I always am unlucky." The optimist says, "I wasn't lucky today."

The second dimension distinguishing pessimists from optimists concerns *pervasiveness*—whether something is universal or specific. Pessimists find universal explanations for bad events and specific explanations for good ones. When something goes wrong, pessimists take this as evidence that everything is wrong, and when something goes right, it is evidence that only that one thing is right. Optimists reverse this pattern. Optimist: "I'm not good at math." Pessimist: "I'm not good at anything." Optimist: "I'm not attractive to him." Pessimist: "I'm just not attractive." Or for good events, optimist: "I'm smart." "I'm attractive." Pessimist: "I'm smart *at math*." "I was attractive *to him*."

The third explanatory dimension is *personalization*—whether or not the person is responsible. Optimists take the credit but not the blame, while pessimists take the blame but not the credit. Optimists are internalizers for good events—they believe that they have made such events happen—but externalizers for bad events, which they regard as beyond their control. Pessimists reverse this pattern. Pessimist: "It's my fault." Optimist: "It's bad luck." Or for a good event, pessimist: "It was a lucky break." Optimist: "I got a clear shot and made the most of it."

Seligman advises that in disputing beliefs, we scan all possible causes and focus on those that are changeable (for example, we were not well enough prepared), specific (this particular competition was a tough one), and nonpersonal (the judging left something to be desired). . . . Here is Seligman's example of a student (Judy) disputing her beliefs, arriving at alternative explanations, and brightening her despair:

Adversity: I recently started taking night classes after work for a master's degree. I got my first set of exams back and I didn't do nearly as well as I wanted.

Belief: What awful grades, Judy. I no doubt did the worst in the class. I'm just stupid. That's all. I might as well face facts. I'm also just too old to be competing with these kids. Even if I stick with it, who is going to hire a forty-year-old woman when they can hire a twenty-three-year-old instead? What was I thinking when I enrolled? It's just too late for me.

Consequences: I felt totally dejected and useless. I was embarrassed I even gave it a try, and decided I should withdraw from my courses and be satisfied with the job I have.

Disputation: I'm blowing things out of proportion. I hoped to get all As, but I got a B, a B+, and a B–. Those aren't awful grades. I may not have done the best in the class, but I didn't do the worst in the class either. I checked. The guy next to me had two C's and a D+. The reason I didn't do as well as I hoped isn't because of my age. The fact that I am forty doesn't make me any less intelligent than anyone else in the class. One reason I may not have done as well is because I have a lot of other things going on in my life that take time away from my studies. I have a full-time job. I have a family. I think that given my situation I did a good job on my exams. Now that I took this set of exams I know how much work I need to put into my studies in the future in order to do even better. Now is not the time to worry about who will hire me. Almost everyone who graduates from this program gets a decent job. For now I need to concern myself with learning the material and earning my degree. Then when I graduate I can focus on finding a better job.

Outcome: I felt much better about myself and my exams. I'm not going to withdraw from my courses, and I am not going to let my age stand in the way of getting what I want. I'm still concerned that my age may be a disadvantage, but I will cross that bridge if and when I come to it. (pp. 218–219)

The Optimistic World of Yes. Optimists live in far richer worlds than pessimists, and as we bring more optimism into our lives, we enhance them. In other words, pessimists live in a world of no and optimists in a world of yes.

Follow-Up

1. *Explain why you believe you are primarily an optimist or a pessimist. What are the effects on your life?*
2. *Choose two statements from this article and provide your interpretation and/or personal application.*

Sarcasm and Apathy

When I was young, *Leave It To Beaver* and *Father Knows Best* were topics of household conversations. There was a lot of admiration for straightforward, innocent, polite people. Sarcasm wasn't something people carried like a badge. Although I have no desire to go back to that era and to give up some of the freedoms we have now, I find myself wishing we could do without some of the sarcasm we have developed. Sometimes the sarcasm that has become such a living, breathing part of our daily lives drives me up the wall.

I grew up on a farm in rural Indiana. For years I actually believed that people could talk to each other without "put-downs." This isn't to say that we never gave opinions—Farmers and small town people can be very frank. But when we talked it was from the heart. Possibly our hearts didn't have so many dark spots. Possibly we were more naive.

By the time I reached high school, the sarcastic revolution had started. Our class had the proud distinction of being the first senior class in the town's history to be released a week earlier than every other grade because of the apathy of the entire senior class. For four years it wasn't "cool" to answer questions in class. It wasn't "cool" to get involved. The administration had an assembly for the senior class to tell us that, after four years of struggling to try and please us and being met with apathy, at last they were tired. They wanted us out.

Eventually I moved to the city and though I had maintained my non-sarcastic attitude, I couldn't keep it forever. One day I was with my sister and she commented on how sarcastic I had become. She was right. I spent a week trying to keep from saying anything sarcastic. Oh, it was tough. I told my son how proud I was of him for doing a chore. He was so confused, he actually asked me if I meant it. Amazingly, though, trying not to be sarcastic has rewards. I felt more real. I felt as if I wasn't trying to cover up my real feelings as much. As a result I was much more relaxed that week. Sometimes, on days when I am in a particularly sarcastic mood, I go to bed wishing that the children were still awake so that I could hold them. On those days I wonder if they know how much I love them. During the week that I was trying not to be sarcastic, I didn't have those down feelings. I went to sleep feeling that my day had been fulfilling.

In my graduate education class I interacted with two other teachers. I noticed the amount of their sarcasm. We all find sarcasm funny so we encourage it, but it was odd to me that these teachers acted in ways that my teachers hated so much in the class of 1970. "Do we have to do this?" "How much of this do we have to do?" "I don't want to do this."

I couldn't help wondering how much sarcasm and apathy they tolerated from their students.

One night in class I sat between these two teachers. We had seen the *Griffin and Phoenix* movie, and they were talking about the movie's "over-kill." After several sarcastic comments, one of them turned to me and asked me what I thought. I feigned that I had been too tired to listen to their conversation. The second woman generously filled me in and I replied, "It was pretty sappy." I couldn't believe myself! I thought about the movie all the way home. In fact, I *cried* about the movie—remembering how some people find living harder than dying. So why did I say that? Probably for the same reason that the woman who had a whole notebook full of writing for one of her papers had said that she hadn't started her papers. It isn't "cool" to be non-sarcastic or non-apathetic.

There is probably a good chance that half of the time people are being sarcastic or apathetic it isn't genuine. Some people probably aren't even comfortable being that way. Comedy clubs, friends, books, and all types of resources help us to develop the idea that sarcasm and apathy should be associated with things that are fun. Sarcasm and apathy are more than just a form of humor—they are becoming a way of life.

Leave It To Beaver has been replaced by Bart Simpson. Bart Simpson is more than a sarcastic underachiever. Bart Simpson is proud to be called that.

—A graduate student and teacher

Follow-Up

1. *The author says that she felt more real when not being sarcastic. Do you agree with this idea?*
2. *Describe the source and effects of any sarcasm and/or apathy in your life.*

My Tyrant

Tom Peyton

In 1776 a handful of hardy and determined souls decided to leave the tyranny of the English government. Their purpose was to find the freedom to live a life they chose, instead of one chosen for them. They sought independence. This past Fourth of July, I discovered the tyrant of my own mind.

I wandered downtown through the crowds of people and watched happy couples embracing. I observed families celebrating together and kids running through the blocked-off city streets. There were smiling faces everywhere—except for mine. The tyrant in my mind spoke: You are alone, Tom. Totally alone. You are all by yourself. Incomplete without a partner, without a spouse. The rest of society is complete. Look at how happy everyone is—it's because they have someone. You, Tom, have no one. The voice beat at my heart and soul. My shoulders tightened and my mood darkened; my body started to feel very tired. My thoughts turned to the incompleteness of the moment and my own incompleteness. My head lowered, heavy with thought. My eyes focused on the blades of grass in front of me, and my thoughts turned to my divorce.

HOPING FOR WHOLENESS

Since my divorce, I have spent more than a year waiting to feel whole again. Waiting for the tyrant in my mind to ease. Waiting for the voice of guilt and shame to quiet. Waiting for something or someone to still the abusive chatter that swirls in your head when you think you have created a situation so ugly, so hideous that you must keep it to yourself. It is a lonely feeling to carry this weight of guilt and shame. This weight is of my own creation, I thought. The guilt is my guilt, and the shame of failure is my shame. I am the one giving it the power to ruin my day. I am the one letting it destroy my mental health. I should be the one to get myself out of this insane dialogue with myself. But I could not. I was trapped, and I surrendered to the rambling in my head. At that moment a drop of rain landed on my forehead, then another and another. In the middle of my self-absorption, it was raining. Perfect, I thought. Perfect?

I looked up and noticed that the sun was still shining. I gazed to the left and saw a beautiful rainbow arching across the sky. A smile crept onto my face.

"Guilt Trip" by tom mcCain. Copyright © 1996.

For a moment, the tyrant stopped. My brain grew quiet, and the only thing that existed was the rainbow. At that moment, my past was in the past, and my future was too far away to see. At that moment, I was completely present with myself. I was no longer searching for my feeling of completeness—I was experiencing it. I was with myself, not by myself.

In the chaos of thousands of people, I understood that I had never been alone. That for 30 years, I have lived this drama we call life, feeling as if I needed someone in my life to feel complete. And for the entire time, that someone was me. I laughed at the irony of it, then felt the sadness of the illusion. To expect someone else to make you whole is a path of misery and depression.

I wrote this very personal column for my own healing. I decided to share it because I know there are people in this world who have the same illusion—that they are alone. I hope, for a moment today, that they understand that they are with themselves, and it's a great place to be. I understand, too, that I will slip and falter along this path of self-acceptance. But, for the rest of the evening, I quietly celebrated with myself. A celebration of independence from the tyranny of my own mind. Freedom on the Fourth of July.

Follow-Up

1. *What is your response to these statements?*
   - *"I have lived this drama we call life, feeling as if I needed someone in my life to feel complete. And for the entire time, that someone was me."*
   - *"You are alone, Tom. Totally alone. . . . The rest of society is complete. Look at how happy everyone is—it's because they have someone. You, Tom, have no one."*
2. *Do you have an inner tyrant at times? How does it influence how you see yourself?*

On the Death of a Father

Sanford Colley

Wednesday, April 29, 1992

My father died last night.

For nearly 2 hours I stood at his bedside, held his hand, and watched the digital readout on a heart machine register an increasingly weaker pulse, slower heart rate, and lower blood pressure. Finally, all three blinked zero.

The ventilator was the only intrusion into what was otherwise a peaceful death. It continued to pump air into his lifeless body in a grotesque parody of breathing. When it was over, my sister asked, "May we turn that damned machine off now?"

Dad, a retired minister, was 85, and he had been in declining health for several years. Dylan Thomas would have been proud of him. He did not go gentle into that good night. A few weeks ago I pushed him in a wheel chair through the halls of a retirement center that had been his home for several months. "Look at all these old people," he snorted. "They're pitiful . . . just pitiful." I did not have the heart to point out the obvious; most were more ambulatory than he.

Two days ago, the morning started like a number of others during the last few months. There was an early morning call from the retirement home, "Your father has fallen again . . . we don't know how serious, but he does appear to be in some pain . . . we've sent for an ambulance . . . you should meet us in the emergency room."

I canceled meetings, rearranged classes, called on wonderfully supportive faculty colleagues to cover appointments, and left a long list of things to do with an accommodating and understanding secretary. X-rays revealed that his hip was broken. The options were to remove the hip joint completely and confine him to a wheelchair or to replace the joint and hope he might regain some of his ability to walk. Although surgery was risky because of his weak heart, the physician recommended joint replacement and surgery was scheduled for the next morning.

I arrived at the hospital in time to see him before the operation. The wait during surgery was long—much longer than my sisters and I had been led to expect. The young surgeon finally came out wearing a thin smile that masked his concern. (Was it only last week I warned my counseling students to never assume a smile means all is well?) He told us that during the operation Dad had gone into cardiac arrest. They had him stabilized, but the next few hours would be critical. At first, Dad improved, then he weakened, and finally, his physician told us, "he's not going to make it."

My two sisters and I stayed with Dad in the intensive care cubicle. His eyes were half closed, but once he shifted his gaze to mine and for a long time we looked at each other intently. I tried desperately to read what was in that gaze. Was it fear? Resignation? Love? Whatever he felt at that moment, I *know* he was aware his three children were there with him.

Dad seemed to sense that his life was nearly over. Last week he told me his days were numbered and asked about his will. I assured him everything was in order. The surgeon seemed to be quite moved when he told us of a comment Dad made to the anesthetist just before surgery. "I'm going to have a heart attack," he said. Those were his last words.

When the ventilator was turned off, I embraced my sisters, and we wept. The last time I cried aloud was 3 years ago when Dad was staying at our home. About 3:00 in the morning I had gotten out of bed and spent nearly an hour struggling to help him to the bathroom. He could hardly stand, much less walk, and he was dead weight in my arms. When I finally returned to bed, exhausted, I saw a guide to the Appalachian Trail (AT) on my bedside table. Dad had always talked about wanting to hike the AT, and I had the guide out because we had talked about spending a couple of days on an accessible part of the trail. That night I knew that he would never realize his dream, and I wept because he *could* have done it when he was in better health had he only chosen to do so. I did a hundred miles on the AT just prior to the American Association of Counseling and Development convention in Baltimore, and realized that I was doing it partly for me and partly for him.

A major concern was how my mother would respond to news of the death. She was in reasonably good physical health, but has experienced a significant reduction in her mental functioning as a result of Alzheimer's disease. She lives in a nursing home, seems to be content and happy, and recognizes members of the family, but she is usually unable to structure her thoughts well enough to form a complete sentence.

I decided it would be best to be direct and unambiguous, so I told her in simple language about the fall, the surgery, and the heart attack. "He's dead, Mom," I concluded, my heart aching.

For a fleeting moment, she seemed to understand. "Oh no," she responded, her eyes filling with tears, an incredibly pained look on her face. Then, almost immediately, she relaxed, her dementia seemingly insulating her from intense grief.

She glanced around the room and pointed to an old tennis shoe in her closet. The mate to it had been lost several weeks earlier. "It's gone, but that one is still there." I was stunned. A shoe with a lost mate; the most gifted and creative writers on our faculty would have been hard pressed to come up with a more striking metaphor for the loss of a spouse. Her thoughts confused and scrambled, Mom had seized that image. Perhaps she had understood.

Friday, May 1, 1992

We buried Dad today.

I woke up early this morning and ran—14 long, leisurely, lung-clearing miles. Halfway through I stopped to watch a hazy sunrise over the Tennessee River. I absorbed the beauty and remembered the fishing trips Dad and I took there when I was a boy. I reflected on his active life, my love for him, and how terribly unhappy he had been confined to the retirement home. When I resumed running, I had acknowledged a feeling of relief that I had not wanted to admit before. I was at peace.

The love and concern we felt at the funeral home last night and at the funeral today was a moving experience. I was overwhelmed that university colleagues would drive so far to express their support. Many individuals spoke of how effectively Dad had ministered to them in their times of grief. One young woman told me of seeing him go by her home every morning during his daily walk to the coffee shop.

"I'll never forget that funny old crooked walking cane he used," she said. "He told me once he wanted to be buried with it."

"I'll tell you a secret," I whispered, "It's with him in the casket."

Sunday, June 21, 1992

Father's Day. My first in 53 years without Dad. It has been nearly 2 months since his death, and the wrenching pangs of grief I experienced initially have started to subside. The healing is not complete, but it has started.

Going through Dad's library has been interesting. I found first editions of Rollo May's 1939 *The Art of Counseling* and Carl Rogers's 1942 *Counseling and Psychotherapy*. A real treasure was an 1892 copy of William James's *Principles of Psychology*, the very first book ever published (initially in 1890) with "psychology" in the title.

Although nothing more than coincidental, I was deeply moved by a book of daily devotionals over 20 years old. I started to chuck it because there were no notations or anything else of apparent value, only a single rusty gem clip on a page with the corner turned down. It marked the devotion for April 28.

That was the date of his death.

Follow-Up

1. *If one or both of your parents have died, compare your initial reactions to those of the author.*
2. *If one or both of your parents are alive, what are some things you'd like them to experience, with or without you, before they die? When will these happen?*
3. *If you are a parent, what are some things you can do now with your child (children) that won't be realistic years from now? When will you do these things?*
4. *Discuss or write about any other point in this article.*

Loss and Mourning

Judith Viorst

We are separate people constrained by the forbidden and the impossible, fashioning our highly imperfect connections. We live by losing and leaving and letting go. And sooner or later, with more or less pain, we all must come to know that loss is indeed "a lifelong human condition."

Mourning is the process of adapting to the losses of our life.

"In what, now," asks Freud in "Mourning and Melancholia," "does the work which mourning perform consist?" He replies that it is difficult and slow, involving an extremely painful, bit-by-bit inner process of letting go. He is talking, as I will be here, about the mourning we do at the death of people we love. But we may mourn in a similar fashion the end of a marriage, the coming apart of a special friendship, the losses of what we'd once had . . . been . . . hoped might be. For, as we shall see, there is an end, an end to much that we have loved. But there can be an end to mourning, too.

How we mourn and how, or if, our mourning is going to end, will depend on what we perceive our losses to be, will depend on our age and their age, will depend on how ready all of us were, will depend on the way they succumbed to mortality, will depend on our inner strengths and our outer supports, and will surely depend on our prior history— on our history with the people who died and our own separate history of love and loss. Nevertheless, there does seem to be a typical pattern to normal adult mourning, despite individual idiosyncrasies. And it seems generally agreed that we pass through changing, though overlapping, phases of mourning and that after about a year, sometimes less but often far longer indeed, we "complete" a major part of the mourning process.

Now many of us find it difficult to hear about phases of mourning without bristling, without the sense that some Julia Child of sorrow is trying to provide us with a step-by-step recipe for the perfect grief. But if we can hear about phases not as something that we—or others—*must* go through, but as something that may illuminate what we—or others— have gone or are going through, perhaps we can come to understand why "sorrow . . . turns out to be not a state but a process."

And the first phase of this process, whether the loss has been anticipated or not, is "shock, numbness and a sense of disbelief." This can't be happening! No, it cannot be! Perhaps we will weep and wail; perhaps we will sit there silently; perhaps waves of grief will alternate with periods of stunned incomprehension. Our shock may be mild if we've lived long and hard with the dead's impending death. Our shock may be less (let's face it) than our relief. But the fact that someone we love no longer exists in time and space is not yet entirely real, is beyond our belief.

Mark Twain, whose daughter Susy—"our wonder and our worship"—died suddenly at the age of twenty-four, writes in his autobiography of that initial state of benumbed disbelief.

> It is one of the mysteries of our nature that a man, all unprepared, can receive a thunderstroke like that and live. There is but one reasonable explanation of it. The intellect is stunned by the shock and but groping gathers the meaning of the words. The power to realize their full import is mercifully wanting. The

mind has a dumb sense of vast loss—that is all. It will take mind and memory months and possibly years to gather the details and thus learn and know the whole extent of the loss.

Although an expected death will usually stun us less than one we are unprepared for, although with a fatal illness our major shock may come when that illness is diagnosed and although in the time preceding the death we may sometimes engage in "anticipatory mourning," we will initially find it difficult—despite such preparation—to assimilate the death of a person we love. Death is one of those facts of life we acknowledge more with our brain than we do with our heart. And often, although our intellect acknowledges the loss, the rest of us will be trying hard to deny it.

Some disbelief, some denial, may continue well beyond the initial shock. Indeed, it may take the entire mourning process to make of the impossible—death—a reality.

After the first phase of mourning, which is relatively short, we move to a longer phase of intense psychic pain. Of weeping and lamentation. Of emotional swings and physical complaints. Of lethargy, hyperactivity, regression (to a needier, "Help me!" stage). Of separation anxiety and helpless hopeless despair. And of anger too.

Annie, age twenty-nine when her husband and daughter were killed by a truck, recalls how angry she was, "how I hated the world. I hated that man in the truck. I hated all trucks. I hated God for making them. I hated everyone, even John [her four-year-old son] sometimes because I had to stay alive for him and if he hadn't been there I could have died too. . . ."

We are angry at the doctors for not saving them. We are angry at God for taking them away. Like Job . . . we are angry at our comforters—what right have they to say that time will heal, God is good, it is all for the best, we'll get over it?

There are those who insist that anger—toward others, and also toward the dead—is invariably a part of the mourning process.

Indeed, a great deal of the anger that we focus on those around us is the anger we feel, but won't let ourselves feel, toward the dead. Sometimes, however, we do express it directly. "God damn you! God damn you for dying on me!" a widow recalls having said to her dead husband's picture. Like her, we love the dead, we miss and need and pine for our dead, but we also are angry at them for having abandoned us.

We are angry at, hate, the dead the way an infant hates the mommy who goes away. And like that infant we fear that it is our anger, our hatred, our badness that drove them away. We have guilt about our bad feelings and we also may have great guilt for what we have done—and what we didn't do.

Guilty feelings too—irrational guilt and justified guilt—are very often a part of the mourning process.

For the ambivalence that is present in even our deepest love relationships tainted our love for the dead while they were alive. We saw them as less than perfect and we loved them less than perfectly; we may even have fleetingly wished that they would die. But now that they are dead we are ashamed of our negative feelings and we start berating ourselves for being so bad: "I should have been kinder." "I should have been more understanding." "I should have been more grateful for what I had." "I should have tried to call my mother more often." "I should have gone down to Florida to visit my dad." "He always wanted a dog, but I would never let him have one, and now it's too late."

Of course there are times when we ought to feel guilt for the way that we treated the dead, appropriate guilt for harm done, unmet needs. But even when we loved them very, very well indeed, we still may find grounds for self-recrimination.

We feel guilt about our failures toward someone we love when he or she dies. We feel guilt about our negative feelings, too. And what we may do to defend against, or alleviate, our guilt is to loudly insist that the person who died was perfect. Idealization—"My wife was a saint," "My father was wiser than Solomon"—allows us to keep our thoughts pure and to keep guilt at bay. It is also a way of repaying the dead, of making restitution, for all of the bad we have done—or imagined we've done—to them.

Canonizing—idealizing—the dead is frequently a part of the mourning process.

Discussing idealization in her excellent book *The Anatomy of Bereavement*, psychiatrist Beverley Raphael gives us Jack, a forty-nine-year-old widower who described his dead wife Mabel in terms of unremitting adulation. She was, he declared, "the greatest little woman ever . . . the best cook, the best wife in the world. She did everything for me."

Anger, guilt, idealization—and attempts at reparation—seem to suggest that we do in fact know the dead died. Yet alternately, or even simultaneously, their death may still continue to be denied. John Bowlby, in his book *Loss*, describes this paradox:

"On the one hand is belief that death has occurred with the pain and hopeless yearning that that entails. On the other is disbelief that it has occurred, accompanied both by hope that all may yet be well and by an urge to search for and to recover the lost person." A child whose mother leaves him will deny the departure, will search for her, Bowlby says. It is in a similar spirit that we—as left, bereft adults—search for our dead.

This searching may express itself unconsciously—as restless random activity. But some of us consciously seek the dead as well. Beth looks for her husband by going again and again to all of the places they'd gone to together. Jeffrey stands in the closet among the clothes his wife used to wear, smelling her smell.

Searching for the dead we sometimes even summon them up: We "hear" their step in the driveway, their key in the lock. We "see" them on the street and eagerly follow them for a block; they turn and we confront . . . a stranger's face. Some of us may bring our dead back to life with hallucinations. Many of us bring our dead back to life in our dreams.

In this acute phase of grief some of us will mourn quietly, some vocally—though it isn't our style to rend garments and tear our hair. But in our own different ways we will have to pass through the terror and tears, the anger and guilt, the anxiety and despair. And in our own different ways, having managed somehow to work our way through our confrontations with unacceptable losses, we can begin to come to the end of mourning.

Starting with shock and making our way through this phase of acute psychic pain, we move toward what is called the "completion" of mourning. And although there still will be times when we weep for, long for, miss our dead, completion means some important degree of recovery and acceptance and adaptation.

We recover our stability, our energy, our hopefulness, our capacity to enjoy and invest in life.

We accept, despite dreams and fantasies, that the dead will not return to us in this life.

We adapt, with enormous difficulty, to the altered circumstances of our life, modifying—in order to survive—our behavior, our expectations, our self-definitions. Psychoanalyst George Pollock, who has written extensively on the subject of mourning, has called the mourning process "one of the more universal forms of adaptation and growth . . ." Successful mourning, he argues, is far more than making the best of a bad situation. Mourning, he says, can lead to creative change.

But he and his colleagues warn us that mourning is rarely a straightforward, linear process. Going through stages of grief, Pastan says, is like climbing a circular staircase—and like learning to climb it "after the amputation." In his record of mourning following the death of his cherished wife, C. S. Lewis uses identical imagery:

> How often—will it be for always?—how often will the vast emptiness astonish me like a complete novelty and make me say, "I never realized my loss till this moment"? The same leg is cut off time after time. The first plunge of the knife into the flesh is felt again and again.

And even when, eventually, we accept and adapt and recover, we may suffer from "anniversary reactions"—recurringly mourning our dead, with feelings of pining and sadness and loneliness and despair, on the day in the calendar year that marks their birth or their death or some special shared occasion. But in spite of setbacks, recurrences and the sense that our sorrow keeps doubling back on itself, there is an end to mourning, to even the seemingly most inconsolable mourning. . . .

It is by internalizing the dead, by making them part of our inner world, that we can at last complete the mourning process.

Remember that, as children, we could let our mother go, or leave our mother, by establishing a permanent mother within us. In a similar way we internalize—we take into ourselves—the people we have loved and lost to death. The "loved object is not gone," psychoanalyst Karl Abraham writes, "for now I carry it within myself. . . ." And while surely he overstates—the touch is gone, the laugh is gone, the promise and possibilities are gone, the sharing of music and bread and bed is gone, the comforting joy-giving flesh-and-blood presence is gone—it is true nonetheless that by making the dead a part of our inner world, we will in some important ways never lose them.

So perhaps the only choice we have is to choose what to do with our dead: To die when they die. To live crippled. Or to forge, out of pain and memory, new adaptations. Through mourning we acknowledge that pain, feel that pain, live past it. Through mourning we let the dead go and take them in. Through mourning we come to accept the difficult changes that loss must bring—and then we begin to come to the end of mourning.

References

Abraham, K. (1927). *Selected papers of Karl Abraham.* New York: Basic Books, Inc.

Bowlby, J. (1980). *Loss.* New York: Basic Books, Inc.

Clemens, S. (1959). *The autobiography of Mark Twain.* New York: Harper.

Freud, S. (1920/1953). *The interpretation of dreams* (Standard edition, Vols 4 and 5). James Strachey (Ed.). London: The Hogarth Press.

Osterweis, M., Solomon, F., and Green, M. (Eds.). (1984). *Bereavement: Reactions, consequences, and care.* Washington, DC: National Academy Press.

Lewis, C. S. (1963). *A grief observed.* New York: Bantam Books.

Raphael, B. (1983). *The anatomy of bereavement.* New York: Basic Books, Inc.

1. *Viorst discusses the characteristics of three phases of mourning: shock, intense psychic pain (anger, guilt, idealization, etc.), and completion. Discuss the validity of these phases from your experience with loss.*
2. *Select two ideas from this article and offer your commentary.*
3. *In other sections of her work, Viorst discusses how mourning may not come to an end. Some people engage in chronic mourning, which takes the form of continual grief or its opposite, denial of grief. Because chronic grief may lead to deep disruptions in regular living, professional help is usually advised. For further information see Viorst's book,* Necessary Losses.

Applied Activities for Section Five

WELL-BEING GAUGE

Cars have oil and heat gauges to indicate fluid levels. A quick glance warns us of possible malfunctioning. Although we do not come equipped with well-being gauges, we can develop them. With this gauge one can spot danger signs in mental and physical functioning.

Directions

1. A model of the Well-Being Gauge is provided. This chart has two dimensions: degree of health and stress (healthy, mild stress, moderate stress, severe stress), and five categories of well-being (physical, emotional, interpersonal, intellectual, miscellaneous).
2. Construct your individualized Well-Being Gauge (enlarge the blank copy provided). Some guidelines:
   a. List *at least* two examples each for the physical, emotional, interpersonal, intellectual, and miscellaneous categories. Then describe how they change according to whether you feel healthy, mildly stressed, moderately stressed, or severely stressed. Note that your examples may be different than those of the model.
   b. The miscellaneous category can include areas such as money management, music preferences, entertainment choices, free time activities, driving attitudes, dreams or fantasies, and so on.
   c. Consider asking others who know you for some examples.

Follow-Up

1. Place an asterisk by your sure-fire indicators of well-being. These are the ones to check out on a weekly basis.
2. Pay particular attention if you reach the moderate stress level. This is when you must try to change how you are living—now—or you will fall into the danger zone.
3. Try to determine the conditions associated with each level of health or stress. What is causing these shifts?
4. Discuss or write about your learnings from this activity.

Model—Well-Being Gauge

Health/ Stress States	Physical	Emotional	Interpersonal	Intellectual	Miscellaneous
Healthy	1. Can fall asleep and wake up with no problems 2. Look in mirror and like what I see 3. Spend a half an hour in morning for makeup 4. Feel good; a lot of energy	1. Feel I am happier and more adjusted than most people 2. Look to future (20 years or more) with expectation and anticipation 3. Participate in church service once a week and feel close to God	1. Enjoy interacting with other people, esp. meeting new people with varied interests 2. Feel I have many friends 3. Feel my marriage is better than most 4. Two parties a week, one in our home 5. Write letters; call friends to talk	1. Tackle problems as they arise 2. Complete tasks ahead of deadlines with some creativity 3. Think of new ways to approach problems, lectures, classes 4. Look for PBS programs of interest; watch local and national news daily 5. Read newspaper daily; read news magazine weekly as well as a women's magazine and journals	1. Feel financially stable; money spent on well-thought gifts* 2. Salary is satisfactory 3. Plan meals weeks in advance; bake bread; cook from scratch 4. Able to tolerate rush hour traffic — part of life
Mild Stress	1. Can fall asleep readily, but have a difficult time waking up in the morning 2. Look in the mirror and add "things I need to improve" to my list according to what I see 3. Spend a half an hour in morning for makeup 4. Feel good; have adequate energy	1. Feel I am as happy and adjusted as most people 2. Look to future (one year) with mixed anticipation and anxiety 3. Attend church once a week and participate as I feel I should	1. Enjoy people, but prefer ones I know, and those with similar interests 2. Feel I have a few good friends 3. Feel marriage is average 4. Do not write letters, but look forward to receiving them	1. Tackle problems as they arise 2. Complete tasks ahead of deadlines as required 3. Utilize previously tested methods for problem-solving, classes, and lectures 4. Watch local and national news, some commercial television 5. Read newspaper daily, but not magazines	1. Financially stable, adequate possessions, seriously consider necessity of gift giving* 2. Salary is inadequate 3. Plan meals weeks in advance but do not bake 4. Rush hour stressful, no one else knows how to drive

*This one turned out to be the guaranteed, sure-fire, always accurate indicator of my states of stress.

Model—Well-Being Gauge

Health/ Stress States	Physical	Emotional	Interpersonal	Intellectual	Miscellaneous
Moderate Stress	1. Fall asleep after half an hour; wake up often during the night, but able to get up in the morning 2. Look in mirror with disgust and despair 3. Put makeup on in the car on the way to work 4. Frequent headaches and stomach aches; loss of energy	1. Feel I am not as happy and adjusted as others 2. Look to short term future (one year) with much anxiety and apprehension 3. Attend church because if I don't things could get worse 4. Think others should take time to help me	1. Interact with people who can help me, do something for me 2. Wonder why I don't have many friends 3. Feel my marriage is poor 4. No social activities; spend time alone with husband 5. Phone calls and letters from friends are bothersome; feel guilty	1. Procrastinate, but meet deadline dates 2. Complete required work, race to meet requirements and deadline dates 3. Avoid thinking of problems, classes 4. Watch only national news on television 5. Only first page of newspaper read	1. Financially insecure; money for rent and food only; do not buy gifts or contribute any money* 2. Salary is inadequate for the work I do 3. Plan meals day by day; must make frequent trips to store 4. Rush hour tolerable; leave work earlier and get home later
Severe Stress	1. Hour or more to fall asleep, wake up after a few hours and cannot return to sleep 2. Avoid mirrors 3. No makeup 4. Frequent headaches, stomachaches, tired, feel I must have cancer	1. Consider counseling or suicide 2. Focus on past bad experiences only 3. Don't attend church because I don't have time 4. Resent others for not helping me or taking time to	1. Do not interact with anyone 2. No one to turn to; no friends 3. Feel I should not be married 4. Spend time alone; no social interaction at all 5. Do not answer phone or open mail	1. Procrastinate and do not meet deadlines 2. Unable to adequately complete required work 3. Try to find someone else to take some of my work load 4. Do not watch TV 5. Do not read newspaper	1. Feel I cannot even afford food; considering going to lower-rent housing* 2. Think about part-time job to supplement income 3. Eat out 4. Leave work an hour late to avoid rush hour

*This one turned out to be the guaranteed, sure-fire, always accurate indicator of my states of stress.

Model—Well-Being Gauge

Health/ Stress States	Physical	Emotional	Interpersonal	Intellectual	Miscellaneous
Healthy					
Mild Stress					
Moderate Stress					
Severe Stress					

EMOTIONAL CHARADES

This activity provides experiences in both emotional and nonverbal expression. For best results, have the instructor prepare the emotion cards (described below). Do *not* look at the list prior to the activity.

1. Participants should divide into groups of four to six members (both genders if possible).
2. Place the emotion cards face down in the middle of the group.
3. Each member selects a card, reads it silently, and then places it face down.
4. Each member has a maximum of two minutes to nonverbally act out the emotion on the card. Only body language is permitted by the sender. The other group members are to identify the emotion expressed. If the emotion is *not* correctly identified within two minutes, go to the next person.
5. Complete this procedure until all the cards are correctly identified. To prepare the emotion cards, write the following emotional states on separate 3 × 5 index cards:

Sorry/remorseful	Embarrassed
Afraid	Withdrawn
Encouraging/supportive	Hesitant/unsure
Bored/apathetic	Disappointed/let down
Arrogant/superior	Angry/hostile
Dominant/showing power, authority	Wonder/amazed
Playful/spontaneous	Eager/enthusiastic
Proud/confident	Content/at ease/relaxed
Friendly/warm	Anxious/nervous
Puzzled/baffled	Romantically interested

Follow-Up

1. Which body parts dominated in expressing emotions? Why were some emotions easier to express than others? What were the effects of this activity on how you worked as a group?
2. Discuss your experience with the whole class.
3. Write a reaction paper on your observations.

EMOTIONS AND PERCEPTION

To demonstrate the power of emotions in your life, try the following activity:

1. Choose a common situation in your life (job, college class, driving, free time, interacting with others).

2. Observe and summarize your perceptions of this situation under different emotional states. (Choose at least two of the following emotional states.)

Situation: _____

Emotion	Perceptions
Happy	
Angry	
Depressed	
Confused	
Anxious	
Confident	

3. Is your emotional state a main factor in how you interpret any given external event? If yes, what are some applications of this finding?
4. Discuss or write about your thoughts on this subject.

LISTENING TO EMOTIONS

With positive emotions like joy and wonder, we usually let them be and do not try to change them. With negative emotions, however, there is a tendency to try to avoid or to change them. Few people enjoy feeling anxious, guilty, or inadequate. Even these negative emotions have their gifts for us. In a sense, they are a special kind of teacher. For example, anxiety can teach us that we need to prepare for whatever we are afraid of facing; anxiety can show us how to be more alert; anxiety tells us that we are alive. Envy can teach us how we judge our own self-worth. Certain kinds of guilt can be helpful in maintaining a life of integrity.

Instead of avoiding or trying to escape negative emotions, it is often helpful to first reflect on what they mean. Reflection enables us to accept and not to deny the teaching power of negative emotions. This does not mean that you have to "like" them. There are several ways to listen to negative emotions as if they were teachers.

1. Ask yourself: What is this emotion attempting to tell me? What is this emotion warning me of in this situation?
2. With a person you trust, share your negative emotion and discuss what it could be trying to "teach you."
3. Write a brief letter to your emotion asking why it is there. Have the emotion write back to you. You will have the opportunity to see the emotion's point of view if you do the latter.
4. Read Thomas Moore's *Care of the Soul* (1992), which discusses how emotions can be teachers.

NONVERBAL OBSERVATIONS

1. While watching a dramatic TV or talk show, turn off the sound and focus on the participants' body language (particularly the face and gestures). Try to guess what emotional states are being expressed. Occasionally turn on the sound to check out your hunches. Record the show for more accuracy.
2. Observe your own ways of expressing various emotions. Some major nonverbal methods include: facial expressions, eye contact, vocal speed/volume/inflection, body positioning and distance, gestures, use of environmental objects (e.g., where you sit). Consider having someone who knows you well offer their observations on how you express various emotions. If you find that you are not expressing a certain emotion as well as you would like, experiment with your nonverbal methods.
3. Discuss or write about what you learned from any of these activities.

ANGER MANAGEMENT

Anger can be a natural emotional response in the following life situations: physical or emotional hurt, blocked needs, unmet expectations, guilt, loss, helplessness, threats, unfulfilled goals/dreams, injustice. Below are constructive and nonconstructive ways to handle anger. Mark the ones that are your typical anger responses.

Constructive Responses

___ Knowing that anger is a natural human feeling and that *you determine* whether to express it.

___ *Delay* any decision or action until your strong anger has subsided.

___ Using *diversion* techniques: Take a deep breath (or even ten) and exhale slowly; count to ten slowly or count slowly backward from fifty; take a walk; engage in physical exercise; tackle a mundane task like laundry or mow a lawn; listen to or play music.

_____ Appropriate *venting:* Talk it out with an understanding friend or colleague; howl at the moon; cry it out; write about it.

_____ Engage in an *incompatible behavior:* Laughter (see a funny movie or TV show, romp with a pet, have fun with a friend); relaxation activities (neck or back rub, a hot bath, view something beautiful); do something you like to do that requires full absorption.

_____ You can say "Yes" to the question: Is your anger in *proportion* to whatever caused it?

_____ Ask and honestly answer: "How much of my life energy is worth being spent in anger at this person or situation?"

_____ Start *problem-solving* strategies if warranted. These could include understanding the underlying causes of your anger; seeing other points of view; initiating constructive, confrontational conversation with the other party after your anger's intensity has lessened; arranging a group meeting to resolve the issue (if it is a problem important to the group); possibly getting a third party to mediate a dispute.

_____ Use the anger as a *positive energy source* and motivation.

_____ Seek qualified guidance if the anger persists in ways that negatively affect your life.

_____ *Observe* and learn how others handle similar anger situations in constructive ways. Also consider talking with them about their approaches.

Nonconstructive Reactions

_____ *Aggression:* Physical attack, ridicule, hostile silence. Aggressive responses almost always evoke strong negative responses in others that add to the problem. Aggressors may even be negatively affected by realizing that their anger increases and/or feelings of guilt result from the aggressive acts.

_____ *Displacement:* Taking out your anger on someone who is not the source of the anger (e.g., yelling at someone at home for a problem at work or school).

_____ *Denial:* Refusing to acknowledge the feeling of anger. If suppressed for a long period, the angry feeling may result in resentment, volatile explosive acts or words, or depression.

_____ Inappropriate *blaming:* Individuals unfairly blame someone or something else for whatever is causing the anger, or they unfairly blame themselves when the cause is truly elsewhere.

_____ *Disproportional* anger expression: Individuals respond with either excessive anger intensity or duration to whatever caused the anger. Also, it means that appropriate anger has not been expressed.

Follow-Up

1. Keep an anger journal. Record the incident, place and time of any anger experience. Do this for at least one to two weeks. Examine your responses using the above guidelines.
2. Add one or more constructive anger management techniques to your repertoire. Decrease or eliminate nonconstructive reactions.
3. Ask people who know you well to describe their perception of your anger management skills. (And don't become angry!)
4. Discuss and/or write about what you've learned about anger management.

THE NEIGHBOR

Twyla Thweebwood couldn't sleep so she made a cup of tea and turned on a late night TV program. It was a crime-watcher documentary. Tonight's show featured prison escapees from her state who were never caught and did not voluntarily return to finish their sentences. Twyla spilled her tea when a photo of her neighbor appeared, although under another name. The neighbor, Delbert Dunkle, had moved to her neighborhood about ten years ago. The documentary said that Delbert had two years left on a forgery conviction. Apparently he just walked away while working in an outer garden in a minimum security correctional facility. Delbert lives with his wife and two school-aged children. He worked his way up to an assistant manager at a local grocery store. He and his wife are members of the PTO and are regular church-goers. They are among the first to help when someone in the neighborhood needs help—shoveling snow, pet-sitting, and so on. They share vegetables from their garden. Overall, the Dunkles appear devoted to their children and are well-liked by their neighbors.

The TV program flashed a number to call if anyone recognized one the featured escapees. Should Twyla notify the authorities about Delbert? Why or why not?

Follow-Up

1. After answering the questions at the end of this piece, attempt to describe the moral rationale of your decision.
2. Discuss your answers with a small group and discuss your reactions. Try to understand each other's point of view. Write your learnings.
3. If you have studied Kohlberg's Stages of Moral Development, relate your (and others') rationale according to Kohlberg's stages. Discuss your learnings.
4. Relate your reactions to this article to "A Matter of Principle" (in this section).

SECTION

SIX

A QUALITY LIFE

If asked what it is we want most from life, most of us shuffle our feet and mumble some words about "happiness," "fulfillment," or "meaning." Whatever "it" is, we feel empty if we do not have it, and if we do have it, the meaning has great difficulty working its way out of our mouths. Many of our best writers have attempted to explain what people want from life. See if you can find an answer close to yours in the following attempts:

The only ones among you who will be truly happy are those who will have sought and found how to serve.

—Albert Schweitzer

How simple and frugal a thing is happiness: a glass of wine, a roasted chestnut, a wretched little brazier, the sound of the sea.

—Nikos Kazantzakis

One should not search for an abstract meaning of life. . . . Life can be made meaningful in a threefold way: first, through what we give to life . . . second, by what we take from the world . . . third, through the stand we take toward a fate we no longer can change. . . .

—Viktor Frankl

This is the true joy in life—being used for a purpose recognized by yourself as a mighty one; being thoroughly worn out before you are thrown on the scrap heap; being a force of nature instead of a feverish, selfish little clod of ailments and grievances complaining that the world will not devote itself to making you happy.

—George Bernard Shaw

299

He who dies with the most toys wins.

—Contemporary slogan

Look at every path closely and deliberately. . . . Does this path have a heart? If it does, the path is good; if it doesn't, it is of no use.

—Carlos Castaneda

If you have the guts to follow the risk . . . if one follows what I call one's "bliss"—the thing that really gets you deep in the gut and that you feel is your life—doors will open up . . . if you follow your bliss, you'll have your bliss, whether you have money or not.

—Joseph Campbell

You must want to be first-class . . . meaning the best, the very best you are capable of becoming. If you deliberately plan to be less than you are capable of being, then I warn you that you'll be deeply unhappy for the rest of your life. You will be evading your own capacities, your own possibilities.

—Abraham Maslow

Something has to matter. Otherwise, a person's life will be miserable and empty. Am I the last one to figure that out? The what that matters is unimportant—God, Coke-bottle collecting, track and field—all are equally useful in staving off the uselessness. For my stepfather, Don, bowling matters. Napoleon wanted to conquer Russia. Lana Sue's mom thinks the quality of her life is directly dependent on the meat prices at Kroger's. Career and love life may be a little trite, but they seem to work as well as anything.

To someone on the outside, your basis may look like a joke, but if you know it's important, really know and go on knowing, you'll never fall into despair.

—Tim Sandlin

All the life you have or ever will have is today, tonight, tomorrow, today, tonight, tomorrow, over and over again . . . and so you had better take what time there is and be very thankful for it.

—Ernest Hemingway

We need others. We need others to love and we need to be loved by them.
—Leo Buscaglia

To live in love is life's greatest challenge. It requires more subtlety, flexibility, sensitivity, understanding, acceptance, tolerance, knowledge and strength than any other human endeavor.

—Leo Buscaglia

When you feel safe enough to try something which requires a risk, it'll probably be too late.

—N. H. Goud

Sometimes we feel that we have paid too high a price for our comfort; that the network of relationships and names which we have become does not leave us room to breathe. The limits which define us for others then seem like prisons. And we suspect, momentarily, that we live in exile from the best part of ourselves.

—Paul Zweig

The human being needs a framework of values, a philosophy of life, a religion or religion-surrogate to live by and understand by, in about the same sense that he needs sunlight, calcium or love.

—Abraham Maslow

Life streamed through him in splendid flood, glad and rampant, until it seemed it would burst him asunder in sheer ecstasy and pour forth generously over the world. The proper function of a man is to live, not to exist. . . .

—Jack London

Every single man is a new thing in the world, and is called upon to fulfill his particularity in this world. Every man's foremost task is the actualization of his unique, unprecedented and never recurring potentialities, and not the repetition of something that another, and be it even the greatest, has already achieved.

—Martin Buber

It's not the critic who counts. . . . The credit belongs to the man who is actually in the arena. . . . And, who, while daring greatly, spends himself in a worthy cause so that his place may never be among those cold and timid souls who have known neither victory nor defeat.

—Theodore Roosevelt

The cost of a thing is the amount of what I call life which is required to be exchanged for it, immediately or in the long run.

—Henry Thoreau

Experience is, for me, the highest authority. . . . No other person's ideas, and none of my own ideas, are as authoritative as my experience. It is to experience that I must return again and again, to discover a closer approximation to truth. . . .

—Carl Rogers

Perhaps some of these passages speak to what you value in life. At this time in your life, which three passages would rank the highest? If none of the above quotes reveal your highest values at this time, add your own. With classmates or with those close to you, share and discuss these top three passages and their meanings.

Unlike the previous sections, you are urged to complete one or more of these Applied Activities *prior* to reading the articles: The Someday List, Talking to Wise Persons, Evolution of a Person #2. By doing so, you should get some ideas on what a quality life means to you. The readings for this section suggest several ideas and strategies for living a quality life.

- Multitasking and fast-forward living versus slowing down and focusing are themes in Nelson Goud's "Having the Time of Your Life."
- Ideas on how time reflects your well-being are offered in "Time Quotes."
- What if one could actually produce happiness in a machine? Award-winning author Ray Bradbury delves into this idea in "The Happiness Machine."
- The classic O. Henry short story "The Last Leaf" explores the power of the will to live.
- Carin Rubenstein and Phillip Shaver explain how "Active Solitude" can lead to a more balanced life.
- See how a natural setting provides hints on how to live in Nelson Goud's "Teachers in the Forest."
- What is your personal style when it comes to gathering and spending money? This idea is covered in "Personality and Money Orientations" by Robert Sullivan.
- "Thoughts on Money" by Nelson Goud offers some practical tips on money management.
- J. William Worden and William Proctor aim to raise your "Personal Death Awareness (PDA)."
- "Silicon Snake Oil" by Clifford Stoll, one of our foremost computer experts, discusses how the computer culture influences our overall well-being.
- "Controlling Your Technologies" presents some tips on increasing your power over multiple technologies.
- James Fearing provides a checklist for computer addiction in "Ten Symptoms of Computer Addiction."
- Nelson Goud contends that we can alter our perceptions by purposely changing what we expect to see in "To See Anew."
- Pianist and author Michael Jones ends the book with a lyrical essay on discovering one's inner essence in "Who Will Play Your Music?"

Having the Time of Your Life

Nelson Goud

Driving to work I found myself switching music stations whenever a commercial or lousy song came on, going over a couple of lesson plans, giving my opinion on the gene pools of a few fellow drivers, gazing at the bare limbs of some maple trees for signs of spring buds, and chomping down an apple.

During one fifteen-minute interval at a faculty meeting I sat next to a colleague who was writing a letter, eating lunch, jotting down dates in a daily planner, looking up and nodding at a point made, making notes on a student's paper, asking a question, and probably wondering why I was observing all of this.

These are examples of multitasking, the simultaneous performance of multiple activities. Some of our more revered persons were multitaskers. Burns (1993) describes a scene of a typical work day in 1621 of the artist Peter Paul Rubens who was simultaneously painting, dictating a letter, having a book read to him, and coherently carrying on a conversation. Rubens was a master multitasker. Burns describes the Busy/Body Syndrome, which is characterized by an intense drive to jam the most activities possible into a single time frame. Underlying this drive is the belief that one of life's most valued commodities, time, is becoming increasingly scarce. Stephan Rechtschaffen (1993) asks people "Do you feel that you have enough time in your daily life?" If you are like 90 percent of his sample, you would not have the time to answer him. You have what is called time-poverty.

We not only do many things at once, but we also like to do things quickly. Social observer Jeremy Rifkin (1987) describes the American cultural pace under one word—speed. "We are a nation in love with speed. We drive fast, eat fast, make love fast. We are obsessed with breaking records and shortening time spans. We digest our life, condense our experiences, and compress our thoughts . . . we are convinced that speed reflects alertness, power, and success" (pp. 58–59). It is like living a life on fast-forward.

Our quality of living is greatly influenced by how we choose to perceive and use time. One choice is the fast-forward, multitasking philosophy. But if it is your *only* choice for how to use time, then you will have restricted life options and, probably, a lower quality of life.

What's so bad about a fast-forward, multitasking approach to life? We get more things done—besides, sometimes there appears to be no other feasible way. In some instances this answer would be right. In other instances this approach works against us. We must be able to distinguish between these instances and employ different time-use strategies.

THE TEMPO OF LIFE EXPERIENCES

Every life experience expresses itself in a particular tempo. If the experience is to be fully understood, one must be in step with this tempo. Enjoying baseball, for example, requires a different mental tempo than enjoying basketball—as does reading Hemingway versus TV channel surfing. Each experience has its preferred and characteristic pace.

The fast-forward, multitasking time strategy is in sync with life experiences that call for instantaneous, multiple responses. Some examples are: a waiter at a popular restaurant during peak times; any first-grade teacher with twenty-five first graders with the energy of caffeine-crazed gerbils; a stock/exchange broker; a wedding consultant handling details one week prior to the wedding; a customer service clerk of a busy department store during the holidays. You can probably think of many others. These activities favor a state of heightened arousal, of adrenaline-pumping intensity, of eyes that can dart like those of a cobra surrounded by hungry mongooses.

The fast-forward, multitasking strategy is completely out of sync with other life experiences. One of my students wanted a book to help her from always feeling overwhelmed and harried by work, school, and family demands. I recommended Anne Morrow Lindbergh's book *Gift from the Sea*. Here was a small book on this very topic that discussed how to center instead of fragment your life. She returned the book the very next class. I asked her if it hadn't been right for her. "Oh it was easy to read," she replied. "I finished reading it in under two hours." After a brief discussion it became apparent that she could not change how she approached life tasks. To complete this reading quickly took precedent over everything else, including her main reason for wanting the book. We then talked about that.

Maybe you are a fast-forward reader and have already finished this article. How did it end? Here is a question for you: How many animals of each species did Moses take on the Ark? Now that is an odd query at this stage of the article. But maybe, just maybe it might slow down any fast-forwarders. The answer, incidentally, is none. It was Noah who built the Ark, not Moses. Ah, a trick question you say. How can it be when it is sitting right there on the page? It is how you approach the question that counts. A fast-forwarding glance at this question will most likely trigger the number two.

Here are some life events that cannot be fully experienced using a fast-forward, multitasking strategy: eating good food; dancing to a ballad with someone special; watching clouds while lounging on the grass; meditating or praying; showing a person that you are really listening to him or her; viewing an art exhibit; rock climbing; holding a newborn infant; watching the sun set over the ocean. Can you think of some others?

HAVING A CHOICE

To be able to adapt your tempo to different kinds of life experiences is essential for a balanced life. In short, we must be able to choose the most appropriate time strategies. Modern life seems to encourage the fast-forward, multitasking time strategy over others. It is the norm to say "I'm so busy" and expect it from others. The busyness syndrome often becomes habitual. Worse, it may eventually control you. Let's say, for example, that you finally have time for a leisurely lunch with a friend. One time choice is to fully absorb yourself into the conversation and the food. Another choice, often when we do not want it, is having the lunch and simultaneously planning your afternoon schedule, gazing around the room, glancing at the TV above your friend, and looking at your watch every ten minutes. Here we have the mismatch between a time strategy and the natural tempo of an experience—and we may even know it but can't stop. Our internal engine is stuck on full throttle even when we're idling.

For many, the fast-forward, multitasking time approach has become a habitual reflex. Life becomes a giant things-to-do list with the goal of crossing off an event as quickly as possible and going on to the next. We are in a hurry to get somewhere, but we never arrive. The fast-forward, multitasking life is one in which each moment is completed and then erased. This produces gaping holes in one's life memory bank. Rechtschaffen (1993) says it this way: "By cramming each moment so full of events, we leave ourselves no time to actually experience them in any meaningful way . . . the past is, in effect, absent from our lives."

Just having had an experience does not mean you will remember it. Without time to savor it, to talk about it, to recall the major aspects and the nuances—without this kind of processing, the experience becomes a memory trace. I have toured Japan twice with a music group within a three-year period. I can remember one tour in vivid detail. The other is basically a blur, except for a grueling fourteen-hour train ride standing up. What was the difference? Was it too much Japanese beer on the forgotten tour? No, I actually had more on the remembered tour. The tour that I remember in detail was one where I kept a journal and took many photos; where musicians and singers talked about their daily experiences with each other; where I discussed the trip often with friends upon my return.

It takes time to remember.

One final clue to whether you are in control of time-use strategies. Think of a situation in which you have no immediate demands, no expected tasks. Down time. For a fast-forward, multitasking person this situation produces anxiety. Instead of enjoying this time with a slower tempo activity, this person is likely to crowd out the anxiety by engaging in a flurry of tasks. Even leisure is pursued with the same relentless intensity. Viktor Frankl, the founder of Logotherapy, calls this the "Sunday neurosis."

The eventual consequences for most people who live full-time in the fast-forward, multitasking mode are physical and emotional exhaustion and/or breakdowns. It may take a while for some, even years, but usually there are heavy costs. Some seek help or develop new time strategies when they cannot satisfactorily answer this question for themselves: What is the purpose of living this way? Or, I accomplish a lot—so why do I feel deep down that something fundamental is missing?

Throughout it has been emphasized that a quality life requires the ability to adapt to the different tempos of life experiences. We must be able to control these time-use strategies instead of being controlled. The fast-forward, multitasking time philosophy strategy is appropriate for some experiences and ill advised for others. It also has a tendency to crowd out and take over all other time-use strategies. In the next section, some ideas on how to implement alternative time-use strategies are presented.

SIMPLIFYING LIFE

Even in 1850 Henry Thoreau was criticizing the hurriedness of people: "Why should we live with such hurry and waste of life? We are determined to be starved before we are hungry. . . . Simplify, simplify . . . I say, let your affairs be as two or three, and not a hundred or a thousand" (in Krutch, 1962, pp. 128, 173). Well, you may comment, this would be easy for him to say, since all he had to do was wander around the woods and look at a pond. That's what old philosophers do. But Thoreau was about thirty when he wrote these remarks and he lived only two years at Walden Pond.

It is possible to simplify. There are two primary time strategies do this: one is to focus, and the other is to slow down. Focusing means to devote your attention and energies to one thing at a time. The phrase that helps me is "Be where you are." The key is to bring your body and mind into the present moment. Do not let yourself wander off into past or future time zones. Be where you are. If you are talking with someone you value, be right there with him or her and show it. For a start, try focusing on a mundane chore; if you are grocery shopping, just do that, be *there*.

Here is a very simple but powerful way to focus, but few can do this the first few times (this is a gentle challenge). The task: Get comfortable and if possible, close your eyes. Take a deep breath and slowly exhale. Do this naturally for ten breaths. Just observe your breathing. If at any time you become distracted and lose count, start over.

How did it go? This breathing focus activity not only is helpful in learning to "be where you are," but is an excellent relaxation and centering experience. Choosing one focusing activity each day will enable you to add this time-use strategy to your repertoire.

SLOWING DOWN

I Need to Stop So I Can Get Somewhere
Countering the fast-forward time strategy means letting up on the accelerator when appropriate. Focusing is often helpful in adjusting your speed. Here are some other ideas for slowing down:

- Apply the concept of *savoring* to selected life activities. Although it normally refers to taste, savoring can be generalized to other domains also. It is the gradual experiencing of an event. Gulping is the opposite of savoring. You gulp Big Macs and savor fine wine. You gulp administrative memos and savor a well-written letter or essay. You gulp local news and savor the stories of a friend or family member. See other examples at the end of the earlier section entitled "The Tempo of Life Experiences."

- Be aware of (and beware) the *paradox* of *time-saving technology*. Electronic communication devices like e-mail, fax, Internet, and voice mail allow us to send and receive more messages in a shorter period than any time in our history. The drawback is that speed has greatly increased the number of messages we receive, consequently creating more demands on our time than ever before. Try to be selective as to which messages really require your quality efforts.

He seemed to have a routine. Fly around the Sebastian Inlet of Florida for a bit, then light on a rock. A rock which had all the appearances of good fishing. And so it was. He would sit there very quietly and very relaxed, but alert. A fish of his liking would swim by and be chosen for a mid-afternoon snack. Sometimes the pelican would let a fish swim by untouched. He was in no hurry. The pelican knew that if he waited, whatever he needed would come along.

Sometimes we need to let life come to us.

"Waiting" by Nelson Goud. Copyright © 1996.

- Let experiences reveal themselves *to you* without imposing your needs and expectations on them first. One of my true life joys is to listen to the jazz trumpeter Maynard Ferguson. If he comes to town, I'm there (even my students call me to let me know, in case I missed the notice). I can remember waiting during a concert with great anticipation for his band to play a certain number that had just appeared on his latest album. Maynard calls out the number. The band roared as usual and Maynard was doing things that all the rest of us trumpeters can do only in dreams. But I was somewhat disappointed. The live version did not sound like the recorded one. I wanted to hear it played like the one on the album. I had fallen into the trap I am writing about. I refused to "let" Maynard play how he felt that night, with that song, at that moment. He did not fit my preconceived expectation. Once I realized this, I could kick back and really get into whatever he and his band were doing that night. I sometimes find myself falling into this trap in meeting friends, or visiting favorite places expecting them to be exactly like they were when . . . , and on it goes until I remember to let others or even nature reveal themselves as they truly are at that moment. So, even if you know how your friend's or parent's story will end, let them finish it, not you. It might be the telling that is important, not that you know the ending.

Solomon observed that there is a time to be born and a time to die. There is a time between also. We have choices in how we conduct ourselves in this interval called life. One of these choices is to enjoy and find meaning in the journey itself. We can take our time.

References

Burns, L. (1993). *Busy bodies.* New York: W. W. Norton.

Krutch, J. (1962). *Thoreau: Walden and other writings.* New York: Bantam Books.

Rechtschaffen, S. (1993). Time-shifting: Slowing down to live longer. *Psychology Today*, November/December, 32–36.

Rifkin, J. (1987). *Time wars.* New York: Henry Holt.

Follow-Up

1. *Goud claims that a fragmented hurriedness is a norm for many in modern times and is used even when not appropriate. Write about or discuss your reactions to this statement based on personal experiences.*
2. *A main idea in the article is that every life experience expresses itself in a particular tempo. Provide some examples of this from your life and describe what happens when you are in sync or out of sync with these tempos.*
3. *The author states that unless we try to remember and communicate major experiences, they become blanks in our memories. Describe a time or two when this has happened to you.*
4. *Attempt the focusing and slowing-down ideas mentioned at the end of the article and report the results.*
5. *Select any other ideas from the article and report your reactions.*

Time Quotes

What is the best use of my time right now?

—Alan Lakein

Nibblers—People are so busy in modern times that the most common length of vacations is 3–5 days (the Travel Industry Association of America calls them "vacation nibblers").

We're constantly doing things faster and saving time. But what are we saving it for? The more things or activities we acquire with our efficiency, our productivity and or time management, . . . the less time we have to savor them.

—David Rohn

Time you enjoy wasting is not wasted time.

—Abraham Maslow

Never attempt to teach a pig to sing; it wastes your time and annoys the pig.
—Robert Heinlein

The high value put upon every minute of time, the idea of hurry-hurry as the most important objective of living, is unquestionably the most dangerous enemy of joy.

—Hermann Hesse

Sunday night anxiety is a real phenomenon, a recognition on Sunday night that the week is going to reappear. . . . Come Sunday night, thoughts about the work week start to intrude, and anxieties of life build . . . there's stuff not done last Friday that's due Monday . . .

—John Herman

Always doing many things quickly means neglecting those things that take time—contemplations, creating, savoring, loving, totally being there for someone.

—N. H. Goud

I am one of a growing number of students who are completing college in three years instead of four—cramming credits in the summer. We're living life on fast-forward without a pause button. . . . I am a member of a generation that is very concerned with saving time but often unaware of why we're doing it.

—Amy Wu

We seem to have lost the knack for dialing down life's speed when a day or weekend or season—summer comes to mind—calls for it. Leisure is eluding us.

—Bob Condor

Time shifting—The key is to step back from the edge, learn to get involved in the process rather than constantly longing for the end result. This does not mean giving up our goal-oriented lives—simply modifying them, finding a balance between our productive and our emotional selves . . . Whatever the activity, slow down, do just one thing, do it well, and allow yourself the sense of accomplishment . . .

—Stephan Rechtschaffen

We yearn for acceleration . . . the feeling of speed . . . the brain-fluid high we miss only when it's gone. Speed is a drug. . . . We want to be velocitized.

—Mark Kingwell

In a fast-paced world we put more energy into arrivals and departures than the experience itself.

—Jay Walljasper

A balanced life—with intervals of creative frenzy giving way to relaxed tranquility—is what people crave.

—Jay Walljasper

Time Sickness—a condition when one is obsessed with the notion that time is getting away, that there isn't enough of it, and that you must pedal faster and faster to keep up. The trouble is the body has limits that it imposes on us.

—Larry Dossey

A man is walking down the street. At a certain moment, he tries to recall something, but the recollection escapes him. Automatically, he slows down. Meanwhile, a person who wants to forget a disagreeable incident he has just lived through starts unconsciously to speed up his pace. There is a secret bond between slowness and memory, between speed and forgetting.

—Milan Kundera

To finish the moment, to find the journey's end in every step of the road, to live the greatest number of good hours, is wisdom.

—Ralph Waldo Emerson

Follow-Up

1. *Select two of these quotes and discuss how they apply to your life now.*

The Happiness Machine

Ray Bradbury

On Sunday morning Leo Auffmann moved slowly through his garage, expecting some wood, a curl of wire, a hammer or wrench to leap up crying, "Start here!" But nothing leaped, nothing cried for a beginning.

Should a Happiness Machine, he wondered, be something you can carry in your pocket?

Or, he went on, should it be something that carries you in *its* pocket?

"One thing I absolutely *know*," he said aloud. "It should be *bright*!"

He set a can of orange paint in the center of the workbench, picked up a dictionary, and wandered into the house.

"Lena?" He glanced at the dictionary. "Are you 'pleased, contented, joyful, delighted'? Do you feel 'Lucky, fortunate'? Are things 'clever and fitting,' 'successful and suitable' for you?"

Lena stopped slicing vegetables and closed her eyes. "Read me the list again, please," she said.

He shut the book.

"What have I done, you got to stop and think an hour before you can tell me? All I ask is a simple yes or no! You're *not* contented, delighted, joyful?"

"Cows are contented, babies and old people in second childhood are delighted, God help them," she said. "As for 'joyful,' Leo? Look how I laugh scrubbing out the sink . . ."

He peered closely at her and his face relaxed. "Lena, it's true. A man doesn't appreciate. Next month, maybe, we'll get away."

"*I'm* not complaining!" she cried. "*I'm* not the one comes in with a list saying, 'Stick out your tongue.' Leo, do you ask what makes your heart beat all night? No! Next will you

ask, What's marriage? Who knows, Leo? Don't ask. A man who thinks like that, how it runs, how things work, falls off the trapeze in the circus, chokes wondering how the muscles work in the throat. Eat, sleep, breathe, Leo, and stop staring at me like I'm something new in the house!"

Lena Auffmann froze. She sniffed the air.

"Oh, my God, look what you done!"

She yanked the oven door open. A great cloud of smoke poured through the kitchen.

"Happiness!" she wailed. "And for the first time in six months we have a fight! Happiness, and for the first time in twenty years it's not bread, it's charcoal for supper!"

When the smoke cleared, Leo Auffmann was gone.

The fearful clangor, the collision of man and inspiration, the flinging about of metal, lumber, hammer, nails, T square, screwdriver, continued for many days. On occasion, defeated, Leo Auffmann loitered out through the streets, nervous, apprehensive, jerking his head at the slightest sound of distant laughter, listened to children's jokes, watching what made them smile. At night he sat on neighbors' crowded porches, listening to the old folks weigh and balance life, and at each explosion of merriment Leo Auffmann quickened like a general who has seen the forces of darkness routed and whose strategy has been reaffirmed. On his way home he felt triumphant until he was in his garage with the dead tools and the inanimate lumber. Then his bright face fell away in a pale funk, and to cover his sense of failure he banged and crashed the parts of his machine about as if they really did make sense. At last it began to shape itself and at the end of the ten days and nights, trembling with fatigue, self-dedicated, half starved, fumbling and looking as if he had been riven by lightning, Leo Auffmann wandered into his house.

The children, who had been screaming horribly at each other, fell silent, as if the Red Death had entered at the chiming of the clock.

"The Happiness Machine," husked Leo Auffmann, "is ready."

"Leo Auffmann," said his wife, "has lost fifteen pounds. He hasn't talked to his children in two weeks, they are nervous, they fight, listen! His wife is nervous, she's gained ten pounds, she'll need new clothes, look! Sure—the machine is ready. But happy? Who can say? Leo, leave off with the clock you're building. You'll never find a cuckoo big enough to go in it! Man was not made to tamper with such things. It's not against God, no, but it sure looks like it's against Leo Auffmann. Another week of this and we'll bury him in his machine!"

But Leo Auffmann was too busy noticing that the room was falling swiftly up.

How interesting, he thought, lying on the floor.

Darkness closed in a great wink on him as someone screamed something about that Happiness Machine, three times.

The first thing he noticed the next morning was dozens of birds fluttering around in the air stirring up ripples like colored stones thrown into an incredibly clear stream, gonging the tin roof of the garage softly.

A pack of multibred dogs pawfooted one by one into the yard to peer and whine gently through the garage door; four boys, two girls, and some men hesitated in the driveway and then edged along under the cherry trees.

Leo Auffmann, listening, knew what it was that had reached out and called them all into the yard.

The sound of the Happiness Machine.

It was the sort of sound that might be heard coming from a giant's kitchen on a summer day. There were all finds of hummings, low and high, steady and then changing. Incredible foods were being baked there by a host of whirring golden bees as big as teacups. The giantess herself, humming contentedly under her breath, might glide to the door, as vast as all summer, her face a huge peach-colored moon gazing calmly out upon smiling dogs, corn-haired boys and flour-haired old men.

"Wait," said Leo Auffmann out loud. "I didn't turn the machine on this morning! Saul!"

Saul standing in the yard below, looked up.

"Saul, did you turn it on?"

"You told me to warm it up half an hour ago!"

"All right, Saul, I forgot. I'm not awake." He fell back in bed.

His wife, bringing his breakfast up, paused by the window, looking down at the garage.

"Tell me," she said quietly. "If that machine is like you say, has it got an answer to making babies in it somewhere? Can that machine make seventy-year-old people twenty? Also, how does death look when you hide in there with all that happiness?"

"Hide!"

"If you died from overwork, what should I do today, climb in that big box down there and be happy? Also tell me, Leo, how is our life? You know how our house is. Seven in the morning, breakfast, the kids; all of you gone by eight-thirty and it's just me and washing and me and cooking and socks to be darned, weeds to be dug, or I run to the store or polish silver. Who's complaining? I'm just reminding you how the house is put together, Leo, what's in it! So now answer: How do you get all those things I said in one machine?"

"That's not how it's built!"

"I'm sorry. I got no time to look, then."

And she kissed his cheek and went from the room and he lay smelling the wind that blew from the hidden machine below, rich with the odor of those roasted chestnuts that sold in the autumn streets of a Paris he had never known. . . .

A cat moved unseen among the hypnotized dogs and boys to purr against the garage door, in the sound of snow-waves crumbling down a faraway and rhythmically breathing shore.

Tomorrow, thought Leo Auffmann, we'll try the machine, all of us, together.

Late that night he awoke and knew something had wakened him. Far away in another room he heard someone crying.

"Saul?" he whispered, getting out of bed.

In his room Saul wept, his head buried in his pillow. "No . . . no . . ." he sobbed. "Over . . . over . . ."

"Saul, you had a nightmare? Tell me about it, son."

But the boy only wept.

And sitting there on the boy's bed, Leo Auffmann suddenly thought to look out the window. Below, the garage doors stood open.

He felt the hairs rise along the back of his neck.

When Saul slept again, uneasily, whimpering, his father went downstairs and out to the garage where, not breathing, he put his hand out.

In the cool night the Happiness Machine's metal was too hot to touch.

So, he thought, Saul was here tonight.

Why? Was Saul unhappy, in need of the machine? No, happy, but wanting to hold onto happiness always. Could you blame a boy wise enough to know his position who tried to keep it that way? No! And yet . . .

Above, quite suddenly, something white was exhaled from Saul's window. Leo Auffmann's heart thundered. Then he realized the window curtain had blown out into the open night. But it had seemed as intimate and shimmering a thing as a boy's soul escaping his room. And Leo Auffmann had flung up his hands as if to thwart it, push it back into the sleeping house.

Cold, shivering, he moved back into the house and up to Saul's room where he seized the blowing curtain in and locked the window tight so the pale thing could not escape again. Then he sat on the bed and put his hand on Saul's back.

"*A Tale of Two Cities?* Mine. *The Old Curiosity Shop?* Ha, that's Leo Auffmann's all right! *Great Expectations?* That *used* to be mine. But let *Great Expectations* be his, now!"

"What's this?" asked Leo Auffmann, entering.

"This," said his wife, "is sorting out the community property! When a father scares his son at night it's time to chop everything in half! Out of the way, Mr. Bleak House, Old Curiosity Shop. In all these books, no mad scientist lives like Leo Auffmann, none!"

"You're leaving, and you haven't even tried the machine!" he protested. "Try it on, you'll unpack, you'll stay!"

"*Tom Swift and His Electric Annihilator*— whose is that?" she asked. "Must I *guess?*"

Snorting, she gave *Tom Swift* to Leo Auffmann.

Very late in the day all the books, dishes, clothes, linens had been stacked one here, one there, four here, four there, ten here, ten there. Lena Auffmann, dizzy with counting, had to sit down. "All right," she gasped. "Before I go, Leo, prove you don't give nightmares to innocent sons!"

Silently Leo Auffmann led his wife into the twilight. She stood before the eight-foot-tall, orange-colored box.

"That's *happiness?*" she said. "Which button do I press to be overjoyed, grateful, contented, and much-obliged?"

The children had gathered now.

"Mama," said Saul, "don't!"

"I got to know what I'm yelling about, Saul." She got in the machine, sat down, and looked out at her husband, shaking her head. "It's not me needs this, it's you, a nervous wreck, shouting."

"Please," he said, "you'll see!"

He shut the door.

"Press the button!" he shouted in at his unseen wife.

There was a click. The machine shivered quietly, like a huge dog dreaming in its sleep.

"Papa!" said Saul, worried.

"Listen!" said Leo Auffmann.

At first there was nothing but the tremor of the machine's own secretly moving cogs and wheels.

"Is Mama all right?" asked Naomi.

"All right, she's fine! There, now . . . there!"

And inside the machine Lena Auffmann could be heard saying, "Oh!" and then again, "Ah!" in a startled voice. "Look at that!" said his hidden wife. "Paris!" and later, "London! There goes Rome! The Pyramids! The Sphinx!"

"The Sphinx, you hear, children?" Leo Auffmann whispered and laughed.

"Perfume!" cried Lena Auffmann, surprised.

Somewhere a phonograph played "The Blue Danube" faintly.

"Music! I'm dancing!"

"Only *thinks* she's dancing," the father confided to the world.

"Amazing!" said the unseen woman.

Leo Auffmann blushed. "What an understanding wife."

And then inside the Happiness Machine, Lena Auffmann began to weep.

The inventor's smile faded.

"She's crying," said Naomi.

"She can't be!"

"She is," said Saul.

"She simply can't be crying!" Leo Auffmann, blinking, pressed his ear to the machine. "But . . . yes . . . like a baby . . ."

He could only open the door.

"Wait." There his wife sat, tears rolling down her cheeks. "Let me finish." She cried some more.

Leo Auffmann turned off the machine, stunned.

"Oh, it's the saddest thing in the world!" she wailed. "I feel awful, terrible." She climbed out through the door. "First, there was Paris . . ."

"What's wrong with Paris?"

"I never even *thought* of being in Paris in my life. But now you got me thinking: Paris! So suddenly I want to be in Paris and now I'm not!"

"It's almost as good, this machine."

"No. Sitting in there, I knew. I thought, it's not real!"

"Stop crying, Mama."

She looked at him with great dark wet eyes. "You had me dancing. We haven't danced in twenty years."

"I'll take you dancing tomorrow night!"

"No, no! It's not important, it *shouldn't* be important. But your machine says it's important! So I believe! It'll be all right, Leo, after I cry some more."

"What else?"

"What else? The machine says, 'You're young.' I'm not. It lies, that Sadness Machine!"

"Sad in what way?"

His wife was quieter now. "Leo, the mistake you made is you forgot some hour, some day, we all got to climb out of that thing and go back to dirty dishes and the beds not made. While you're in that thing, sure, a sunset lasts forever almost, the air smells good, the temperature is fine. All the things you want to last, last. But outside, the children wait on lunch, the clothes need buttons. And then let's be frank, Leo, how long can you *look* at a sunset? Who *wants* a sunset to last? Who wants perfect temperature? Who wants air smelling good always? So after awhile, who would notice? Better, for a minute or two, a sunset. After that, let's have something else. People are like that, Leo. How could you forget?"

"Did I?"

"Sunsets we always liked because they only happen once and go away."

"But Lena, that's sad."

"No, if the sunset stayed and we got bored, that would be a real sadness. So two things you did you should never have. You made quick things go slow and stay around. You brought things faraway to our backyard where they don't belong, where they just tell you, 'No, you'll never travel, Lena Auffmann, Paris you'll never see! Rome you'll *never* visit.' But I *always* knew that, so why tell me? Better to forget and make do, Leo, make do, eh?"

Leo Auffmann leaned against the machine for support. He snatched his burned hand away, surprised.

"So now what, Lena?" he said.

"It's not for me to say. I know only so long as this thing is here I'll want to come out, or Saul will want to come out like he did last night, and against our judgment sit in it and look at all those places so far away and every time we will cry and be no fit family for you."

"I don't understand," he said, "how I could be so wrong. Just let me check to see what you say is true." He sat down inside the machine. "You won't go away?"

His wife nodded. "We'll wait, Leo."

He shut the door. In the warm darkness he hesitated, pressed the button, and was just relaxing back in color and music, when he heard someone screaming.

"Fire, Papa! The machine's on fire!"

Someone hammered the door. He leaped up, bumped his head, and fell as the door gave way and the boys dragged him out. Behind him he heard a muffled explosion. The entire family was running now. Leo Auffmann turned and gasped, "Saul, call the fire department!"

Lena Auffmann caught Saul as he ran. "Saul," she said. "Wait."

There was a gush of flame, another muffled explosion. When the machine was burning very well indeed, Lena Auffmann nodded.

"All right, Saul," she said. "Run call the fire department."

Everybody who was anybody came to the fire. There was Grandpa Spaulding and Douglas and Tom and most of the boarders and some of the old men from across the ravine and all the children from six blocks around.

And Leo Auffmann's children stood out front, proud of how fine the flames looked jumping from the garage roof.

Grandfather Spaulding studied the smoke ball in the sky and said, quietly, "Leo, was that it? Your Happiness Machine?"

"Some year," said Leo Auffmann, "I'll figure it and tell you."

Lena Auffmann, standing in the dark now, watched as the firemen ran in and out of the yard; the garage, roaring, settled upon itself.

"Leo," she said, "it won't take a year to figure. Look around. Think. Keep quiet a little bit. Then come tell me. I'll be in the house, putting books back on shelves, and clothes back in closets, fixing supper, supper's late, look how dark. Come, children, help Mama."

When the firemen and the neighbors were gone, Leo Auffmann was left with Grandfather Spaulding and Douglas and Tom, brooding over the smoldering ruin. He stirred his foot in the wet ashes and slowly said what he had to say.

"The first thing you learn in life is you're a fool. The last thing you learn in life is you're the same fool. In one hour, I've done a lot of thinking. I thought, Leo Auffmann is blind! . . . You want to see the *real* Happiness Machine? The one they patented a couple thousand years ago, it still runs, not good all the time, no! but it runs. It's been here all along."

"But the fire—" said Douglas.

"Sure, the fire, the garage! But like Lena said, it don't take a year to figure; what burned in the garage don't count!"

They followed him up the front-porch steps.

"Here," whispered Leo Auffmann, "the front window. Quiet, and you'll see it."

Hesitantly, Grandfather, Douglas, and Tom peered through the large windowpane.

And there, in small warm pools of lamplight, you could see what Leo Auffmann wanted you to see. There sat Saul and Marshall, playing chess at the coffee table. In the dining room Rebecca was laying out the silver. Naomi was cutting paper-doll dresses. Ruth was painting water colors. Joseph was running his electric train. Through the kitchen door, Lena Auffmann was sliding a pot roast from the steaming oven. Every hand, every head, every mouth made a big or little motion. You could hear their faraway voices under glass. You could hear someone singing in a high sweet voice. You could smell bread baking, too, and you knew it was real bread that would soon be covered with real butter. Everything was there and it was working.

Grandfather, Douglas, and Tom turned to look at Leo Auffmann, who gazed serenely through the window, the pink light on his cheeks.

"Sure," he murmured. "There it is." And he watched with now-gentle sorrow and now-quick delight, and at last quiet acceptance as all the bits and pieces of this house mixed, stirred, settled, poised, and ran steadily again. "The Happiness Machine," he said. "The Happiness Machine."

A moment later he was gone.

Inside, Grandfather, Douglas, and Tom saw him tinkering, make a minor adjustment here, eliminate friction there, busy among all those warm, wonderful, infinitely delicate, forever mysterious, and ever-moving parts.

Then smiling, they went down the steps into the fresh summer night.

Follow-Up

1. *Written over forty years ago, Bradbury's* The Happiness Machine *foreshadows contemporary virtual reality technology. Many thinkers have warned if you "seek happiness for its own sake, you will not find it" (Tyron Edwards). Have your attempts to directly find happiness also been unsuccessful? Try to find the underlying reasons for when you feel happiness, and why.*

2. *Leo Auffmann was driven to build his machine even though it created large problems between him and those closest to him. Have you ever been so driven that similar results occurred? If yes, describe the reasons why, the effects, and whether you will do that again.*

3. *The story implies that happiness is meant to be short lived, that permanently happy conditions would eventually get boring, and that one's Happiness Machine is essentially where you are and those most important to you. Write about or discuss your reactions to these points.*

4. *Select any other aspect of the story to write about or discuss.*

The Last Leaf

O. Henry

In a little district west of Washington Square the streets have run crazy and broken themselves into small strips called "places." These "places" make strange angles and curves. One street crosses itself a time or two. An artist once discovered a valuable possibility in this street. Suppose a collector with a bill for paints, paper and canvas should, in traversing this route, suddenly meet himself coming back, without a cent having been paid on account!

So, to quaint old Greenwich Village the art people soon came prowling, hunting for north windows and eighteenth-century gables and Dutch attics and low rents. Then they imported some pewter mugs and a chafing dish or two from Sixth avenue, and become a "colony."

At the top of a squatty, three-story brick Sue and Johnsy had their studio. "Johnsy" was familiar for Joanna. One was from Maine; the other from California. They had met at the table d'hote of an Eighth street "Delmonico's," and found their tastes in art, chicory salad and bishop sleeves so congenial that the joint studio resulted.

That was in May. In November a cold, unseen stranger, whom the doctors called Pneumonia, stalked about the colony, touching one here and there with his icy finger. Over on the east side this ravager strode boldly, smiting his victims by scores, but his feet trod slowly through the maze of the narrow and moss-grown "places."

Mr. Pneumonia was not what you would call a chivalric old gentleman. A mite of a little woman with blood thinned by California zephyrs was hardly fair game for the red-fisted, short-breathed old duffer. But Johnsy he smote; and she lay, scarcely moving, on her painted iron bedstead, looking through the small Dutch window-panes at the blank side of the next brick house.

One morning the busy doctor invited Sue into the hallway with a shaggy, gray eyebrow.

"She has one chance in—let us say, ten," he said, as he shook down the mercury in his clinical thermometer. "And that chance is for her to want to live. This way people have of lining-up on the side of the undertaker makes the entire pharmacopeia look silly. Your little lady has made up her mind that she's not going to get well. Has she anything on her mind?"

"She—she wanted to paint the Bay of Naples some day," said Sue.

"Paint?—bosh! Has she anything on her mind worth thinking about twice—a man, for instance?"

"A man?" said Sue, with a jewsharp twang in her voice. "Is a man worth—but, no, doctor; there is nothing of the kind."

"Well, it is the weakness, then," said the doctor. "I will do all that science, so far as it may filter through my efforts, can accomplish. But whenever my patient begins to count the carriages in her funeral procession I subtract 50 per cent from the curative power of medicines. If you will get her to ask one question about the new winter styles in cloak sleeves I will promise you a one-in-five chance for her, instead of one in ten."

After the doctor had gone Sue went into the workroom and cried a Japanese napkin to a pulp. Then she swaggered into Johnsy's room with her drawing board, whistling ragtime.

Johnsy lay, scarcely making a ripple under the bedclothes, with her face toward the window. Sue stopped whistling, thinking she was asleep.

She arranged her board and began a pen-and-ink drawing to illustrate a magazine story. Young artists must pave their way to Art by drawing pictures for magazine stories that young authors write to pave their way to Literature.

As Sue was sketching a pair of elegant horseshow riding trousers and a monocle on the figure of the hero, an Idaho cowboy, she heard a low sound, several times repeated. She went quickly to the bedside.

Johnsy's eyes were open wide. She was looking out the window and counting—counting backward.

"Twelve," she said, and a little later "eleven;" and then "ten," and "nine;" and then "eight" and "seven" almost together.

Sue looked solicitously out of the window. What was there to count? There was only a bare, dreary yard to be seen, and the blank side of the brick house forty feet away. An old, old ivy vine, gnarled and decayed at the roots, climbed half way up the brick wall. The cold breath of autumn had stricken its leaves from the vine until its skeleton branches clung, almost bare, to the crumbling bricks.

"What is it, dear?" asked Sue.

"Six," said Johnsy, in almost a whisper. "They're falling faster now. Three days ago there were almost a hundred. It made my head ache to count them. But now it's easy. There goes another one. There are only five left now."

"Five what, dear? Tell your Sudie."

"Leaves. On the ivy vine. When the last one falls I must go, too. I've known that for three days. Didn't the doctor tell you?"

"Oh, I never heard of such nonsense," complained Sue, with magnificent scorn. "What have old ivy leaves to do with your getting well? And you used to love that vine so, you naughty girl. Don't be a goosey. Why, the doctor told me this morning that your chances for getting well real soon were—let's see exactly what he said—he said the chances were ten to one! Why, that's almost as good a chance as we have in New York when we ride on the street cars or walk past a new building. Try to take some broth now, and let Sudie go back to her drawing, so she can sell the editor man with it, and buy port wine for her sick child, and pork chops for her greedy self."

"You needn't get any more wine," said Johnsy, keeping her eyes fixed out the window. "There goes another. No, I don't want any broth. That leaves just four. I want to see the last one fall before it gets dark. Then I'll go, too."

"Johnsy, dear," said Sue, bending over her, "will you promise me to keep your eyes closed, and not look out the window until I am done working? I must hand those drawings in by to-morrow. I need the light, or I would draw the shade down."

"Couldn't you draw in the other room?" asked Johnsy, coldly.

"I'd rather be here by you," said Sue. "Besides, I don't want you to keep looking at those silly ivy leaves."

"Tell me as soon as you have finished," said Johnsy, closing her eyes, and lying white and still as a fallen statue, "because I want to see the last one fall. I'm tired of waiting. I'm tired of thinking. I want to turn loose my hold on everything, and go sailing down, down, just like one of those poor, tired leaves."

"Try to sleep," said Sue. "I must call Behrman up to be my model for the old hermit miner. I'll not be gone a minute. Don't try to move 'till I come back."

Old Behrman was a painter who lived on the ground floor beneath them. He was past sixty and had a Michael Angelo's Moses beard curling down from the head of a satyr along the body of an imp. Behrman was a failure in art. Forty years he had wielded the brush without getting near enough to touch the hem of his Mistress's robe. He had been always about to paint a masterpiece, but had never yet begun it. For several years he had painted nothing except now and then a daub in the line of commerce or advertising. He earned a little by serving as a model to those young artists in the colony who could not pay the price of a professional. He drank gin to excess, and still talked of his coming masterpiece. For the rest he was a fierce little old man, who scoffed terribly at softness in any one, and who regarded himself as especial mastiff-in-waiting to protect the two young artists in the studio above.

Sue found Behrman smelling strongly of juniper berries in his dimly lighted den below. In one corner was a blank canvas on an easel that had been waiting there for twenty-five years to receive the first line of the masterpiece. She told him of Johnsy's fancy, and how she feared she would, indeed, light and fragile as a leaf herself, float away when her slight hold upon the world grew weaker.

Old Behrman, with his red eyes plainly streaming, shouted his contempt and derision for such idiotic imaginings.

"Vass!" he cried. "Is dere people in de world mit der foolishness to die because leafs dey drop off from a confounded vine? I haf not heard of such a thing. No, I will not bose as a model for your fool hermit-dunderhead. Vy do you allow dot silly pusiness to come in der prain of her? Ach, dot poor leetle Miss Johnsy."

"She is very ill and weak," said Sue, "and the fever has left her mind morbid and full of strange fancies. Very well, Mr. Behrman, if you do not care to pose for me, you needn't. But I think you are a horrid old—old flibbertigibbet."

"You are just like a woman!" yelled Behrman. "Who said I vill not bose? Go on. I come mit you. For half an hour I haf peen trying to say dot I am ready to bose. Gott! dis is not any blace in which one so schones at Miss Yohnsy shall lie sick. Some day I vill baint a masterpiece, and ve shall all go away. Gott! yes."

Johnsy was sleeping when they went upstairs. Sue pulled the shade down to the window-sill, and motioned Behrman into the other room. In there they peered out the window fearfully at the ivy vine. Then they looked at each other for a moment without speaking. A persistent, cold rain was falling, mingled with snow. Behrman, in his old blue shirt, took his seat as the hermit-miner on an upturned kettle for a rock.

When Sue awoke from an hour's sleep the next morning she found Johnsy with dull, wide-open eyes staring at the drawn green shade.

"Pull it up; I want to see," she ordered, in a whisper.

Wearily she obeyed.

But, lo! after the beating rain and fierce gusts of wind that had endured through the livelong night, there yet stood out against the brick wall one ivy leaf. It was the last on the vine. Still dark green near its stem, but with its serrated edges tinted with the yellow of dissolution and decay, it hung bravely from a branch some twenty feet above the ground.

"It is the last one," said Johnsy. "I thought it would surely fall during the night. I heard the wind. It will fall to-day, and I shall die at the same time."

"Dear, dear!" said Sue, leaning her worn face down to the pillow, "think of me, if you won't think of yourself. What would I do?"

But Johnsy did not answer. The lonesomest thing in all the world is a soul when it is making ready to go on its mysterious, far journey. The fancy seemed to possess her more strongly as one by one the ties that bound her to friendship and to earth were loosed.

The day wore away, and even through the twilight they could see the lone ivy leaf clinging to its stem against the wall. And then, with the coming of the night the north wind was again loosed, while the rain still beat against the windows and pattered down from the low Dutch eaves.

When it was light enough Johnsy, the merciless, commanded that the shade be raised.

The ivy leaf was still there.

Johnsy lay for a long time looking at it. And then she called to Sue, who was stirring her chicken broth over the gas stove.

"I've been a bad girl, Sudie," said Johnsy. "Something has made that last leaf stay there to show me how wicked I was. It is a sin to want to die. You may bring me a little broth now, and some milk with a little port in it, and—no; bring me a hand-mirror first; and then pack some pillows about me, and I will sit up and watch you cook."

An hour later she said:

"Sudie, some day I hope to paint the Bay of Naples."

The doctor came in the afternoon, and Sue had an excuse to go into the hallway as he left.

"Even chances," said the doctor, taking Sue's thin, shaking hand in his. "With good nursing you'll win. And now I must see another case I have downstairs. Behrman, his name is—some kind of an artist, I believe. Pneumonia, too. He is an old, weak man, and the attack is acute. There is no hope for him; but he goes to the hospital to-day to be made more comfortable."

The next day the doctor said to Sue: "She's out of danger. You've won. Nutrition and care now—that's all."

And that afternoon Sue came to the bed where Johnsy lay, contentedly knitting a very blue and very useless woollen shoulder scarf, and put one arm around her, pillows and all.

"I have something to tell you, white mouse," she said. "Mr. Behrman died of pneumonia to-day in the hospital. He was ill only two days. The janitor found him on the morning of the first day in his room downstairs helpless with pain. His shoes and clothing were wet through and icy cold. They couldn't imagine where he had been on such a dreadful night. And then they found a lantern, still

"Ode to the Last Leaf"

There it stands alone. The last leaf of autumn. At the top of a branch of a young broadleaf oak, it is hanging on for a while longer than the others. Maybe it likes the view. It does not seem to mind that its edges are frayed and that you can even see through it. But soon it will join its comrades below. Below, where it will add a little color to the ground. Then slowly, very slowly, get smaller until it becomes part of the soil. It will not be forgotten. In the spring the bare oak branch will gather sustenance from the soil. It will sprout buds and then leaves—leaves which exist because of the last leaf of autumn.

You will leave a legacy. What will it be?

lighted, and a ladder that had been dragged from its place, and some scattered brushes, and a palette with green and yellow colors mixed on it, and—look out the window, dear, at the last ivy leaf on the wall. Didn't you wonder why it never fluttered or moved when the wind blew? Ah, darling, it's Behrman's masterpiece—he painted it there the night that the last leaf fell."

Follow-Up

1. *One's "will to live" is often connected to a commitment to something larger than oneself (another person, group, vocation, incompleted work). Johnsy had lost this connection. What in your life gives you this sense of being involved in something larger than yourself? How do you function when this connection is weak?*

2. *Johnsy believed that when the last leaf fell she would die. Reflect on a time when you let something or someone determine your life direction versus you taking the initiative. Would you characterize yourself as primarily outer-directed or inner-directed concerning major life decisions? Explain your answer.*

3. *Behrman, the old painter, can easily be negatively rubricized (see "Rubricizing," Section One). Think of a time when you negatively rubricized someone who eventually turned out to be a good guy. Discuss this idea.*

4. *Select a statement or idea from this story and offer your commentary.*

———

Active Solitude

Carin Rubenstein
and Phillip Shaver

For some people, being alone automatically implies loneliness; for them, the word *solitude* evokes images of isolation, panic, fear, inability to concentrate, numbness, or boredom. For others—poets and artists, for example—solitude carries almost the opposite meaning: bliss, relaxation, personal integration, a feeling of warm connectedness with the world and other people, creativity, and reflection. What are the differences between these people—or between times in the life of a particular person when one rather than another reaction predominates?

The difference is partly one of perspective. Sometimes, because of past or recent experiences, we conceive of aloneness as being cut off, bereft, alienated from others, the way a child feels after being sent to his or her room for punishment. (As the poet Coleridge put it in "The Rime of the Ancient Mariner": "Alone, alone, all, all alone, / Alone on a wide wide sea! / And never a saint took pity on / My soul in agony.") In this state of mind, we feel a keen sense of loss and powerlessness—loss of other people's approval and company, and powerlessness to do anything about it. The loss calls attention to deficiencies in ourselves; we are "bad," unworthy of love, deserving of rejection, vulnerable and helpless. In this state, self-esteem is diminished; we become frightened and defensive. We can't relax or be creative.

In contrast, the orientation we call active solitude emphasizes the positive side of being alone. In solitude, you are together with yourself, physically but not psychologically cut off from other people; free to explore thoughts and feelings without regard for anyone else's im-mediate reactions. You can hear your own mental voice and react to your own subtle desires and moods. Oddly enough, the result is often a deeper affection for other people. One of our respondents in Billings, Montana, wrote us, for example, that she spends ten days in total solitude each year—causing rumors among her neighbors that her marriage is on the rocks. Leaving husband, children, dog, and three canaries back home, she retreats to a mountain cabin by herself—to think, read, and write. "I have a ball—no obligations and no distractions. No radio, no TV, no screaming kids or pesky husband. For ten days I have just me. I love being away from it all for those days. Funny thing is though, I appreciate them a whole lot more when I get back—a year's worth of appreciation builds up in just ten days."

One of the people we interviewed told us: "Odd as it sounds, I'm more able to be by myself when I feel most in tune with my lover. It's easier to concentrate on work, to be creative. I know when we're apart that we'll soon be together, that she's there if I need her. And we're more valuable to ourselves and get along better when we've spent time alone."

Although the words "alone" and "lonely" come from the same middle English root—meaning "all one" (or only one)—they are not psychological synonyms. Many people—for example, those trapped in unhappy marriages or forced to live with relatives who "don't understand"—are much lonelier living with others than are the hundreds of thousands who live alone but have close ties with friends and family. It's clearly possible to be lonely without being alone and alone without being lonely.

Many people find that the first few minutes or hours of solitude are unsettling. While working individually on this book, for example, having set aside time for reflection and writing, we often spent the first half hour (at least) with unnecessary phone calls, irrelevant reading, and distracting, time-wasting trips to the bathroom or refrigerator. The urge to avoid self-confrontation, to escape the feeling of aloneness that solitary thought requires, is powerful indeed. In the first few moments of solitude, many people make a hasty decision to go shopping or turn on the television set, and they immediately lose the opportunity for creativity and self-renewal. If this pattern becomes habitual, their sense of identity and personal strength is eroded and they become chronically afraid of solitude.

The writings of religious hermits throughout history reveal that they too suffered an initial period of doubt, agitation, and panic when they first got out into the wilderness by themselves. Most of them, however, like most of us in our successful attempts at creative solitude, waited out this temporary anxiety and found themselves moved and enriched by the rewards of solitude.

In extreme forms, solitude has often been used in *rites de passage* to transform boys into men. In many primitive societies, pubertal boys were sent off into the forest, jungle, or plains, and ordered to remain alone for periods ranging from overnight to several months. The boys were thought to die a symbolic death and become transformed: when they returned to the world of the living as men, their boyhood ignorance and dependence were gone forever. If this sounds barbaric, consider that Outward Bound, a popular American recreation group for men and women of all ages, requires its participants to take solo wilderness trips; the experience of solitary survival is assumed to foster independence and self-sufficiency.

Some researchers have tested the idea that solitude can be strengthening. During the six-ties and seventies, John Lilly experimented with "restricted environmental stimulation" by placing people in immersion tanks full of warm salt water, asking them to remain inside for hours, even days, at a time. Psychologist Peter Suedfeld claimed more recently that REST, or *Restricted Environmental Stimulation Therapy*, calms mental patients, helps overweight people lose weight, smokers quit smoking, alcoholics reduce their drinking, and stutterers speak more clearly. REST simply places patients in dark, sound-proof rooms for about eight hours without radios, books, or other diversions.

Strangely enough, meditation and reflection—although usually solitary activities—are almost the opposite of what we normally think of as self-consciousness or self-preoccupation. When properly pursued, they aren't at all narcissistic. When we are self-conscious in the usual sense (anxious or embarrassed), the self that occupies our attention is, meditation experts say, a figment of our social imagination; it is the self of the adolescent conformist wondering nervously if he is accepted by the group. Surprisingly, when we are alone and allow ourselves to pass through the initial period of agitated discomfort, this social pseudo-self eventually evaporates, revealing a more relaxed and substantial self underneath. This genuine self needs no outside approval and is not simply a social creation. People who make contact with this deeper self find that their subsequent social relations are less superficial, less greedy, less tense. They have less need to defend their everyday social selves, their social masks.

Our first piece of advice, then: *When you are alone, give solitude a chance. Don't run away at the first sign of anxiety, and don't imagine yourself abandoned, cut off, or rejected.* Think of yourself *as with yourself, not without* someone else. Allow yourself to relax, listen to music that suits your feelings, work on something that you've been neglecting, write to a friend or for yourself in a journal, or just lie back and be at peace. If you are religious, your solitude may take the form of conversations with God or meditation on religious ideas. Whatever the content of your solitude, if you allow the first burst of anxiety to fade, you will open a door to many rewarding hours: of quiet prayer or contemplation; full enjoyment of music, sketching, or painting; total involvement in a novel or book of poetry; recording your own thoughts, feelings, songs, or poems. This solitude is a far cry from loneliness.

If you think about this, you can begin to see why active solitude and intimacy are related. In solitude, we experience our most genuine needs, perceptions, and feelings. We listen to our deepest selves. Intimacy involves the disclosure of this deeper self to trusted friends or lovers, and really listening, in turn, to their needs, thoughts, and feelings. In other words, in solitude we are intimate with ourselves in a way that enhances our intimacy with other people.

If you find that you can't be comfortable with yourself, you are probably a dissatisfying friend and lover as well. Perhaps you fear there is really nothing very interesting about you; your value is assured only when you are with and approved by someone else. This idea was taken to a supernatural extreme by Henry James, in a story called "The Private Life." Lord Mellifont completely vanishes when he is left alone. "He's there from the moment he knows someone else is." Mellifont is "so essentially, so conspicuously and uniformly the public character" that he is simply "all public" and has "no corresponding private life." Discovering this horrible fact, the narrator of the story feels great sympathy for Mellifont. "I had secretly pitied him for the perfection of his performance, had wondered what blank face such a mask had to cover, what was left to him for the immitigable hours in which a man sits down with himself, or, more serious still, with that intenser self his lawful wife."

We know from our research that adults who have suffered painful losses or rejections in the past are more likely to feel this way and to panic when they are alone; we also know that such people tend to have self-esteem problems. But as long as they cling desperately to others rather than confronting and overcoming their fears and feelings of inadequacy, they are unlikely to become confident and independent. For these people, spending time alone is an essential part of overcoming loneliness.

We don't want to oversell solitude. In fact, for some people solitude replaces normal social life, causing them to become self-contained, fussy, and rigid. Psychiatrist George Vaillant described such a man, in his late forties at the time they talked: "During college he had dealt with his very real fear of people by being a solitary drinker. He enjoyed listening to the radio by himself and found math and philosophy his most interesting courses. Although afraid to go out with girls, he was very particular about his appearance. . . . Thirty years later, [he] was less interested in clothes, but had become terribly preoccupied with keeping fit. He admitted that in his life 'things had taken the place of people' and that he loved to retreat into the 'peace and quiet of a weekend alone.' Approaching old age with no family of his own, he daydreamed of leaving his rare book collection to a favorite young cousin; but he had made only a small effort to get to know this cousin personally." Vaillant went on: "Not only had he never married, but he never admitted to being in love. Unduly shy with women in adolescence, at forty-seven [he] was still put off by 'eager women' and still found 'sex distasteful and frightening.' He had gone through life without close friends of any kind, male or female, and . . . still found it difficult to say good-bye to his mother."

How can you tell if solitude is leading you toward or away from other people? In general, if you find yourself soothed and strengthened by solitude, more *aware of your love for other people,* and less frightened or angry in your dealings with them, then solitude is a healthy part of your social balance. If you find, on the other hand, that you use solitude as a chronic escape from other people, and if people generally seem to you to be scary, selfish, cruel, or too messy, then you are retreating into a shell of solitude. We say this not because we wish to impose some superficial standard of sociability on everyone, but because studies like Vaillant's indicate that long-term defensive withdrawal from other people leads to unhappiness, alcohol and [other] drug abuse, underachievement, and vulnerability to illness.

Practice active solitude, then, *but not to the detriment of intimacy, friendship, or community.* Let active solitude be the ground from which your feelings of intimacy and community grow.

Follow-Up

1. *Write about or discuss your views of one or more of these statements:*
   - *"It is clearly possible to be lonely without being alone and alone without being lonely."*
   - *"The urge to avoid self-confrontation, to escape the feeling or aloneness that solitary thought requires, is powerful."*
   - *"If you find that you can't be comfortable with yourself, you are probably a dissatisfying friend and lover as well."*
2. *The authors warn that solitude can become a vice in the form of chronic escape from other people. Write or discuss your reactions to this idea.*
3. *Attempt one or more periods of active solitude. If you are not used to being alone, start with a period of two hours. Gradually increase the duration of your solitude. Take note of any resistance in the form of doubt, anxiety, or "antsiness." For some interesting insights, try a twenty-four-hour "solo," where you spend a full day and night away from normal activities and distractions. Report your reactions and what you learned from any of these activities.*
4. *For further reading on this topic see Anne Morrow Lindbergh's* Gift from the Sea *and* The Stations of Solitude *by Alice Koller.*

Teachers in the Forest

Nelson Goud

Coming upon my first forest Titan I stopped, stared, and whispered something like "ZZANG!" The Titan, a giant sequoia, appeared to materialize from a secluded space in the forest. It was so colossal that "tree" did not seem to be a proper designation. Its cinnamon hued trunk, as wide as a two-car garage, rose to a point beyond which I could see. Nature writer Barry Lopez bows to wildlife and landscape features. He considers them to be part of his moral universe and a bow is a way of acknowledging a spiritual connection. I agree with Lopez's sentiment, but how do you bow to a tree hundreds of feet above you?

It was mid-October and I was prowling the Giant Forest region of the Sequoia National Park. This is the home of the largest concentration of the sequoias, scientifically known as Sequoia-dendron giganteum. Sequoias grow only on the western slope of California's Sierra-Nevada mountains at about 6,500 feet elevation. I went there to experience directly these trees that have fascinated me from afar. Little did I know that I was also to be a student. Below are a few of the learnings encountered from my Titan teachers.

1. *The sequoia challenges one's concept of the possibilities of growth.* The massiveness of a sequoia stuns a first time beholder. Up close a mature sequoia will require all of your peripheral vision, and the ability to bend your back like a Slinky to even approach seeing its summit. For example, the General Sherman sequoia qualifies as the world's largest living thing. It is approximately 275 feet high, has a 37-foot base diameter, and weighs about 2.5 million pounds. For a comparison, a good sized maple

or oak tree will be about 90 feet tall and 5–7 feet in diameter. Earth's heaviest animal, the blue whale, weighs in at 300,000 pounds, eight times lighter than General Sherman. General Sherman is 2,600 years old. This sequoia was middle-aged when Shakespeare was writing, and nearly 2,400 years old when Thomas Jefferson was writing the Declaration of Independence. And it is not the oldest sequoia. Astoundingly, the life force in the General Sherman sequoia is as potent as a young twig; it adds new wood equivalent to a 60 foot oak each year. The sequoia had no qualms about realizing its potential; its essence is the process of growth and has been since a seedling.

2. *Balanced growth is valued by the sequoia.* To remain standing as it ascends toward the clouds, the sequoia relies on an intricate system of equalizing forces. Its root system may extend for an acre but it is very shallow, rarely more than five feet deep. The trunk is straight and the sequoia's mammoth branches cluster at the upper third of the trunk and act as counterbalances. The sequoia demonstrates the wisdom of a life with balance.

3. *Sequoias beckon you to come to your senses.* If you hike the trails away from the tourist stops, you will encounter sequoias that have existed for thousands of years. Some sequoias stand with other trees—white pine, red fir, incense cedar, and often surrounded by braken fern. In sequoia groves there is little other vegetation, and the ground cover is a deep needle layer that has a spongy feel as you walk over it. Small, dark cones lie scattered on the needles. If you are lucky, one of these forest Titans

will invite you to take a break there. The first thing you notice is the sequoia's bark. Furrows crease into the bark and some have so much depth that it is possible to cushion a daypack in them. The bark can be as much as 30 inches deep. Its color is a reddish-brown except for black scars from hundreds of years of battling forest fires. Sequoias are among the most fire resistant organisms on earth. The surface of the bark is soft and crumbly to the touch; the wood underneath is hard but brittle. (This, thankfully, made sequoias somewhat undesirable in pre-national park years to harvest, although some were used for things like fencing, toothpicks, and even a dance floor).

It is cloudy and a mist winds its way through the grove simultaneously darkening and magnifying the sequoias. When the clouds depart, openings in the canopy allow streaks of sunlight to fuse with the sequoia bark, which now radiates a cinnamon tinge. You are not just looking at trees and the sun and shadows this October, but watching what it has been like for a couple thousand years in this same place. You are observing time as well as space. The only new object is you.

A distinct scent from a controlled burning pierces the giant sequoia grove and if you hang around these Titans for a couple days, this scent seems to go with you. The bottom of my hiking shoes and a couple of sequoia cones have retained this scent and when I need to remember how it was in the grove, I smell them. Unlike the smell of a campfire or fireplace, the sequoia grove scent is a burned muskiness. It is tempting to call it a primordial smell, but this would be a bit difficult to verify. You could possibly come close to the smell if you burned some dry mushrooms, bark, and pine needles in an earthen pit—and then kept re-burning them for a couple hundred years. The sequoia tree itself does not have this pungent aroma (you can smell the remnant of fire on the charred trunk segments). Other trees in the area have treats for the olfactory devotees and among the suggested actions is to whiff the bark of an incense cedar.

On the back trails there is little sound. Any noise becomes exaggerated in these environs. Cones falling through branches sound like baseballs cracking against bats and when one hits the ground it resounds with a concussive Whump! Scampering squirrels and chipmunks may have you twitching the first few instances, especially when you have just finished reading about what to do if a bear or cougar is encountered on a trail. But the most enticing sound comes from another wild creature. If you shaped a piece of the darkest night into a bird, you would create a raven. Slightly larger than a crow, ravens call to each other in the empty groves. Unlike the higher pitched caw-caw of the crow, the raven's call is a series of low, reverberating croaks. The raven's sound is closer to a big frog than a crow. The raven calls were initially intrusive. Then I eventually realized that this sound is natural to the grove. But the sound that endeared me to the raven was its flight. I have never heard a bird fly. When a raven flies directly overhead you hear a soft WHOOSH-WHOOSH from its wings. Each time this happened I would look up and smile. Barry Lopez would bow. Once a flock of over 80 ravens flew overhead and the dozens of whispering WHOOSH-WHOOSH sounds made me feel like I was beneath scores of silent helicopters with feathered blades.

A large part of what many value most in life is best experienced directly—love, beauty, music, nature, our bodies. Modern living emphasizes indirect modes of knowing and interacting with the world: electronic communications, virtual realities, and working with abstractions. The sequoias remind us that we are sensory beings too, and that direct experience is necessary for a full, balanced life.

4. *When the sounds of the grove vanish, there is total silence.* The silence deepens into stillness. No sound, no motion—quietude. The sequoias stand in the thick hush that now dwells in the grove. "It is stillness and yet it echoes," says Ira Progoff (1992, p. 389).

For some, silence is to be avoided; it makes us feel lonely and makes us turn inward and we may not like what we find there. Or silence is a reminder of nothingness, death. One then turns to noises that mask the silence. Listen about you at any moment of the day. Sounds. Many sounds. Some are nice sounds, but there are many intruding annoyances.

Where can one go to find silence, or at least relative quiet on a consistent basis? The news had a feature about a man who was attempting to get federal protection in each state for one simple thing: "one square inch of silence." In most states this would mean protecting many miles of landscape to attain the one square inch of silence. We may not find that perfect space of silence, but we do need something close to it. It is silence that can create something from nothing. Only in stillness can one hear the faint voices from our deepest sources. And consider the power of the pause, that quiet interval between notes of music or in conversation. Finally, as Thoreau (1854/1962) tells us, "there are many fine things which we cannot say if we have to shout" (p. 209).

5. *There is a connectedness among living things.* Experiencing the stillness of a sequoia grove is disorienting for a few moments. Watching the silent harmony of everything in the grove and how natural the stillness is for them marks you as an outsider. If you sit quietly for a while this strangeness dissolves. Sitting in stillness *with* the Titans will eventually yield a sense of acceptance—that it is all right for you to be there, too. More moments pass in the stillness and you begin to be aware of another change. Time suspends itself so that there is only this moment, and the moment extends into infinity. The boundaries between you and the things in the grove become less distinct. You share a common identity somehow—a merge at a deeper level.

Others have commented on this common identity among humans and nature. In 1836, Emerson (1926/1951) wrote that "the greatest

delight which the fields and woods minister is the suggestion of a mystical relation between man and the vegetable" (p. 381). Thomas Moore (1992), a Jungian therapist and former monk, claims that "when we disallow soul to the simple things around us, we lose that important source of soul for ourselves. Concretely, a tree can tell us much . . . in the way it presents itself as an individual. But in this expression of itself, it is also showing us the secrets of our own souls, for there is no absolute separation between the world's soul and our own" (p. 214). Nikos Kazantzakis's Zorba asks "Can you make it out, boss? It's beyond me. Everything seems to have a soul—wood, stones, the wine we drink and the earth we tread on. Everything, boss, absolutely everything!" (1952, p. 77).

Even biology hints at this fundamental linkage between living things. Carl Sagan (1980) states that "at the very heart of life of Earth—the proteins that control cell chemistry, and the nucleic acids that carry the hereditary instructions—we find these molecules to be essentially identical in all plants and animals. An oak tree and I are made of the same stuff. If you go far enough back, we have a common ancestor" (p. 33). You, the raven, and the giant sequoia have identical genetic building blocks—the variations come in the coding. One song, many instruments.

6. *Living with paradox.* This lesson begins with one of the Titan's smallest forest companions, the chickaree (Douglass squirrel). Larger than a chipmunk but smaller than a squirrel, the perky chickaree is two million pounds lighter than the giant sequoia. But many Titans exist because of this furry Lilliputian. This is because chickarees get hungry. Chickarees cannot resist a tasty sequoia cone. Whether snatching one from the ground or from a sequoia branch, the chickaree holds the ends of the cone between its paws and spins it while munching the outer layers—somewhat like a kid eating a buttery ear of corn at a state fair.

The seeds from the sequoia cone are released and scattered by the chickaree's snacking. The cones contain about 200 seeds and one sequoia tree will produce about 2,000 cones. The sequoia seed itself is unexpectedly tiny. I just placed one on the word *seed* and it covered only the first three letters. Paradox. The giant sequoia exists because of small things.

Paradox occurs in other dimensions of the Titan's existence. Very few giant sequoias are destroyed by fire. Hundreds of years of fires have left scorch marks on the sequoia trunks—some are blackened gouges over a foot deep and 10 feet long. Still, the Titan will not burn for long. Sequoias have built in fire departments. Tannins, the chemicals which turn the bark a cinnamon brown, are potent fire retardants. The tannins also repel insects and fungus growth. By withstanding fire, the sequoia benefits from its after effects. Forest fires prepare mineral-rich seedbeds; they open holes in the canopy allowing more sunlight to reach the soil; fires reduce competition from less fire resistant plants. Fires dry sequoia cones, which makes them open and disperse their seeds. The Titan instructs us how to make a potentially destructive force into an ally.

7. *Aging.* No giant sequoia dies from aging. As mentioned earlier, the sequoia's life force is as vigorous at 2,000 years old as it was as a sprig of 200. But sequoias do die. A small percentage are destroyed by natural disasters, and some were destroyed in the 1800s by lumbermen. But no sequoia has ever been confirmed of dying of old age. The main cause of death is by toppling. The root system that is essential to the sequoia's balance may be undercut by natural or human-made soil erosion. It may take a few hundred years, but without its counter-balancing roots a sequoia will fall, usually without notice. The sequoia teaches how to die: grow until you topple.

8. *Wonder.* Sequoias emanate a sense of silent dominion. Their immensity and mysteriousness cause one, says John Steinbeck (1963)

"Sequoia"

"to go under a spell." Some ask, what is the purpose of a sequoia anyway? It is a query that the Titans do not address. The sequoias are content to *be.* In *Apology To Wonder* (1969), Sam Keen contends that the primal source of all wonder is the jarring realization that something actually exists in the first place. It could, in short, not exist. The sequoias being here is a triumph over nonbeing or nothingness. It is, continues Keen, a cause for "rejoicing in the presence of things rather than going beyond them" (p. 29). Similarly, *you* are here. But why you? One man produces billions of sperm in a lifetime and one woman produces several hundred ovum. You began by the joining of just one of these sperm and ovum. If another sperm swimming right next to yours had been a jot quicker, you would not be here and someone else would be. Your existence, too, is a case for wonder.

And so ended my seminar with the sequoias. I had confirmed Thoreau's conclusion that "we need the tonic of wildness" and to be "refreshed by the sight of inexhaustible vigor, vast and titanic features . . . We need to witness our own limits transgressed, and some life pasturing freely where we never wander" (Thoreau, 1854/1962, p. 339).

You do not have to go among the sequoias to learn some life lessons. The idea is to find a place where wonder dwells and drop in for a spell.

References

Emerson, R. (1926/1951). *Emerson's essays.* I. Edman (Ed.). New York: Perennial Library.

Kazantzakis, N. (1952). *Zorba the Greek.* New York: Simon and Schuster.

Keen, S. (1969). *Apology for wonder.* New York: Harper & Row.

Moore, T. (1992). *Care of the soul.* New York: Harper Perennial.

Progoff, I. (1992). *At a journal workshop.* New York: Jeremy P. Tarcher/Perigee.

Sagan, C. (1980). *Cosmos.* New York: Random House.

Steinbeck, J. (1963). *Travels with Charley.* New York: Bantam.

Thoreau, H. (1854/1962). *Thoreau: Walden and other writings.* J. W. Krutch (Ed.). New York: Bantam Books.

Follow-Up

1. *Select two statements from this article and offer your commentary.*
2. *Describe how two of the lessons mentioned in this article have relevance in your life.*
3. *Goud claims that much of what we value most in life is experienced directly instead of indirectly. Explain if this is true for you. Why or why not?*
4. *Explain how you relate to silence. Is it needed, as the author claims, to hear our deeper voices? Comment on this question.*
5. *The author describes how the sequoia turns a destructive force (fire) into a constructive one. Describe how you have turned a crisis, problem, or adversarial situation into a positive stance.*

Personality and Money Orientations

Robert Sullivan

Complete this quiz before reading further.

MONEY ORIENTATION QUIZ

A. I'd rather be safe than sorry in my investment decisions 0

 I believe in taking financial risks to get ahead 1

 If you answered 1, then you are a hunter.

 If you answered 0, then go to question B.

B. When it comes to money, a person has to look out for himself first 0

 Even with financial matters, it is important to think of others before yourself 1

 If 0, continue to question C.

 If 1, skip to question G.

C. Wealth makes a person more attractive. (1 = *disagree completely;* 7 = *agree completely*)

 1   **2**   **3**   **4**   **5**   **6**   **7**

 If you answered 1, 2, 3, 4, or 5, continue to question D.

 If you answered 6 or 7, then you are a striver.

D. I most enjoy buying luxury items 0

 I most enjoy buying things that are practical and sensible 1

 If you answered 0, then you are a splurger.

 If you answered 1, skip to question E.

E. With money, I feel it is more important to plan for the future than to enjoy what I have now. (1 = *disagree completely;* 7 = *agree completely*)

 1   **2**   **3**   **4**   **5**   **6**   **7**

 If you answered 1, 2, or 3, then you are a nester.

 If you answered 4, continue to question F.

 If you answered 5, 6, or 7, then you are a gatherer.

F. How to do you feel about assessing your options when it comes to buying life insurance?

1. Quite competent
2. Somewhat competent
3. Uncertain
4. At a loss

If you answered 1, 2, or 3, then you are a gatherer.

If you answered 4, then you are a nester.

G. My top priority is to get ahead financially. (1 = *disagree completely*; 7 = *agree completely*).

| **1** | **2** | **3** | **4** | **5** | **6** | **7** |

If you answered 1 or 2, then you are an idealist.

If you answered 3 or 4, then continue to question H.

If you answered 5, 6, or 7, then you are a protector.

H. How do you feel about assessing your options when choosing a sound investment?

1. Quite competent
2. Somewhat competent
3. Uncertain
4. At a loss

If you answered 1 or 2, then you are a protector.

If you answered 3 or 4, then you are an idealist.

The following are descriptions of seven money orientations. See if your quiz score matches the description of your orientation. Keep in mind that not all characteristics may fit, but the overall picture should be relatively accurate.

Hunter: 13% of the population; have the highest average income; aggressive and eager to make, spend, and invest money; money means happiness, achievement, power; feels competent in money management skills; willing to risk; can tend toward extravagance.

Gatherer: 19% of the population; conservative attitude toward money matters (hold tight to what you earn, take low risks in investing); money means security; high competence in money management and high spending discipline; often seen as miserly; can be overly cautious in money matters.

Protector: 16% of the population; providing for others is the primary value of money (others take precedence regarding expenditures); have the second highest incomes of all types; adverse to money risk-taking; financial success is *not* a measure of self-worth.

Splurger: 14% of the population; money is a means to consumption; more indulgent than practical in money expenditures; wants to go "first class" concerning clothing, dining, travel, etc; tend to make low risk investments; may purchase items even if they cannot be afforded.

Striver: 13% of the population; money is the controlling force of their life; money success is due to luck or who you know; has the lowest average income of all the types; most do *not* feel competent in money management skills; money is equated with power and happiness; tend to be jealous of those with more money.

Nester: 14% of the population; wants just enough to get by; has low emotional attachment to money; money is not equated with status, worth or happiness; have minimal money management skills; most likely of all groups to quit jobs if winning a large lottery.

Idealist: 10% of the population; least materialistic of all types; has second lowest average income; money is seen as one of life's necessities but not related to happiness or self-worth; close to Nesters with the difference being that Idealists are more generous with their money if they have it; most likely group to have term life insurance and savings accounts but few investments; generally indifferent to money.

*Editor's Note: For a more complete description of these money types, see "Americans and Their Money" by Robert Sullivan. *Worth,* June 1994.

Follow-Up

1. *Explain why you agree or disagree with your quiz score and/or orientation description. You may have characteristics of more than one orientation; however, there should be a dominant one.*
2. *Consider having a significant other rate you according to the money orientation descriptions. See if they agree with your self-scoring. Discuss your learnings.*
3. *Have you always tended to have your current money orientation or has it changed over the years? Discuss your answer.*
4. *How would you describe your parents' (guardians') money orientations? How have these influenced your orientation?*
5. *If you are married or in an intimate relationship, what is your partner's money orientation and its compatibility with yours? Discuss your answer.*
6. *If you are dissatisfied with your money orientation, consider talking with others with differing orientations and discuss your learnings.*
7. *See Section Four, "Human Relationships," for a related article by Dianne Hales entitled "Are Money Fights Ruining Your Marriage?"*
8. *Describe how your money orientation influences your well-being, relationships, and growth.*

Thoughts on Money

Nelson Goud

The cost of a thing is the amount of what I call life which is required to be exchanged for it, immediately or in the long run.

—*Henry Thoreau,* Walden

Thoreau so desired to live to experience philosophy, nature, and writing, that he spent his mornings reading (and occasionally conversing with townspeople), his afternoons walking and observing in woods and fields and ponds, and evenings writing in his journal (which eventually yielded two million words). He could work six weeks per year to fulfill his material needs.

But for most of us, working six weeks per year will just not provide for our material wants. We need more money. Money is more than a primary means for obtaining goods; it also has great psychological and symbolic significance. With few exceptions, telling someone how much money you make is an act of high disclosure—for many it is a mark of your worthiness and status, whether we like it or not. Money is related to power, security, hope, generosity, and interpersonal dynamics. Most know that money is a central part of their existence but do little to really understand their financial decisions. How we behave toward money issues tells us much about our identity and what we value. Money is often cast as an evil force when by itself it means nothing—we attach the meanings. And as Thoreau pointed out above, a certain proportion of our life force is spent in the pursuit of the material.

In addition to the articles by Dianne Hales (Section Four) and Robert Sullivan (Section Six), here are some additional thoughts on money:

- "Every money question is also a profound life question, and in my life I want to seek a deep understanding about important issues like security, power, comfort. . . . Money issues—the hard need to save, invest, and manage my resources—push me out of my private safety zone and into a reeling world of contradiction, choices, and concerns. . . . I realize now that it helps me find out what sort of human being I am—what I am willing to do to obtain material security and what I am not willing to do." (Jon Spayde, *Utne,* July–August 2003, p. 60)
- The average U.S. credit card debt in 2001 was over $8,000 per household (triple the amount just ten years earlier). The average household has over ten credit and debit cards.

- Imagine that a person offers you $80 for $100. Would you make the deal? Of course not. But this is what you do when paying off most credit card debts. Take $5,000 in credit card balance with a 16 percent interest rate. If you make only minimum payments each month, it will take you 28.5 years to pay it off. The initial $5,000 you received has now cost you $12,000.

- Almost all financial advisors focus on credit cards as the primary way to effectively manage your money. One way to think of a credit card purchase is to see it for what it is—a *loan*. Each time you purchase something with a credit card, you are taking out a loan. This is why most advisors say to use a credit card for only essential needs.

Try spending actual money instead of using a card for daily purposes (e.g., food, normal living expenses) and see how much you save. Physically handing over the money registers differently in our brains than swiping a card. By using actual money, you also eliminate the credit card illusion that you "have the money."

- Beware of the traps of "entitlement." Many persons rationalize large expenses because they believe they are entitled to make them. Here are a few forms of entitlement spending: "I've been working so hard or been having a tough time, so I deserve *X*," "Others 'less worthy' have *X* so I deserve it," "You only live once" (yes, but you can live it without crushing debts).

- Bankruptcies have increased 400 percent over the past 25 years (it is projected that one in seven families will file for bankruptcy by 2010).

- Basic guides for spending (Jane Bryant Quinn, *Newsweek*, Sept. 15, 2003)
    1. Spend no more than 36 percent of your gross monthly steady income toward regular debt repayment (credit cards, car, and housing).
    2. Spend no more than 2.5 times your income on a home.
    3. Place at least 5 percent of your income in savings. This will aid in building a safety net for emergencies such as illness, losing a job, arrival of a child, etc.
    4. If buying a more expensive house, have at least six months' worth of mortgage payments available.

People who manage their money in productive ways are content; they don't let their money manage them.

—*Jean Chatzsky*

Recommended Readings on Money Management

Chatzky, J. (2003). *You don't have to be rich: Comfort, happiness and financial security on your own terms.*

Opdyke, J. (2004). *Love & money.*

Warren, E., & Warren Tyagi, A. (2003). *The two-income trap.*

Zimmerman, S. (2004). *The power in your money personality: 8 ways to balance your urge to splurge with your craving for saving.*

Follow-Up

1. *What psychological qualities do you associate with money?*
2. *What is your greatest difficulty in money management? How could you im-prove? What is one of your strengths in money management?*
3. *How does "entitlement trap" relate to you and your spending?*
4. *Select at least one statement from this article and apply it to your life.*

Personal Death Awareness (PDA)

J. William Worden and William Proctor

Personal Death Awareness Index

Your Personal Death Awareness is a fluctuating phenomenon, moving up and down daily. Some days, you'll be more aware of your own limited life span, and other days you may act and think as though you're going to live forever.

Most of us usually register quite low on the awareness index because we tend to shy away from thoughts of our own death. Consciously or subconsciously, we deny that someday our lives must end. The more intense our denial, the lower our PDA.

I am purposely asking you to raise your Personal Death Awareness so that you can begin to perceive an entire range of choices about your life and death that you might not have been aware of before.

Just as there are extremes of introversion and extroversion, there are extremes of Personal Death Awareness. You may have willingly experienced only one polarity—the low side of the awareness index. Any high death awareness you've experienced was probably associated with something very unpleasant, such as the death of a friend or loved one, and that makes you resist increasing your death awareness. But I've often found that if a person *willingly* increases his own Personal Death Awareness and looks his mortality squarely in the face, he seldom prefers to return to his previous state of unawareness.

SELECTED PDA EXERCISES

1. Draw a line of any length, a straight one with a beginning and an end.

   Consider this line to be your total life span. Place a slash mark at any point along the line where you think you are today in your life's chronology. Now, complete the following sentences by filling in the blanks:

   I expect to live until age _____

   I am currently age _____

When you compare your present age with the age at which you expect to die, how much of your life do you find you've already lived? A third, a half, two-thirds, or more? Now look back at the line with the slash mark. How does your estimate of the time you have left to live on the life-span line compare with your numerical estimate?

Many people who have done this exercise have found that they placed the slash mark at an earlier age than their written guess. When you see your life starkly depicted on a line in front of you, like a race-track or a road map, the tendency is to give yourself more time to live than you know you probably have.

How did it feel to commit yourself to a definite life span? Some people worry that they may jinx themselves by doing this. Old superstitions rise up and haunt them. Does this concern you?

2. Take a few minutes to compose your own obituary-eulogy. No, don't close the book yet! Many of my students who have taken the time for this exercise have been impressed with its value, especially with the way it makes death personal for them. You can use your own format or the one suggested below. If you use the one below, take your time and fill in the blanks thoughtfully.

OBITUARY-EULOGY

_____ died today at the age of _____. A native of _____, he/she died _____.
He/she is best remembered for _____

_____

_____

_____.

He/she is survived by _____

_____

_____.

Details of the funeral and the burial are as follows: _____

_____

_____

_____.

What was it like for you to compose your own obituary? Did you feel anxious or upset? Did any of the questions make you think about things you had refused or neglected to think about before? . . .

How did you see yourself dying? Was it a so-called "natural" death, a terminal illness, or a quick, violent death, as in an accident or homicide? Perhaps you chose a self-inflicted death like suicide?

Some people find how they want to be remembered a particularly hard question, so they insert something funny. Humor can eliminate the sting, the uncomfortable feelings invoked by a serious issue.

In writing your own obituary one of the most difficult details is listing survivors. It's fairly easy for most people to conceive of living longer than their parents and not living as long as their children. But when it comes to surviving brothers and sisters, that's a much harder matter. Who among your siblings still living do you expect to die before you? Who will outlive you? If you are married, do you anticipate outliving your spouse?

An awareness of your own mortality can also help you live a more effective life in the here and now:

- You can deal with feelings and not have to hide them.
- You can identify what it is specifically about dying that is causing you anxiety. Once you've pinpointed the cause, you can proceed to do something about it.
- You can take more advantage of opportunities which happen your way. A healthy Personal Death Awareness will prevent you from postponing until tomorrow tasks which can *only* be done today. Tomorrow may be too late.

If you remember that you and your loved ones won't live forever, you can have more significant, less superficial, personal relationships. But if you postpone expressing appreciation and love, death may intervene to make your temporary delay a permanent thing. Or if you harbor long-standing grudges, the grave may prevent them from being resolved. In psycho-therapy sessions, I often have to work with people who have profound resentments which they never expressed to their parents. The parents are now dead, but the resentments linger on and have to be worked out in therapy.

I think psychologist Rollo May understood the place of death in life when he wrote, "The confronting of death gives the most positive reality to life itself. It makes the individual existence real, absolute, and concrete. Death is the one fact of my life which is not relative but absolute, and my awareness of this gives my existence and what I do each hour an absolute quality."

People often ask me if working with the dying is a depressing experience. It can be a *sad* experience, especially with a person to whom I am particularly close. But on the positive side, working with the dying has increased my awareness of the brevity of life and the importance of living my life now and not postponing things until tomorrow.

As you allow yourself to experience a healthy increase in your own Personal Death Awareness, you too may find yourself reaching out for life with a new healthy zest.

Follow-Up

1. *Discuss your learnings from one or more of the PDA exercises explained by Worden and Proctor.*
2. *Discuss the way in which the subject of death was (is) dealt with in your family. Do you find that this is how you want to remain, or do you want to change certain aspects?*
3. *Explain why you agree or disagree with the thesis that increasing your PDA is helpful.*

Silicon Snake Oil

Clifford Stoll

Me, an Internet addict? Hey—I'm leading a full life, with family, friends, and a job. Computers are a sideline, not my life.

Jupiter is rising in the east, looking down on the Connecticut farm where I'm vacationing. On one side, a forest; on the other, a cornfield. Three guys are talking about the Knicks in the next room; in the kitchen, several women are buttering popcorn. One of them just called my name. But I don't care.

Fingers on the keyboard, I'm bathed in the cold glow of my cathode-ray cube, answering e-mail. While one guy's checking the sky through binoculars, and another's stuffing himself with popcorn, I'm tapping out a letter to a stranger across the continent. My attention's directed to the Internet.

Tonight, twenty letters want replies, three people have invited me to chat over the network, there's a dozen newsgroups to read, and a volley of files to download. How can I keep up?

I see my reflection in the screen and a chill runs down my spine. Even on vacation, I can't escape the computer networks.

I take a deep breath and pull the plug.

For fifteen years, I've been online, watching as thousands of computers joined hands to form a ubiquitous global network. At first, the nascent Arpanet seemed like an academic toy, a novelty to connect inanimate computers across the continent. Later, this plaything began supplying electronic mail and an occasional data file from other astronomers.

As the Arpanet grew into the Internet, I began to depend on e-mail to keep up with colleagues and friends. The Usenet brought news from around the continent. It became a whole new way to communicate.

Then, in 1986, while managing a computer system in Berkeley, I stumbled on a group of hackers breaking into computers. No ordinary cyberpunks, these: they sold their discoveries to the Soviet KGB.

It took a year to chase them down. During that time, I realized that our networks aren't simple connections of cables and computers; they're cooperative communities.

Since then, the Internet has become a most inviting and intriguing neighborhood. E-mail and chat lines keep me in touch with friends around the world; data transfers let me exchange information with colleagues. I join in discussions over the Usenet, posting queries and answering questions. One click of the mouse and I can read the daily news or a monthly report. At once it's fun and challenging.

But what a price! Simply keeping track of this electronic neighborhood takes a couple of hours every night. I find myself pawing through Internet archives or searching for novelties over the World Wide Web. I spend still more time downloading files and following newsgroups. Bit by bit, my days dribble away, trickling out my modem.

But for all this communication, little of the information is genuinely useful. The computer gets my full attention, yet either because of content or format, the network doesn't seem to satisfy.

I can't turn my back on the network. Or can I? Right now, I'm scratching my head, wondering.

Perhaps our networked world isn't a universal doorway to freedom. Might it be a distraction from reality? An ostrich hole to divert our attention and resources from social problems? A misuse of technology that encourages passive rather than active participation? I'm starting to ask questions like this, and I'm not the first.

And so I'm writing this free-form meditation out of a sense of perplexity. Computers themselves don't bother me, it's the culture in which they're enshrined.

What follows, I suppose, shows my increasing ambivalence toward this most trendy community. As the networks evolve, so do opinions toward them, and my divergent feelings bring out conflicting points of view. In advance, I apologize to those who expect a consistent position from me. I'm still rearranging my mental furniture.

I suspect I'll disappoint science-fiction romantics as well. Nobody can offer utopia-on-a-stick, the glowing virtual community that enhances our world through discovery and close ties while transcending the coarseness of human nature.

Oh, I care about what happens to our networked neighborhood. However, I care more about—and am affected more by—what's happening in our larger society. So do parents, professors, teachers, librarians, and, yes, even politicians.

When I put on my cone-shaped thinking cap, I wonder what I would have said fifty years ago, when the interstate highway system was first proposed. Plenty of people favored it: truckers, farmers, and shippers wanted to break the railroad monopoly. Political subdivisions, car makers, and construction unions knew it would generate money. Politicians from every state felt highways were universally good things.

Who spoke out against the superhighway system? I don't remember anyone saying, "Hey, these beltways will destroy our cities. They'll pave over pristine lands and give us hour-long commutes. They'll change our society from one of neighborhoods to that of suburbs."

In advance, then, here are my strong reservations about the wave of computer networks. They isolate us from one another and cheapen the meaning of actual experience. They work against literacy and creativity. They will undercut our schools and libraries.

Forgive me. I don't want to pontificate. But I do want people to think about the decisions they're making. It'd be fun to write about the wonderful times I've had online and the terrific people I've met through my modem, but here I'm waving a flag. A yellow flag that says, "You're entering a nonexistent universe. Consider the consequences."

It's an unreal universe, a soluble tissue of nothingness. While the Internet beckons brightly, seductively flashing an icon of knowledge-as-power, this nonplace lures us to surrender our time on earth. A poor substitute it is, this virtual reality where frustration is legion and where—in the holy names of Education and Progress—important aspects of human interactions are relentlessly devalued.

End of philippic. I don't mean to lay down an unwelcome mat. Nor do I feel that I'm entitled to technogoodies and others aren't. Quite the contrary: I look forward to the time when our Internet reaches into every town and trailer park. But the medium is being oversold, our expectations have become bloated, and there's damned little critical discussion of the implications of an online world.

The popular mythos tells us that networks are powerful, global, fast, and inexpensive. It's the place to meet friends and carry on business. There, you'll find entertainment, expertise, and education. In short, it's important to be online.

It ain't necessarily so.

Our networks can be frustrating, expensive, unreliable connections that get in the way of useful work. It is an overpromoted, hollow world, devoid of warmth and human kindness.

The heavily promoted information infrastructure addresses few social needs or business concerns. At the same time, it directly threatens precious parts of our society, including schools, libraries, institutions.

No birds sing.

For all the promises of virtual communities, it's more important to live a real life in a real neighborhood.

I began this meditation with a perplexed ambivalence toward computers, networks, and the culture that enshrines them.

At first, I wanted to think about technical issues. But I found myself returning to the same themes: real life and authentic experience mean much more than anything the modem can deliver. The culture of information isn't knowledge. Electronic networks erode important parts of our community.

Computer networks, like cars and televisions, confer a most seductive freedom, the "freedom to." As I step back from the insistent messages beckoning from across my computer, I'm beginning to wonder about a different kind of freedom—call it a "freedom from."

Certainly, few will toss out their computers or back away from their keyboards. Our networks are far too useful, and there's so much available over the modem.

Oh?

It's late on an October evening in Oakland; I smell popcorn in the kitchen.

I'm done meditating.

Follow-Up

1. *Stoll is one of the most famous and skilled computer experts in the United States. He now sees the computer and Internet as both a help and a hindrance. Choose one or more of these statements and offer your views:*
   - *"Real life and authentic experience mean much more than anything the modem can deliver."*
   - *"Simply keeping track of this electronic neighborhood takes a couple of hours every night."*
   - *"Perhaps our networked world isn't a universal doorway to freedom. Might it be a distraction from reality? A diversion from social problems? A misuse . . . that encourages passive rather than active participation?"*
2. *How does the "electronic neighborhood" positively and negatively influence the way you live?*

Controlling Your Technologies

Nelson Goud

For most of us, forms of technology play a major part in existence. The question is not should we use technology, but instead whether you control your technologies. Is "technology creep" (gradual takeover) now a large part of your life? Below is a way to test how much control you exert with your technologies.

Step 1:   Check off each item that you use.

        ____ Cell phone(s)

        ____ Pager

        ____ E-mail

        ____ voicemail

        ____ instant messaging

        ____ Internet use

        ____ Fax machine

        ____ Others

Step 2:   Rate each of the above according to the scale below.

C   You definitely control when and how to use this device.

O   Out-of-control. The device seems to have more power than you in how it is used. For example, you check e-mail even if not necessary.

+–   You share the power about equally with the device, an approach–avoidance dynamic.

Step 3:   If you choose to gain more control over one or more of these technologies, try this idea:

Select one device and gradually use it less frequently each day. For example, if you check e-mail five times per day, then start by checking it 4 times, then 3 . . . until you feel in control. Do the same for another device. For overuse of the cell phone, start by turning it off for ten minutes during the day.

(This approach is a modification of one suggested by Tim O'Brien of Knight Ridder Newspapers, May 2, 2004).

Ten Symptoms of Computer Addiction

James Fearing

1. A demonstrated "loss of control" when trying to stop or limit the amount of time on the computer. (Breaking promises to self or others. Promising to quit or cut down and not being able to do so.)
2. Being dishonest or minimizing the extent of the time you stay on the computer, or covering up or being dishonest about what activities you participate in when on the computer.
3. Negative consequences experienced by the computer user or his/her friends or family as a direct result of time or activities spent on the computer.
4. Participation in high risk or normally unacceptable behaviors when using the computer. Compromising your morals and values based on the opportunity to remain anonymous and protected on the computer. (A good test for this is to ask yourself if your spouse, partner, or family would approve of what you were doing on the computer.)
5. An overdeveloped sense of importance for the computer in your life. Defending your right to use the computer as much as desired, regardless of the fact that people in your life are feeling left out and neglected. (Denial of the problem and justification; not being able to hear or feel what the other people are saying regarding your computer behavior.)
6. Mixed feelings of euphoria (a "rush"), combined with feelings of guilt, brought on by either the inordinate amount of time spent on the computer or the abnormal behavior acted out while using the computer.
7. Feelings of depression or anxiety when something or someone shortens your time or interrupts your plans to use the computer.
8. Preoccupation with the computer and computer activities when you are not using the computer. (Thinking about the computer and its activities when doing something else; i.e., having a family dinner, working on project deadline, etc.)
9. Finding yourself using the computer at times when you are feeling uncomfortable, irritated, or sad about something happening in your life. (Feeling uncomfortable in your relationship, so you will self-medicate and "hide out" on the computer.) Using time on the computer to become externally focused as a way to avoid facing what is

happening in your life and avoid feeling the appropriate feelings inside yourself (self-medicating).

10. Experiencing financial concerns or problems in your life as a result of money being spent on computer hardware, computer on-line charges, or any other costs associated with computers.

After honestly answering, if you said yes to one question you *may* have a problem with computer addiction. If you said yes to two questions, there is a *good chance you do* have a problem with computer addiction. If you answered yes to three or more, you are demonstrating a pattern of behavior which would suggest that *you are addicted to your computer* and/or the activities you participate in when you are using it. If you are experiencing problems in this area of your life, it is important for you to contact a psychotherapist in your area who has experience in working with addictive behaviors. A safe place to start would be to have an assessment done to help you and your therapist gain insight into what's happening in this area of your life. Based on this evaluation, the appropriate plan can be formulated for help in your specific situation.

To See Anew

Nelson Goud

Reading outside of my field often surfaces long-held beliefs and shows them to be false. How we see things for example. I assumed that to see, you needed two things: a functioning eye and a light source. Then I read about experiments where people peered into a fabricated box containing pure light. What did they see? Darkness. How could this be since they had functioning eyes and were gazing into pure light? It was explained that light itself is invisible; an object reflecting the light is necessary for vision to occur (e.g., when a stick was placed into the box of light, the subjects saw it). Astronauts report that in the completely sunlit outer space, they see only darkness until a tool or part of the spaceship passes in their line of vision.

Persons blind since birth who then undergo restorative eye surgery often cannot see objects placed before them. Shape, size, and distance are beyond their capabilities even though they have functioning eyes, light, and objects to perceive. One machinist who learned his trade through touch was brought to his lathe a few days after his eye surgery. He could not see the lathe even though he knew it was in front of him. Only after he touched the lathe did the machine begin to take shape. The shapeless and blurry world of the newly sighted is so disorienting that many revert to their former ways of touching and hearing to navigate the world (e.g., many turn out the lights in their homes).

Sight is not a purely sensory act. We must literally train the brain to see. Physicist Arthur Zajonc says that the world presents itself to us, and then our brains translate these stimuli into form and meaning. Seeing, in short, requires an active participation of the brain. Recently, a mother told me that her six month old son attempts to grasp airplanes when he sees them in the sky. By trial and error, he is learning about size and distance; he is training his brain.

In its broader sense, seeing also refers to understanding, knowing, and foresight (Do you see what I mean?). We train our brains in the non-physical world and, much like the newly sighted, often prefer familiar ways of perceiving and thinking. Existing, but not seen, are other possibilities and realities. Most of us are so set in our going-to-work routine, for example, that we would not see an elephant perched on a telephone pole on the way. Occasionally we are jolted out of perceptual patterns by a death, a birth, an illness, winning a lottery or dazzled by an epiphany. But most of these new points of view are out of one's immediate control. What can one do to purposely train the brain to see anew?

What we see is greatly determined by our perceptual sets. A perceptual set is a highly tuned readiness to detect particular stimuli. For example, you hear your name called and others next to you do not; or when love fails, somehow every other song relates to this loss; and why is it that each time you purchase a different car, many others just like it suddenly appear on the streets? Perceptual sets are strongly influenced by past learnings, current needs, and expectations. Perceptual sets act as screeners and filters and help us to focus. But in this screening, a number of perceptual options are missed or disregarded. Seeing anew is enhanced when we become aware of how our perceptual sets affect our attention.

Everyday activities are fertile sources for expanding our perceptual sets. Observe what other people select and respond to in a wide range of settings (restaurant, ballgame, TV/movie, a speech or lecture, nature stroll, people-watching, etc.). What claims the attention of young children that seems to slip under your radar screen? By seeing through others' perceptual sets, you will soon detect other possibilities of a given situation.

Intentionally developing a new perceptual set will also make things appear that did not exist before. You may not be fully aware, for instance, of all the "little joys" that are encountered in a daily existence: the taste and aroma of a good cup of coffee or tea, a bird's chirping, someone lets you in line, a cool breeze on a hot day, fresh sheets, a child's laughter, a pet greeting you, the sun rose again and you are here to see it. Many studies have shown that recognizing little joys is essential to a sense of well-being. Try this: purposely make a perceptual set to spot all the little joys in a day (and especially for those days which are likely to be peppered with grumbling and mumbling).

An anthropology professor once said, "Every human is like all other humans, like some other humans, and like no other human." However, we tend to give priority to just one of these dimensions when perceiving others. By modifying our perceptual sets, the same human may appear to possess qualities formerly unseen. Think of a friend, family member, colleague, and even someone you do not like. For each, think of ways that they are alike (e.g., basic needs, having dreams and hopes, having worries, hobbies and interests, etc.). How are they like some humans but not others (e.g., age, gender, race, occupation, where they live, etc.). How are these persons unique? What we see in others often depends on which of these perspectives we emphasize. It even alters how we perceive ourselves.

The opposite of a truth, say the sages, is another truth. "Love is blind" it is said, and everyone but the lovers can see the obvious. Abraham Maslow observed, though, that "love may make it possible to see qualities in the loved person of which others are completely oblivious." The Maslow principle also holds true for knowledge. A higher degree of knowledge permits the knower to perceive in ways not available to those without the knowledge. A dentist shows me an X-ray, and all I can see are cloudy shadings, but he sees things I wish he did not. A trombone buddy and I, a trumpeter, relish listening to jazz bands with brassy, let-it-rip horn sections. Once he almost toppled off his chair exclaiming, "Did you hear that bass trombone riff?" I told him I could not hear the difference between the bass trombone and the other trombones. In the next song, he would point and say "there, and there" until I could hear the difference. He taught me how to hear what entered my ears but went unheard.

One potent method for learning new knowledge is through the little used art of listening. It is easy to blurt your views and easy to listen to someone who believes like you, but these paths rarely lead to new knowledge. It is hearing a new or even contrasting point of view that creates the greater probability of an expanded world. True listening means that one attempts to understand another without interjecting or mentally thinking of counterarguments while another is speaking. "The greatest compliment that was ever paid to me," said Thoreau, "was when one asked me what I thought and attended to my answer." Granted, listening to Uncle Lester drone on about his 31 years in a tweezer factory will not likely trigger a life altering revelation. Instead, choose a topic where you have strong beliefs and talk with a few people who differ from you and attempt to really hear them. You may not change your original stance, but now you have alternative angles and have at least given a compliment à la Thoreau. Who knows, perhaps someone may even return the compliment.

Our culture rewards goal-setting. Goals, if valued, provide clear directions and are powerful motivators. However, they may also function as blinders if they become all consuming. A folk tale illustrates this problem.

> A Chippewa brave was told by the tribal chief to seek the elk herds in preparation for a major hunt. After three weeks of journeying through forests and over mountains, the brave returns. He reports that he located the elk herd and then described their number and location. The chief then asks him, "Were there any fruits and nuts on the trees along the way?" The brave answered, "I do not know. I was not seeking them." The chief paused and replied, "You must learn how to see things you are not looking for. Go out again and tell me what you see."

Like the brave, we may allow a goal to so dominate our thoughts that we do not see other life offerings. Examine your goal-setting style and judge whether it is primarily a positive or negative force in perceiving the world.

Finally, intentionally experimenting with perceptual sets may yield a few surprises. Consider attempting one more of the following activities:

• Soundscape awareness. In at least two settings, close your eyes for a minute and become aware of sounds. What difference is there compared to your eyes being open? How compatible are these soundscapes with your overall well-being?

• By yourself, stroll in your surroundings (outside if possible). In a relaxed manner, look for something that reflects you as a person. Do not force this parallel, instead let it present itself. This symbolic reflection may take a few minutes or even a half hour or so. If this symbolic reflection appears, pause and think about it for awhile; write your thoughts. If no symbolic reflection appears on your stroll, try again sometime.

• Alternative focus strategy. Faced with a crisis in World War II, England's Winston Churchill told a colleague that "It will all look different after a good lunch, a cigar, and a nap." When overwhelmed with a problem and decision, often the best idea is to engage in an unrelated activity. Even simple breaks—a walk, a short talk with a friend, reading, a movie—have the potential to create perceptual shifts which make a difference. Poet Wallace Stevens pointed out that "sometimes the truth depends on a walk around a lake."

• Personification. In a page or less, describe the world of something besides yourself. It can be a live or an inanimate object. Try to imagine what it would be like to be in its world and how it would perceive things. Try not to name your subject in your writing (then you can have someone else guess what it is).

In *Steppenwolf*, Hermann Hesse (1929) said that humankind walks in the midst of a garden with a hundred kinds of trees, a thousand kinds of flowers, and a hundred kinds of fruit and vegetables. "Suppose then that the gardener of this garden knew no other distinction than between edible and inedible, nine-tenths of this garden would be useless to him" (p. 75).

Relying on our habitual ways of seeing may find us with the restrictive choices of Hesse's gardener. If one desires to be more aware of life's offerings, then we must train our brains to occasionally see anew. This could mean experiencing the odd or the unexpected or we could be startled by something which exists beyond our usual limits of the possible. Or it could involve intentionally experimenting with ways of perceiving to allow the appearance of alternate views. Ed Abbey reminds us that "out there is a different world which is older and greater and deeper by far than ours." Perhaps we should take a look.

Reference

Hesse, H. (1929/1969). *Steppenwolf*. New York: Bantam Books.

Follow-Up

1. *Choose two of the main points that the author presents and offer your commentary and/or personal application.*
2. *At the end of the article, four techniques are described for altering perceptual sets. Attempt one and report your results and offer some commentary.*

Who Will Play Your Music?

Michael Jones

Although I spent long periods of time playing my own music, I was uncomfortable performing for others, with the exception of close friends. Instead, I did covers of other people's music and relied upon these arrangements when I played in public.

It was one of these arrangements I was exploring while sitting at a piano in a hotel lobby one quiet evening. I had been at the hotel for several days, leading a management seminar. We had given ourselves the night off. Now, I sat for a time, lost in my musings. The building around me appeared to be so quiet and empty that I even felt free to let some of my own music weave in and out of these musical conversations.

It wasn't *that* empty, however. Soon an old man walked unsteadily out of the nearby lounge and plopped himself into a big easy chair beside the piano. There, he slowly sipped his wine and watched me play. I felt distracted and uneasy, trapped on the bench, where any moment he might request one of his favorite tunes, one I most likely did not know how to play.

"What's that?" he asked when I was done.

"Oh, a little bit of 'Moon River,'" I replied.

"Yeah, I recognized that," he said. "But there was something else before it, what was that?"

"That was some of my own music," I replied. "I don't have a name for it yet."

"You should," he said. "It deserves one." He looked thoughtful for a moment, then he said, "Your music is beautiful, but you're wasting your time with that other stuff."

His comment dropped into my lap so quickly I wasn't sure I fully understood what I'd just heard.

"What do you mean?" I asked.

"It's *your* music that brought me out here."

"But . . ." I said, cutting him off. "It's the other music that people want to hear."

"Not when they hear this," he replied. "Please, play some more." Then he closed his eyes and sat back in his chair.

When I am being deeply heard, playing my music feels less like a performance and more like an intimate act of love. I become more conscious of being carried along by a current of feelings, and following these feelings becomes more important than holding to the accuracy of the notes. Perhaps it is when we are in the company of another, particularly one whose appreciation for our work knows no bounds, that this love is most likely to be found.

When I finished playing, he and I sat together quietly for a long time. Slowly, he opened his eyes and sipped again from his glass.

"What are you doing with your music?" he asked.

"Nothing," I said. "It's just something I do for myself."

"Is that *all?*" he replied, surprised by my words.

Then I explained briefly what had brought me to the hotel.

"But how many others can do this consulting work?" he asked.

"Oh, perhaps twenty or thirty," I said, adding quickly, "but I don't want to give it up; my mission through this work is to change the world."

"I'm sure it is," he said. He seemed unmoved by the forced conviction of my words. Then he set his wineglass down on the table and looked directly at me.

"But who will play your music if you don't do it yourself?"

"It's nothing special," I protested.

"No," he agreed. "But it's you, and the world will be poorer without it."

I was about to offer other excuses when, with fire in his eyes and a voice sober and clear, he said, "This is your gift—don't waste it."

With that, he stood up, steadied himself by resting his hand on my shoulder for a moment, raised his glass in a silent toast, and then weaved slowly back to the lounge.

I sat frozen on the bench. Who will play my music? I asked myself over and over again. An hour or so passed, but I was still in shock. In his memoirs, Chilean poet Pablo Neruda speaks of how people who have lived unfulfilling lives sometimes complain that no one gave them any advice. No one warned them in advance that they were off course. But this was no longer true for me—I had just been warned.

Later, I went in search of this man, to insist that he tell me more. But he was gone, and a part of me suspected that perhaps he had never been there. If I had not heard his advice on the bench that evening, something else might have happened—a dream, perhaps, or an accident—to get my attention. For some people, it is the ending of a relationship or the onset of an unexpected illness—something comes along that brings our lives up short. What we had always thought secure suddenly becomes finite. In that moment, the larger universe, of which we have always been a part but often ignored, has our full attention. Its presence can be as dramatic and frightening as a raging storm at sea or as gentle as the intimate act of kissing the princess awake. It knows how to find the weak point, the undefended part where we are most likely to yield. This one wake-up call is enough to set us on a path. Following this path as it spirals inward and outward, and honoring it, even though the purpose of it and the final result may remain unclear, becomes our new

work. "The truth dazzles gradually," as Emily Dickinson says, "or else the world would [be] blind."

Often, I imagined that my true vocation was to be a painter, or a poet, or something else equally remote or extraordinary. When friends asked about the music, I was emphatic in my reply. "No," I would say. "This is something *special*." But there is no mystery to the work that is ours to do. Although it may appear to be some attribute situated in the heavens somewhere, it is often found in the familiar and ordinary and located close at hand. Indeed, it is the idea that it should be special and extraordinary, that it is something out there—remote, elusive, and difficult to do—that throws us off track.

What is ours to do comes so easily, because from the very beginning it has always been there. It may not necessarily be a special talent like writing or music; it may instead be a quality of caring that we offer, a capacity for listening deeply to others, or simply the wonder and beauty we bring to the world through how we give our attention to a piece of music, a flower, or a tree. Our purpose is to give ourselves to the world around us—including people, musical instruments, trees, and words—and through the attention we bring to them help them blaze to life. When we offer ourselves to the world, the world gives itself back to us. In the words of D. H. Lawrence, "Life rushes in."

What is it that we desire to do that brings an increase to life? This often offers a clue as to where our gifts are to be found. Beneath the long list of things we *must* do is a deeper purpose, one that involves being present with ourselves and, in so doing, bringing some aspect of the world to life. But we cannot do it alone, for the recognition of who we truly are is most often found through the other. "The mystery of creation was always between two," Laurens van der Post writes, "in an awareness that there was always both a 'thou' and an 'I.'" We all need at least one other person to recognize this spark in ourselves, to make us the one we were meant to be. For me, it was that man in the lobby of the hotel.

Who is it that offers the act of confirmation in your life, the one willing to hold the match to light the fire to set your gift to the world ablaze? And who, or what, does your gift serve? As Laurens van der Post says, "most of us indeed have become distorted into knowing only the 'I' of ourselves and not the 'thou.'" Yet, once ignited, the flame that burns within us does so with such intensity that we would go blind if we looked upon ourselves directly. Our "thou" is seen through the actions of others in relation to us; they are the moons that reflect back to us the intensity of our sun.

When I said yes to that moment, I was relearning how to say yes to the pleasure I knew the music would bring. But I was also opening myself to the fulfillment of larger intentions, ones that were not entirely my own. I trembled at the thought. Sometimes others have already tried to set our lives ablaze, and we have not accepted the match. We know that once the genie is out of the bottle, our lives will never be quite the same. There is burning that takes place, burning that has the power to transform to ashes old, limiting beliefs and everything else that we hold to be true. Nothing is exempt; everything may change, including even the smallest of acts.

I could neither push forward nor go back. When we reach this step in our creative life, we are often asked to go beyond our skills, to do the opposite of what has gone before. If we have been unfocused, it's time to focus; if we have been driven, as I had been from time to time, it's time for space. Nourish the longing, Kabir says to us, for it is the intensity of the longing that does all the work.

Yet we cannot be casual about this step, either. To turn our attention from our longing, even for a moment, may be one moment too long.

How many of us have turned away from living an imaginative life? How many of us would rather sacrifice ourselves to the security of institutional life than engage with the volatility of a soulful one? What is it that so often compels us to turn away from our longing rather than into it? Perhaps the dream seems so distant from the reality we live with day to day that we simply don't know where to begin or how to find a convenient time to start. There is also an awkwardness in our initial attempts to put ourselves into our art. We can feel unsure and self-conscious—quick to judge our progress and ready to admit defeat in the presence of those who say what we are doing is silly or frivolous, or through the constant pesterings of our own self-doubt.

When we take these first tender and delicate steps into our own imaginative life, we often need a bold and fiery image, one large and intense enough to make it a part of our-

"Trumpet" by Nelson Goud. Copyright © 1996.

selves until our own small, gentle fire is strong enough to burn on its own.

The encounter with the old man had encouraged my return to music, but it offered something more. Being at the piano had opened a pathway in which I could feel once again the tenderness that lay deep within my heart. And as my heart opened, it, in turn, offered an invitation to a wedding—a marriage between the ambitions of my intellect and the yearning for a deeper truth that was emerging within my soul. I was learning to love the other half of my self.

Could I, like Beethoven, hold a vision large enough to fill the entire span of my life? Could I say yes to it all despite the setbacks and confusion and self-doubt? Could I not only accept but embrace the uncertainty, not only tolerate but engage the ambiguity? Could I step forward and meet the suffering, the bliss, and the frustration? Could I willingly receive the future with a humble and prayerful acceptance and say, as philosopher Rudolph Steiner once said, that "whatever the next hour or day may bring, I cannot change it by fear or anxiety, for it is not yet known"? The terrors I feel may simply be shadow images from a more limiting past, not predictors of times to come.

When I left consulting to begin sitting at the piano again, I believed that I played poorly. And I had little experience with writing when I later took time from music to begin working on this book. Perhaps this is what life asks of us—to step faithfully into that very place in our lives where we can no longer fall back on our cleverness or wits. To serve the impulse to create is to accept that it may ask everything from us and offer little assurance in return. Moses guided his people into the Red Sea on faith; they were apparently up to their necks before the sea finally parted. Perhaps it is only when we have emptied ourselves of all guarantees that life finds us.

As I experienced their joining together, I was saddened by the years that had been lost, the times I had willfully struggled to try to get everything right when I didn't know what right was. They were times of planting seeds and then impatiently digging them up to see if they had grown, of trying to figure out what others wanted from me instead of asking what I most wanted for myself, of feeling the fear of not knowing where this was all going to lead, of believing that I needed to rely upon the individualistic and achieving parts of my nature to do all of the work, because I did not believe in asking for help.

Learning to trust that these terrifying leaps of faith are in fact *of* life and not *against* it came slowly for me. And I am grateful now for knowing that perhaps it is when we feel truly lost, groping our way somewhere between the in breath and the out breath that the gods are most near.

How do we discover in words the same depth of truth and inspiration that flows from our hands when we paint or our dancing when our feet touch the floor? Is it possible to suspend our schedules and routines to experiment with the deeper insights that can emerge when we are free to bring our different voices forward without fear of embarrassment or concern? Can we share our most deeply held beliefs with the possibility that behind them lies an even greater truth, one which, once revealed, might allow us to live in a more imaginative and peaceful world?

When I set aside my consulting practice to return to music, I could not foresee where it would lead. But over time, the painful uncertainties have evolved into a wonderful dance that elegantly weaves together all of the various significant but seemingly separate strands of my life. Finding the marriage between my intellect and my soul could not have been planned, at least not by me. It would have been too complex and perhaps too terrifying for my strategic mind to grasp. But perhaps, just as Wagner spoke of Beethoven's spontaneous and deeply felt performances as being "child's play" for him, creating our lives so that they are a reflection of what we love is child's play for the heart.

So now when I join these groups, I don't bring charts and theories and projectors as I did before. Instead, I simply bring myself and a nine-foot-six-inch concert grand. And as we form into a circle, I'm careful to save a place beside the piano for the old man from the lobby of the hotel.

Editor's Note: Michael Jones, pianist and composer, is a founding artist of Narada Productions and has released ten recordings. He is also an organizational consultant with DIA Logos in Cambridge, MA.

Follow-Up

1. *Choose one or more of these statements and apply them to your life:*
   - *"There is no mystery to the work that is ours to do . . . because from the very beginning it has always been there."*
   - *"Our purpose is to give ourselves to the world around us—including people, musical instruments, trees, and words. . . . When we offer ourselves to the world, the world gives itself back to us. . . . What is it that we desire to do that brings an increase to life?"*
   - *"Perhaps this is what life asks of us—to step faithfully into that very place in our lives where we can no longer fall back on our cleverness or wits. . . . Perhaps it is only when we have emptied ourselves of all guarantees that life finds us."*
2. *Jones states that we all need at least one other person to recognize our gifts, our life work. Comment on this idea and explain if it is true for your life.*
3. *Select any other idea(s) from the article and write about and/or discuss your reactions.*
4. *Who will play your music?*

Applied Activities for Section Six

THE SOMEDAY LIST

Between now and your death there are (and will be) many things you hope to experience and accomplish. Listing some of these often reveals some themes that can be helpful as you seek to understand your life. Below is a technique for finding these themes.

1. List at least twenty things you would like to experience or accomplish before you die that you have not started or completed at this time. Note that an accomplishment is a goal-oriented effort, whereas an experience refers to just being there (letting something happen). Here are a few examples to clarify the difference:

    Accomplishments—earning a degree, writing an article/book, mastering a skill, building something, changing a habit

    Experiences—attending a concert or art exhibit, having a child or grandchild, feeling inner harmony, standing on a mountain top, riding in a hot air balloon

    It may be difficult to complete this list at one sitting. Do as many as you can in a free-associating manner. No one will see your list. Include "unrealistic" items as well as expected ones. Include fantasies and dreams. Leave this task for a while or even a few days and go back to it. Try to list items from several categories of life.

2. Analysis and interpretation suggestions:

    a. Identify common themes (patterns or clusters) among your listed items. For example, you may have a few items with the theme of physical challenge and excitement, or creativity, or family/interpersonal relationships, or professional goals, or inner states of being, and so on. In a list of twenty-five items, there are usually four or five themes. Some individual items may fit under more than one theme. Once you have identified the themes, label them.

    b. Think of your themes as *unmet needs* that are present *now* (instead of the future). Do you think this list would be the same as one written five years ago? Why or why not?

    c. When will you begin to do the things on your list? Some will, realistically, have to be started later. Others, though, can be started now. Beware of the "wait until" illusion. People keep putting off desired life actions until certain conditions occur—but they may never occur just by waiting. The most common wait until conditions are time and money. "I'll be able to X when I finish school." Five years later: "When I don't have so many demands at work," or "When the kids are grown." This can continue until the "wait until" becomes a "wish I had . . . ," or "if only. . . ." If an item has existed for a few years, it probably falls under the wait until illusion.

Consider items with short time frames. Physical challenges such as high-level athletics or performance dancing have short lifespans. Many items are very difficult to do with family responsibilities. In short, pay close attention to valuable experiences that have small windows of opportunity.

d. Activate your themes in some manner. Remember that the themes act as unmet needs that call for some attention. Choose one or two themes that seem to shout the loudest. If the actual items under the theme are not truly feasible, think of a substitute activity that fulfills the spirit of this theme. For example, if you cannot begin a book, start a chapter or even a short story. If you cannot travel to Europe with a loved one for two months now, plan a nice escape weekend in a location you both like. Any theme can be activated by creating similar, substitute activities.

e. Try at least one activity per theme over the next month.

3. Discuss your things to do list and themes in small groups and/or with the whole class. Write about your themes, possible wait until traps, and your attempts to activate the themes.

For further reading on this activity and additional ideas, see *Strategies for Experiential Learning: Book Two* (1981) by Louis Thayer (Ed.), published by LT Resources, 8594 Sleepy Hollow Dr., Saline, MI 48176.

TALKING TO WISE PERSONS

A wise person has deep knowledge and understanding and is capable of profound insight and judgment. A wise person may or may not be a highly educated person in the traditional sense. A wise person is one from whom we seek some guidance that will aid us in moments when wisdom is needed. There are many ways in which we can hear from those who are wise. One of these ways is described below. All that is required is a willingness to hear what these wise persons have to say to you.

1. Think of three persons who have the qualities of wise persons as described above. You may have known them as a grandparent, aunt, parent, teacher, neighbor, or mentor. Or, they may be known indirectly to you as a philosopher, religious leader, writer, or historical figure. Somehow these persons connect with you on a deep, inner level. Name these three wise persons:

_____ , _____ , _____ .

2. Select one of these wise persons with whom you would like to talk at this time. This wise person would be able to offer answers for a current decision, dilemma, or just life in general.

3. Recall the qualities of this person whom you respect so much. Try to remember a couple of instances when he or she was helpful to you in the past. Sense his or her presence with you now.
4. On a sheet of paper, start a dialogue by first greeting this wise person and stating why you are requesting guidance. Continue the dialogue with the wise person's imagined response. Continue your conversation in a natural manner. Do not force any words. Let the conversation flow in the manner you think it actually would with this person. You may reach a natural stopping point. If this happens, stop the conversation and pick it up at a later time.
5. If desired, complete steps 2–4 with other wise persons in your life.
6. Follow-up ideas: What ideas or actions resulted from your dialogue(s) with this wise person? Can you now contact this wise person more readily?

This idea is an adaptation of a technique from *A Journal Workshop* by Ira Progoff (1992), Jeremy Tarcher/Perigee Books.

EVOLUTION OF A PERSON #2

1. *Lifeline* (from now to death): List the events you *expect* and *want* to occur during the rest of your life. Try to estimate your age at each event (including your death). Consider the following major events: career/education changes, marriage/family plans, loss of significant others, lessening mental/physical powers, places you want to visit, special goals or dreams.
2. Follow-up questions: What are the one or two things that stand out to you on your projected lifeline? Which part of your life has the most incomplete predictions and what do you think this means? How does your estimate of your age at death influence how you are living now and in the near future?
3. Consider completing this activity during some time of "active solitude" (see the article entitled "Active Solitude" in this section).
4. Discuss or write a reaction paper on what you've learned from this activity.

Epilogue

Healthy growth means living in a stream of change. We are continually modifying and discarding ways of being. Sometimes we determine when and how we will change, sometimes not. What was fitting in one era of our lives may not be in the next. Even Thoreau ended his experiment at Walden Pond: "I left the woods for as good a reason as I went there. Perhaps it seemed to me that I had several more lives to live, and could not spare any more time for that one" (Thoreau, 1854/1962, p. 343).

We face our time to leave the woods when current ways of being no longer provide the needed stimulus for growth. Courage must be summoned for the challenge of re-inventing ourselves. The alternative is sameness and stagnation. If you peer deeply, the way will eventually reveal itself. Like a distant star, the light may be faint but its source is strong. A glimmer is all you need. You may discover, like Thoreau, that "if one advances in the direction of his dreams, and endeavors to live the life which he has imagined, he will meet with a success unexpected" (Thoreau, 1854/1962, p. 343).*

Whatever you can do, or dream you can, begin it.
Boldness has genius, power and magic in it.
                                                            —Goethe

*Thoreau, H. (1854/1962). *Thoreau: Walden and other writings*, J. W. Krutch, Ed. New York: Bantam Books, Inc.